WASHINGTON
Our Home
TEACHER EDITION

➤ GIBBS SMITH EDUCATION
TO ENRICH AND INSPIRE HUMANKIND

Published by
Gibbs Smith Education
PO Box 667
Layton, UT 84041
801.544.9800
www.gibbs-smith.com/education

TEACHER EDITION
Curriculum Developer: Megan Hansen
Editor: Courtney Thomas, Susan A. Meyers, Charlene Reyes
Designer: Alan Connell, Jeremy Munns

STUDENT EDITION
Project Editor: Courtney Thomas
Editorial Assistants: Susan A. Meyers
Photo Editor: Wendy Knight, Janis Hansen
Cover design: John Vehar
Book design: Alan Connell, Robert A. Jones, Jeremy Munns

Cover Photo Credits: Mount Rainier sparkles on a clear day.
Photograph by Jeffzenner/Shutterstock.

Gibbs Smith books are printed on either recycled, 100% post-consumer
waste, FSC-certified papers, or on paper produced from a 100%
certified sustainable forest/controlled wood source.

Printed and bound in Korea
ISBN-10: 1-4236-0615-9
ISBN-13: 978-1-4236-0615-4

15 14 13 12 11 10 09   10 9 8 7 6 5 4 3 2 1

TEACHER EDITION CONTENTS

TEACHER EDITION FEATURES

CHAPTER PLANNER

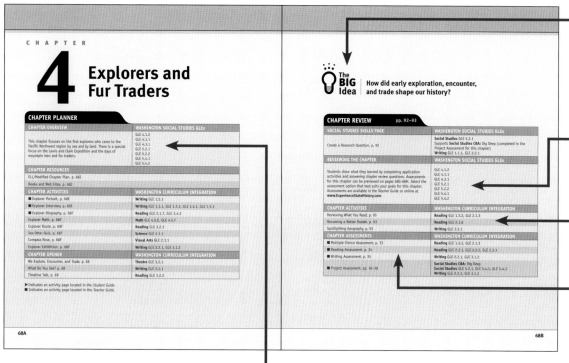

Chapter Overview
The Chapter Overview provides a quick look at the key learning of the chapter.

The Big Idea
The Big Idea focuses the learning of the chapter. The answer to the Big Idea is found in the standards-based Key Ideas. The standards-based Key Ideas support the Big Idea.

Social Studies Standards
Each chapter and lesson addresses specific Social Studies Standards.

Activities List
The Activities List includes curriculum integration.

Activity Pages and Assessments
Symbols indicate, at a glance, available activity pages and assessments.

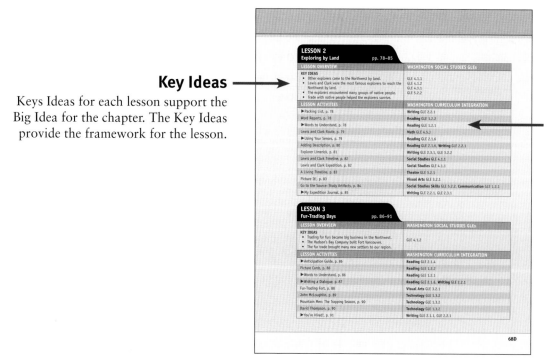

Key Ideas
Keys Ideas for each lesson support the Big Idea for the chapter. The Key Ideas provide the framework for the lesson.

Curriculum Integration
All activities in each lesson address the Social Studies Standards. In addition, each activity integrates with another curriculum area. This Curriculum Integration chart provides a quick glance at ways to integrate and meet standards in other curriculum areas.

GIBBS SMITH EDUCATION
TO ENRICH AND INSPIRE HUMANKIND

CHAPTER ACTIVITIES

Chapter Activities

The Chapter Activities provide a unifying theme and integrated activities in all the major subject areas: reading, writing, math, art, science, and social studies. The Chapter Activities also include a Set the Stage feature, Introductory Activity, and a Culminating Activity. The Set the Stage feature provides ideas for preparing your classroom for the theme of the chapter. The Introductory Activity sparks students' interest in the topic of the chapter. The Culminating Activity provides a way for students to show what they learned from reading the chapter in a fun and engaging manner. Worksheets for Chapter Activities are available in the *Teacher Guide*.

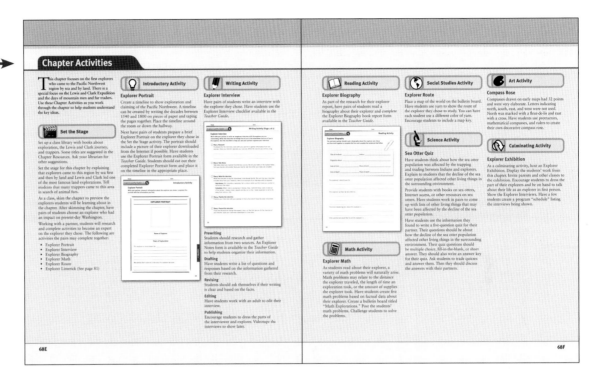

ASSESSMENT OPTIONS

Assessment Options

A preview of the assessment options—Multiple Choice Assessment, Reading Assessment, Writing Assessment, and Project Assessment—is provided. The assessments are available online at **www.ExperienceStateHistory.com** or in the *Teacher Guide*.

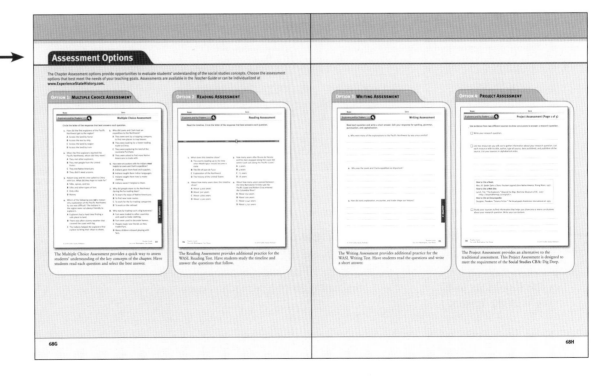

ELL/Modified Chapter Plan

The ELL/Modified Chapter Plan is an overview of the modified lesson that is available in the *Teacher Guide*. The modified chapter lesson can be used with ELL and exceptional, gifted, or special needs learners or as a fast track when time prohibits completion of the whole chapter.

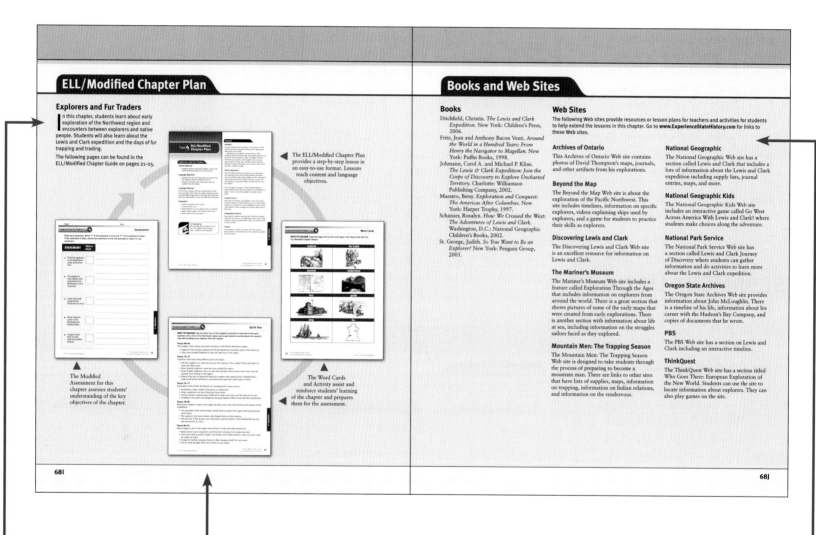

Lesson Overview

The Lesson Overview provides a quick look at the Key Ideas to be taught in the lesson.

Preview of ELL/Modified Chapter Pages

A preview of each page of the ELL/Modified Chapter Plan pages is available with an explanation of how each is used.

Books and Web Sites

The Books and Web Sites page provides reading resources and web sites available to help teachers extend their lessons for some of the topics in the chapter.

UNIT OPENER

The Unit Opener spread is used to introduce chapters in the book that follow the same theme. Each Unit Opener includes an activity or discussion to introduce students to the theme of the unit.

INTRODUCING THE CHAPTER

Use the Chapter Opener to introduce the Big Idea of the chapter. All Chapter Openers include a Big Idea activity and a Put Yourself in the Picture activity. History chapters also include a chapter timeline.

TEACHING THE LESSON

Each lesson is organized into three main areas of focus: Prepare, Teach, and Reflect.

Lessons

Every chapter is divided into short, manageable lessons. Each lesson has a title, page references for the *Student Edition* and *Student Guide*, Key Ideas, and a correlation of standards.

Prepare

This section provides ideas for both preparing the instructor to teach the lesson and preparing the students to learn the content.

Teach

This section provides strategies and content extensions for use in teaching the lesson.

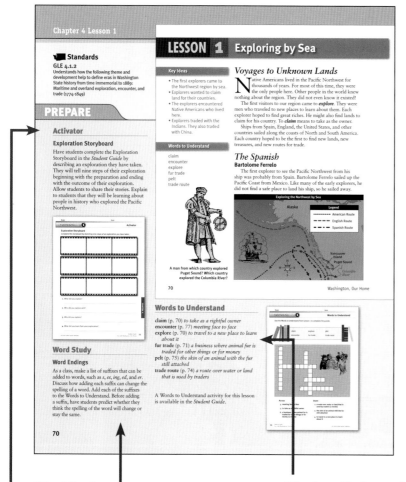

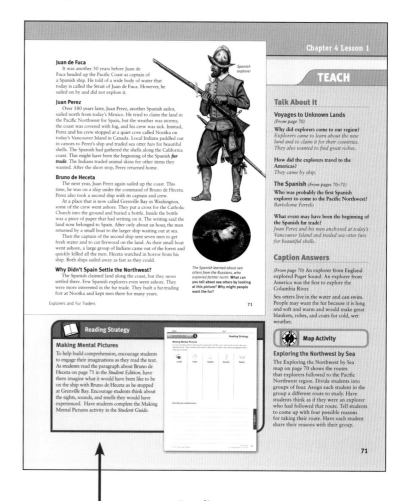

Word Study

The Word Study activity helps students learn key vocabulary found in the Words to Understand section.

Activator

This pre-reading activity engages students in a warm-up discussion or activity about lesson content. It allows students to activate prior knowledge and practice prediction skills.

Words to Understand

The Words to Understand are defined for teacher reference.

Reading Strategy

These are activities that encourage higher-level thinking and build reading comprehension.

Reading strategies in each chapter are related. Reading strategies begin with simple comprehension strategies and build upon one another through the course of the book.

Reflect

This section provides strategies for helping students review the standards-based lesson objectives.

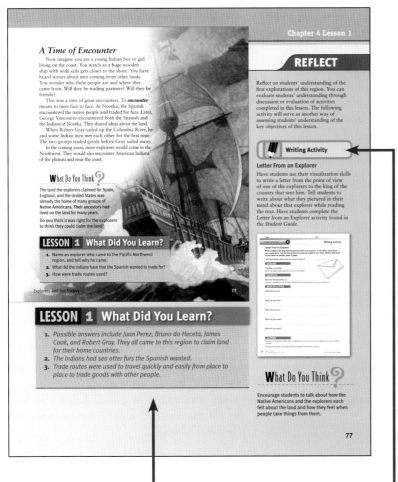

Go to the Source

This primary and secondary source-based feature asks questions that help students develop critical thinking skills and understand the significance of primary and secondary sources.

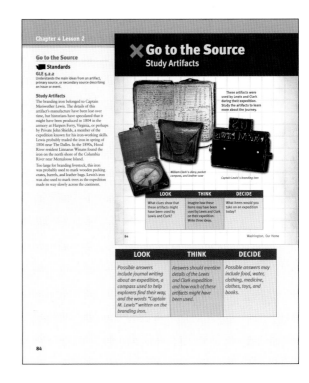

What Did You Learn?
This section provides answers to the What Did You Learn? lesson review questions.

Writing Activity
Each Reflect section includes a Writing Activity that allows students to apply critical thinking and writing skills to show what they learned through their reading of the lesson.

CHAPTER REVIEW

This section provides activities that help students review and recall the chapter's main ideas.

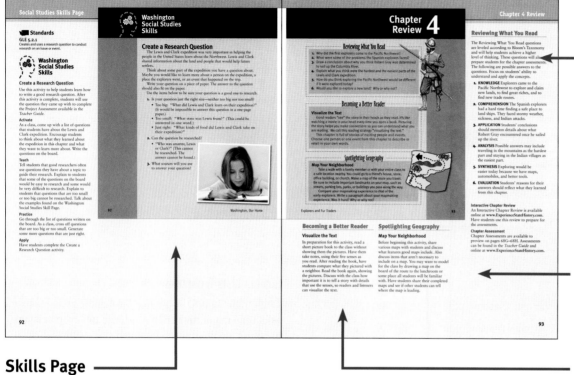

Skills Page

The Skills Pages are based on the Washington Social Studies Skills Standards and promote critical and creative thinking.

Reviewing the Chapter

This section provides answers to the Chapter Review section in the *Student Edition.*

Spotlighting Geography

This section offers possible answers and extensions to critical and creative thinking exercises related to geography.

Becoming a Better Reader

This section offers strategies to strengthen information-reading and content-reading skills.

Answers

Answers to *Student Guide* pages and to the assessments can be found in the *Teacher Guide.*

GIBBS SMITH EDUCATION
TO ENRICH AND INSPIRE HUMANKIND

ADDITIONAL FEATURES AND ACTIVITIES

Throughout the *Teacher Edition*, icons are provided as a visual to highlight a variety of activities and curriculum subjects. Look for these icons to help you meet your specific curriculum goals.

 Art
Art Activities focus on art, crafts, music, and theater.

 Background Info
Background Info provides the teacher with more information to better prepare him or her to teach the lesson.

 **Cooperative Groups**
Cooperative Group activities give students a chance to work together in an activity based on the content of the chapter. Each student's role in the group is essential to the activity.

 Differentiated Paths
Differentiated Paths include activities that can be completed by students at varying levels of ability.

 Literature Link
Literature Links incorporate an activity using a book to address the key objectives of the lesson.

 Map Activity
Map Activities support the maps in the Student Edition by providing discussion questions and further investigations.

 Math Activity
Math Activities challenge students to use their math skills within the social studies curriculum.

 Reading Activity
The Reading Activities provide many options for students to practice their fluency and comprehension.

 Science Activity
Science Activities ask students to use scientific processing skills to investigate science topics as they relate to the social studies themes.

 Social Studies Activity
Social Studies Activities support the objective of the lesson.

 Technology Tie-In
Technology Tie-In Activities provide ideas for online investigations.

 Writing Activity
Writing Activities provide many options for students to practice the writing process, review writing elements, and engage in a variety of writing applications.

STUDENT EDITION FEATURES

CHAPTER OPENER

All chapters begin with a Chapter Opener that provides a visual introduction to the material covered in the chapter. The Big Idea encompasses the overall theme of the chapter.

The BIG Idea

How did early exploration, encounters, and trade shape our history?

The title of this painting is *Sacajawea Guiding the Lewis and Clark Expedition. It took over two years for the expedition to travel from St. Louis to the Pacific Northwest and back. Study the painting.* **Which men might be Lewis and Clark? What do you think Sacajawea is pointing at?**

Explorers and Fur Traders

CHAPTER 4

Strong winds blew against the tall white sails of the first explorers' wooden ships. The winds pushed the ships up the foggy coast of the Pacific Northwest. The men on the ships were eager to explore and trade. They wanted the thick furs of sea otters that swam in the ocean.

After a time, Lewis and Clark led a group of explorers by land. Wide rivers carried them to the ocean in long wooden canoes. These explorers did not come to trade for furs. They came to learn about the land and people who lived here.

Timeline of Events

1500 Many groups of Native Americans live across the Pacific Northwest.

These are the years the explorers first came to the Pacific Northwest. Some explorers came more than once.

1542 Bartolome Ferrelo

1592 Juan de Fuca

1774 Juan Perez

1775 Bruno de Heceta

1776–1778 James Cook

1789 Robert Gray

1792 George Vancouver

1804–1806 Lewis and Clark

1825 Fort Vancouver is built.

1780s–1840s The fur trade

68   69

The Big Idea
The Big Idea reflects the standards-based curriculum covered in the chapter.

Chapter Timeline
The Chapter Timeline is essential because most dates have been taken from the text. This improves readability and, therefore, comprehension. The timeline also allows students to understand sequence and cause and effect.

Introductory Text
The Introductory Text provides a quick summary of the main topics discussed in the chapter.

GIBBS SMITH EDUCATION
TO ENRICH AND INSPIRE HUMANKIND

Lesson

Lesson Title
Each lesson's title reflects the standards covered in that lesson.

LESSON 1 Exploring by Sea

Key Ideas
- The first explorers came to the Northwest region by sea.
- Explorers wanted to claim land for their countries.
- The explorers encountered Native Americans who lived here.
- Explorers traded with the Indians. They also traded with China.

Words to Understand
claim
encounter
explore
fur trade
pelt
trade route

A man from which country explored Puget Sound? Which country explored the Columbia River?

Voyages to Unknown Lands
Native Americans lived in the Pacific Northwest for thousands of years. For most of this time, they were the only people here. Other people in the world knew nothing about the region. They did not even know it existed!

The first visitors to our region came to ***explore***. They were men who traveled to new places to learn about them. Each explorer hoped to find great riches. He might also find lands to claim for his country. To ***claim*** means to take as the owner.

Ships from Spain, England, the United States, and other countries sailed along the coasts of North and South America. Each country hoped to be the first to find new lands, new treasures, and new routes for trade.

The Spanish
Bartolome Ferrelo
The first explorer to see the Pacific Northwest from his ship was probably from Spain. Bartolome Ferrelo sailed up the Pacific Coast from Mexico. Like many of the early explorers, he did not find a safe place to land his ship, so he sailed away.

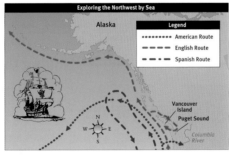

Exploring the Northwest by Sea

Alaska

Legend
- - - - - - - - American Route
- - - - - English Route
- - - - Spanish Route

Vancouver Island
Puget Sound
Columbia River

70   Washington, Our Home

Juan de Fuca
It was another 50 years before Juan de Fuca headed up the Pacific Coast as captain of a Spanish ship. He told of a wide body of water that today is called the Strait of Juan de Fuca. However, he sailed on by and did not explore it.

Juan Perez
Over 180 years later, Juan Perez, another Spanish sailor, sailed north from today's Mexico. He tried to claim the land in the Pacific Northwest for Spain, but the weather was stormy, the coast was covered with fog, and his crew was sick. Instead, Perez and his crew stopped at a quiet cove called Nootka on today's Vancouver Island in Canada. Local Indians paddled out in canoes to Perez's ship and traded sea otter furs for beautiful shells. The Spanish had gathered the shells along the California coast. This might have been the beginning of the Spanish ***fur trade***. The Indians traded animal skins for other items they wanted. After the short stop, Perez returned home.

Bruno de Heceta
The next year, Juan Perez again sailed up the coast. This time, he was on a ship under the command of Bruno de Heceta. Perez also took a second ship with its captain and crew.

At a place that is now called Grenville Bay in Washington, some of the crew went ashore. They put a cross for the Catholic Church into the ground and buried a bottle. Inside the bottle was a piece of paper that had writing on it. The writing said the land now belonged to Spain. After only about an hour, the men returned by a small boat to the larger ship waiting out at sea.

Then the captain of the second ship sent seven men to get fresh water and to cut firewood on the land. As their small boat went ashore, a large group of Indians came out of the forest and quickly killed all the men. Heceta watched in horror from his ship. Both ships sailed away as fast as they could.

Why Didn't Spain Settle the Northwest?
The Spanish claimed land along the coast, but they never settled there. Few Spanish explorers even went ashore. They were more interested in the fur trade. They built a fur-trading fort at Nootka and kept men there for many years.

Spanish explorer

The Spanish learned about sea otters from the Russians, who explored farther north. **What can you tell about sea otters by looking at this picture? Why might people want the fur?**

Explorers and Fur Traders   71

Words to Understand
Words to Understand are grade-level-appropriate, standards-based vocabulary words. Familiarity with these new terms is essential for comprehension of chapter content.

Key Ideas
Each lesson has one to four Key Ideas that summarize the standards-based content within the chapter text.

Captions and Visual Literacy Questions
Engaging photographs and illustrations promote visual literacy through thought-provoking captions. These captions include questions that prompt students to connect photo content to chapter text.

A Northwest Passage That Did Not Exist

For a long time, Europeans thought there must be a way to sail from the Atlantic Ocean to the Pacific Ocean all the way across North America. The country that found this route would have an easier way to sail between Europe and Asia. The control of this route would bring riches and power. People started to call this route the Northwest Passage.

Many explorers, including Captain Cook, tried to find a northwest passage. They searched all along the coasts of North and South America. They sailed into bays and up rivers, but the rivers always came to an end. There was no way for ships to cross North or South America. No one found the Northwest Passage because it did not exist.

The Spanish started a fur trade with Indian people at Nootka. Captain Cook stopped there for a short time, but he never went ashore. What activities are going on in this picture?

The English
Captain James Cook

Other countries did not like it when Spain started claiming land in the Pacific Northwest. Each country wanted to be the most powerful by claiming the most land.

Captain James Cook was an important English explorer. Before coming to the Northwest, he had already sailed around the world twice. On one of his trips, he found the sunny islands we now call Hawaii. He called them the Sandwich Islands.

When Cook later sailed by the Northwest, he kept his ships far offshore. However, he did stop for a short time in the harbor at Nootka. He saw, to his dismay, that the Spanish were already there, trading with the Indians for sea otter furs.

Feeling that his trip had been a failure, Cook sailed once again to the Sandwich Islands. Just as he was leaving one of the islands, he was killed by native people.

72   Washington, Our Home

Sidebars

Sidebars highlight interesting facts about places, events, or people.

What Do You Think?

What Do You Think? questions are open-ended and encourage students to critically consider different points of view.

Finally, Gray left China and sailed around Asia and Africa and across the Atlantic Ocean to Boston. He sold the Chinese goods in Boston at high prices.

Gray Enters the Columbia River

After only six weeks in Boston, Gray again sailed to the Pacific Northwest. He traded up and down the coast. One day, through the fog, Gray saw what seemed to be a wide river. Could he sail into the river? His crew tried, but the water was very rough. Long sandbars blocked the way.

A month later, the men came back. They waited until the ocean tides were high enough to carry a boat over the sandbars. This time they made it! Gray sailed up the river and claimed all the land around it for the United States.

Indians took their canoes out to meet the explorers. Gray gave them nails and other metal objects in exchange for salmon, deer meat, and 450 sea otter pelts. A **pelt** is an animal skin with the fur still on it. After 10 days, Gray left and sailed to China again.

Gray was the first non-Indian to sail up the Columbia River. He was also the first American to sail around the world—twice. He started an important trade route to China. He also gave the United States a stronger claim to the Northwest.

Gray named the Columbia River after his ship, the Columbia.

What Do You Think?

What do you think the Indians thought when they first saw the explorers, who had lighter skin and hair and wore different clothes?

Gray's Trade Route to China

What route did Gray follow from Boston to China?

Boston

Explorers and Fur Traders   75

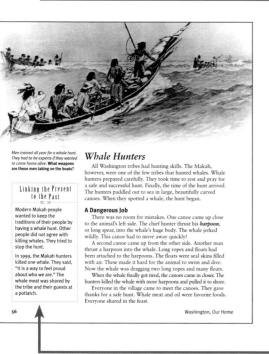

Men trained all year for a whale hunt. They had to be experts if they wanted to come home alive. **What weapons are these men taking on the boats?**

Linking the Present to the Past

Modern Makah people wanted to keep the traditions of their people by having a whale hunt. Other people did not agree with killing whales. They tried to stop the hunt.

In 1999, the Makah hunters killed one whale. They said, "It is a way to feel proud about who we are." The whale meat was shared by the tribe and their guests at a potlatch.

56

Whale Hunters

All Washington tribes had hunting skills. The Makah, however, were one of the few tribes that hunted whales. Whale hunters prepared carefully. They took time to rest and pray for a safe and successful hunt. Finally, the time of the hunt arrived. The hunters paddled out to sea in large, beautifully carved canoes. When they spotted a whale, the hunt began.

A Dangerous Job

There was no room for mistakes. One canoe came up close to the animal's left side. The chief hunter thrust his **harpoon**, or long spear, into the whale's huge body. The whale jerked wildly. This canoe had to move away quickly!

A second canoe came up from the other side. Another man thrust a harpoon into the whale. Long ropes and floats had been attached to the harpoons. The floats were seal skins filled with air. These made it hard for the animal to swim and dive. Now the whale was dragging two long ropes and many floats.

When the whale finally got tired, the canoes came in closer. The hunters killed the whale with more harpoons and pulled it to shore.

Everyone in the village came to meet the canoes. They gave thanks for a safe hunt. Whale meat and oil were favorite foods. Everyone shared in the feast.

Washington, Our Home

Linking the Present to the Past

This informative feature helps students connect unfamiliar events or historical concepts to familiar things in their lives today. By accessing this prior knowledge, the unknown becomes relevant, and students begin to understand how events from the past affect the present.

Washington Portraits

Because the story of Washington's history is actually the story of its people, Washington Portraits provide biographical information about people who made significant contributions to the state or the nation.

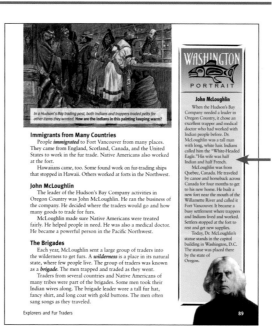

In a Hudson's Bay trading post, both Indians and trappers traded pelts for other items they wanted. **How are the Indians in this painting keeping warm?**

Immigrants from Many Countries

People **immigrated** to Fort Vancouver from many places. They came from England, Scotland, Canada, and the United States to work in the fur trade. Native Americans also worked at the fort.

Hawaiians came, too. Some found work on fur-trading ships that stopped in Hawaii. Others worked at forts in the Northwest.

John McLoughlin

The leader of the Hudson's Bay Company activities in Oregon Country was John McLoughlin. He ran the business of the company. He decided where the traders would go and how many goods to trade for furs.

McLoughlin made sure Native Americans were treated fairly. He helped people in need. He was also a medical doctor. He became a powerful person in the Pacific Northwest.

The Brigades

Each year, McLoughlin sent a large group of traders into the wilderness to get furs. A **wilderness** is a place in its natural state, where few people live. The group of traders was known as a **brigade**. The men trapped and traded as they went.

Traders from several countries and Native Americans of many tribes were part of the brigade. Some men took their Indian wives along. The brigade leader wore a tall fur hat, fancy shirt, and long coat with gold buttons. The men often sang songs as they traveled.

Explorers and Fur Traders   89

WASHINGTON PORTRAIT
John McLoughlin

When the Hudson's Bay Company needed a leader in Oregon Country, it chose an excellent trapper and medical doctor who had worked with Indian people before. Dr. McLoughlin was a tall man with long, white hair. Indians called him the "White-Headed Eagle." His wife was half Indian and half French.

McLoughlin was from Quebec, Canada. He traveled by canoe and horseback across Canada for four months to get to his new home. He built a new fort near the mouth of the Willamette River and called it Fort Vancouver. It became a busy settlement where trappers and Indians lived and worked. Settlers stopped at the fort to rest and get new supplies.

Today, Dr. McLoughlin's statue stands in the capitol building in Washington, D.C. The statue was placed there by the state of Oregon.

Go to the Source

Go to the Source allows students to analyze a primary or secondary source document or artifact that relates to the content of the chapter. The questions help students develop critical thinking skills.

Skills Pages

The Skills Pages are standards-based and ask students to apply critical and creative thinking to social studies content.

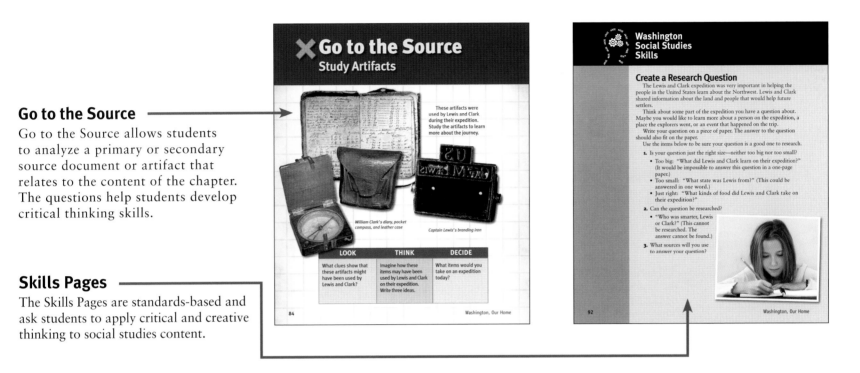

CHAPTER REVIEW

Each Chapter Review allows students to review the key objectives of the chapter and to evaluate understanding of chapter content.

Reviewing What You Read

The Reviewing What You Read questions assess students' understanding of the chapter's main ideas.

Becoming a Better Reader

These activities reinforce the learning of the reading strategies used throughout the chapter.

Spotlighting Geography

This feature connects the content of the chapter to geography skills.

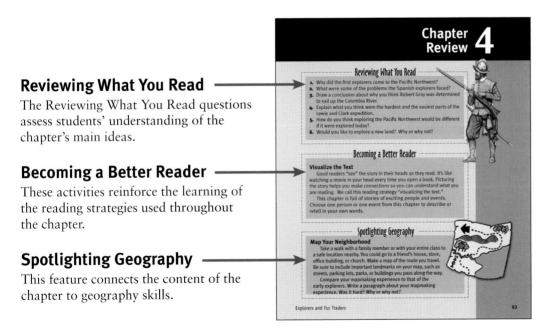

STUDENT GUIDE FEATURES

STUDENT GUIDE FEATURES

Each lesson within the *Student Guide* will contain the following four components:

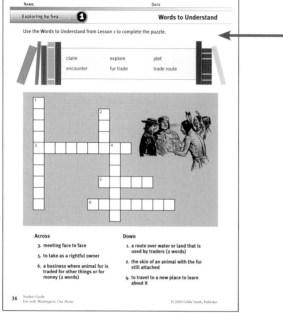

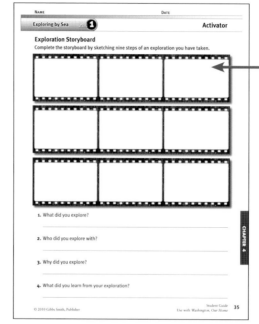

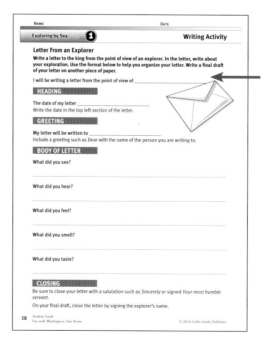

Words to Understand

This activity gives students an opportunity to apply their understanding of new content vocabulary.

Activator

Use this pre-reading activity to activate students' prior knowledge and to give students an opportunity to practice their prediction skills.

Reading Strategies

Use these activities to encourage higher-level thinking and to build reading comprehension.

Writing Activity

This activity provides a fun way for students to practice the writing process, review writing elements, and engage in a variety of writing applications.

GIBBS SMITH EDUCATION
TO ENRICH AND INSPIRE HUMANKIND

DIGITAL RESOURCES

AUDIO BOOK

The Audio Book CD for *Washington, Our Home*, contains an audio recording of the entire text of the *Student Edition*.

WEB SITE: WWW.EXPERIENCESTATEHISTORY.COM

www.ExperienceStateHistory.com is where you will find electronic resources specifically designed for *Washington, Our Home*. This site supports the textbook, enhances students' learning, and provides user-friendly ways to incorporate technology into your social studies instruction. The following are some of the features found at the site.

- Online *Student Edition*
- Audio recording of the *Student Edition*
- *Teacher Guide* pages
- *Student Guide* pages
- Image Bank: downloadable photos, maps, charts, and more
- ExamView® test-generating program
- Correlation to the state standards
- Links to chapter resources used in the *Teacher Guide*

What Is History?

CHAPTER PLANNER

CHAPTER OVERVIEW	WASHINGTON SOCIAL STUDIES GLEs
Students will learn what history is and that history can be found in many different places. They will also learn that historians use tools such as primary and secondary sources to study history from different points of view.	GLE 4.1.1 GLE 4.3.1 GLE 5.1.1 GLE 5.1.2 GLE 5.2.2

CHAPTER RESOURCES	
ELL/Modified Chapter Plan, p. 2I	
Books and Web Sites, p. 2J	

CHAPTER ACTIVITIES	WASHINGTON CURRICULUM INTEGRATION
You as a Primary Source, p. 2E	**Writing** GLE 2.2.1
Artifacts of a Typical Student, p. 2E	**Communication** GLE 2.2.2
■ Washington Biography, p. 2E	**Reading** GLE 2.1.7, GLE 4.2.1
Who Are We?, p. 2E	**Math** GLE 4.4.E
A Traveling Adventure, p. 2F	**Writing** GLE 1.1.1, GLE 1.2.1, GLE 1.3.1, GLE 1.4.1, GLE 1.5.1
■ Family Resemblance, p. 2F	**Writing** GLE 2.2.1, **Science** GLE 4-5 LS3B
All About Me, p. 2F	**Visual Arts** GLE
Family History Day, p. 2F	**Writing** GLE 2.2.1, GLE 3.1.2

CHAPTER OPENER	WASHINGTON CURRICULUM INTEGRATION
Many Things Have History, p.4	**Visual Arts** GLE 2.3.1
Postcard From Washington, p. 5	**Writing** GLE 3.2.1

►Indicates an activity page located in the *Student Guide*
■ Indicates an activity page located in the *Teacher Guide*

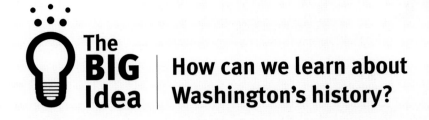

The BIG Idea | How can we learn about Washington's history?

CHAPTER REVIEW	pp. 16–17
SOCIAL STUDIES SKILLS PAGE	**WASHINGTON SOCIAL STUDIES GLEs**
Reading and Creating a Timeline, p.16	**Social Studies** GLE 4.1.1 **Reading** GLE 3.1.1 **Writing** GLE 2.2.1
REVIEWING THE CHAPTER	**WASHINGTON SOCIAL STUDIES GLEs**
Students show what they learned by completing application activities and answering chapter review questions. Assessments for this chapter can be previewed on pages 2G–2H. Select the assessment option that best suits your goals for this chapter. Assessments are available in the *Teacher Guide* or online at **www.ExperienceStateHistory.com**.	GLE 4.1.1 GLE 4.3.1 GLE 5.1.1 GLE 5.1.2 GLE 5.2.2
CHAPTER ACTIVITIES	**WASHINGTON CURRICULUM INTEGRATION**
Reviewing What You Read, p. 17	**Reading** GLE 1.3.2, GLE 2.1.3
Previewing a Textbook, p. 17	**Reading** GLE 2.1.5
Family History, p. 17	**Writing** GLE 2.2.1
CHAPTER ASSESSMENTS	**WASHINGTON CURRICULUM INTEGRATION**
■ Multiple Choice Assessment, p. 3	**Reading** GLE 1.3.2, GLE 2.1.3
■ Reading Assessment, p. 4	**Reading** GLE 2.1.3, GLE 2.1.5
■ Writing Assessment, p. 5	**Writing** GLE 2.2.1, GLE 3.1.2
■ Project Assessment, pp. 6–8	**Writing** GLE 2.2.1, GLE 3.1.2

LESSON 1
Many Kinds of History pp. 6–9

LESSON OVERVIEW	WASHINGTON SOCIAL STUDIES GLEs
KEY IDEAS: • History is the story of the past. • Places, people, and objects have stories to tell.	**GLE 4.3.1** **GLE 5.1.1** **GLE 5.2.2**

LESSON ACTIVITIES	WASHINGTON CURRICULUM INTEGRATION
▶What Do You Know About Washington?, p. 6	**Writing** GLE 2.2.1
Grouping Words, p. 6	**Reading** GLE 1.3.1
▶Words to Understand, p. 6	**Reading** GLE 1.3.1
How Seattle Got Its Name, p. 7	**Communication** GLE 3.3.1
Flag About Me, p. 7	**Visual Art** GLE 3.1
▶Previewing a Textbook, p. 7	**Reading** GLE 2.2.2, GLE 2.2.4
▶My Washington Portrait, p. 8	**Writing** GLE 3.1.1, GLE 3.2.2
Mary Low Sinclair, p. 9	**Communication** GLE 1.2.1
Review Memory, p. 9	**Reading** GLE 1.3.1, GLE 1.3.2

LESSON 2
Tools of History
pp. 10–15

LESSON OVERVIEW	WASHINGTON SOCIAL STUDIES GLEs
KEY IDEAS: • Historians use tools to discover what happened in the past. • Historians use primary sources, secondary sources, and timelines. • People have different points of view.	**GLE 4.1.1** **GLE 5.1.1** **GLE 5.1.2** **GLE 5.2.2**

LESSON ACTIVITIES	WASHINGTON CURRICULUM INTEGRATION
▶Guess Who?, p. 10	**Writing** GLE 2.2.1
Word Parts, p. 10	**Reading** GLE 1.2.2
▶Words to Understand, p. 10	**Reading** GLE 1.3.1
▶Previewing to Find Main Ideas, p. 11	**Reading** GLE 2.2.2
Examine a Certificate, p. 12	**Reading** GLE 3.1.1
Primary Source Learning, p. 12	**Reading** GLE 3.1.1
Go to the Source: Study a Photograph, p. 13	**Communication** GLE 1.2.1
Tell the Story of a Picture, p. 13	**Writing** GLE 2.3.1, GLE 3.2.2
How Historians Study the Past, p. 14	**Writing** GLE 2.2.1
▶Writing From Another Point of View, p. 15	**Reading** GLE 2.1.1, GLE 2.2.1

Chapter Activities

This chapter focuses on history and how we study it. Attention is given to helping student understand primary and secondary sources. Use these Chapter Activities as you work through the chapter to help students understand the key ideas.

 Set the Stage

Before you begin this chapter, create a bulletin board titled "Washington, Our Home." Download pictures from the Internet of people doing different activities in Washington. Invite students to draw or bring pictures from home to add to the bulletin board.

 Introductory Activity

You as a Primary Source

Start this chapter about history and the way we study history by presenting your own family history to the class. Show students pictures and artifacts that tell where your ancestors came from and what your family is like today. Help students see that history is not just about people in the long-ago past. History shapes who we are today. Following your presentation, have students write a few sentences in their journals telling about the similarities and differences between your family history and their own.

 Social Studies Activity

Artifacts of a Typical Student

Have students set up a mini-exhibit showing artifacts of a typical student.

As a class, brainstorm artifacts that show the life of a typical fourth-grade student. Artifacts may include books, backpacks, student identification cards, library cards, popular magazines, CDs of favorite music, or DVDs of favorite movies. Encourage students to be creative. Students may want to dress a doll or draw a picture on a poster showing how a typical student dresses. You may want to divide the boys and the girls into separate groups and have each group set up their own exhibit showing the typical boy or girl student.

 Reading Activity

Washington Biography

Have students read a biography of someone with a connection to Washington. After reading the book, students should prepare a report about the person. A Washington Biography book report form is included in the *Teacher Guide*. Have students use information from their reports to present an oral book report to the class in first person. Encourage students to dress the part of the person and talk about the life of the person as if they are the person.

NAME _____ DATE _____

What Is History? **1** Reading Activity

Washington Biography
After reading a biography of someone with a connection to Washington, complete this form.

Title of Book: _____
Author: _____
Biography about: _____
Date of Birth: _____
Place of Birth: _____
Date of Death: _____
Place of Death: _____
This person is best known for: _____

People would describe this person as: _____
_____
_____

The most interesting fact about this person is: _____

One question I would ask the person if I met him or her is: _____

I admire/don't admire (circle one) this person because: _____

I would/would not (circle one) recommend this book because: _____
_____
_____

© 2010 Gibbs Smith, Publisher   Teacher Guide   1
Use with *Washington, Our Home*

CHAPTER 1

 Math Activity

Who Are We?

People from Washington are not the same! Begin by looking at the people in your own classroom. First ask, *Who are we?* Students may describe themselves by age, gender, location, interests, or preferences. As a class, create a list of possible survey questions, such as:

- Where were you born?
- What is your favorite _____?
- How many siblings do you have?
- How tall are you?

After choosing questions, students should collect data. To do this, they will survey their classmates and record their responses to the questions. Show students how to collect and record data by taking a quick survey (show of hands) of the birthdays of the students in your class. Draw a graph like the one below on your board. Point out the title of the graph and the two labels. Complete the graph showing the information you collected from the class. Ask questions about the information on the graph. Allow students to collect data and record what they find in graph form. Challenge: Encourage student to find the mean, median, and mode of the number of siblings students they surveyed have.

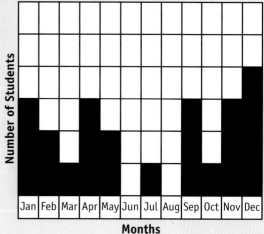

Months of Birthdays

(Number of Students / Months: Jan Feb Mar Apr May Jun Jul Aug Sep Oct Nov Dec)

A Traveling Adventure

Ask students why they think the textbook is called *Washington, Our Home*. To help students get thinking about the textbook, have them write a one-page essay on a traveling adventure they have had in Washington.

Prewriting

Have students brainstorm different places in Washington they have lived in or visited, including places they have visited on vacation, field trips, or even someplace near where they live. Have them talk with a partner to narrow their list down to the place they want to write about.

Drafting

Provide time for students to write a first draft of their essay on their traveling adventure. Write the following on the board and tell students that their essay should cover each item:

1. Where they went
2. Why they went there
3. What they took with them
4. What they did

Revising

Have students use the four points listed above when revising their essays. They should check to make sure that each point is covered. They should also revise to include more details about their adventures.

Editing

Have students work in pairs to edit their essays for spelling, grammar, capitalization, and punctuation. You may choose to have students erase and make changes to their first draft, or rewrite the first draft if there were a lot of changes.

Publishing

Have students share their essays with the class or with a partner.

Family Resemblance

Our parents give us their history, and they also give us our physical appearance. Skin color, eye color, hair color, even whether the bottom of our ear lobes attach to our heads are traits we receive from our parents. This introductory lesson on genetics will help students understand why we look the way we do.

Have students complete the Family Resemblance activity available in the *Teacher Guide*. Place a chart on the board for students to record their information. Have students compare the differences and similarities between themselves and their classmates. They should complete the second part of the activity with their families at home. Have students write about the similarities and differences in their families.

For more on this topic, go to the Kids Genetics Web site. This Web site has lots of interesting information and games kids can play to learn more about the science of genetics. Go to **www.ExperienceStateHistory.com** for a link to this site.

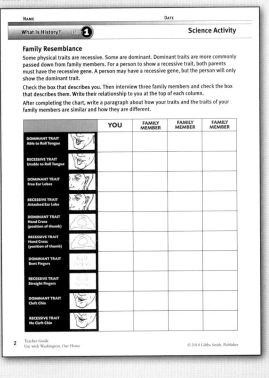

All About Me

Create a silhouette of each student. To do this, tape a large piece of paper to the wall. Have each student sit in a chair so the side of the student's head is next to the paper. Shine a lamp so you can see the shadow of the student on the paper, and trace around the shadow. Then give the silhouette to the student and have him or her trace around the silhouette with a thick, black marker, and then cut it out. When all the students have their silhouettes, they should fill them with words and pictures that tell about who they are, including their personal history.

 Culminating Activity

Family History Day

To culminate the learning in this chapter, display students' work and invite other classes and parents to view their projects. If you recorded the students' giving oral presentations from their Family History projects from the *Teacher Guide*, have a TV available to play the presentations for visitors. (Have a couple of students write up a list so visitors can fast-forward to the presentation they are most interested in viewing.) Students can also display their interviews and artifacts on their desks and be available to talk about their projects with visitors. The following projects may also be included in the display:

- Family Resemblance recording sheets
- Artifacts of a Typical Student displays
- All About Me silhouettes
- My Washington Portrait
- Family History Projects (Project Assessment)

Assessment Options

The Chapter Assessment options provide opportunities to evaluate students' understanding of the social studies concepts. Choose the assessment options that best meet the needs of your teaching goals. Assessments are available in the *Teacher Guide* or can be individualized at www.ExperienceStateHistory.com.

OPTION 1: MULTIPLE CHOICE ASSESSMENT

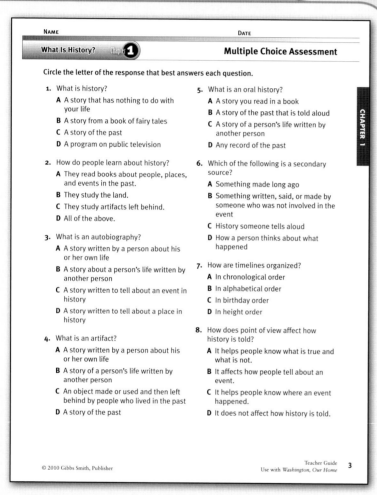

The Multiple Choice Assessment provides a quick way to assess students' understanding of the key concepts of the chapter. Have students read each question and select the best answer.

OPTION 2: READING ASSESSMENT

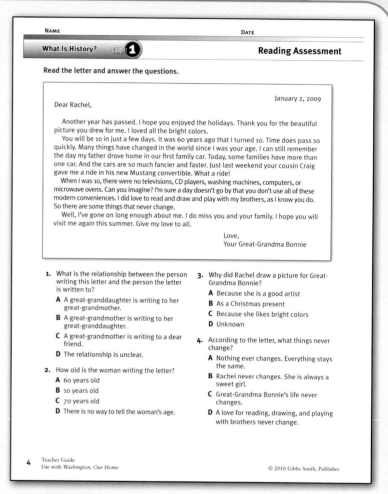

The Reading Assessment provides additional practice for the WASL Reading Test. Have students read the passage and answer the questions that follow.

NAME _____ DATE _____

What Is History? Chapter **1**   **Writing Assessment**

Read each question and write a short answer. Edit your responses for spelling, grammar, punctuation, and capitalization.

1. How do people learn about the past?

_____

_____

_____

_____

2. What is the difference between primary and secondary sources? Give two examples of each.

_____

_____

_____

_____

_____

3. What is point of view and how does it affect how history is told?

_____

_____

_____

_____

_____

_____

The Writing Assessment provides additional practice for the WASL Writing Test. Have students write a short answer to each question about the chapter.

NAME _____ DATE _____

What Is History? Chapter **1**   **Project Assessment (Page 1 of 3)**

Research your family history, and prepare a Family History Report. Use this checklist to help you organize your project. Check off the steps as you go.

Family History Project

☐ **Create a Family Tree**
With help from an adult in your family, complete your family tree to the best of your knowledge. Your teacher will provide a form to use. Have the adult who helped you sign here:

_____

☐ **Interview a Family Member**
Interview the oldest family member you are able to talk with either in person, on the telephone, or through e-mail. Use the form your teacher provides to do the interview. Using the responses from the interview, write an essay about the person. The final draft should be typewritten, with few or no errors in punctuation, capitalization, grammar, and spelling. Have an adult help you edit. Have the adult who helped you edit sign here:

_____

☐ **Present Your Family History**
Prepare a five-minute oral presentation about your family history. First, write your family history. Practice your presentation to a family member before you present it to the class. Have the family member sign here:

_____

☐ **Find a Family Artifact**
Find an artifact that shows something of your family history. A photograph, a certificate, or newspaper article are some examples of possible artifacts. On the day of your oral presentation, bring the artifact to class.

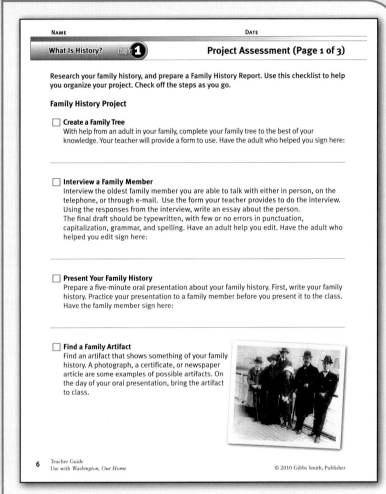

The Project Assessment provides an alternative to the traditional assessment. Have students read the checklist to plan their Family History Project.

ELL/Modified Chapter Plan

What Is History?

In this chapter, students will learn that history is the story of the past. Students will also learn that historians use primary and secondary sources to learn about history.

The following pages can be found in the ELL/Modified Chapter Guide on pages 3–7.

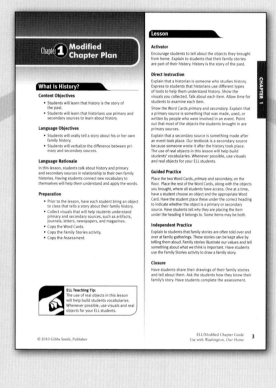

The ELL/Modified Chapter Plan provides a step-by-step lesson in an easy-to-use format. Lessons teach content and language objectives.

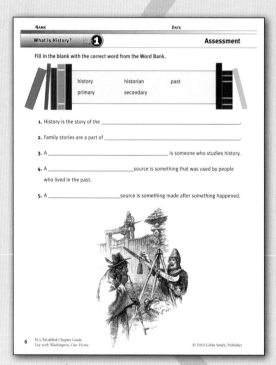

The Modified Assessment for this chapter assesses students' understanding of the key objectives of the chapter.

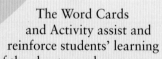

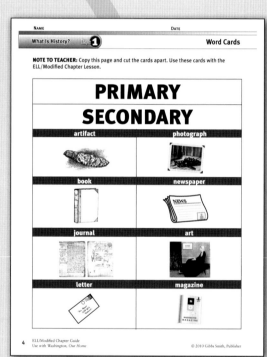

The Word Cards and Activity assist and reinforce students' learning of the chapter and prepares them for the assessment.

Books and Web Sites

Books

Edinger, Monica. *Seeking History: Teaching with Primary Sources in Grades 4-6.* Portsmouth: Heinemann, 2000.

Hoose, Phillip. *We Were There, Too! Young People in U.S. History.* New York: Farrar, Straus and Giroux, 2001.

Smith, Roland. *E is for Evergreen: A Washington State Alphabet.* Chelsea: Sleeping Bear Press, 2004.

Web Sites

The following Web sites provide resources or lesson plans for teachers and activities for students to help extend the lessons in this chapter. Go to **www.ExperienceStateHistory.com** for links to these Web sites.

America's Story from America's Library

The America's Story Web site provides information for teachers and students about amazing people and historic events in America.

History Matters

The History Matters Web site provides teachers with strategies for analyzing online primary materials as well as interactive exercises for students.

Kids Genetics

On the Kids Genetics Web site, students can learn more about the science of genetics and play some fun games.

The Library of Congress, American Memory

This Library of Congress, American Memory Web site provides lesson plans for teachers to help students understand how to use primary sources.

The National Archives

The National Archives Web site provides several online exhibits and primary documents.

National History Day

The National History Day Web site enables students to ask questions about a topic's significance in history. Students can creatively interpret primary sources to answer questions about these topics.

Primary Source Learning

The Primary Source Learning Web site has a wealth of information to help teachers use online primary sources with confidence. It also has a brief online video for students that reinforces how and why historians use primary sources.

We Were There, Too!

The We Were There, Too! Web site provides interesting stories for teachers and students from the point of view of young people in history.

Unit Opener Activity

Scenes from History

Have students study the picture on the pages of the Unit Opener. Use the caption question to lead the class in a discussion.

 Put Yourself in the Picture

Act Out History

After discussing some of the events in the picture, have students work in groups to create a short skit for one of the events. Their skits should show what they know about the event or any questions they might have about the event. After the class shares their skits, have students write a short paragraph about how they think the events in the Unit Opener might affect Washington's state history.

Caption Answer

The students are wearing clothes from different time periods. They also have props that are clues to what events they are acting out.

UNIT 1

Have you ever seen a play? People decorate the stage to help tell the story. They act out a story from a certain time and place.

History is made up of stories that happened at certain times and places. If our history were a play, our land would be the stage. It is the setting for our state's story.

These school children are dressed up in costumes. They are putting on a play about events in history. **What clues tell you what some of the events might be?**

2

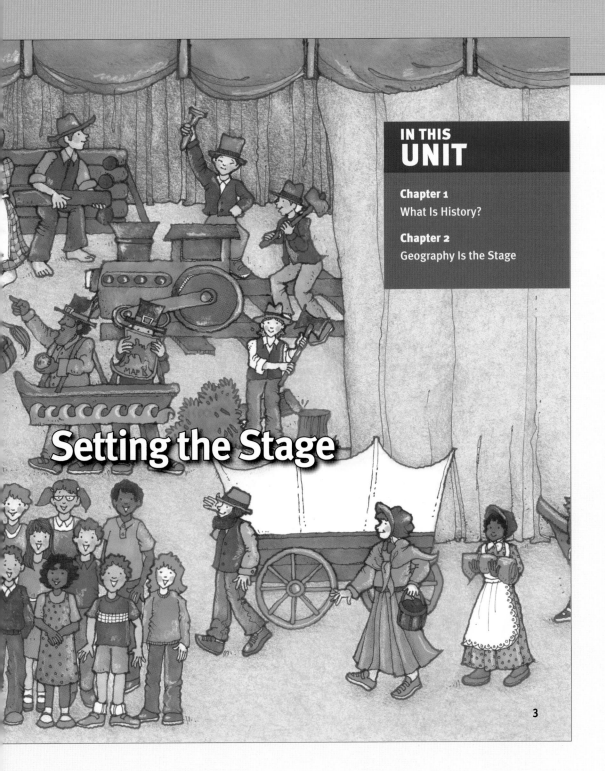

Setting the Stage

3

The BIG Idea

Many Things Have History

Ask students to turn to a partner and briefly discuss the meaning of the word *history*. Bring the class back together and ask for volunteers to share some ideas they discussed. Explain to the class that history is the story of the past.

As a class, brainstorm a list of different stories, such as stories about families, students, countries, and pets. Write the list on the board. Have students choose a word from the list and draw a picture to depict its history. Ask students to share their drawings with the class or in a small group. After sharing drawings, explain to students that this year they will be learning about Washington's stories of the past.

Caption Answer

You can learn how people used to dress, what buildings used to look like, and how people used to travel in early Seattle.

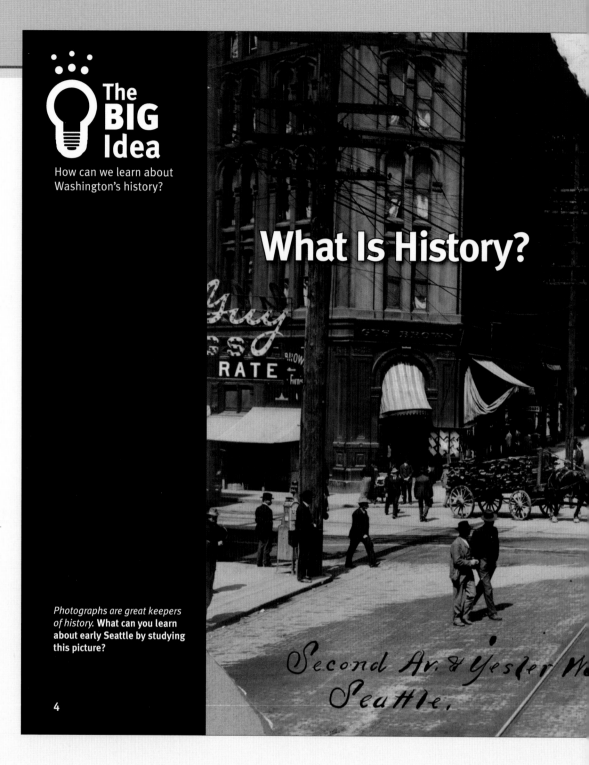

The BIG Idea

How can we learn about Washington's history?

What Is History?

Photographs are great keepers of history. **What can you learn about early Seattle by studying this picture?**

4

Second Av. & Yesler W
Seattle,

CHAPTER

1

 Put Yourself in the Picture

Postcard from Washington

As a class, study the picture from the Chapter Opener. Have students choose a person in the photograph and think about what that person might have been doing, thinking, and feeling. Tell students they will be writing a postcard to tell about what is happening in the picture from the perspective of the person they chose. They may choose to write to a friend or member of that person's family who doesn't live in Washington or who lives in another area of Washington.

Talk about the elements of a postcard, including the picture on front, the message on the back, a place for an address, and a place for a stamp. Encourage students to draw a picture on the front that represents Washington. Allow students to share their postcards with the class.

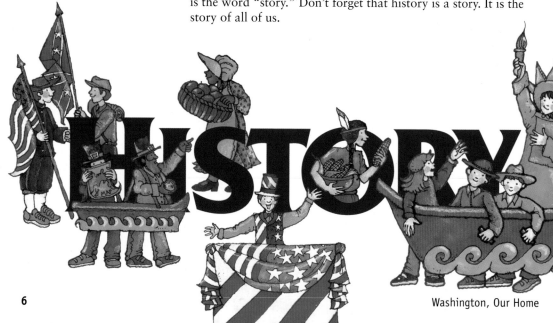Washington, Our Home

Standards

GLE 4.3.1
Understands that there are multiple perspectives regarding the interpretation of historical events and creates an historical account using multiple sources.

PREPARE

Activator

What Do You Know about Washington?

Ask students to think about what *Washington, Our Home* will be about. Using the KWL chart found in the *Student Guide,* have students write down anything they know about Washington's history in the left column. In the middle column, have students write down anything they'd like to know about Washington's history. Keep these pages in a file to access at the end of the year. At that time, have students complete the last column with information they learned about Washington's history.

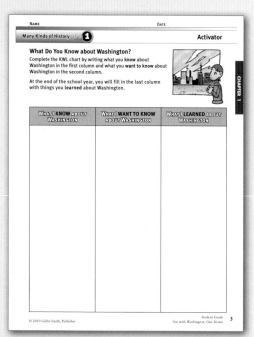

Word Study

Grouping Words

Pair students, and have them put the Words to Understand into related groups. Have students label each group. For example, autobiography, biography, history, and oral history could be grouped together as stories about people. Encourage students to come up with different ways to group the words.

LESSON 1 Many Kinds of History

Key Ideas

- History is the story of the past.
- Places, people, and objects have stories to tell.

Words to Understand

artifact
autobiography
biography
history
oral history
portrait

One State, Many Stories

People are not all the same. We do not think the same thoughts. We do not wear the same clothes. Some people were born in Washington and have lived here their whole lives. Other people have come to live here from many different places. Each person adds to the story of our state.

History, the Story of the Past

What do you think when you hear the word "story"? Do you think of a story you have read? Do you think of a story your parents read to you?

Perhaps you can tell a story of something that happened to you when you were little. Can you remember your first day of school? Maybe you remember the first time you rode a bike or went bowling. What is your favorite story?

History is the story of the past. Look at the word "history." Take off the first two letters of the word. What word is left? It is the word "story." Don't forget that history is a story. It is the story of all of us.

6

Words to Understand

artifact (p.8) *an object made or used by people of the past*

autobiography (p.8) *a book written by a person about his or her own life*

biography (p.8) *the story of a person's life as written by another person*

history (p.6) *the story of the past*

oral history (p.9) *a story told aloud and passed down from person to person*

portrait (p.8) *a picture of a person in words, art, or photograph*

A Words to Understand activity for this lesson is available in the *Student Guide.*

Stories of Place

Places have stories. A town is a place. So is a state. What places have you lived in? What places have you visited? All of these places have a history.

Who first started the place where you live? Have you ever wondered how your town or city got its name? To answer these questions, we need to search for the stories of the place.

How Seattle Got Its Name

Chief Sealth was a leader of two Indian tribes. He was also a friend to white settlers when they came to find new places to live. Later, the settlers wanted the Indians to move to a different place. Chief Sealth asked his people to go peacefully. Seattle was named for this Indian man. See if you can find other towns that were named for Indian people or Indian words.

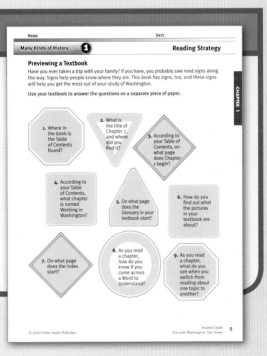

Seattle was named for Chief Sealth. **How can you tell this photo was taken in modern times?**

What Is History?

7

TEACH

Talk About It

One State, Many Stories *(From page 6)*

What is history?
History is the story of the past.

Stories of a Place

What are some places that have stories?
Possible answers include classrooms, kitchens, parks, cities, and states.

Caption Answer

There are a lot of tall buildings. Many buildings are lit up.

 Social Studies Activity

How Seattle Got Its Name

As a class, talk about how your school, city, or nearby sites got their name. Then have students turn to a partner and discuss how they got their names. Were they named after someone in their family? Were they named after someone in history? Ask for volunteers to share what they discussed.

 Art Activity

Flag About Me

Have students divide a white sheet of paper into fourths. Instruct students to draw something different in each quarter representing 1) their name 2) how they got their name 3)what their name means, and 4) some of their favorite things. Display the flags in the classroom.

Reading Strategy

Previewing a Textbook

Tell students that good readers preview a textbook before reading it. A preview is a quick look through the book. Explain that this textbook has certain features to help readers better understand the text. The features include a **title page, table of contents, chapters, photo captions, Glossary,** and **Index.** Explain to the students how each feature is helpful. After providing instruction, students will complete the Previewing a Textbook activity in the *Student Guide*.

7

Standards

GLE 5.2.1
Understands the concepts used in documents and sources.

GLE 5.2.2
Understands the main idea from an artifact, primary source, or secondary source describing an issue or event.

Talk About It

Stories of People

What is the difference between a biography and an autobiography?

A biography is a story of a person's life written by another person. An autobiography is a story someone writes about his or her own life.

Stories from Artifacts

What is an artifact that might tell about your life?

Encourage students to tell about things that are important to them.

Stories from Photographs

Why do you think photographs are helpful in giving details about history?

Photographs give us a visual picture of the event.

Stories Told Aloud *(From page 9)*

What is oral history?

It is history told aloud.

WASHINGTON
PORTRAIT

Mary Low Sinclair

Mary wrapped up her baby son in a warm blanket. Then she carried him onto a small steamship. The ship crossed Puget Sound and then went up the Snohomish River.

When the ship stopped next to a deep forest, Mary and her baby joined Mary's husband. He had bought some land and built a small home. It had no windows and only a dirt floor.

Mary was the first white woman to live in what was later called Snohomish City. There were no schools, so Mary taught children in her own home. She also learned to speak Indian languages and taught Indian children.

8

Stories of People

Washington's story includes the stories of ordinary people and heroes. By learning a person's story, we can understand what problems he or she faced. We can learn what has changed over time and how our lives today are different. We can also learn about things that have stayed the same.

One way to learn about a person is through a *biography*. A biography is the story of a person's life that was written by another person. Most people love to read these exciting true stories.

In this book you will see short biographies of important people. They are called Washington Portraits. A *portrait* is usually a photograph or painting of a person, but in this book we also tell about the person in words.

Some people write books about their own lives. This kind of book is called an *autobiography*. What would you write in your autobiography?

Stories from Artifacts

Long ago, people made tools, pottery, jewelry, and other things. Sometimes the people moved and left the objects behind. Sometimes they dropped a ring or toy and never found it. Many years later, it was found.

Objects that people made or used and then left behind are called *artifacts*. We can study artifacts for clues about Washington's story.

Stories from Photographs

Have you ever picked up an old photograph and wondered, "What would these people tell me if they could speak to me?" The photograph does speak, but the words are silent.

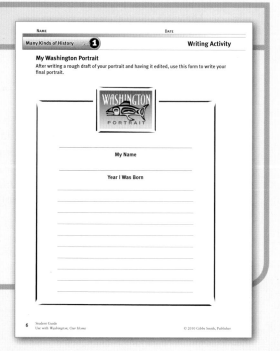

Washington, Our Home

Writing Activity

My Washington Portrait

Discuss the meaning of portraits and the "Washington Portrait" feature of this textbook with the class. Then have students write a short portrait about themselves. Use this activity as an opportunity to take your class through the writing process:

First, have students brainstorm some key traits about themselves.
Next, have students choose two of these traits as main ideas to write about.
Encourage students to start each paragraph with a topic sentence relating to a main idea, followed by three or more supporting sentences.

Discuss purpose and audience when writing a biography.

Have students write a draft and edit. After editing, have students write their finished essay on the My Washington Portrait form available in the *Student Guide*. Either encourage students to bring a photograph to go with their portraits or take photos of the students. Use their finished portraits to create a bulletin board titled, "Our Washington Portraits."

Family stories are told aloud and passed down from person to person.
How might this grandfather's oral history stories help his grandchildren?

Stories Told Aloud

Have you ever listened to an older person tell a story from his own life? These stories passed from person to person down through time are called *oral history*. The stories are told aloud.

Oral histories are important ways to learn history. However, when people tell stories from memory, they might forget exactly what happened. Or, they might change the story a little. When Uncle John tells about the time he caught his first fish in a mountain stream, he might forget to tell about how small the fish was. He might also change the story just a little bit.

Even if they are not exactly true, oral histories are great clues to the past. They tell us how people saw the world.

LESSON 1 What Did You Learn?

1. What things can have a history?
2. What can we learn by studying history?
3. How do we learn about history?

What Is History?

LESSON 1 What Did You Learn?

1. *History is the story of the past.*
2. *We can learn how people before us lived.*
3. *We can learn about history by studying primary and secondary sources and other artifacts.*

REFLECT

Reflect on students' understanding of history as a story of the past and the idea that places, people, and objects have stories to tell. You can evaluate students' understanding through discussion or evaluation of activities completed in this lesson. The following activity will serve as another way of assessing students' understanding of the key objectives of this lesson.

 **Social Studies Activity**

Review Memory

Have students work in pairs, and write the following terms on a set of flashcards: artifact, autobiography, biography, history, oral history, photograph, and portrait.

Next, have students create a second set of flashcards by either drawing or writing examples for each term on a card.

Tell students to mix both sets of cards and lay them face down. Students take turns flipping over two cards at a time to try to find the term and the example it matches. The student with the most matches at the end is the winner.

Caption Answer

His grandchildren will learn about their family history from his stories. This will help them understand their family.

WASHINGTON
PORTRAIT

Mary Low Sinclair *(from page 8)*

As a class, discuss what effects Mary Low Sinclair may have had on future residents of Snohomish City.

Have students work in pairs to discuss people in your community's history that have had an effect on how things are today. Encourage students to share their ideas with the class.

Standards

GLE 5.2.2
Understands the main ideas from an artifact, primary source, or secondary source describing an issue or event.

PREPARE

Activator

Guess Who?

Choose an adult whom all the students know personally. Perhaps it could be the principal, the librarian, or a third-grade teacher. Ask the person for some artifacts that tell about his or her life and put them in a bag. Show the students each artifact, one at a time.

Then ask students to complete the Guess Who? activity page available in their *Student Guide*. Using the clues from the artifacts, have students guess who the artifacts belongs to.

Word Study

Word Parts

Write the words Primary and Secondary on the board. Explain that the word part *pri* means first, and the word part *second* means second. Make a list of words and ways these word parts are used.

Key Ideas

- Historians use tools to discover what happened in the past.
- These tools include primary sources, secondary sources, and timelines.
- People have different points of view.

Words to Understand

chronological
century
decade
era
document
historian
point of view
primary source
secondary source

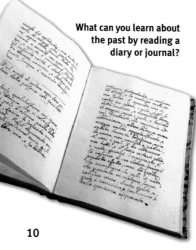

What can you learn about the past by reading a diary or journal?

10

LESSON 2 Tools of History

Be a History Detective

You have just read about different kinds of stories that tell about the past. **Historians** are people who study history. In some ways, they are like detectives. They try to find clues about what happened in the past. You can be a history detective by asking:

- **What** happened?
- **Where** did it happen?
- **When** did it happen?
- **Who** was there?
- **Why** did it happen?

Primary Sources

Historians have special words for the things they study. They call them primary sources and secondary sources.
Primary sources were made by people who were there at the time. Pretend that your great-great-grandmother lived on a farm. In her diary, she wrote about how cold it was when she had to go outside in the dark to use the outhouse. (Her house did not have a bathroom indoors.) The diary is a primary source.

Papers and forms are called *documents*. A birth certificate is a document. It was written at the time you were born. It tells the names of your parents and when and where you were born. It is a primary source about you.

Here are some examples of primary sources:

- Artifacts
- Diaries and journals
- Letters
- Photographs
- Autobiographies
- Interviews done at the time and place an event happened
- Certain newspapers and magazines

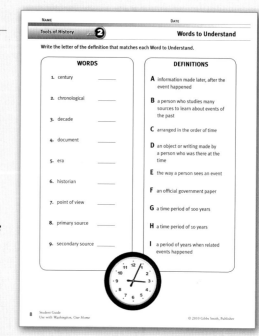

Washington, Our Home

Words to Understand

century (p. 14) *a time period of 100 years*
chronological (p. 14) *arranged in the order of time*
decade (p. 14) *a time period of 100 years*
era (p. 14) *a period of years when related events happened*
document (p. 10) *an official government paper*
historian (p. 10) *a person who studies many sources to learn about events of the past*
point of view (p. 15) *the way a person sees an event*
primary source (p. 10) *an object or writing made by a person who was there at the time*
secondary source (p. 11) *information made later, after the event happened*

A Words to Understand activity for this lesson is available in the *Student Guide*.

Secondary Sources

Secondary sources are made later, after the event happened. The person creating the secondary source was NOT involved in the event at all. To understand history, we need to study both primary and secondary sources.

If, for example, you wanted to write a book about whale hunting 100 years ago, you would read other books about the subject. You would search for photographs of whale hunters out in their boats. You might go to a museum to study spears or other tools the whale hunters used.

You could also try to find someone whose great-grandfather had been on a whale hunt. Maybe he or she remembers hearing the story of the dangerous hunt. Maybe the story even explained what whale meat tasted like!

The book you write on whale hunting will be a secondary source. Here are some other examples of secondary sources:

- Textbooks
- Biographies
- Movies
- Encyclopedias
- Internet sites

In the past, movies came to theaters on large reels of film like the one in the picture. No one had DVDs to watch at home. People liked to watch movies, but books were the main way people got information. **Why are movies and books often secondary sources?**

What Is History?   **11**

TEACH

Talk About It

Be a History Detective (From page 10)

What is a historian?
A person who studies history.

How can you be a history detective?
By asking what happened? Where did it happen? When did it happen? Who was there? Why did it happen?

Primary Sources (From page 10)

What is a primary source?
Objects or stories made by people who were there at the time of an event.

What are documents?
Government papers and forms.

What are some examples of primary sources?
Answers may include artifacts, journals, letters, photographs, autobiographies, interviews, and newspapers.

Secondary Sources

What is a secondary source?
Objects or stories that are written, said, or made after the time of an event.

What are some examples of a secondary source?
Answers may include textbooks, biographies, movies, encyclopedias, art, magazines, and Internet sites.

Reading Strategy

Previewing to Find Main Ideas

Use a student book to show the students examples of headings, subheadings, images, photo captions, and special features such as bold words. Tell students they will be previewing the text with the help of these features to find specific information.

Have students look at the chapter titles in the Table of Contents and make predictions about the main ideas of the chapters. Have students flip through the first few chapters and make predictions about the main ideas of the lessons. Have students use headings, bolded words, images, and captions to help make predictions about the paragraphs' main ideas. Have students complete the Previewing to Find Main Ideas page in their *Student Guide*.

NAME _____ **DATE** _____

Tools of History **2**   **Reading Strategy**

Previewing to Find Main Ideas
Use pages 10–15 in your textbook to answer the questions.

1. What does the heading of Lesson 2 tell you about what you will be reading?

2. From the heading on page 10, what do you think the main idea of this paragraph is?

3. Under the subheading, "Primary Sources" on page 10, what do the bulleted words make you think this section will be about?

4. Using the images and heading on page 13, what do you think this Go to the Source activity will ask you to do?

5. By only looking at the images on page 14, what do you think the main ideas of these paragraphs will be?

6. After viewing different parts of Lesson 2, write a new title for the lesson that will tell readers what this lesson will be about.

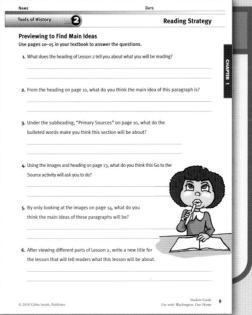

© 2010 Gibbs Smith, Publisher   Student Guide **9**
                                Use with *Washington, Our Home*

Talk About It

Primary or Secondary Source?

Is the first newspaper article a primary or a secondary source?
The article includes accounts from people who were there when the earthquake happened, so it would be a primary source.

Is the second newspaper article a primary or secondary source?
The article includes information from many sources who may or may not have been present at the time of an earthquake, so it is a secondary source.

Ask students if they can think of any other examples of primary and secondary sources. Write their suggestions on the board in a two-column chart.

Historians Use Many Sources

Can you see how using many different sources helps Amber learn about pioneer children?
Accept answers that explain what Amber could have learned from the sources she studied.

What other primary and secondary sources could Amber have used?
Amber could have used encyclopedias, artifacts, other books, letters, and Internet sites.

Caption Answers

The title, pictures, and story give clues to tell if it is a primary or secondary source.

Technology Activity

Primary Source Learning

Have students go online to the Primary Source Learning Web site to investigate the types of primary source documents this site contains. See **www.ExperienceStateHistory. com** for a link to this site.

Primary or Secondary Source?

Some items, such as newspapers, magazines, and paintings, can be either primary or secondary sources. It all depends on when and where the item was written or painted.

Let's look at an example. A newspaper reporter goes to a city just after an earthquake. She sees a building that has just crashed to the ground. She takes photographs of what she sees. She talks to people who just watched the building fall. Some of the people might have escaped from the shaking building just in time! They tell the reporter what happened to them.

Then the reporter writes a story, or article, that describes what just happened and what the city looks like after the earthquake. She includes quotes from people who talked to her. Do you think her newspaper article will be a primary source or a secondary source?

Now let's say another reporter in a different city 10 years from now is writing a story about earthquakes. He reads a lot of old newspaper stories and some magazine articles. He reads some facts on the Internet about all of the earthquakes in Washington over the past 100 years.

Then the reporter writes a newspaper article about earthquakes. Do you think his newspaper article will be a primary source or a secondary source? Why?

Historians Use Many Sources

Amber loves to read, so she goes to the library and checks out an exciting book. It is the story of a pioneer boy who moved to Washington a long time ago. Then she visits a museum and sees an old covered wagon with very large wheels. She sees a pioneer boy's faded shirt and old straw hat.

Later, Amber's teacher shows a map of wagon trails. Then Amber's class reads a diary of a red-haired 10-year-old boy. He helped drive two oxen that pulled his family's wagon over a muddy trail. The class is very sad when they read the part that says the boy's father drowned trying to get their wagon across a raging river.

Can you see how using many different sources helps Amber learn about pioneer children? What other primary and secondary sources could Amber have used?

Newspapers have all kinds of stories called articles. **How would you know if an article is a primary or secondary source?**

12

 Reading Activity

Examine a Certificate

Encourage students to bring in copies of their birth certificates or certificates of adoption. If students are unable to bring in their own certificates, they can work in pairs with students who have a copy of their certificate. Write the following questions on the board:

- What is the full name of the person on the certificate?
- When was the person born?
- Where was the person born?
- Who are the parents listed on the certificate?
- If a historian looked at this certificate 100 years from now, what could he or she learn about this person?

Go to the Source
Study a Photograph

This is a photograph of an Indian girl in Washington's White River Valley. Study the photograph to see what you can learn about the girl from this picture.

White River Valley

LOOK	THINK	DECIDE
What do you see in the photograph that gives clues about the time and the place it was taken?	Using clues from the photograph, what do you think might have happened before this picture was taken and after it was taken?	What can you infer (guess) about the girl's life, based on what you see in the picture?

What Is History?   13

Standards

GLE 5.1.2

Evaluates the accuracy of primary and secondary sources.

Study a Photograph

This photograph was taken sometime between 1902 and 1907. We know very little about where the photo was taken or the little girl in the photo. Encourage students to think like a historian using the Writing Activity below the student page.

Writing Activity

Tell the Story of a Picture

We don't know much about the little girl in this picture. We can only use clues from the picture to infer, or make guesses, about her story. Have students write a short biography about this little girl, making their most educated guesses about her life. Encourage them to use clues from the picture and the caption as they tell the story. Allow students to share what they wrote in small groups and see how different or similar their stories are.

LOOK	THINK	DECIDE
The color and quality of the photo tell us that the picture is old. The trees, basket, and clothing can give us clues to where the little girl was from.	Students' answers should be supported by clues from the photo.	The girl's family probably worked in fields. They probably didn't have a lot of money.

13

 Standards

GLE 4.1.1

Understands and creates timelines to show how historical events are organized into time periods and eras.

Talk About It

Chronological Order

What is chronological order?
The order in which things happened.

What are examples of things we list in chronological order?
Possible answers include birthdays, calendar events, and our daily schedules.

Events

What are some examples of events that might happen during a day at school?
Possible answers include saying the Pledge of Allegiance, reading a book, going outside to recess, solving math problems, eating lunch, and cleaning up for the day.

Time Periods and Eras

What year does the timeline start?
2001

What year does the timeline end?
2010

Point of View *(From page 15)*

What is point of view?
Point of view is a person's view or opinion of an event.

What are some events that take place during a school day that you and a classmate could have a different point of view about?
Possible answers include lessons in class, games at recess, opinions of current events, and presentations the students might give.

Caption Answers

It is the 21st century.

(From page 15) No, you have different points of view. You and the monkey each see different things.

A Timeline of MY LIFE

I was born.
I got my dog.
my family moved to washington.
I spent the summer at my grandmother's house.

2001 2002 2003 2004 2005 2006 2007 2008 2009 2010

I started kindergarten.
My baby sister was born.
I started the fourth grade.

What Century Is It?

Century	Years
18th	1700s
19th	1800s
20th	1900s
21st	2000s

HINT: To know the century, go up one number from the year. For example: 1600s = 17th century.

Understand Dates and Timelines

Chronological Order

Timelines are another tool historians use. A timeline helps us see the order in which events happened. This is called *chronological* order. The timeline above shows what happened first, next, and so on.

Events

What is an event? It is something that happens on an exact date in an exact place. Your birth was an important event. What day and year was it? However, growing older is not an event. Can you tell the difference?

Time Periods and Eras

Timelines are divided into equal parts that stand for a certain number of years. Each part could stand for 1 year, 5 years, 10 years, or 100 years!

Another timeline might show a group of dates called an era, such as the era of inventions or the era of space travel.

There are words, almost like shortcuts, that describe periods of time.

A *decade* is 10 years.

A *century* is 100 years.

An *era* is a period of years when related events happened.

14   Washington, Our Home

Differentiated Paths

How Historians Study the Past

One of the key objectives of this lesson is to understand the difference between a primary and secondary source, and to understand that historians use many sources to learn about the past.

ELL and Special Needs

Refer to the ELL/Modified Chapter Lesson in the ELL/Modified Chapter Guide for an activity to teach this concept.

Gifted Learners

Have your students write a How to Study History manual using the information from this textbook and other resources. Students can work together to decide on the Table of Contents for the manual. Then each student can take one chapter or section to write. Encourage students to download pictures to include in their manuals.

Point of View

Pretend you and your friend go to the zoo. When you come home, you each tell your families a different story of what happened at the zoo. Why would you do this if you were both there at the same time?

Here is what happened. You spent a lot of time watching the silly little monkeys jump from tree to tree. Then you realized your friend and her mother had left you at the monkey cage. You were worried. You just wanted to go home.

However, your friend and her mother got tired of watching the monkeys, and they went over to see the huge apes peeling oranges. When you wanted to leave, they still wanted to stay.

Can you see why each of you had a different story about the zoo? What if you had dropped your ice cream cone on the ground? Would you feel even worse about the trip to the zoo?

Each person has a ***point of view***. This means that people see an event from their own experiences. Often adults and children have different points of view. So do people on different sides of a game. Historians keep in mind different points of view when they try to learn what happened in the past. In this book, you will see that there are many sides to a story.

You are looking at the monkey. The monkey is looking at you! **Do you and the monkey have the same point of view?**

LESSON 2 What Did You Learn?

1. What do historians try to learn by studying history?
2. What is the difference between a primary and secondary source?
3. Why is it important to study history by using many different sources?

"In seeking truth, you have to get both sides of the story."
—Walter Cronkite, TV reporter

What Is History?

15

LESSON 2 What Did You Learn?

1. *A historian is a person who studies history.*
2. *Primary sources are things made or used by people during the time an event took place. Secondary sources are things that are written, said, or made after the time an event took place.*
3. *It is important to study history from many different sources so that we can learn from different points of view and get more information on a topic.*

Reflect on students' understanding of how historians use primary and secondary sources to study the past. Encourage students to state the importance of point of view when using primary and secondary sources. You can evaluate students' understanding through discussion or evaluation of activities completed in this lesson. The following activity will serve as another way of assessing students' understanding of the key objectives of this lesson.

 Writing Activity

Writing from Another Point of View

Divide the class into pairs. Students will use the Writing from Another Point of View page in the *Student Guide* to write a paragraph about an event that happened in your class or school. Challenge students to think about how their partner saw the event and how he or she felt about what happened.

Have students share their paragraphs with their partner. Encourage partners to talk about whether or not the paragraph tells the event from their point of view. Have students edit to better show the correct point of view.

NAME _____ DATE _____

Tools of History 2 **Writing Activity**

Writing from Another Point of View
Complete the organizer to help you tell about an event from your partner's point of view.

Who was there?	
What happened?	
Were you a part of this event?	
What role did you play?	
Why did it happen?	
How did you feel?	

10 Student Guide
Use with *Washington, Our Home*   © 2010 Gibbs Smith, Publisher

Standards

GLE 4.1.1

Understands and creates timelines to show how historical events are organized into time periods and eras.

Washington Social Studies Skills

Reading and Creating a Timeline

Use this activity to help students become familiar with reading and creating timelines.

Activate

Draw a simple timeline of your own life on the board. Ask students what events from your life you included on the timeline. Ask students to discuss with a neighbor why they think you chose to include those events on your timeline. Tell students about the events on your timeline.

Teach

As a class, read the first paragraph of the Student Edition page Reading and Creating a Timeline. Use your timeline on the board to show students the parts of a timeline. Ask students questions about the timeline: What year was I born? How old was I when I started school? How many years have I taught school? Lead the class in a discussion about how to read and interpret a timeline.

Practice

Have students work in pairs to finish reading the section Reading a Timeline in their Student Edition and answer the questions. Go over the answers to the questions as a class.

Apply

Have students complete the Creating a Timeline activity.

Washington Social Studies Skills

Reading and Creating a Timeline

Timelines show important events that occurred during a specific time period. We read a timeline from left to right. Events that happened first are on the left.

Marcus, a fourth grader, created this timeline about his own life. Notice that not every event of Marcus's life is included on his timeline. He included events he thought were the most important. Use the timeline to answer the questions.

1. What year was Marcus's baby sister born? How old was Marcus when she was born?
2. What else happened to Marcus the year his sister was born?
3. How many years does Marcus's timeline show?
4. Based on this timeline, would you conclude that Marcus never went to first, second, or third grade? Why do you think he didn't include those grades on his timeline?

Creating a Timeline

Make a timeline of your own life. Decide what year to start and end your timeline. Make sure the marks on your timeline show equal amounts of time in between each one. Choose 10 of the most important events in your life. Put the events in the order in which they happened. You may want to include pictures on your timeline.

Chapter Review 1

Reviewing What You Read

1. List three ways you can learn about Washington's history.
2. Explain why an autobiography can tell us a lot about a person's history.
3. Write three sentences explaining what a historian does.
4. Explain the differences between a primary and a secondary source.
5. Create a list of three different sources, and tell why each is important.
6. Why is it important to study history from many points of view?

Becoming a Better Reader

Previewing a Textbook

Previewing is a reading strategy good readers use to become familiar with a book before they read it. You previewed Chapter 1 as you looked for images, headings, and special features to help you understand the chapter.

Now preview the rest of this book. Then write two sentences about what you might learn by reading it. Get ready for a great adventure!

Spotlighting Geography

Family History

Living in Washington is part of your family history. Write a few sentences that tell about the first people in your family to live in Washington. Who were they? Where did they come from? Why did they come?

With a small group, share what you wrote about your family history.

What Is History? 17

Reviewing What You Read

The Reviewing What You Read questions are leveled according to Bloom's Taxonomy and will help students achieve a higher level of thinking. These questions will also prepare students for the chapter assessment. The following are possible answers to the questions. Focus on students' ability to understand and apply the concepts.

1. **KNOWLEDGE** Possible Answers: By talking to people who have lived in Washington for a long time, by reading old newspapers from Washington, by studying textbooks such as this one.

2. **COMPREHENSION** An autobiography is a book someone wrote about his or her own life.

3. **APPLICATION** A historian studies history. They study primary and secondary sources to learn about history. A historian learns about history from different points of view.

4. **ANALYSIS** Primary sources were made by people who were there at the time an event took place. Secondary sources are written, said, or made after the time an event took place.

5. **SYNTHESIS** Students' answers should include three primary or secondary sources and tell why each source is important.

6. **EVALUATION** It is important to study history from many points of view so we can get correct details about events from history.

Spotlighting Geography

Family History

Talk about how people and our surroundings influence us when we are making decisions. Share your personal story about the first people in your family who lived in Washington and why they decided to come here. Break students into small groups to share their stories. As a class, discuss some of the similarities and differences between all the stories.

Becoming a Better Reader

Previewing a Textbook

Students may not realize it, but they have already learned a lot by simply previewing the book. Ask students what they have already learned. Have students share their sentences about what they might learn while studying from *Washington, Our Home* this year.

Interactive Chapter Review

An Interactive Chapter Review is available online at **www.ExperienceStateHistory.com**. Have students use this review to prepare for the assessments.

Chapter Assessment

Chapter Assessments are available to preview on pages 2G–2H. Assessments can be found in the *Teacher Guide*. They can also be found online at **www.ExperienceStateHistory.com**.

2 Geography Is the Stage

CHAPTER PLANNER

CHAPTER OVERVIEW	WASHINGTON SOCIAL STUDIES GLEs
This chapter focuses on the geography of Washington. Attention is given to the land, people, and regions of our state.	GLE 3.1.1 GLE 3.1.2 GLE 5.2.2

CHAPTER RESOURCES	
ELL/Modified Chapter Plan, p. 18I	
Books and Web Sites, p. 18J	

CHAPTER ACTIVITIES	WASHINGTON CURRICULUM INTEGRATION
Tour of Washington, p. 18E	**Communication** GLE 1.1.2
■ Border Lines, p. 18E	**Reading** GLE 3.2.1, **Visual Arts** GLE 2.1.1
■ How Far Is It?, p. 18E	**Math** GLE 4.4.B
Regions Relief Map, p. 18E	**Visual Arts** GLE 2.1.1
Environmental Poster, p. 18F	**Writing** GLE 3.2.1, GLE 1.2.1, GLE 1.3.1, GLE 1.4.1, GLE 1.5.1, GLE 1.6.1
Map of the Perfect Community, p. 18F	**Social Studies** GLE 3.1.1, **Visual Arts** GLE 2.1.1
A Tasting Party, p. 18F	**Health** GLE 1.4.1b
Regions Festival, p. 18F	**Reading** GLE 2.1.7
CHAPTER OPENER	WASHINGTON CURRICULUM INTEGRATION
Chart the Effects of Geography, p. 18	**Communication** GLE 1.2.1
Write the Caption, p. 18	**Writing** GLE 2.2.1

▶ Indicates an activity page located in the *Student Guide*
■ Indicates an activity page located in the *Teacher Guide*

The BIG Idea | How does geography shape the way we live?

CHAPTER REVIEW   pp. 42–43

SOCIAL STUDIES SKILLS PAGE	WASHINGTON SOCIAL STUDIES GLEs
Create a Map, p. 42	**Social Studies** GLE 3.1.1 Use with the Chapter 2 Project Assessment Supports **Social Studies CBA:** People on the Move (completed in the Chapter 5 Project Assessment)

REVIEWING THE CHAPTER	WASHINGTON SOCIAL STUDIES GLEs
Students show what they learned by completing application activities and answering chapter review questions. Assessments for this chapter can be previewed on pages 18G-18H. Select the assessment option that best suits your goals for this chapter. Assessments are available in the *Teacher Guide* or online at **www.ExperienceStateHistory.com**.	GLE 3.1.1 GLE 3.1.2 GLE 5.2.2

CHAPTER ACTIVITIES	WASHINGTON CURRICULUM INTEGRATION
Reviewing the What You Read, p. 43	**Reading** GLE 1.3.2, GLE 2.1.3
Becoming a Better Reader, p. 43	**Reading** GLE 2.3.2
Spotlighting Geography, p. 43	**Writing** GLE 1.1.2

CHAPTER ASSESSMENTS	WASHINGTON CURRICULUM INTEGRATION
■ Multiple Choice Assessment, p. 14	**Reading** GLE 1.3.2, GLE 2.1.3
■ Reading Assessment, p. 15	**Reading** GLE 3.2.2
■ Writing Assessment, p. 16	**Writing** GLE 2.2.1, GLE 2.3.1
■ Project Assessment, pp. 17–18	**Social Studies** GLE 3.1.1

LESSON 1
Where in the World Are We?   pp. 20–23

LESSON OVERVIEW	WASHINGTON SOCIAL STUDIES GLEs
KEY IDEAS • Washington is on the continent of North America. • Washington is a state in the country of the United States of America. • Maps help us see where places are located.	GLE 3.1.1 GLE 3.1.2

LESSON ACTIVITIES	WASHINGTON CURRICULUM INTEGRATION
▶My Place in the World, p. 20	**Writing** GLE 2.2.1
Word Roots, p. 20	**Reading** GLE 1.2.2
▶Words to Understand, p. 20	**Reading** GLE 1.3.1
▶Using a KWL Chart, p. 21	**Reading** GLE 2.3.2
Near or Far?, p. 22	**Reading** GLE 3.2.2, **Communication** GLE 2.2.2
Create a Map, p. 22	**Visual Arts** GLE 2.1.1
▶Washington's Place in the World, p. 23	**Writing** GLE 2.3.1

LESSON 2
The Land We Call Home   pp. 24–33

LESSON OVERVIEW	WASHINGTON SOCIAL STUDIES GLEs
KEY IDEAS • Places can be described by their land and people. • Natural resources are important to everyone. • Climate affects where and how people live.	GLE 3.1.2

LESSON ACTIVITIES	WASHINGTON CURRICULUM INTEGRATION
▶Snapshots of Washington, p. 24	**Visual Arts** GLE 2.1.1
Picture Flash Cards, p. 24	**Reading** GLE 1.2.2
▶Words to Understand, p. 24	**Reading** GLE 1.3.2
▶Using an Anticipation-Reaction Guide, p. 25	**Reading** GLE 4.4.D
Graphing Rivers, p. 26	**Math** GLE 2.1.5
Hydroelectricity, p. 26	**Science** GLE 3.1.2, **Technology** GLE 1.3.2
Make Your Own Hydropower, p. 26	**Science** GLE 3.1.2
Washington's Waterways, p. 27	**Writing** GLE 2.3.1
Drawing Ocean Creatures, p. 27	**Visual Arts** GLE 2.1.1
Create Landforms, p. 28	**Visual Arts** GLE 2.1.1
Paper Mache Landforms, p. 28	**Visual Arts** GLE 2.1.1
The Important Book, p. 29	**Writing** GLE 2.2.1, **Reading** GLE 3.2.1
The Magic School Bus Blows its Top, p. 30	**Reading** GLE 3.1.1, **Technology** GLE 1.3.2
Go to the Source: Compare a Photo and a Map, p. 31	**Social Studies** GLE 5.2.2
Mount St. Helens 25-Years Later, p. 31	**Social Studies** GLE 5.2.2, **Technology** GLE 1.3.2
Climate Experiment, p. 32	**Science** GLE 2.1.4
Scrapbook of Washington Climate, p. 32	**Technology** GLE 1.1.1, GLE 1.3.2
▶Washington for Sale!, p. 33	**Writing** GLE 2.2.1, GLE 2.3.1

LESSON 3
Land Regions
pp. 34–41

LESSON OVERVIEW	WASHINGTON SOCIAL STUDIES GLEs
KEY IDEAS • Regions can share physical or cultural characteristics. • Washington's land regions share common characteristics.	GLE 3.1.2

LESSON ACTIVITIES	WASHINGTON CURRICULUM INTEGRATION
▶Regions Survey, p. 34	**Writing** GLE 2.1.1, **Communication** GLE 2.2.2
Word Endings, p.34	**Reading** GLE 1.2.2
▶Words to Understand, p. 34	**Reading** GLE 1.2.2
▶Summarize and Synthesize, p. 35	**Reading** GLE 2.3.2
Washington's Land Regions, p. 35	**Social Studies** GLE 3.1.1
Puget Sound Shorelines, p. 36	**Science** GLE 3.2.4, **Technology** GLE 1.3.2
Cascade Eruptions, p. 37	**Math** GLE 4.5.E, GLE 4.5.F
Webbing the Columbia Plateau, p. 38	**Reading** GLE 2.1.7
Design a License Plate, p. 38	**Visual Arts** GLE 2.1.1
Where Would You Live?, p. 38	**Writing** GLE 2.2.1
E is for Evergreen, p. 39	**Reading** GLE 3.2.1, **Writing** GLE 2.3.1
Compare and Contrast, p. 39	**Writing** GLE 2.2.1
Regions Brochure, p. 40	**Technology** GLE 1.1.1, GLE 1.3.2
▶Tanka Poem, p. 41	**Writing** GLE 2.2.1, GLE 2.3.1

Chapter Activities

This chapter focuses on Washington's geography and place in the world. Attention is given to the physical and cultural characteristics of Washington's five land regions. As you work through the chapter, use these Chapter Activities to help students understand the key ideas.

Set the Stage

Set up a class library with books that show the physical and human characteristics of Washington. Some titles are suggested in the Chapter Resources on page 18J. Ask your librarian for other suggestions.

Introductory Activity

A Tour of Washington

As an introduction to this chapter on the physical and cultural characteristics of Washington, take your students on a virtual tour of our state. Depending on the technology available at your school, there are many ways to do this. Talk with your media specialist about the options available to you. With a computer, Internet connection, VGA cable, and a video projector, you have images of Washington literally at your fingertips. Possibilities for creating a virtual tour include making a PowerPoint presentation of images downloaded from the Internet. Pinnacle Studios, Microsoft MovieMaker, and PhotoStory are software systems that can be used for this purpose.

If technology at your school is limited, you can "show" students Washington through pictures in books and magazines available at the library. After the "tour," have students write about their favorite place in Washington. For links to Web sites with pictures of Washington you can download, see **www.ExperienceStateHistory.com.**

Reading Activity

Border Lines

Read the poem "Border Lines" by Dr. Alberto Alvaro Rios. A Border Lines Activity page is available in the *Teacher Guide*. After reading the poem, have students answer the questions.

Then have students create puzzles of Washington. An outline of Washington is available in the *Teacher Guide*. Have students glue their maps to poster board or construction paper. You may want students to label their maps with key features, cities, and landmarks throughout the state. Then have students cut their maps into about 10 pieces to create a puzzle. Puzzle pieces can be placed in a plastic bag or envelope. Have students exchange puzzles and put a classmate's puzzle together.

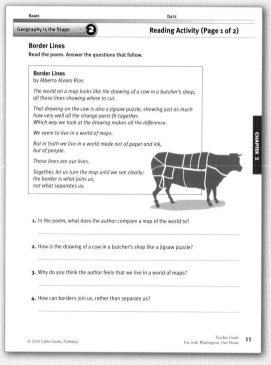

Math Activity

How Far Is It?

Using the map of Washington on page 22 of the *Student Edition,* have students determine the direction and miles to and from places on the map. A How Far Is It? activity page is available in the *Teacher Guide.*

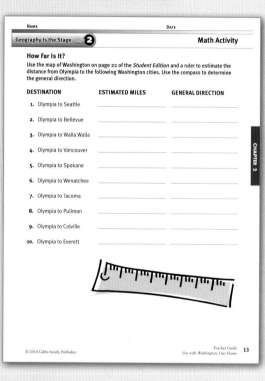

Art Activity

Regions Relief Map

Using this Salt Dough recipe, have students create a relief map of Washington.

Salt Dough Recipe
4 cups flour
1 cup salt
1 cup hot water
2 teaspoons vegetable oil

Stir flour and salt together. Slowly add water and oil. If the dough is sticky, add more flour. If it doesn't stick together well, add a little water. Knead the dough into balls.
Use a board as a base. Have students form the dough into the shape of Washington and its landforms. Allow the dough to dry. Have students paint the rivers, lakes, and other landforms.

Writing Activity

Environmental Poster

Explain to students that as the leaders of tomorrow, it is their job to help care for our resources. Have students create a poster describing an environmental problem and presenting a solution to the problem.

Prewriting
Brainstorm a list of land, air, or water issues in your town, county, or state. Have each student choose a problem and come up with a solution to the problem.

Drafting
Have students design a draft for a poster that states the problem and the solution. Students should also think about ways of making their posters attention-getting. Encourage them to use graphics and fonts that are eye-catching. At this stage, students should sketch their ideas on a piece of paper.

Revising
In groups, have students share their drafts. Encourage students to point out the attractive features of each poster. Encourage students to suggest one way to make each poster better.

Editing
Students should edit their drafts to incorporate the group's suggestions for improvement.

Publishing
Have students make a final copy of their poster on the poster board. If possible, display the posters in public places throughout the school, such as the library, hallways, office, or cafeteria.

 Social Studies Activity

Map of the Perfect Community

Talk with students about what people need to live. Tell students to imagine they have just discovered an uninhabited piece of land. Challenge students to design the perfect community on the land. Have students imagine what the perfect community would look like, how the people of the community would use the land to meet their needs and wants, and what rules they would have concerning the use of the land.

Have students draw a map to show their perfect community. Along with the map, students should include an outline of the features of the land, how the land meets the needs of the people, and the rules of the land.

 Science Activity

A Tasting Party

Geography is the study of the Earth's land and people. The food we eat is influenced by where we live. Different foods are available to people in different land regions in Washington. Although each land region has access to grocery stores with many foods, each land region still has different foods that are unique to that region.

Schedule a Tasting Party to go along with the Regions Festival (see Culminating Activity). Have different groups gather the food to represent different regions in Washington, preparing enough for everyone to have a sample. Ask for food donations and parent volunteers. Be sure to have small cups, napkins, and plastic utensils available.

Talk about how the foods from different regions provide for the nutritional needs of the people. Help students understand that if basic nutritional needs are not met, people will become ill.

 Culminating Activity

Regions Festival

Divide your class into five groups. Assign each group to one of the land regions of Washington State to research. Groups should present the information they gather in a booth at a Regions Festival. Each booth should be decorated to show cultural and physical characteristics of the region. In addition, each booth should include:

- Special landforms in the region
- General climate of the region
- Natural resources in the region
- Large cities and special attractions in the region
- Businesses and industries unique to the region
- Famous people from the region (past and present)
- Arts or crafts from the region
- Foods common to the region
- Recreational activities common to the region
- Special music, dance, or literature common to the region
- Festivals or holidays common to the region

Assessment Options

The Chapter Assessment options provide opportunities to evaluate students' understanding of the social studies concepts. Choose the assessment options that best meet the needs of your teaching goals. Assessments are available in the *Teacher Guide* or can be individualized at **www.ExperienceStateHistory.com**.

OPTION 1: MULTIPLE CHOICE ASSESSMENT

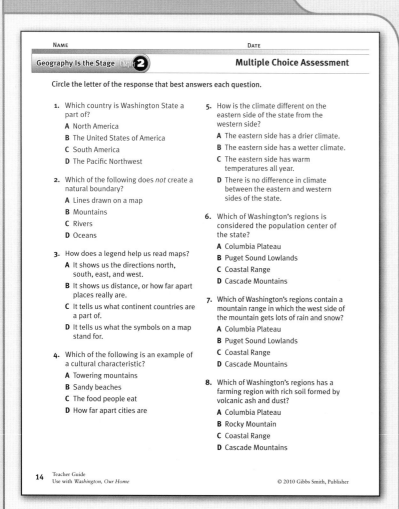

The Multiple Choice Assessment provides a quick way to assess students' understanding of the key concepts of the chapter. Have students read each question and select the best answer.

OPTION 2: READING ASSESSMENT

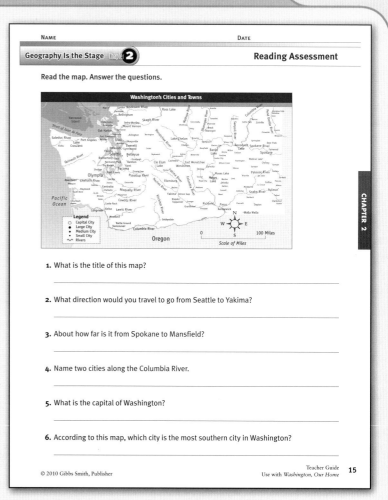

The Reading Assessment provides additional practice for the WASL Reading Test and allows students to apply their map-reading skills learned during the study of this chapter. Have students study the map and answer the questions that follow.

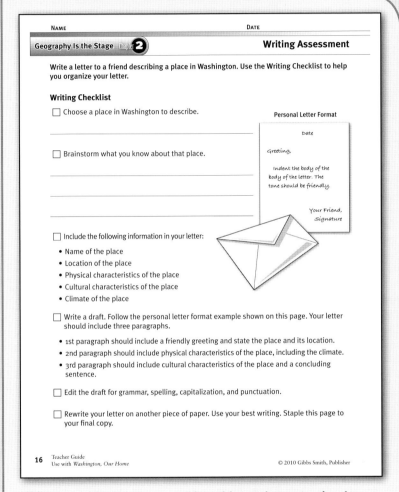

NAME   DATE

Geography Is the Stage Chapter **2**   **Writing Assessment**

Write a letter to a friend describing a place in Washington. Use the Writing Checklist to help you organize your letter.

Writing Checklist

☐ Choose a place in Washington to describe.

☐ Brainstorm what you know about that place.

Personal Letter Format

Date

Greeting,

Indent the body of the body of the letter. The tone should be friendly.

Your Friend,
Signature

☐ Include the following information in your letter:

• Name of the place
• Location of the place
• Physical characteristics of the place
• Cultural characteristics of the place
• Climate of the place

☐ Write a draft. Follow the personal letter format example shown on this page. Your letter should include three paragraphs.

• 1st paragraph should include a friendly greeting and state the place and its location.
• 2nd paragraph should include physical characteristics of the place, including the climate.
• 3rd paragraph should include cultural characteristics of the place and a concluding sentence.

☐ Edit the draft for grammar, spelling, capitalization, and punctuation.

☐ Rewrite your letter on another piece of paper. Use your best writing. Staple this page to your final copy.

16 Teacher Guide
Use with *Washington, Our Home*   © 2010 Gibbs Smith, Publisher

The Writing Assessment provides additional practice for the WASL Writing Test. Have students use the checklist to write a friendly letter describing a place in Washington.

NAME   DATE

Geography Is the Stage Chapter **2**   **Project Assessment (Page 1 of 2)**

Follow the steps to construct a map of Washington.

Construct a Map

☐ Choose a type of map to create: relief map of physical characteristics, elevation map, climate map, map of cities and places of interest, or other type approved by your teacher.

☐ Write the type of map you will be creating: _____

☐ Give your map a title: _____

☐ Research and find at least two sources to help you complete your map. Write the sources:

☐ Brainstorm what places or features you will need to include in your map.

☐ Assign symbols to the places or features you will include on your map.

☐ Using the outline of Washington provided by your teacher, create your map. Be sure to include the following:

• Title
• Legend
• Compass
• Labels

CHAPTER 2

© 2010 Gibbs Smith, Publisher   Teacher Guide 17
                                     Use with *Washington, Our Home*

The Project Assessment provides an alternative to the traditional assessment. Encourage students to follow the checklist as they construct their maps.

Geography Is the Stage

Students will learn about the human and land features found in each of Washington's five land regions. In this lesson, students will increase their understanding of key geography words.

The following pages can be found in the ELL/Modified Chapter Guide on pages 9–13.

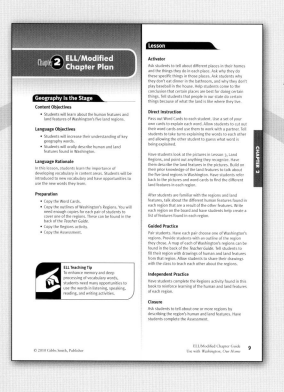

The ELL/Modified Chapter Plan provides a step-by-step lesson in an easy-to-use format. Lessons teach content and language objectives.

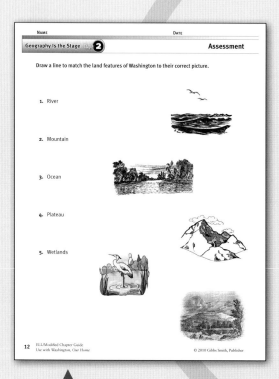

The Modified Assessment for this chapter assesses students' understanding of the key objectives of the chapter.

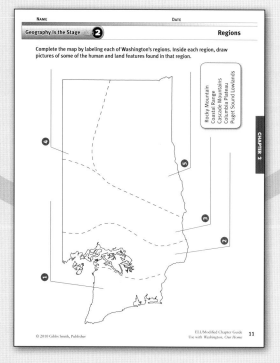

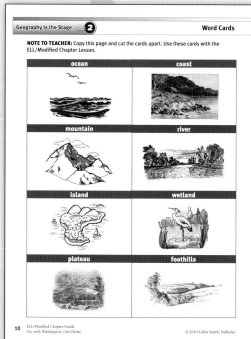

The Word Cards and Activity assist and reinforce students' learning of the chapter and prepares them for the assessment.

Books and Web Sites

Books

Brown, Margaret Wide and Leonard Weisgard. *The Important Book*. New York: Haper Collins, 1990.

Cole, Gary Ed and Bruce Degen. *Magic School Bus Inside the Earth (Magic School Bus Series)*. Redmond: Scholastic, Inc., 1989.

Cole, Joanna and Bruce Degen. *A Guide for Using the Magic School Bus Inside the Earth*. Huntington Beach: Teacher Created Materials, 1995.

Deviny, John. *Exploring Washington's Backroads: Highway and Hometowns of the Evergreen State*. New York: Wilder Publications, 2005.

Herman, Gail. *The Magic School Bus Blows Its Top*. New York: Scholastic Paperbacks, 1996.

Marsh, Carole. *Washington Geography Projects: 30 Cool Activities, Crafts, Experiments, & More for Kids to Do to Learn About Your State*. Peachtree City: Gallopade International, 2003.

McHugh, Erin. *State Shapes: Washington*. New York, Black Dog & Leventhal, 2008.

Newton, James R. and Susan Bonners. *Rain Shadow*. New York: Crowell, 1983.

Smith, Roland. *E is for Evergreen: A Washington State Alphabet*. Chelsea: Sleeping Bear Press, 2004.

Stamper, Judith, Joanna Cole, and John Speirs. *Voyage to the Volcano (Magic School Bus Chapter Books Series #15)*. New York: Scholastic, Inc., 2003

Webster, Christine. *Washington*. New York: Children's Press, 2002.

Web Sites

The following Web sites provide resources or lesson plans for teachers and activities for students to help extend the lessons in this chapter. Go to **www.ExperienceStateHistory.com** for links to these Web sites.

Blows Its Top

This Scholastic Web site features a game called Blows Its Top that students can play after reading the book by the same title, or just to learn fun facts about volcanoes.

Cascade Eruptions During the Past 4000 Years

This Web site from the U.S. Geology Survey has a great page with a graph called Cascade Eruptions During the Past 4000 Years. In this graph, students can see all of Washington's five major volcanoes and how long ago they last erupted. Other volcanoes in the Cascade Range in Oregon and California are also shown.

Energy Matters

This Thinkquest Web site is titled Energy Matters and includes pictures and illustrations explaining how hydropower works.

Foundation for Water and Energy Education

The Foundation for Water and Energy Education has a lesson plan on their Web site called Make Your Own Hydropower. Use this lesson plan along with your teaching of Lesson 2 of this chapter. Use the directions from this lesson plan to create a hydropower model, and use it to teach your class about hydropower.

HistoryLink.org

HistoryLink.org contains an article about Washington's record-cold temperatures in Washington's past called *Cold Weather Freezes Wharves and Rivers in Washington in January 1875*. Use this article as you talk about the importance of water as a natural resource for Lesson 2.

Marine Life Center

The Marine Life Center in Bellingham has a Web site with a page called Animals and Exhibits that includes pictures and descriptions of common sea animals found off the coast of Washington.

Mount St. Helens Twenty-Five Years Later

This Web site was created by the Daily News to commemorate the eruption of Mount St. Helens. The site includes secondary source accounts of witnesses to the eruption, along with many pictures of the catastrophe and what the area looks like more recently.

Puget Sound Shorelines

This Web site from the Department of Ecology has a page called Puget Sound Under Ice. On this page, students can read about how the shorelines of Puget Sound were carved out by glaciers over many years.

The BIG Idea

Chart the Effects of Geography

Share the definition of *geography* with the class: the study of the land, where places are located, and how people use the land. Make a three-column chart on the board, labeling the sections Land, Places, People. Ask students to think about how the study of land, places, and people affects their lives. Write students' responses on the chart in the place in which they belong. Examples may include geographers who study land to make maps that make travel easier, or geographers who study people in the places where our ancestors came from.

 Put Yourself in the Picture

Write the Caption

Tell the students to think as if they are reporters for a newspaper in Washington. The photo from the Chapter Opener is going to be used on the front page of tomorrow's newspaper. They are to write a caption for the picture telling the who, what, where, why, and when for this photo. As they write their captions, encourage students to consider why this photo may have made the front page of the paper. Have students share their captions in small groups.

Caption Answer

You would see mountains and hills as you looked down. If you looked our further, you would see cities. You could tell the people use the land to live, work, and play.

The BIG Idea

How does geography shape the way we live?

If you were to look down from the top of Mt. Rainier, would you wonder who else had stood on this very peak? **What might the land look like below? Through the clouds, what could you tell about how people use the land?**

18

 Background Info

Washington's National Historic Parks

Washington has several national historic parks. Here is information on some of the most popular.

Klondike Gold Rush National Historic Park

Klondike Gold Rush National Historic Park is located in downtown Seattle. The park tells the city's historic role as the beginning site for trips to the Alaskan gold fields in the mid-1800s.

San Juan Island National Historic Park

San Juan Island National Historic Park is the site of the British and American military campsites from the time when the United States and Great Britain both claimed the islands.

Whitman Mission National Historic Site

Whitman Mission National Historic Site is where Marcus and Narcissa Whitman started an Indian mission and were later massacred. The Whitmans provided education and religious instruction to the native people and assistance to pioneers on the Oregon Trail.

Geography Is the Stage

If our history were a play, our geography would be the stage. As you read this book, think about the kinds of places you are reading about. Think about how the land is part of the story.

19

Background Info

Washington's National Parks

Olympic National Park, Created 1938
Olympic National Park has a constant wet climate. On the ocean beaches of the park, you can search for interesting rocks and shells and climb on huge driftwood logs. Just beyond the beaches, a rain forest, thick and green and full of many kinds of plants, is unique in North America.

Mt. Rainier National Park, Created 1899
Mt. Rainier National Park was the first national park in Washington and one of the first in the United States. A giant volcano is covered with glaciers. Lower slopes are decorated with dense forests and flowering meadows. Skilled mountain climbers find this highest peak

in the state—and one of the highest in North America—a challenge.

North Cascades National Park, Created 1963
North Cascades National Park is a breathtakingly beautiful place to visit. Jagged glaciated peaks loom above an alpine region of meadows, forests, fast-running streams, and spectacular waterfalls. The park is rich in wildlife.

Standards

GLE 3.1.1
Constructs and uses maps to explain the movement of people.

GLE 3.1.2
Understands the physical, political, and cultural characteristics of places, regions, and people in the Pacific Northwest, including the difference between cities, states, and countries.

PREPARE

Activator

My Place in the World

Have students complete the My Place in the World activity in the *Student Guide*.

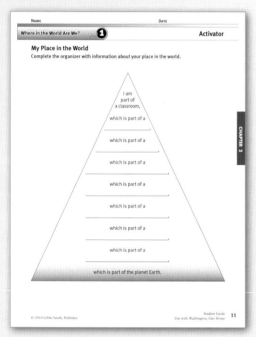

Word Study

Word Roots

The word *geography* is made up of two roots. The root *geo* means earth. Write the words *geology*, *geode*, *geologist*, and *geometry*. Talk about these words. The root *graphy* means written, representing, or recording. Write the words *photography*, *biography*, and *choreography*. Talk about the meanings of these words.

Words to Understand

compass (p. 23) *a symbol that shows direction on a map (north, south, east, west)*

continent (p. 20) *one of the earth's seven large land areas almost surrounded by water*

country (p. 20) *a land region under the control of one government*

geography (p. 20) *the study of the Earth and the people, animals, and plants living on it*

legend (p. 23) *on a map, a key to the meaning of symbols*

natural boundary (p. 22) *a boundary line formed by a natural landform such as a river, coast, or mountain range*

political boundary (p. 22) *a boundary line decided by people*

scale (p. 23) *on a map, the ruler that compares distance on the map to the actual distance on the land*

state (p. 20) *a part of a country that makes some of its own laws; a political region of a country*

symbol (p. 23) *a mark or design that stands for something else*

LESSON 1 — Where in the World Are We?

Key Ideas

- Washington is on the continent of North America.
- Washington is a state in the country of the United States of America.
- Maps help us see where places are located.

Words to Understand

compass
continent
country
geography
legend
natural boundary
political boundary
scale
state
symbol

The Land We Call Home

Washington State seems very large. Yet it is just one small part of the world. Because we live in Washington, it is important to us. It is our home. People all over the world live in places that are important to them.

In this chapter, you will learn about where Washington is located in the world. You will study Washington's land and waterways. You will learn about some of the plants and animals that live here. You will see how people in Washington live and work.

All of these things are part of our geography. *Geography* is the study of the land, where places are located on the land, and how people use and change the land.

Why is it important to know about the geography of a place? Because geography affects where we live and how we live.

Where Is Washington?

We all know we live on the planet Earth. But just where on Earth do we live?

Washington State is located on one of the world's *continents*. Continents are very large land areas. They have oceans on many sides. Washington is on the continent of North America.

Washington is part of a *country* on that continent. A country is a land region under the control of one government. Our country is the United States of America. Canada is the country to the north of us. Mexico is the country to the south of us.

Our country is divided into 50 *states* that each have a state government and make some of their own laws. Within the states are communities called **cities** and **towns**. They may be large or small. What city or town do you live in? Or do you live on a farm away from a town?

A Words to Understand activity for this lesson is available in the *Student Guide*.

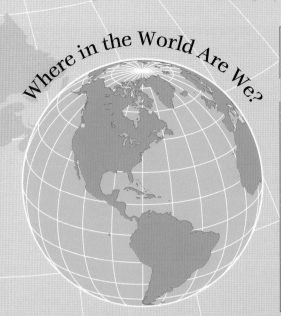

Where in the World Are We?

1. Our **world** is the planet Earth.

2. Our **continent** is North America.

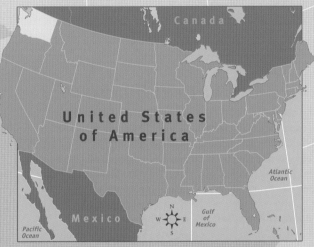

Canada

United States of America

Atlantic Ocean

Mexico

Pacific Ocean

Gulf of Mexico

3. Our **country** is the United States of America. What countries are north and south of us?

Canada

Washington

Montana

Oregon

Idaho

4. Our **state** is Washington. What states are next to Washington?

Geography Is the Stage

21

Reading Strategy

Using a KWL Chart

Without a strategy for managing information in a textbook, students lose their motivation and ability to comprehend the text. To prevent information overload, give students a purpose for reading. Using a KWL chart gives students a chance to activate prior knowledge they have on a topic. It also gives students a purpose for reading as they look for new things they learned to add to the chart after reading. A Using a KWL Chart activity is available in the *Student Guide*.

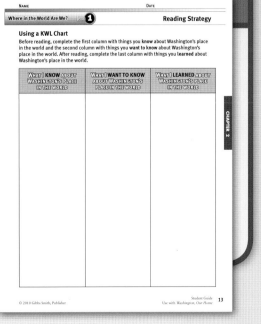

NAME   DATE

Where in the World Are We? | Lesson 1 | **Reading Strategy**

Using a KWL Chart

Before reading, complete the first column with things you **know** about Washington's place in the world and the second column with things you **want to know** about Washington's place in the world. After reading, complete the last column with things you **learned** about Washington's place in the world.

WHAT I **KNOW** ABOUT WASHINGTON'S PLACE IN THE WORLD	WHAT I **WANT TO KNOW** ABOUT WASHINGTON'S PLACE IN THE WORLD	WHAT I **LEARNED** ABOUT WASHINGTON'S PLACE IN THE WORLD

CHAPTER 2

© 2010 Gibbs Smith, Publisher

Student Guide **13**
Use with *Washington, Our Home*

TEACH

Talk About It

The Land We Call Home *(From page 20)*

Why is Washington important to us?
We live in Washington, it is our home.

What is geography?
Geography is the study of the land, where places are located on the land, and how people use and change the land.

Why is it important to know about the geography of a place?
Geography affects where we live and how we live. Encourage to share ways that geography affects students personally.

Where Is Washington? *(From page 20)*

What is a continent?
A continent is a very large land area. There are seven continents on the planet Earth. Continents have oceans on many sides.

On which continent is Washington located?
Washington is located on the continent of North America.

What is a country?
A country is a land region under the control of one government.

In which country is Washington located?
Washington is in the United States of America.

What is a state?
A state is a part of a country that makes some of its own laws; a political region of a country. There are 50 states in the United States of America.

Caption Answers

Canada is the country north of Washington, and Mexico is the country south of Washington.

Idaho is the state next to Washington on the right or east, and Oregon is the state south of, or below, Washington.

Talk About It

Natural and Political Boundaries

What are some things that can form natural boundaries?
Mountains, rivers, and oceans can form natural boundaries.

Which rivers form part of Washington's natural boundaries?
The Columbia and Snake Rivers form part of our boundaries with Idaho and Oregon.

How are political boundaries decided on?
Political boundaries are decided by government leaders and can only be seen on maps.

Reading a Map *(From page 23)*

How do the symbols found on maps help us?
A compass shows the directions north, south, east, and west. A legend explains what the symbols on the map mean. A scale shows distances, or how far apart places really are.

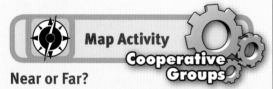

Map Activity

Cooperative Groups

Near or Far?

Have students work in small groups to study the map of Washington on this page. Tell students to locate their current city on the map. Next have each student in the group choose one other city in Washington they have been to. Have a recorder in each group write each group member's choice. Tell the students in the group to help each other use the scale and measure the distance from their current city to the city they have been to. Have the recorder write the distances to each city. Allow a reporter from each group to share the findings with the class.

Caption Answer

Have students work in pairs to locate their city, rivers, the Strait of Juan de Fuca, and the Pacific Ocean.

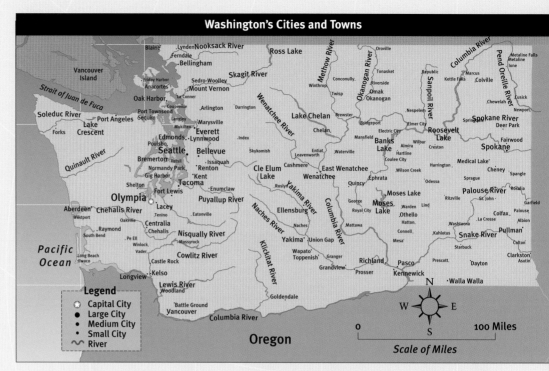

Washington's Cities and Towns

Legend
- ⬡ Capital City
- ● Large City
- ● Medium City
- ○ Small City
- ~ River

This map shows many of the towns and cities of our state. The map also shows a lot of water! **Where is your city on the map? Can you find the rivers, the Strait of Juan de Fuca, and the Pacific Ocean?**

Natural and Political Boundaries

Mountains, rivers, and oceans form *natural boundaries* (outside edges) of countries and states. The Columbia and Snake Rivers form part of our boundaries with Oregon and Idaho. It is easy for everyone to see and understand these boundaries because they are marked by something in nature. What ocean forms one of Washington's boundaries?

Other boundaries were decided by government leaders. These lines are *political boundaries.* You see them only on maps. If you were to walk from Washington into Idaho, you would see no line on the land.

22   Washington, Our Home

Differentiated Paths

Create a Map

The teaching of map skills can be approached from many different entry points.

ELL and Special Needs

Copy a blank outline map of Washington for each student. A copy of this map can be found in the back of the *Teacher Guide*. Have students draw a compass on the map showing the directions north, south, east, and west. Tell students to locate, draw, and label the capital city and two other large cities with an appropriate symbol. Have students locate, draw, and

label two major rivers. Have students finish the map with a legend that includes all the symbols they used.

Gifted Learners

Without the use of a map or a globe, challenge gifted learners to tear colored paper into the shapes of the seven continents and glue them on a large piece of paper. Have them compare their continents to those of other students and then to those on a map or globe.

Reading a Map

Maps help us get where we want to go. They help us see where places are.

There are many kinds of maps. Can you think of some? Perhaps you first thought of a road map. You might use it on a vacation. Your classroom has maps of the world and the United States. You could draw a map to get from the school to your home.

It is important to know how to read a map. Most maps have *symbols* you need to know about. Here are some of them:

Compass: A *compass* on a map shows the directions north, south, east, and west. Most maps have north at the top. Then west will always be on the left side of the map, and east will be on the right side of the map. Can you find the compass on the map of Washington's cities and towns?

Legend: Symbols stand for certain things such as cities, rivers, freeways, campgrounds, and airports. Whenever there are symbols, there is a *legend* that explains what the symbols mean. What do the symbols on the legend of this map represent?

Scale of Miles: To show us distances, or how far apart places really are, map makers use a *scale*. One inch on a map might mean 100 miles on real land. Or, on a map of the world, one inch might stand for 1,000 miles or more.

Look at the map of Washington's cities and towns to see how many miles are represented by one inch on the scale of miles. Then look at a globe in your classroom and see how many miles one inch represents.

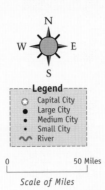

Legend
- Capital City
- Large City
- Medium City
- Small City
- River

0   50 Miles

Scale of Miles

LESSON 1 What Did You Learn?

1. Washington is a part of what country?
2. Give three examples of natural boundaries.
3. How does a compass help you read a map?

LESSON 1 What Did You Learn?

1. *Washington is part of the United States of America.*
2. *Natural boundaries can be formed by mountains, rivers, and oceans.*
3. *A compass helps us read maps by showing us the directions north, south, east, and west.*

REFLECT

Reflect on students' understanding of Washington's place in the world and of how to read a map. You can evaluate students' understanding through discussion or evaluation of activities completed in this lesson. The following activities will serve as another way of assessing students' understanding of the key objectives of this lesson.

Writing Activity

Washington's Place in the World

Tell students that the back cover of books usually include a summary of what the book is about. The author makes this interesting so people will want to read their book. Tell students that they will be writing a summary for the back of a book about Washington's place in the world. Encourage students to give the book a title and write an interesting summary. Allow students to decorate the back cover.

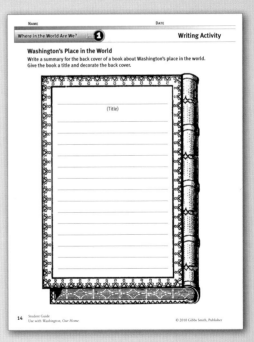

LESSON 2 The Land We Call Home

GLE 3.1.2
Understands the physical, political, and cultural characteristics of places, regions, and people in the Pacific Northwest including the difference between cities, states, and countries.

PREPARE

Activator

Snapshots of Washington

To access students' prior knowledge about the natural resources, landforms, and other physical characteristics of Washington, have them complete the Snapshots of Washington activity in the *Student Guide*.

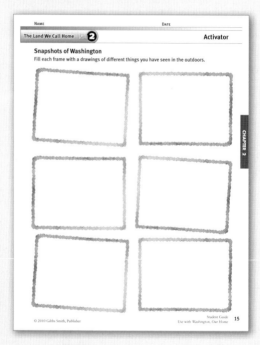

Word Study

Picture Flash Cards

Have students create picture flash cards to study the Words to Understand. Tell students to write the word on one side of the card and draw a picture that represents the meaning of the word on the other side. Have students show the pictures to a partner and have the partner guess what word it describes.

Key Ideas

- Places can be described by their land and people.
- Natural resources are important to everyone.
- Climate affects where and how people live.

Words to Understand

climate
cultural characteristic
elevation
landform
natural resource
physical characteristic
population
rural
urban

What Kind of Place Is Washington?

You have learned about where our state is located in the world. Now you will learn about the land and the people.

Physical Characteristics

The people of Washington State are lucky. We live in a beautiful place. Our state has sandy beaches, beautiful islands, towering mountains, deep lakes, and sparkling rivers. All of these things are natural features of the land. They are called *physical characteristics.*

Cultural Characteristics

Wherever people live, there are *cultural characteristics.* These reflect the people's culture, or lifestyle. The jobs people do, the kind of food they eat, and their belief in what they feel is important are all part of culture.

Language is also part of culture. All over the world, people speak different languages. English is the main language in our state. Spanish and Asian languages are spoken in many homes. In big cities, you can hear languages from around the world.

The *population* of Washington is all the people who live in the state. Children and adults are all part of the population. Most of our people live in large cities that spread out for miles from Puget Sound. In other parts of the state, people live in smaller towns.

Urban or Rural?

Busy cities, with many large buildings, stores, apartments, and homes, are *urban* places. But if a place is *rural,* it means there are only a few homes and a lot of open land. Farmland is rural. Do you live in an urban or rural place?

Birds enjoy the water on this beach in Olympic National Park.
What physical characteristics do you see in this photograph?

24

Washington, Our Home

Words to Understand

climate (p. 32) *the weather pattern year after year*
cultural characteristic (p. 24) *a feature that has to do with the way people live*
elevation (p. 33) *how high the land is above the level of the ocean*
landform (p. 28) *a natural feature of the land*
natural resource (p. 25) *something found in nature that people use, such as trees, water, minerals*
physical characteristic (p. 24) *a feature that has to do with the natural land and landforms*
population (p. 24) *all the people who live in a particular area*
rural (p. 24) *having to do with the countryside rather than a town or city*
urban (p. 24) *having to do with a city*

A Words to Understand activity is available in the *Student Guide.*

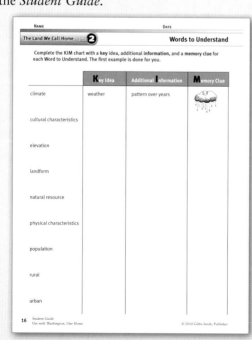

People have jobs cutting down trees, sawing logs into lumber, and making products from wood. Trees are one of Washington's important resources. **What is happening in this photograph?**

Natural Resources

Natural resources are things found in nature that are useful to people. They are part of our state's physical characteristics. No one can make a natural resource. People can only discover where they are and learn how to use them.

Washington's forests are a good example. People have jobs cutting down trees and sawing logs into lumber. Workers get paid to build homes and other buildings from wood.

Gravel and stone are other examples of natural resources. Stone is used to make buildings. Gravel is used to make cement. It is also used to pave roads. Look around your school. How many ways are gravel, stone, and cement used?

Rich soil for farming and family gardens is another natural resource. Our soil makes it possible for farmers to grow wheat, peas, potatoes, berries, apples, cherries, and beautiful flowers. They are shipped out and sold in places around the world.

The Pacific Ocean, wide rivers, and smaller streams are very important natural resources, too. Salmon, crabs, and other seafood provide food for people. Catching them and selling them provides jobs for workers.

What natural resources are important to the people where you live?

Reading Strategy

Using an Anticipation-Reaction Guide

An Anticipation-Reaction Guide gives readers some idea about what they will be reading and what to look for as they read. Readers have the opportunity to go back to the guide and change their responses after reading. An Anticipation-Reaction Guide for this lesson is available in the *Student Guide.*

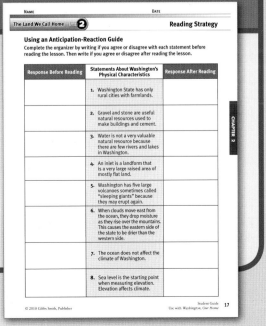

© 2010 Gibbs Smith, Publisher

TEACH

Talk About It

Physical Characteristics *(From page 24)*

What are some examples of physical characteristics?
Possible answers include beaches, islands, mountains, lakes, rivers, and animals.

Cultural Characteristics *(From page 24)*

What are some examples of cultural characteristics?
Possible answers include jobs people have, food people eat, beliefs, language, and traditions.

What are some ways the population of Washington is different from city to city?
The population may be bigger or smaller, it may be close or spread out, it may have people with similar or different cultural characteristics.

Urban or Rural? *(From page 24)*

What is the difference between rural and urban cities?
Urban cities have many buildings and people and are very busy. Rural cities have fewer homes and a lot of open land. They often have farmland.

Natural Resources

What are some of Washington's most important natural resources?
Some of Washington's most important resources include water, fish and other seafood, forests, soil, gravel and stone, and minerals.

Caption Answers

(From page 24) The physical characteristics include large rocks jutting up out of the water, trees, and ocean water.

Small boats are guiding log rafts down a river. One boat may be pulling the log rafts, but this is not clear from the photograph.

Talk About It

Water is Important for Transportation

In what ways does water provide transportation?
Answer should explain that boats travel on rivers, lakes, and the ocean near Washington. The boats carry people and things from place to place.

Water Is a Source of Food

What are some of the foods that come from the ocean?
Fish, oysters, clams, crabs, and mussels are all examples of foods from the ocean.

What is our most important fish, and where does it come from?
Our most important fish is salmon. It spends part of its life in freshwater and part of its life in the ocean.

Rivers Help Make Electricity

How does electricity come from rivers?
River waters run through dams. As the water runs through, it makes giant machines turn. This produces electricity.

Why is the Columbia River so important?
The Columbia River is the state's largest river and its most important source of electricity.

Water Is Great for Having Fun!

What are some ways that people have fun on the water?
Possible answers include swimming, sailing, boating, windsurfing, and fishing.

A Place by the Water

Julia B
Westport docks

Columbia Gorge

A dam on the Skagit River

26

Water is one of our most valuable natural resources. We cannot live without water. How does water help the people of our state?

Water Is Important for Transportation

Before there were cars, trains, or airplanes, canoes and other boats were one of the main ways to get from one place to another. People didn't have to clear the trees and rocks to make a path like they did on land. Instead, they could just ride the river currents. Today, large ships and smaller boats carry many products in and out of our harbors and up and down our large rivers. Water is still important today.

Water Is a Source of Food

Fish, oysters, clams, crabs, and mussels are examples of foods from the salty sea. Fish also live in our lakes, rivers, and streams. Rivers are not salty like the ocean. Our most important fish—salmon—lives part of its life in freshwater and part of its life in the ocean.

Rivers Help Make Electricity

As river water rushes through dams, it helps make electricity. Inside a dam are giant machines. As water flows through the dam, it powers the machines so they can make electricity.

The Columbia River is the state's largest river and its most important source of electricity, but electricity is also made in dams on other rivers.

Water Is Great for Having Fun!

Of course, oceans, rivers, and lakes are also great places to play! Swimming, sailing, boating, windsurfing, and fishing are popular water sports here. How do you like to have fun in the water?

Math Activity

Graphing Rivers

Using the Internet or resource books, have students research the names and lengths of the most important rivers in Washington. As a class, work together to put the information on a graph. Talk about what type of graph would be most useful (a bar graph), the title of the graph, and ways to organize the data (rivers by length or alphabetically).

Technology Activity

Hydroelectricity

The Thinkquest Web site called Energy Matters has a simple and understandable page on hydroelectricity. This page includes images that explain how dams produce hydroelectricity. After sharing this site with students or allowing students to explore the site, have students write a short paragraph explaining how hydroelectricity is produced. Visit **www. ExperienceStateHistory.com** for a link to this site.

Science Activity

Make Your Own Hydropower

The Foundation for Water and Energy Education Web site contains a lesson plan called Make Your Own Hydropower. This lesson will work best for fourth grade if you make the model beforehand and have the class study it to answer the following questions:

- What is the source of energy for this hydropower model?
- What do you see that tells you that?
- What parts of the model create the electricity or energy?

A link to the Foundation for Water and Energy Education site can be found at **www.ExperienceStateHistory.com**.

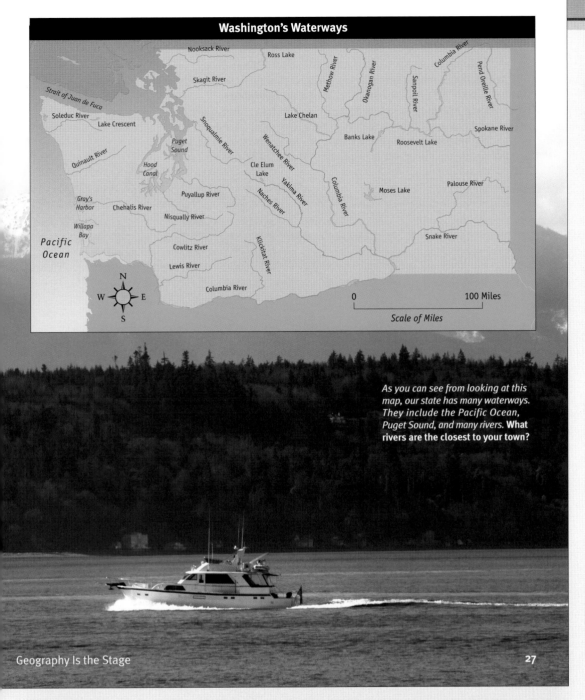

Washington's Waterways

Nooksack River
Ross Lake
Columbia River
Methow River
Okanogan River
Sanpoil River
Pend Oreille River
Skagit River
Strait of Juan de Fuca
Soleduc River
Lake Crescent
Lake Chelan
Spokane River
Snoqualmie River
Quinault River
Puget Sound
Wenatchee River
Banks Lake
Roosevelt Lake
Hood Canal
Cle Elum Lake
Yakima River
Columbia River
Puyallup River
Naches River
Moses Lake
Palouse River
Gray's Harbor
Chehalis River
Nisqually River
Willapa Bay
Pacific Ocean
Cowlitz River
Klickitat River
Snake River
Lewis River
Columbia River

N W E S

0   100 Miles
Scale of Miles

*As you can see from looking at this map, our state has many waterways. They include the Pacific Ocean, Puget Sound, and many rivers. **What rivers are the closest to your town?***

Geography Is the Stage   27

Washington's Waterways

As a class, study the map of Washington's waterways. Discuss the number of rivers, lakes, bays, and harbors.

Have students write an acrostic poem using the word *waterways* to describe the waterways of Washington. Tell students to write *waterways* vertically down a piece of paper. They will need to write one describing word or phrase that begins with each letter in the word *waterways*.

To differentiate this activity, students can write a poem for the word *water* to make it more simple, or for the words *Washington's waterways* to make it more challenging.

 Art Activity

Drawing Ocean Creatures

The Marine Life Center of Bellingham has detailed pictures and information on a number of sea creatures found off the coast of Washington. Have students explore the site, or share the site with the class. Encourage students to use previously learned art concepts to draw their favorite ocean creature. Allow students to share their completed drawings with the class, along with some interesting facts about the animal. A link to this site can be found at **www.ExperienceStateHistory.com.**

Caption Answer

Display a physical map of Washington. Help students locate their town on the map. Have them work with a partner to find which rivers are close to their town.

Background Info

The Columbia River

The river has its headwaters at Columbia Lake, high in British Columbia, Canada. The river enters Washington flowing south, then sweeps around the "Big Bend" to its meeting place with the Snake River. The Columbia River then carries the water of both rivers west to the Pacific Ocean. The river's huge volume of water, together with its very steep fall in elevation, makes it the most powerful river in North America in terms of hydroelectric energy. Major dams on the river produce more electricity than in any other state. By the late 1900s, the Columbia had been so altered by dams it was called an "engineered" river.

Talk About It

Landforms

Ask students to name landforms they can see around the school.

You may want to have the class look out the windows or take the class for a walk outside. Discuss what landforms are seen around the school. Encourage students to think of other landforms in their city/town that are not seen from the school grounds.

What places outside of Washington have you been to where you have seen similar landforms?

Allow students to share experiences they have had in traveling. Encourage students to describe the landforms they have seen.

What is the difference between a mountain and a plateau?

A mountain is a high landform that comes to a peak. A plateau is a raised area of flat land.

What is the difference between a peninsula and an island?

A peninsula is land that has water on three sides and an island is land that has water on all sides.

What is the difference between a strait and an inlet?

A strait is a narrow stretch of water between larger bodies of water. An inlet is a small or narrow bay of water, part of the shoreline of a large body of water.

 Social Studies Activity

Create Landforms

Have each student select at least five landforms to make out of clay. You can have students make the landforms on a paper plate and label each landform with a flag created with toothpicks, tape, and small pieces of paper.

This activity is an easy, hands-on way to assess students' understanding of landforms. You may want to pour a small amount of water on the finished landforms to see if any lakes, rivers, or other bodies of water will form.

Landforms

Look at the shapes of the land around you. What do you see? Are there tall mountains and low valleys? Are there many hills or flat plains? All of these natural features are *landforms*.

Even bodies of water, such as rivers and lakes, are sometimes called landforms. They are part of the shape of the land.

Washington has all of the landforms in this picture. The next time you take a trip, see how many of these landforms you see.

Mountain: a very high land formation. Washington is divided by the high Cascade Mountains. The Olympic Mountains are near the ocean. Millions of years ago, some mountains were pushed up from the earth. Others were formed when volcanoes erupted and lava built up a mountain.

Wetland: an area that is usually soaked with water

Harbor: a sheltered part of a body of water deep enough for anchoring ships

Peninsula: land that has water on three sides

Inlet: a small or narrow bay

Washington, Our Home

 Art Activity

Paper Mache Landforms

Let students help you make a list of the landforms they've studied. Then allow each student to choose at least four different landforms from the list. Students will create a paper mache representation of the landforms they chose.

First have students create the base form for their landforms. For rounder, hollow landforms, students can create their paper mache landforms on inflated balloons. Most other shapes can be created by bending cardboard and holding it in place with masking tape.

To create the paper mache paste, use white glue mixed with a bit of water. Mix using about 1 part water with 2 parts glue. Use strips of newspaper to dip in the paste and layer over the base forms. After the landforms dry, students can paint and label them.

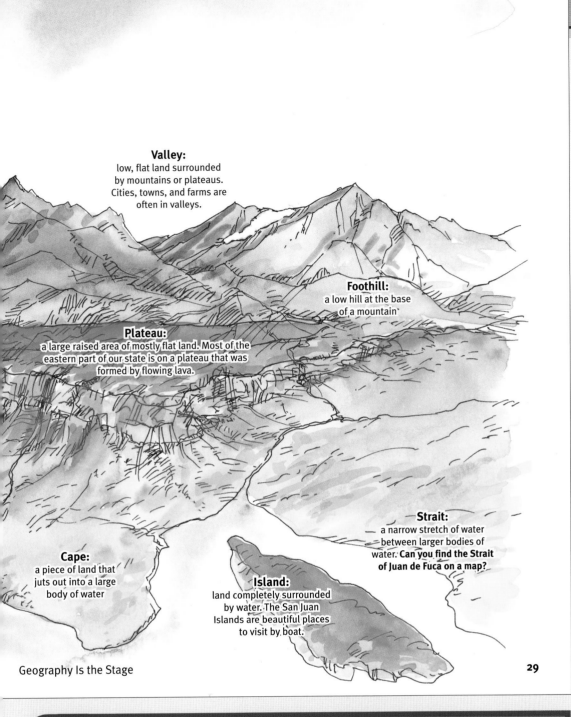

Valley:
low, flat land surrounded
by mountains or plateaus.
Cities, towns, and farms are
often in valleys.

Foothill:
a low hill at the base
of a mountain

Plateau:
a large raised area of mostly flat land. Most of the
eastern part of our state is on a plateau that was
formed by flowing lava.

Strait:
a narrow stretch of water
between larger bodies of
water. **Can you find the Strait
of Juan de Fuca on a map?**

Cape:
a piece of land that
juts out into a large
body of water

Island:
land completely surrounded
by water. The San Juan
Islands are beautiful places
to visit by boat.

Geography Is the Stage

29

Literature Link

The Important Book

Share *The Important Book* by Margaret Wise Brown with your class. This book encourages students to think about why some of the most common things are important.

After reading the book, have students create a foldable booklet to illustrate the important things about six of Washington's landforms. Each student will need an 18 x 20-inch piece of paper to fold and cut as shown below. Students should title the booklet *The Important Book About Landforms* on the front cover. Have students illustrate and label a different landform on each of the six pages inside the book they created.

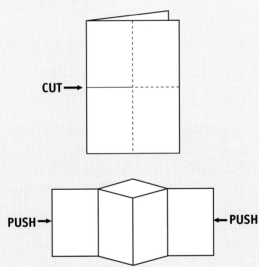

CUT →

PUSH → ← PUSH

Background Info

Forming Our Mountains

Tectonic forces are strong forces in the Earth that cause landmasses to move. They also cause the earth to fold and crack. The Earth's crust may be made up of around 20 moving plates. These plates carry both the Earth's continents and pieces of the ocean floor. In some places plates spread apart, and in other places the collided with, or scraped against, each other. Mountain ranges were uplifted, tilted, and folded in various ways. You can see the folded and tilted layers of rock as you explore mountain canyons. The uplifting is partly the result of the tectonic forces that pushed huge ridges of land against each other. Where the two landmasses met, land ridges were forced upward.

Talk About It

Mt. Saint Helens Erupts!

What were some of the signs of danger on Mt. Saint Helens before it erupted?
Some small earthquakes shook the land, towers of steam rose from the mountaintop, and scientists could tell that the mountain was swelling.

What were some of the effects of the eruption of Mt. Saint Helens?
Possible answers include a huge explosion, a nine-mile high fountain of ash rose in the sky, ash filled the sky and blocked the sun, some places grew dark during the day, some highways, schools, and businesses were closed, people had to stay indoors, and melted snow mixed with dirt to create mud that carried away houses and caused huge floods.

Other Volcanoes

Why are Washington's five other volcanoes sometimes called "sleeping giants?"
They are not active volcanoes right now, but they may erupt again.

 Literature Link

The Magic School Bus Blows its Top

Read the book the *Magic School Bus Blows its Top*. This book will give students more information about how volcanoes work. After reading the book, students can visit the Scholastic Web site to play an educational game called, Blows Its Top. In this game, students learn facts about volcanoes while making a volcano erupt. A link to the Scholastic Web site can be found at **www.ExperienceStateHistory.com**.

This is how Mt. Saint Helens looks today. Great rivers of mud and blasts of hot gas killed most of the plants. **Can you see the large crater where the top of the mountain used to be?**

Other Volcanoes

Washington has five large volcanoes. They are Mt. Rainier, Mt. Baker, Mt. Adams, Mt. Saint Helens, and Glacier Peak. The volcanoes are sometimes called "sleeping giants" because they may erupt again.

- Mt. Baker
- Glacier Peak
- Mt. Rainer
- Mt. Adams
- Mt. Saint Helens

30

Mt. Saint Helens Erupts!

Mountains are very important landforms in Washington. Some of our mountains are actually volcanoes.

In early 1980, there were signs of danger on Mt. Saint Helens. Some small earthquakes shook the land. Towers of steam rose from the mountain top. Scientists could tell that the mountain was swelling. Everyone was told to leave the area. Most people did. Still, no one knew exactly what might happen, or when.

On May 18, they found out. There was a huge explosion. Its force broke rocks into fine gray dust called ash. A fountain of ash shot nine miles into the sky. Winds blew the ash across the state. The ash filled the sky and blocked the sun. In the middle of the day, some places were as dark as night.

Highways, schools, and businesses closed. People had to stay indoors. Meanwhile, snow on the mountain melted, mixed with dirt, and formed gooey mud. Great rivers of mud carried away houses and caused huge floods.

Washington, Our Home

i **Background Info**

Our Most Dangerous Volcano

Geologists today are concerned about Mt. Rainier, Washington's largest dormant volcano. Mt. Rainier, a towering pile of loose rocks and a cubic mile of glacier ice, looms over the Puget Sound region near Seattle and Tacoma. Rainier's capacity for destruction is truly frightening. Geologists consider the mountain to be dangerously unstable. If Rainier collapses in an earthquake or the volcano erupts, an avalanche of red-hot lava and ash will sweep down the mountain. Huge lahars of mud and ice will travel swiftly down the river valleys. Thousands of people will have less than an hour to flee the destruction. Geologists predict a one-in-seven chance of that happening in the lifetime of anyone living in the potential path of destruction.

✖ Go to the Source
Compare a Photo and a Map

Compare the photograph and map of Mt. Saint Helens to learn what is happening in this picture.

LOOK	THINK	DECIDE
What is happening in this photograph?	What clues from the photograph tell you that something big is happening?	How do you think this event changed the land shown on the map?

Geography Is the Stage

31

Go to the Source

🏴 Standards

GLE 5.2.2
Understands the man ideas from an artifact, primary source, or secondary source describing an issue or event.

Compare a Photo and a Map

On May 18, 1980, Mt. Saint Helens awoke with an eruption equal to 21,000 atomic bombs. The mountain had been fairly active over the past 300 years. A few months earlier, tremors deep in the mountain signaled that an eruption was likely. By early May, a large bulge began to form on the mountain's north side. A week later, a large patch of the mountain turned into a churning brown liquid mass and began to slide downward. Then came an enormous explosion and a chain reaction of catastrophic events.

All of the wild land animals, fish, and birds around the mountain were killed. Fifty-seven people lost their lives. The north fork of the Toutle River was filled with debris 600 feet deep. The Cowlitz River carried debris down to the Columbia River, where the mud clogged up the river, closing it to ocean-going vessels. In Spokane, 200 miles to the east, visibility was reduced to 10 feet and the airport was forced to close. There were many other consequences from the blast.

 Technology Activity

Mount St. Helens Twenty-Five Years Later

Have students visit the Mount St. Helens Twenty-Five Years Later Web site to find more information and photos of Mount St. Helens. Under the Stories link, students will find newspaper articles about Mount St. Helen's activity in more recent years, as well as secondary source articles from eyewitnesses remembering the eruption of 1980. For a link to the Mount St. Helens site, visit **www.ExperienceStateHistory.com**.

LOOK	THINK	DECIDE
Possible answers include the eruption of Mt. Saint Helens, a volcano eruption, an explosion, and smoke and ashes being shot into the air.	*Answers should mention details about the huge cloud of smoke rising from the mountain and possibly the lava running down the mountainside.*	*Possible answers include a change in the slope or shape of the mountain, a change to the shape of the land and lakes around the mountain, and movement of debris from the mountain to the areas around it.*

Talk About It

Wet or Dry?

How do we describe a region's climate?
A region's climate is what its weather is like year after year. We can describe a region's climate by how much rain it receives. The usual number of hot days in the summer and cold days in the winter are another way to describe the climate of a region.

Why is the climate of eastern Washington dryer than the climate of western Washington?
Clouds traveling east over the state drop their moisture in the west as they rise to pass over the Cascade Mountains. There is little moisture left to fall on the eastern part of the state.

Climate and the Ocean

Why is the air near the ocean cooler in summer and warmer in winter?
The ocean's temperature changes more slowly than air does. This keeps the air above and next to the ocean more like the temperature of the water. It takes the air near the ocean longer to change temperature with the change of the seasons.

Climate and Elevation *(From page 33)*

What is the starting point for measuring elevation?
The level of the ocean, called sea level, is the starting point for measuring elevation.

How does the elevation of land affect its climate?
The higher in elevation you go, the colder it gets.

32

Wet or Dry?

Climate is important to a place. *Climate* is what the weather is like year after year. The amount of rain or snow that falls each year is part of the climate. The usual number of hot days in summer and cold days in winter are part of climate, too.

Washington's climate has an interesting story. The story begins far out over the Pacific Ocean. As air passes over the ocean, it picks up moisture, or water. Wet ocean winds blow over Washington from west to east.

When the air reaches the mountains, it must rise. As air rises, it cools, and cool air cannot hold so much moisture. The water falls to the ground as rain or snow.

By the time the winds reach the other side of the mountains, the air has very little moisture left. This is why the eastern side of the state, on the other side of the Cascade Mountains, is much drier than the western side.

Climate and the Ocean

The ocean affects our climate in another way. Large bodies of water change temperature more slowly than the air does. This means that the ocean helps keep the air near it cooler in summer and warmer in winter.

Part of our state is near the ocean. It rains often. Moss grows in wet places. **In this rain forest in Olympic National Park, can you see the moss growing on the trees?**

Washington, Our Home

 Science Activity

Climate Experiment

Have students investigate whether water or soil holds heat longer. Before doing the experiment, have students make their predictions. You will need two empty soup cans. Fill one with water and one with soil. Place a thermometer in each can. Record the temperatures of the soil and the water. Place both cans under a lamp. Record the temperatures of the soil and water every 3 minutes. Do this for 15 minutes. After 15 minutes, turn off the lamp and continue to record the temperatures every 3 minutes, for an additional 15 minutes. Have students write their conclusions. Ask them to compare their conclusions to their predictions.

 Writing Activity

Cooperative Groups

Scrapbook of Washington Climate

For this activity, students will need access to the Internet. Divide the class into cooperative groups. Assign each group a specific place in Washington. The groups should create a scrapbook about the place's climate. The scrapbooks should include maps showing annual rainfall; charts of average temperatures; extremes in temperatures or precipitation; and photographs, newspaper clippings, and illustrations of weather events in the place. Students can also include recreational activities that occur in the place during different seasons.

Reflect on students' understanding of Washington's natural resources, landforms, and factors that affect Washington's climate. Students should be able to distinguish between Washington's physical and cultural characteristics. You can evaluate students' understanding through discussion or evaluation of activities completed in this lesson. The following activity will serve as another way of assessing students' understanding of the key objectives of this lesson.

Climate and Elevation

Elevation means how high the land is above the level of the ocean. This is called sea level. It is the starting point for measuring elevation.

Washington has both low land and high land. Parts of the coastline are just a few feet above sea level. The mountains are thousands of feet higher.

Have you ever hiked on a mountain trail and felt cooler as you climbed higher? This is because the elevation of the land affects the climate. The higher you go, the colder it gets. Have you seen high mountains covered with snow all year, even when it is warm in the city below?

On the plateau, it is too dry for forests to grow. Sagebrush, however, is a desert plant. Since it does not need much water, it grows wild in dry climates.

How are climate and weather different? Climate is the general pattern of weather, year after year. Weather is what we get each day. Each day's weather can be sunny or rainy, warm or cold, windy or calm.

 Writing Activity

Washington for Sale!

Have students apply what they learned about the land in Washington State to write and illustrate an ad to sell the state of Washington. Encourage students to be persuasive in their writing and to focus on the many natural resources and features of the land. Have students complete the Washington for Sale! activity in the *Student Guide*.

LESSON 2 What Did You Learn?

1. Describe some physical and cultural characteristics.
2. Name two natural resources and tell how they are used.
3. How are weather and climate related?

LESSON 2 What Did You Learn?

1. *Examples of physical characteristics include anything that is a natural feature of the land. Examples of cultural characteristics should describe people's culture or lifestyle.*
2. *Answers should include a natural resource and its use discussed in this lesson. Possible answers include trees for building lumber, gravel and stone to make buildings and cement, soil for farming and family gardens, and seafoods to provide food.*
3. *Climate is the big picture that includes the day-to-day weather patterns year after year.*

LESSON 3 Land Regions

Standards

GLE 3.1.2
Understands the physical, political, and cultural characteristics of places, regions, and people in the Pacific Northwest including the difference between cities, states, and countries.

PREPARE

Activator

Regions Survey

Have students study the map on this page. Ask students what cities and other landmarks are in each region. Have students complete the Regions Survey activity in the *Student Guide* by surveying other students in the class.

Word Study

Word Endings

Explain to students that the meaning of a word can change simply by changing the ending of the word. Write the following word endings and their meanings on the board: *s* or *es*, plural (more than one); *er*, more; *est*, most; *ing*, in the act of doing something; *al*, of or relating to. Explain how the spelling and the meaning of the words *jump*, *high*, *family*, and *fox* are changed when some of these word endings are added to them. Explain that not all word endings can be added to every word.

Key Ideas

• Regions can share physical or cultural characteristics.
• Washington's land regions share common characteristics.

Words to Understand

agriculture
industry
irrigation
region
timber
tourism

Washington's Land Regions

Regions are another way to divide up the land. A land region usually has one important physical characteristic, such as the coast, mountains, or a plateau. Regions also have cultural characteristics, such as a common language or the kinds of jobs people have.

If you were a bird flying over our state, you would see that some places look very different from other places. You would glide over Puget Sound and the San Juan Islands. Don't get wet—it rains a lot by the water! Watch out for the highest mountains. It's cold up there! Now fly down over the valleys and the wide plateau. What a beautiful place Washington is.

Washington's Five Land Regions

Each of Washington's land regions is different from the others. The name of each region gives clues to its landforms.
• Coastal Range
• Puget Sound Lowlands
• Cascade Mountains
• Columbia Plateau
• Rocky Mountain

Washington's Land Regions

Find Washington's land regions on the map. **Which region do you live in?**

Words to Understand

agriculture (p. 36) *the business of raising crops and animals to sell*
industry (p. 36) *a certain kind of business, such as manufacturing, shipping, tourism, etc.*
irrigation (p. 38) *bringing water to crops from a river or a lake*
region (p. 34) *a land division based on common characteristics*
timber (p. 37) *wood (from trees) that is used for building*
tourism (p. 36) *the industry of making money by supplying the needs of visitors*

A Words to Understand activity for this lesson is available in the *Student Guide.*

Coastal Range

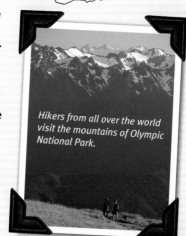

Landforms and Natural Resources

Some parts of the coastline are rough and rocky. In other parts you can walk along wide, sandy beaches. If you are on the coast, you won't have to travel far to see the towering, snow-capped Olympic Mountains. They are covered with thick forests. The ocean is another important natural resource.

Climate

Washington's coastal region is the wettest part of the state. The elevation varies from sea level up to the snowy peaks of the Olympic Mountains. The plants and animals that live in these places need a lot of water to grow.

Cultural Characteristics

Few people live in this land region, so there are only a few small towns. People in the towns earn money by working in restaurants and hotels for visitors.

Hikers from all over the world visit the mountains of Olympic National Park.

When the tide comes in, tidal pools like this one hold ocean water. **What will happen when the tide goes out?**

35

TEACH

Talk About It

Washington's Land Regions
(From page 34)

What sets one region apart from another region?
A region usually has one important physical characteristic that is different from other regions. A region also has its own cultural characteristics such as a common language or the kinds of jobs people have.

What do the names of each region tell us?
The names of each region give us clues to its landforms.

Coastal Range

What is the climate of the Coastal Range like?
The Coastal range is the wettest part of the state.

Why do you think few people live in this land region?
Encourage students to think about which characteristics of this region may prevent people from living here.

Caption Answers

(From page 34) There are five land regions shown on the map. Help students determine which region they live in.

The tidal pool will dry up. There may be plant and animal life left behind from the ocean water.

Map Activity

Washington's Land Regions
(From page 34)

Have students create a map of Washington's land regions, using the map on page 34 as a guide. Maps of Washington are available in the back of the *Teacher Guide*. Have students draw, label, and color each of the five regions. Tell students to include symbols of what landforms each region is known for.

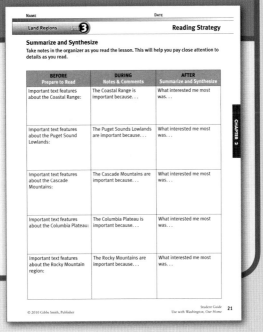

Reading Strategy

Summarize and Synthesize

Summarizing and synthesizing information after reading is a great way to increase and sustain reading comprehension. If students know they will be summarizing what they read, they pay closer attention to details while reading. Have students take interactive notes while reading to complete the Summarize and Synthesize activity available in the *Student Guide*.

Talk About It

Puget Sound Lowlands

What are some of the physical characteristics of the Puget Sound Lowlands?

It is a region of valleys and low hills. The coastline is shaped by miles of bays. Islands dot the water. There are flowing rivers and rich farmland. Mt. Rainier is a prominent landform in this region.

What are December and January like in the Puget Sound region?

During December and January, it rains or snows almost every day.

What is meant by the phrase "population center of the state?"

Large cities such as Seattle, Tacoma, Bellevue, Bremerton, Bellingham, Everett, and Olympia are found in this region, making the population of this region larger than the others.

What are some examples of industry in the Puget Sound Lowlands?

Shipping, building airplanes, boats, and trucks, computer programming, tourism, and farming, and agriculture are examples of some of the industries in this region.

Science Activity

Puget Sound Shorelines

The Washington Department of Ecology has a Web site called Puget Sound Shorelines in which they have a page explaining how the shorelines were formed. Have students read and study the images on this site to learn about how the Puget Sound Lowlands were carved out by glaciers. Have students journal about their findings and compare what they found with a partner. A link to this site can be found at **www.ExperienceStateHistory.com.**

Caption Answers

There are many buildings built close together.

Ships are able to bring many goods to Seattle. This allows for trading of goods between Seattle and ships from other locations.

Puget Sound Lowlands

Tacoma is a large port city on Puget Sound. **How can you tell that Tacoma is a busy urban place?**

Landforms and Natural Resources

This region of valleys and low hills stretches out from the shores of Puget Sound. The coastline is shaped by miles of bays. Islands dot the water. The rolling ocean, flowing rivers, and rich farmland are valuable natural resources.

Climate

If you live in this region, you know that in July and August, it hardly ever rains. But in December and January, you get rain or snow almost every day. You get more rain than any other region.

Cultural Characteristics

Large cities such as Seattle, Tacoma, Bellevue, Bremerton, Bellingham, Everett, and Olympia (the state capital) make this region the population center of the state.

People move here from many places in the world to work in different industries. An ***industry*** is a certain kind of business. Shipping is a major industry. Every day, huge ships carrying products to sell move in and out of the seaports on Puget Sound.

Many people make products to sell. Airplanes, boats, and trucks are built here. Computer programs are developed. ***Tourism*** is the industry of making money by providing hotels, food, transportation, and activities for visitors, or tourists.

Farming, or ***agriculture***, is an important industry in the Skagit River Valley. Tulips and daffodils are the most famous crops. Peas, carrots, broccoli, and other crops are grown for their seeds or are canned or frozen to sell. Raising animals is also part of agriculture. Dairy cows and chickens are raised and sold here, too.

How does Seattle's location on the water help industry in the region?

36

Background Info

Seattle

Seattle is the heart of the region. Home to Microsoft, one of the world's largest corporations, this region boasts one of the highest per capita income levels in the country. Traffic congestion is considered one of the worst in the country. This is a bustling, crowded, exciting, prosperous region.

Cascade Mountains

Landforms and Natural Resources

The tall, rugged Cascade Mountains divide our state. There are five famous mountains in this region. They are Mt. Saint Helens, Mt. Rainier, Mt. Adams, Mt. Baker, and Glacier Peak.

Forests of hemlocks, fir, and cedar trees grow on the wet western side of the mountain. Their *timber*, or wood, is a natural resource.

Climate

Winters are long and cold, and the summers are short. The west side of the mountains gets a lot of rain and snow. Traveling through the high mountains in winter used to be very frightening. Now wide freeways make traveling over Snoqualmie Pass much easier and safer.

Cultural Characteristics

There are no big cities in this region of steep mountains. However, Leavenworth is an example of the smaller towns that depend on tourists. It is built to look like a village in the mountains of Germany. Ellensburg has a university and a famous rodeo that brings tourists from other towns and other states.

People also visit the region to hike, camp, fish, and ski. In some small communities, farming, ranching, and forest jobs are important. Creating electricity in dams is an important industry.

Snoqualmie Pass

Mt. Rainier can be seen in Seattle, Tacoma, and other cities, but it is part of the Cascade Mountains region.

Glacier Peak is reflected in a clear mountain lake. **What natural resources are in this photograph?**

37

Background Info

Mountain Travel

The Cascades are not the great obstacle they were in the past years, though two of the five mountain passes are closed in the winter. Early wagon roads across the mountains were a dangerous adventure. Railroad access came only late in the 1800s. Now the 14-lane Interstate 90 traverses the mountains through Snoqualmie Pass. When winter snows pile up and the threat of avalanches is great, however, Snoqualmie Pass can be closed for days at a time. Travelers will have to wait.

Talk About It

Cascade Mountains

What are some of the physical characteristics of the Cascade Mountain region?
The tall, rugged Cascade Mountains with five famous mountains are in this region. Forests of hemlock, fir, and cedar trees grow on the wet western side of the mountain.

What is the climate of the Cascade region like?
Winters are long and cold, and the summers are short. The western side of the mountains get a lot of rain and snow.

Why do you think there are no big cities in this region?
Answers should mention something about the steep mountains in the region.

What are some reasons tourists come to the Cascade region?
Leavenworth is a town built to look like a village in Germany, and Ellensburg has a university and a famous rodeo. There are places to hike, camp, fish, and ski.

Math Activity

Cascade Eruptions

The U.S. Geological Survey has a Web site that shows volcanic eruptions in the Cascades during the past 4,000 years. The graph showing the eruptions includes the Cascade's five major mountains. Mountains in the Cascade regions of Oregon and California are also included.

Have students study the graph on this site and come up with five math-related questions they get from studying the graph. Tell students to exchange their five math questions with a partner and answer each other's questions. Allow students to check their answers with their partner. A link to the U.S. Geological Survey site can be found at **www.ExperienceStateHistory.com**.

Caption Answer

There is a lake with water and fish, soil, grass, trees, rock, and snow.

Talk About It

Columbia Plateau

What are some of the most valuable natural resources in the Columbia Plateau region?

Large, winding rivers and rich soil for farming are some of the most valuable natural resources.

How are farmers able to take care of their crops with very little rain and snowfall?

Farmers dig ditches to bring water from lakes and streams to their plants.

What are some of the industries found in this region?

Health care, education, research, Washington State University, fruit-growing, farming, and cattle ranching are all industries in the Columbia Plateau region.

Caption Answers

There are many buildings and busy roads.

There is no water falling over the cliff. In former years, during a time of great flooding, the cliffs would be covered with waterfalls.

Social Studies Activity

Webbing the Columbia Plateau

After reading about the Columbia Plateau, have students summarize their learning by creating a web. A web is available in the graphic organizer section of the *Teacher Guide*. Have students fill the web with details about the physical and cultural characteristics of the Columbia Plateau.

Art Activity

Design a License Plate

Our current license plate reads, "Evergreen State." Or, " Lighthouses." Challenge students to create a new license plate using information from this lesson about the physical and cultural characteristics of our state. Have students create their license plates on stiff white paper and display the finished products around the room.

Columbia Plateau

If you were looking down from the window of an airplane, you would see this view of Spokane. **How can you tell that this photograph shows an urban place?**

Can you see why this place on the plateau is called Dry Falls?

38

Landforms and Natural Resources

On the east side of the Cascades is the wide, flat, plateau that covers most of eastern Washington. Large winding rivers are important, valuable resources.

The Palouse is a farming region on the plateau. Palouse soil was formed thousands of years ago from volcanic ash and dust. The soil is the most valuable natural resource here.

Climate

Very little water falls on the land here. The land is the driest in the state. In many places, miles of grassland and scattered trees are all you can see.

Since there is so little rain, farmers dig ditches to bring water from lakes and streams to their plants. This is called *irrigation.*

Cultural Characteristics

Spokane is the largest city in this region and is a center for the health care industry. Pullman is a center of education and research. Washington State University is here. Yakima and Wenatchee are centers for the fruit-growing industry. Smaller towns include the Tri-Cities of Richland, Pasco, and Kennewick.

In rural places, farming is big business. Wheat, corn, alfalfa, apples, cherries, and grapes are grown to sell to people around the world. Do you like hamburgers? Where ranchers raise cattle, meat is an important product.

A combine harvests wheat in the rolling hills of the Palouse farming region of the plateau.

Differentiated Paths

Where Would You Live?

Have students imagine they could live in any region of Washington. Tell them to think about which region they would choose, and why they would choose that region.

ELL and Special Needs

Encourage ELL and Special Needs students to write words or statements explaining why they chose a certain region. Allowing students to illustrate their reasons along with their writing will add to students' understanding of the characteristics of the region.

Gifted Learners

Have gifted learners write a persuasive essay convincing their family to either move to or stay in the region of their choice. Encourage students to use descriptive language to describe the physical and cultural characteristics they enjoy most about the region that they chose.

Rocky Mountain

Landforms and Natural Resources

This region lies at the foothills of the great Rocky Mountains. The Rockies are the largest mountain range in North America. Forests are a natural resource that cover some of the highlands. Grazing land is also a rich resource.

Climate

Since most of this region has a high elevation, it is cool in the summer, but there are many thunderstorms. It is much colder in the winter. The deep snow from November doesn't melt until the air warms in April.

Cultural Characteristics

There are no large cities here, but there are small towns and many ranches. To earn money in this rural region, people farm, raise cattle, cut timber, and mine lead and zinc.

What Do You Think ?

Why do you think most people in Washington live in the Puget Sound Lowlands instead of the Rocky Mountain region?

The land next to the mountains is dotted with cattle. **What kind of industry is shown in this region?**

39

Talk About It

Rocky Mountain

What physical characteristics are found in the Rocky Mountain region?
The region lies at the foothills of the Rocky Mountains. Forests cover some of the highlands. There is plenty of grazing land.

What are summers like in the Rocky Mountain region?
Most of this region has a high elevation, so it is cool in the summer.

How do most people in this region make a living?
This is a rural region where people farm, raise cattle, cut timber, and mine lead and zinc.

What Do You Think ?

Encourage students to think about what natural resources are available in each region as they answer the question.

Literature Link
Cooperative Groups

E is for Evergreen

The alphabet book, *E is for Evergreen*, by Marie Smith, Roland Smith, and Linda Ayriss is all about Washington State. There are great illustrations of physical and cultural characteristics of Washington. After sharing the book, divide the class into cooperative groups to create alphabet books about the geography of our state. Have students divide the letters of the alphabet up within the group. Encourage students to use information from this textbook, other books from the library, and the Internet to make their books interesting.

Caption Answer

Cattle ranching is shown in the picture.

Writing Activity

Compare and Contrast

Using a Venn diagram, have students compare the Rocky Mountain region of Washington to one of its other regions. Encourages students to think about and list each region's physical and cultural characteristics that make it unique. A Venn diagram is available in the graphic organizer section of the *Teacher Guide*.

Talk About It

Other Land Regions

What other two states are part of the Pacific Northwest region?
Idaho and Oregon are also part of the Pacific Northwest region.

What characteristics might states in the American West region have in common?
Display a physical map of the United States. Encourage students to think about what landforms, resources, jobs, and other characteristics these states may have in common.

The Pacific Rim Region *(From page 41)*

Why do you think countries along the Pacific Rim do so much trading with each other?
The ocean between the countries provides easy transportation for boats that can carry lots of goods to trade.

What are some of the countries along the Pacific Rim that trade with each other?
Possible answers include United States of America, Japan, China, Korea, regions of the Australian continent, and countries in South America.

Caption Answer

(From page 41) The region is named for the Pacific Ocean. Asia, Australia, North America, and South America are around the Pacific Rim.

Art Activity

Regions Brochure

Washington is a great place to live and work. Divide your class into groups. Have each group design a brochure showcasing the benefits of living and working in one of the regions of Washington. Encourage students to think about the physical and cultural characteristics of their region. Have students design their brochures on the computer for a professional look. There is a lot of software available with templates to design brochures. Ask your computer specialist or a parent for help if you are unfamiliar with designing brochures on a computer.

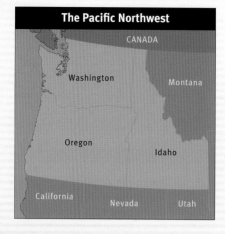

The Pacific Northwest

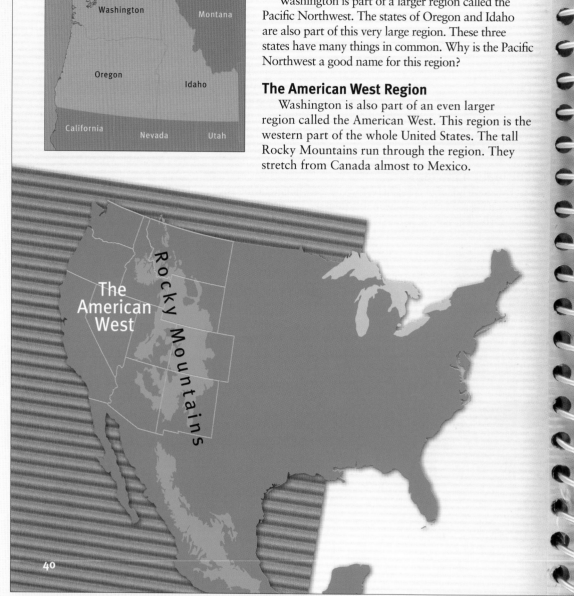

40

Other Land Regions

The Pacific Northwest Region

Washington is part of a larger region called the Pacific Northwest. The states of Oregon and Idaho are also part of this very large region. These three states have many things in common. Why is the Pacific Northwest a good name for this region?

The American West Region

Washington is also part of an even larger region called the American West. This region is the western part of the whole United States. The tall Rocky Mountains run through the region. They stretch from Canada almost to Mexico.

Background Info

The Pacific Rim

Each country around the rim makes products the other countries want to buy. For example, people in the United States buy clothing made in China and the Philippines. We buy cars, televisions, and electronic equipment made in Japan. Washington exports aircraft, wheat, fruit, and computer software to China, Japan, Korea, and many other countries on the Pacific Rim.

Goods in large metal cases are constantly being shipped across the Pacific. The ships move in and out of the port cities in Washington, Oregon, and California. Ships from the East Coast and Europe come here too, passing first through the Panama Canal. In our port cities, goods are loaded onto trucks and trains and moved to other places in the United States and Canada.

The Pacific Rim Region

Find the Pacific Ocean on a globe or a world map. Then find Washington State in North America and all the other continents that touch the Pacific Ocean. These lands make up a large region called the Pacific Rim.

Japan, China, and Korea are countries in Asia. They lie along the Pacific Rim. The United States and many other countries are part of the Pacific Rim, too.

Each day, hundreds of ships and airplanes travel back and forth between the cities of the Pacific Rim. Visit a busy seaport in Washington, and you might see a ship bringing cars from Japan. You might see Washington farm products being loaded and shipped to China. You might see airplanes full of tourists and business people.

All of this selling and buying with people who live along the Pacific Rim is important. This is the way people get the things they want. This is also the way many people earn money for their families. You will learn more about this trading region in a later chapter.

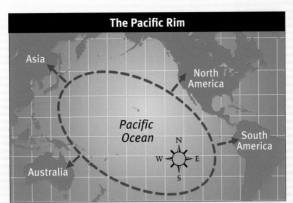

The Pacific Rim

Asia · North America · Pacific Ocean · South America · Australia

Look at the map. **What ocean is the region named for? What continents border the Pacific Rim?**

LESSON 3 What Did You Learn?

1. How many land regions does Washington have? Name them.
2. Describe the climate of the Puget Sound Lowlands.
3. What are some important natural resources of the Columbia Plateau?
4. Why is it important for Washington to buy from and sell to other countries on the Pacific Rim?

41

REFLECT

Reflect on students' understanding of the physical and cultural characteristics of Washington's five land regions. You can evaluate students' understanding through discussion or evaluation of activities completed in this lesson. The following activity will serve as another way of assessing students' understanding of the key objectives of this lesson.

Writing Activity

Tanka Poem

A tanka is a poem of 31 syllables in five lines. There are five syllables in lines 1 and 3 and seven syllables in lines 2, 4, and 5. Have students write a tanka poem about two of the land regions in Washington. Encourage students to choose two regions in order to showcase their differences in the poems. Have students complete the Tanka Poem activity in the *Student Guide*.

Example:
Washington regions
There are five regions in all
Each one is unique
Some have mountains, some are flat
Some are wet and some are dry

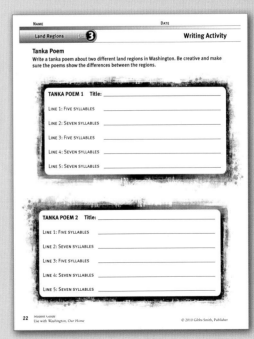

LESSON 3 What Did You Learn?

1. *Washington has five land regions: Coastal Range, Puget Sound Lowlands, Cascade Mountains, Columbia Plateau, and Rocky Mountain.*
2. *It hardly rains in July and August, but in December and January, you get rain or snow almost every day.*
3. *Large, winding rivers and Palouse soil are two of the Columbia Plateau's most important natural resources.*
4. *Washington trades with other countries on the Pacific Rim to get goods that we need that aren't available in our area. Trade also helps Washington workers make money when they sell their goods.*

Washington Social Studies Skills

Washington Social Studies Skills

Standards

GLE 3.1.1
Constructs and uses maps to explain the movement of people.

Create a Map

Use this activity to support the **Social Studies CBA:** People on the Move (completed in the Chapter 5 Project Assessment).

Activate

Gather and share different maps with the class. Ask students to discuss what each map is showing and how it would be useful.

Teach

Remind students that in order for a map to be helpful, is should include symbols, a compass, a legend, and a scale. Write each of these terms on the board and explain why each is useful when reading a map.

Have students work in pairs or small groups to locate each of the features on the maps gathered for the Activate activity. Encourage students to compare the scales and legends on different maps.

Practice

Have students continue working in pairs or small groups to write five questions about their maps. Tell students to write five questions that another student would be able to answer by using the features of the map.

Have students exchange maps and questions between the pairs or groups. Give students time to answer the other group's questions.

Apply

Have students create a map, following the directions on the Social Studies Skill Page. Be sure to explain that their maps will not include a scale because that is an advanced map-making skill.

Create a Map

In this chapter, you learned that maps are useful in helping us get from place to place. For a map to be the most helpful, it should include symbols, a compass, and a legend.

Create a map of your school grounds that a person who has never been to your school could use to find his or her way around. Be sure to include the school, the playground, the parking lot, the flagpole, and other important things.

☐ Make a list of things you want to include on your map.

☐ Draw a symbol for each thing. (These symbols will be included in your legend.)

☐ On a large piece of paper or poster board, draw the map of your school grounds.

☐ Draw the symbols on the map and in the legend.

☐ Give your map a title.

☐ Put a compass on your map.

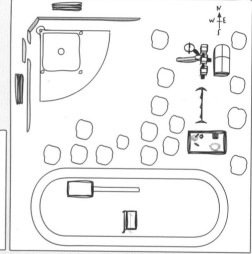

Washington, Our Home

Chapter Review 2

Reviewing What You Read

1. On which country, continent, and planet is Washington State located?
2. What ocean and large river form part of our state's boundaries?
3. Choose one feature of a map and tell how it is helpful.
4. How would life in Washington be different if it weren't located next to the ocean?
5. Predict what might happen if one of Washington's volcanoes were to erupt.
6. Choose three of our state's landforms and evaluate their importance to your city or town.

Becoming a Better Reader

Set a Purpose for Reading

Good readers always set a purpose for reading. Part of setting a purpose for reading is thinking about what you already know about a subject.

The next chapter in this book, Chapter 3, is about Native Americans. Using the KWL chart your teacher provides, show what you know and what you want to know about Native Americans in Washington. After you have studied the chapter, you will complete your chart by writing what you learned.

Spotlighting Geography

Geography Is All Around You!

Watching the news is a good way to learn what is going on around you. At home, watch the news and write down the stories that have to do with geography. These might include traffic reports, weather reports, and reports of events in your town and your state. Some reports might include maps. Share your work with the class.

Geography Is the Stage

43

Reviewing What You Read

The Reviewing What You Read questions are leveled according to Bloom's Taxonomy and will help students achieve a higher level of thinking. These questions will also prepare students for the chapter assessment. The following are possible answers to the questions. Focus on students' ability to understand and apply the concepts.

1. **KNOWLEDGE** Washington State is located in the United States of America, on the North American continent, on the planet Earth.

2. **COMPREHENSION** The Pacific Ocean and the Columbia River form part of our state's boundaries.

3. **APPLICATION** Possible answers include a compass shows the directions, a legend tells what symbols on a map stand for, and a scale of miles tells how far apart places really are.

4. **ANALYSIS** If Washington weren't located next to the ocean the plant and animal life would be different, some people would have different jobs, people might travel differently to get here, we would have different natural resources, and the climate would be different.

5. **SYNTHESIS** Students' answers should describe how an eruption would affect the land, people, plants, and animals.

6. **EVALUATION** Students' answers should reflect an understanding of the landforms they chose and should describe how each landform affects life in their city or town.

Interactive Chapter Review

An Interactive Chapter Review is available online at www.ExperienceStateHistory.com. Have students use this review to prepare for the assessments.

Chapter Assessment

Chapter Assessments are available to preview on pages 18G–18H. Assessments can be found in the *Teacher Guide*. They can also be found online at www.ExperienceStateHistory.com.

Becoming a Better Reader

Set a Purpose for Reading

Students should always set a purpose for reading. This will help them become more engaged and aid comprehension. Encourage students to set a purpose for reading throughout the year. There are a number of graphic organizers available in the back of the *Teacher Guide* that you can use to help set a purpose for any reading activity.

Spotlighting Geography

Geography Is All Around You!

Have students create a three-column chart labeling the sections Land, Places, People. As students share the stories they found in the news, have the class decide if it is a story about land, a place, or people. Then have students write a phrase describing the story in the column in which it belongs.

3 Native People

CHAPTER PLANNER

CHAPTER OVERVIEW	WASHINGTON SOCIAL STUDIES GLEs
This chapter focuses on the early people of the Pacific Northwest. Attention is given to the Coastal and Plateau groups of Indians as well as how archaeological research adds to our understanding of history.	GLE 4.1.2 GLE 5.1.2 GLE 5.2.1 GLE 5.4.2

CHAPTER RESOURCES
ELL/Modified Chapter Plan, p. 44I
Books and Web Sites, p. 44J

CHAPTER ACTIVITIES	WASHINGTON CURRICULUM INTEGRATION
History on the Line, p. 44E	**Visual Arts** GLE 2.1.1
Read Native American Legends, p. 44E	**Reading** GLE 3.2.1, **Theatre** GLE 3.2.1
Studying Bones, p. 44E	**Science** GLE 1.1.6
Totem Poles, p. 44E	**Visual Arts** GLE 2.1.1
Dig It!, p. 44F	**Math** GLE 4.4.D
Future Artifacts, p. 44F	**Reading** GLE 3.2.1
■ Write a Legend, p. 44F	**Writing** GLE 2.3.1
Early People of Washington Potlatch, p. 44F	**Reading** GLE 2.1.7

CHAPTER OPENER	WASHINGTON CURRICULUM INTEGRATION
Picture Washington Long Ago, p. 46	**Visual Arts** GLE 3.2.1
Think About the Painting, p. 46	**Visual Arts** GLE 4.4.1
Timeline Talk, p. 47	**Reading** GLE 3.2.2

▶Indicates an activity page located in the *Student Guide*
■ Indicates an activity page located in the *Teacher Guide*

The BIG Idea | Who were the first people in Washington, and how did they use the environment to meet their needs?

CHAPTER REVIEW   pp. 66–67

SOCIAL STUDIES SKILLS PAGE	WASHINGTON SOCIAL STUDIES GLEs
How to Cite Sources, p. 66	**Social Studies** GLE 5.4.2 Use with the Chapter 3 **Project Assessment**

REVIEWING THE CHAPTER	WASHINGTON SOCIAL STUDIES GLEs
Students show what they learned by completing application activities and answering chapter review questions. Assessments for this chapter can be previewed on pages 44G-44H. Select the assessment option that best suits your goals for this chapter. Assessments are available in the *Teacher Guide* or online at **www.ExperienceStateHistory.com**.	GLE 4.1.2 GLE 5.1.2 GLE 5.2.1 GLE 5.4.2

CHAPTER ACTIVITIES	WASHINGTON CURRICULUM INTEGRATION
Reviewing What You Read, p. 67	**Reading** GLE 1.3.2, GLE 2.1.3
Becoming a Better Reader, p. 67	**Reading** GLE 2.3.1
Spotlighting Geography, p. 67	**Writing** GLE 3.2.1

CHAPTER ASSESSMENTS	WASHINGTON CURRICULUM INTEGRATION
■ Multiple Choice Assessment, p. 22	**Reading** GLE 1.3.2, GLE 2.1.3
■ Reading Assessment, p. 23	**Reading** GLE 2.3.3
■ Writing Assessment, p. 24	**Writing** GLE 2.2.1, GLE 3.1.2
■ Project Assessment, pp. 25–26	**Social Studies** GLE 5.2.1, **Writing** GLE 1.1.1, GLE 1.2.1 GLE 1.3.1, GLE 1.4.1, GLE 1.5.1, GLE 1.6.1

LESSON 1
The First People
pp. 48–51

LESSON OVERVIEW	WASHINGTON SOCIAL STUDIES GLEs
KEY IDEAS • The first people to live in the Pacific Northwest were Paleo-Indians. • The Paleo-Indians were skilled stone workers and hunters. • Archaeologists study clues to learn about people of the past. • Changes in climate changed how the early Indian groups lived.	GLE 4.1.2

LESSON ACTIVITIES	WASHINGTON CURRICULUM INTEGRATION
▶Digging for Treasure, p. 48	**Visual Arts** GLE 2.3.1, **Writing** GLE 2.2.1
Word Clues, p. 48	**Reading** GLE 1.2.1
▶Words to Understand, p. 48	**Reading** GLE 1.3.1
▶Text to Self Connection, p. 49	**Reading** GLE 2.3.1
Monitor Your Reading Rate, p. 50	**Reading** GLE 2.1.3
▶Venn Diagram, p. 51	**Reading** GLE 3.2.1, **Writing** GLE 2.2.1
Archaeologists Dig For Clues, p. 51	**Reading** GLE 2.1.7

LESSON 2
Coastal People
pp. 52–60

LESSON OVERVIEW	WASHINGTON SOCIAL STUDIES GLEs
KEY IDEAS • The ocean helped the Coastal people meet their needs. • Coastal people celebrated many traditions and passed along legends.	GLE 4.1.2 GLE 5.1.2

LESSON ACTIVITIES	WASHINGTON CURRICULUM INTEGRATION
▶Details About Me, p. 52	**Writing** GLE 2.2.1
Vocabulary Notebook, p. 52	**Reading** GLE 1.2.2
▶Words to Understand, p. 52	**Reading** GLE 1.3.1
▶Text to Text Connection, p. 53	**Reading** GLE 2.3.1
Think Like an Archaeologist, p. 54	**Science** GLE 2.1.5
Coastal People Food Pyramid, p. 55	**Health** GLE 1.4.1
How to Hunt Whales, p. 56	**Writing** GLE 2.3.1
Go to the Source: The Ozette Dig, p. 57	**Social Studies** GLE 5.1.2
Virtual Tour of the Ozette Dig, p. 57	**Technology** GLE 1.3.2
Legend Role Play, p. 58	**Theatre** GLE 3.2.1
Family Legends, p. 59	**Writing** GLE 2.2.1, GLE 2.3.1
Expand the Legend, p. 59	**Writing** GLE 2.2.1, GLE 2.3.1
▶What If . . ., p. 60	**Writing** GLE 3.1.1, GLE 3.1.2

LESSON 3
Plateau People pp. 61–65

LESSON OVERVIEW	WASHINGTON SOCIAL STUDIES GLEs
KEY IDEAS • Plateau people used the land to meet their needs. • Plateau people had strong spiritual beliefs. • The people got things they wanted by trading with other groups.	GLE 4.1.2

LESSON ACTIVITIES	WASHINGTON CURRICULUM INTEGRATION
▶Differences in Cultures, p. 61	**Reading** GLE 2.1.4
Synonyms, p. 61	**Reading** GLE 1.2.1
▶Words to Understand, p. 61	**Reading** GLE 1.3.1
▶Text to World Connection, p. 62	**Reading** GLE 2.3.1
Plateau Art and Legends, p. 63	**Technology** GLE 1.3.2
How Far Is a Mile?, p. 63	**Math** GLE 4.5.E
Farming Could Have Helped, p. 64	**Technology** GLE 1.3.2
▶A Great Place to Live, p. 65	**Writing** GLE 3.1.1

Chapter Activities

This chapter focuses on the early people of the Pacific Northwest. Attention is given to the Coastal and Plateau Indians and archaeology. As you work through the chapter, use these Chapter Activities to help students understand the key ideas.

Set the Stage

Before you begin the study of the early people of the Pacific Northwest, decorate your room with pictures of artifacts from the different groups of people. You can download images from the Internet. Be sure to have a map of Washington easily accessible to note the regions mentioned in the textbook.

Set up a class library with books that support and enrich the concepts presented in the chapter. Some titles are suggested in the Books and Web Sites on page 44J. Ask your librarian for other suggestions.

Introductory Activity

History on the Line

This chapter begins our study of Washington's history. Place a large timeline around the room. You should include dates beginning with 10,000 B.C. through the current year. Talk about the timeline and how it is used. As you read through the history chapters, have students draw pictures of the different people and events covered in the textbook, and place them on the timeline. The timeline will provide a visual to help students understand more about Washington history.

Reading Activity

Read Native American Legends

In this chapter, students learn that many Native Americans told legends to teach lessons, share history, and give explanations for why some things happen. Share with your class the book *Spider Spins a Story: Fourteen Legends from Native America* by Jill Max. Read some of the legends aloud. Allow students to talk about the meanings of the legends or the lessons learned.

Then, ask students to respond to the legends by role playing. Depending on your class, you may want to divide students into groups and have each group read a legend and act it out. The First People Web site also includes lots of legends from many different tribes. See **www.ExperienceStateHistory.com** for a link to this site.

Science Activity

Studying Bones

Locate several different kinds of bones. You can use chicken, cow, or pig bones left over from dinner, or you may be able to get access to bones from the science department of your local high school, college, or museum. Your district's resource center or local library may also have suggestions for locating bones to use for this lesson.

Ask students to look at the bones carefully. Students should make a sketch of the bones, noting any interesting distinctions or characteristics. Have students try to determine which animal the bones came from and what part of the animal they are. Students should write about their findings and their conclusions.

Art Activity

Totem Poles

Although not actually produced by Indians of today's Washington, totem poles were created by people in the northern Pacific Northwest region to tell stories of their history. Each animal on the pole told a different story.

Have students work in groups to design and illustrate a totem pole. Have each member of the group draw an animal on a piece of sturdy construction paper to represent that story. After the animals have been drawn, attach them to a paper towel roll. Hang each paper towel roll on the bulletin board, stacking the groups' animals on to of each other. Allow students to share the stories of their totem pole with one another.

Math Activity

 Writing Activity

 Culminating Activity

Dig It!

Explain to students that when archaeologists have reason to believe a particular site might have historical significance, they organize a dig. A dig is an archaeological site with ongoing excavations. An excavation is an organized way of uncovering and searching for artifacts.

Find a location on the school grounds for students to simulate a dig. Bury "artifacts" for students to find. Students will need graph paper, a measuring tape, string, and stakes to hold the string. Encourage students to wear old clothes and bring digging tools.

Prior to starting the dig, have students make a plan, using graph paper to create a grid of the site. Once outside, have students section off the area, using their plan as a guide. Assign pairs of students sections of the area to investigate. Explain that archaeologists dig very slowly and carefully, so as not to miss or damage artifacts.

As students locate items, they should record what and where they were found on the grid. Have students write about how each item may have ended up where it was found and who might have left it.

 Social Studies Activity

Future Artifacts

Remind students that one way we know about ancient people is by the artifacts they left behind. Have students think about artifacts they could leave behind for people in the future to study. As a class, fill a metal container (such as a coffee can) with artifacts that tell about the students. Some suggestions include a class picture, newspaper clipping, kids' magazine, and a wrapper from a favorite food item. Decorate the can, being sure to include the date. Finally, help students bury the container on the playground for people in the future to find.

Write a Legend

After reading some Native American legends, ask students to brainstorm a list of events or things to write a legend about. For example, students can write a legend about why snow falls from the sky or why their hair grows longer. Have each student write a legend explaining something in his or her life. Instruct students to illustrate their legends and share them in small groups.

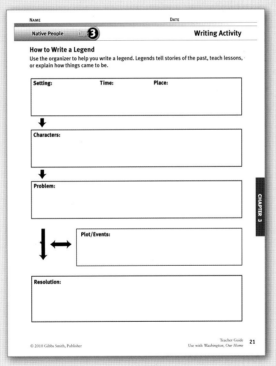

Early People of Washington Potlatch

Lead your class in hosting a potlatch. Invite family members or guests from other classes to join in the potlatch. Allow students from your class to create invitations for the potlatch and deliver them to other fourth grade classes. Encourage students in your class to dress up for the potlatch. If possible, have food and small gifts available to share with guests.

Once guests have arrived, have students stationed at different areas around the room to tell guests about the many projects on display. Have students research to learn and perform Native American songs and dances. Then have groups of students role play their legends. Share any other performances from the study of this chapter. The following are items you may want to display and share with guests:

- Timeline (See History on the Line)
- Legends (See Write a Legend)
- Grids and Artifacts (See Dig It!)
- Collection of bones and explanations (See Studying Bones)
- Totem Poles (See Totem Poles)
- Research Reports (See the Project Assessment available in the *Teacher Guide.*)

Assessment Options

The Chapter Assessment options provide opportunities to evaluate students' understanding of the social studies concepts. Choose the assessment options that best meet the needs of your teaching goals. Assessments are available in the *Teacher Guide* or can be individualized at www.ExperienceStateHistory.com.

OPTION 1: MULTIPLE CHOICE ASSESSMENT

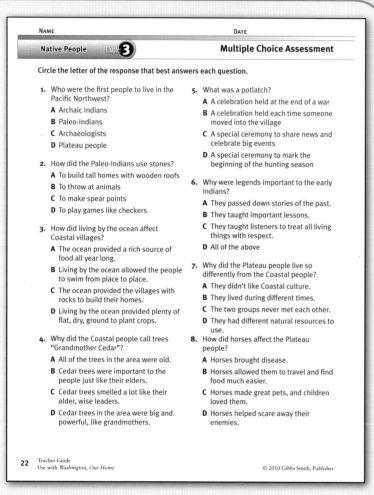

The Multiple Choice Assessment provides a quick way to assess students' understanding of the key concepts of the chapter. Have students read each question and select the best answer.

OPTION 2: READING ASSESSMENT

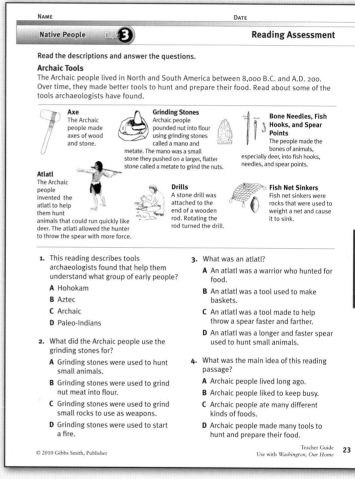

The Reading Assessment provides additional practice for the WASL Reading Test. Have students study the information and answer the questions that follow.

OPTION 3: WRITING ASSESSMENT

NAME DATE

Native People Chapter 3 **Writing Assessment**

Choose one of the groups of people you learned about in Chapter 3. Write a paragraph about how the group lived and the contributions the people made. Use the Writing Checklist to help you organize your paragraph. Check off the steps as you go.

Writing Checklist

- ☐ Write a sentence stating the main idea of your paragraph.
- ☐ Write three to six sentences to support the main idea.
- ☐ Write one sentence to conclude your paragraph. Your conclusion should restate the main idea.
- ☐ Review your writing. Be sure you have used correct grammar, spelling, capitalization, and punctuation. Be sure your writing makes sense and includes facts about the people you are describing.
- ☐ Rewrite your paragraph on another piece of paper. Be sure to use your neatest writing. Staple this page to your final copy.

24 Teacher Guide Use with *Washington, Our Home* © 2010 Gibbs Smith, Publisher

The Writing Assessment provides additional practice for the WASL Writing Test. Have students use the checklist to write a paragraph about one of the groups of people from the chapter.

OPTION 4: PROJECT ASSESSMENT

NAME DATE

Native People Chapter 3 **Project Assessment (Page 1 of 2)**

Use the checklist to write a research report that addresses your research question from the Social Studies Skills Page, How to Cite Sources, on page 60 of the *Student Edition.* Use information from the resources you gathered for the Social Studies Skills Page.

Research Report

Prewriting

- ☐ **Write Your Research Question**
- ☐ **Research**
  For this report, you will use your textbook and at least two other sources. From the Social Studies Skills Page, write the two sources you will use.

CHAPTER 3

© 2010 Gibbs Smith, Publisher Teacher Guide Use with *Washington, Our Home* 25

The Project Assessment provides an alternative to the traditional assessment. Have students follow the checklist to plan and write a research report. Have students complete the Skills Page activity on page 66 to support this assessment.

ELL/Modified Chapter Plan

Native People

Native people lived in today's Washington long before white settlers came. Students will learn about the different groups of early people who lived in the Pacific Northwest long ago.

The following pages can be found in the ELL/Modified Chapter Guide on pages 15-19.

The ELL/Modified Chapter Plan provides a step-by-step lesson in an easy-to-use format. Lessons teach content and language objectives.

The Modified Assessment for this chapter assesses students' understanding of the key objectives of the chapter.

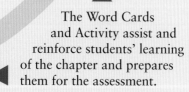

The Word Cards and Activity assist and reinforce students' learning of the chapter and prepares them for the assessment.

Books and Web Sites

Books

Barbeau, Marius. *Art of the Totem*. Blaine: Hancock House Publications, 2006.

Bartok, Mira. *Northwest Coast Indians*. Glenview: Good Year Books, 1996.

Duke, Kate. *Archaeologists Dig for Clues*. Let's-Read-and-Find-Out, Science 2. New York: Harper Trophy, 1997

Kamma, Anna. *If You Lived with the Indians of the Northwest Coast*. Danbury, Scholastic, 2002.

Max, Jill. *Spider Spins a Story: Fourteen Legends of Native America*. Flagstaff: Rising Moon, 1997.

Newmann, Dana. *Ready-to-Use Activities and Materials on Coastal Indians*. Englewood: Prentice Hall Direct, 1996.

Panchyk, Richard. *Archaeology for Kids: Uncovering the Mysteries of the Past*. Chicago: Chicago Review Press, 2001.

Smithyman, Kathryn and Bobbie Kalman. *Nations of the Northwest Coast (Native Nations of North America)*. New York: Crabtree Publishing Company, 2003.

Taylor, Colin F. *Native American Weapons*. Norman: University of Oklahoma Press, 2005.

Web Sites

The following Web sites provide resources or lesson plans for teachers and activities for students to help extend the lessons in this chapter. Go to **www.ExperienceStateHistory.com** for links to these Web sites.

British Columbia Folklore Society

This Web site from the British Columbia Folklore Society lists several examples of legends from the Plateau people.

The Burke Museum of Natural History and Culture

This Web site from the Burke Museum of Natural History and Culture contains an online Plateau collection with many pictures of Plateau art.

The Coastal and Plateau Indians

This Coastal and Plateau Indians Web site was created for teachers. It includes links and instructions to take students through a research project of the Coastal and Plateau Indians.

Dig on Site

The Dig on Site Web site is designed for budding archaeologists and includes information on how to subscribe to *Dig It!* an archaeology magazine for kids.

First People

The First People Web site is filled with information about Native Americans. It also includes lots of legends from many different tribes.

Kidz World

Students can use the Kidz World Web site to search for information on Native Americans from the Pacific Northwest. This site includes images and kid-friendly information.

My Pyramid

The My Pyramid government Web site contains explanations and examples of the food guide pyramid to use in the Coastal People Food Pyramid activity on page 49.

Native Americans

The Native Americans Web site has information for teachers on various Native American tribes. A list of biographies on Native Americans is also available.

Unit Opener Activity

Becoming Washington

Use this activity to help students understand that Washington has not always been a state and has changed over many years. It has taken a lot of time for Washington to become what it is today.

Ask students to think of something they are good at. It may be a sport, a game, or a subject in school. Ask for volunteers to share something they do well. Have students work in small groups to talk about how each of them have become better at a sport, a game, a musical instrument, or a subject in school.

Explain to students that developing these talents was a process that took a lot of time. There were probably a lot of mistakes made that students learned from. Explain that Washington has gone through similar processes as it has changed over the years. Washington is a great place to live now, but throughout its history, there were a lot of good things and bad things that happened.

Caption Answer

Life was much different than it is now. The buildings were different, people dressed different, and there were no cars or paved roads.

UNIT 2

For thousands of years, Native Americans lived across the Pacific Northwest. After a long time, explorers came by sea and by land. The Native Americans and the explorers met each other for the first time.

Soon an unending stream of traders and settlers came to the Northwest. **The settlers started towns like this one. What can you learn about life in early Washington by studying this picture?**

44

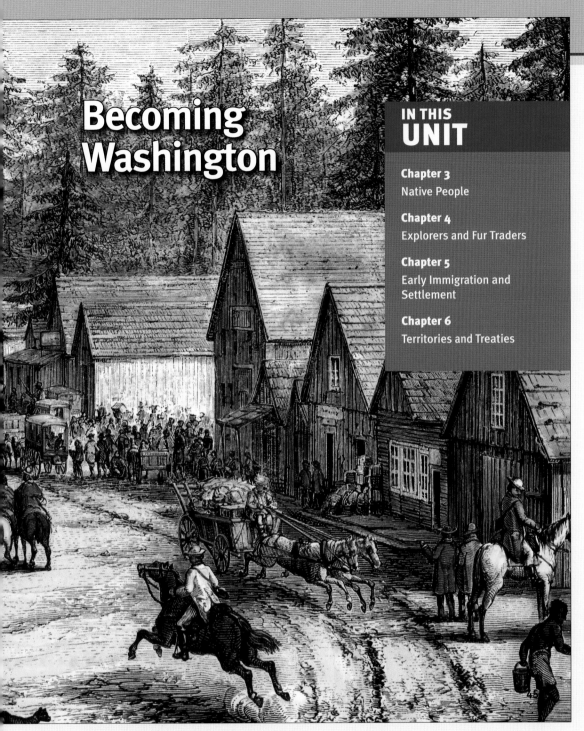

Becoming Washington

 Put Yourself in the Picture

I Spy

Have students work in pairs or small groups to play I Spy with the picture from the Unit Opener. One student begins the game by choosing an item from the picture and saying, "I spy, with my little eye..." The student will then continue to describe the details of the item they chose until the other students guess what is being described.

The BIG Idea

Picture Washington Long Ago

Before opening their textbooks, have students draw pictures of what they think Washington looked like many years ago. Encourage students to think about the following questions when creating their pictures:

- Were there buildings in this region hundreds of years ago?
- Did the early people look, act, and dress like we do today?
- How did the early people live on and use the land?
- Did the land look the same hundreds of years ago as it does today?

Have students share their pictures with the class and discuss similarities and differences between pictures.

 Put Yourself in the Picture

Think About the Painting

As a class, study the painting. Use these questions to lead your class in a discussion about the it. Encourage students to explain their ideas with a partner. Ask for volunteers to share their answers with the class.

- What is going on in this painting?
- What does it look like the people in the picture are doing?
- What do you see that makes you say that?
- Who do you think the people in the picture are?
- What was happening in history during the time shown in this painting?
- What do you think interested the artist about this subject?
- How does this picture compare to the picture you drew in the Picture Washington Long Ago activity?

Caption Answer

The people from this picture stayed in teepees.

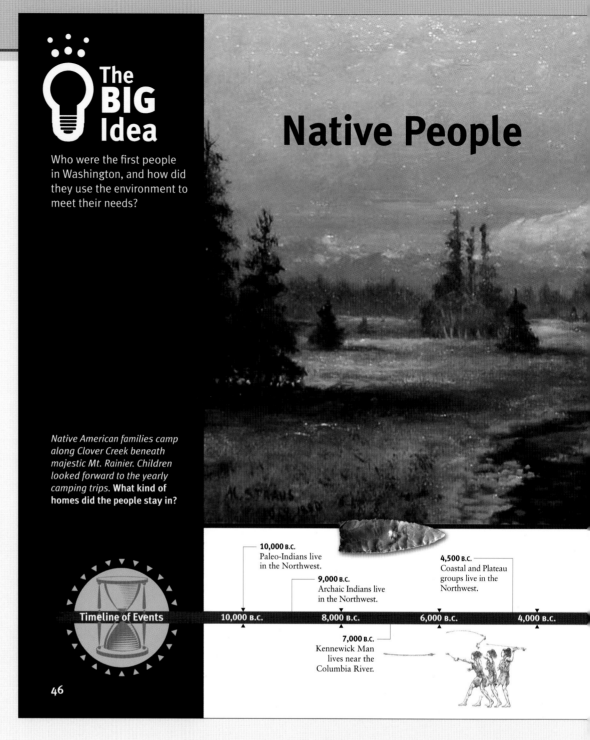

The BIG Idea

Who were the first people in Washington, and how did they use the environment to meet their needs?

Native People

Native American families camp along Clover Creek beneath majestic Mt. Rainier. Children looked forward to the yearly camping trips. **What kind of homes did the people stay in?**

Timeline of Events

10,000 B.C.
Paleo-Indians live in the Northwest.

9,000 B.C.
Archaic Indians live in the Northwest.

7,000 B.C.
Kennewick Man lives near the Columbia River.

4,500 B.C.
Coastal and Plateau groups live in the Northwest.

| 10,000 B.C. | 8,000 B.C. | 6,000 B.C. | 4,000 B.C. |

46

CHAPTER

3

Close your eyes for a minute, and go back in time. There are no cities, no cars, no stores. You see forests all around you. Look closely, and you might see a line of smoke curling up into the sky. You hear a fire crackle. You come upon a group of people sitting around the fire. These are the first people to live in the land we call Washington. That's why they are called native people.

1500
A mudslide covers part of the village at Ozette.

1800s ─────▶
The first settlers live in the Northwest.

| 2,000 B.C. | A.D. 1500 | A.D. 1600 | A.D. 1700 | A.D. 1800 |

1500 B.C.
Coastal people begin to hunt seals and whales.

1700s ─────▶
Explorers come to what is now Washington.

47

Timeline Activity

Timeline Talk

Direct students' attention to the timeline. Talk about the information that can be learned from the timeline. Remind students they learned about reading timelines in their Skill Page in Chapter 1. Engage students in a discussion about the information on the timeline.

What year did the first people shown on the timeline live in the Northwest?
10,000 B.C.

How many years passed between the time the Archaic Indians lived in the Northwest and the time the Coastal and Plateau groups lived in the Northwest?
4,500 years

How long did the Coastal people live in the Northwest before they began to hunt seals and whales?
3,000 years

About how long did native people live in the Northwest region before the first settlers came in the 1800s?
About 11,800 years

🔷 **Standards**

GLE 4.1.2
Understands how the following theme and development help to define eras in Washington State history from time immemorial to 1889: Growth of northwest coastal and plateau tribes prior to treaties (time immemorial to 1854).

PREPARE

Activator

Digging for Treasure

Before beginning this lesson, ask students if they have ever dug outside anywhere. Explain to students that any items they found while digging have a story to tell about the past. Have students complete the Digging for Treasure page in their *Student Guide* and share their stories about digging.

Word Study

Word Clues

Write the Words to Understand on the board. Ask students to share what they know about each of the words. Write the information under each word. Help students gather clues about the meanings of the words from different word parts. Next, read each definition aloud and have the class guess which word it belongs to, using the clues they gathered about the words.

LESSON 1 The First People

Who Were the First People?

The first people in the Pacific Northwest probably came here in small family groups. Scientists call them Paleo-Indians. Native Americans call them the Ancient Ones. *Ancient* refers to the earliest time, long, long ago.

The people moved from place to place to find the best places to hunt large animals for food. They also gathered wild roots, berries, and nuts for their families.

We don't know much about these men, women, and children. They left no written stories of their lives. However, they did leave clues about how they lived. They left spear points and other tools made from stone and bone. They left shells and bones from their food. They also left ashes from their cooking fires. Scientists study these clues to learn about the people of the past.

Skilled Stoneworkers

The people made spear points by chipping away at small pieces of hard rock with sharp tools they made from other stones. Large stone spear points are some of the most beautiful and unusual artifacts found in Washington. Many have been found in East Wenatchee.

The people also made tools to carve designs into large rocks. Rock carvings are called *petroglyphs*. If you know where to look, you can see this rock art in many places in Washington.

Long ago, people carved pictures that are still here today. We can only guess at what the pictures mean. **What natural resources in this place might have been helpful to people?**

48

Washington, Our Home

Words to Understand

ancient (p. 48) *relating to a time long, long ago*
archaeologist (p. 49) *a scientist who studies clues to learn how people lived in the past*
atlatl (p. 51) *a tool used to throw a spear farther and faster*
descendant (p. 51) *children, grandchildren, great-grandchildren, and so on*
extinct (p. 50) *no longer living anywhere on the Earth*
native (p. 51) *being born or raised in a certain place or region*
petroglyph (p. 48) *a rock carving*

A Words to Understand activity for this lesson is available in the *Student Guide*.

Archaeologists

Archaeologists are scientists who study clues to learn how people lived in the past. Many of these clues are artifacts buried in the earth. An artifact is something people made and left behind.

How do archaeologists work? First, they mark off the site they will study. They want to know just where an object was found. This might give them clues about how an object was used.

Carefully, archaeologists remove one layer of dirt at a time. They keep careful notes about what they find. Even the smallest item may have a story to tell. It might give clues to what the people ate and what tools they made.

Stone spear points are among the oldest artifacts found in Washington. Many are about 12,000 years old.

Layer by layer, these students dig carefully into the ground. They are looking for artifacts left behind by people long ago. **What tools are they using?**

Stone spear points are some of the oldest artifacts. They last a very long time.

Native People

49

TEACH

Talk About It

Who Were the First People?
(From page 48)
What do scientists call the first people who lived in the Pacific Northwest?
Scientist call the first people Paleo-Indians; Native Americans call them the Ancient Ones.

How did the Paleo-Indians get food?
They moved from place to place to find the best places to hunt large animals for food. They also gathered wild roots, berries, and nuts for their families.

Skilled Stoneworkers *(From page 48)*
What were some ways the Paleo-Indians used stoneworking?
They made spear points and they carved petroglyphs into large rocks.

Archaeologists
Why do you think archaeologists' work is so important?
Possible answers include archaeologists find artifacts and clues about the past, and they help us learn more about the places where we live.

Caption Answers

(From page 48) Rocks and trees would have been helpful for making tools and for building.

They are using a hoe and a shovel to search for artifacts.

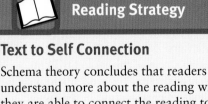

Reading Strategy

Text to Self Connection

Schema theory concludes that readers understand more about the reading when they are able to connect the reading to their personal experiences, knowledge, and emotions. Good readers draw on prior knowledge and experience to help them understand the text. In this Reading Strategy, students are asked to make personal connections between the text and themselves. A Text to Self Connection activity is available in the *Student Guide*.

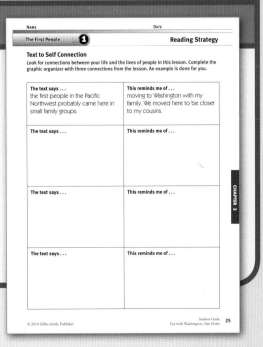

Talk About It

Hunting Ancient Animals

Why were ancient animals different from animals of today?

Long ago, the climate was very different. The animals that lived then were able to survive in those conditions. Today's animals could not live in that cold climate.

Why don't we see mammoths and mastodons on the land today?

Mammoths and mastodons are extinct.

An Ancient Man

What clues about history do you think archaeologists can gather from the Kennewick Man?

Possible answers include learning about what people from that time looked like, when they lived, and maybe how they lived. By comparing the bones with bones from other ancient people in other parts of the world, archaeologists try to figure out where Kennewick Man came from.

Archaic Indians *(From page 51)*

What caused the Archaic Indians to change their ways of living?

Both the land and the climate changed over time.

Why did the populations of these Indian groups grow about 4,500 years ago?

The climate grew warmer, and life was easier.

Two Indian Cultures Grow

(From page 51)

Most of today's Native Americans who live in Washington State are descendants of what two Indian groups?

Most of Washington's Native Americans are descendants of the Coastal Indians or the Plateau Indians of the Pacific Northwest.

Mammoths and mastodons provided food for ancient people.

The saber-tooth tiger hunted smaller animals.

Ancient bison were larger than the buffalo we know today.

Hunting Ancient Animals

When the Paleo-Indians lived all across North America, the land looked different than it does today. The climate was also very different. It was cool and wet.

Because the land and the climate were very different from what we see today, the animals were also very different. Huge mammoths and mastodons walked over the land. Large wildcats as big as lions and tiny horses as small as dogs lived in North America. All these animals are now ***extinct***. This means they no longer live anywhere on Earth.

The first people may have come here following the wild animals. The people were skilled hunters who killed large and small animals for food.

An Ancient Man

Archaeologists have found the bones of mammoths and other animals with spear points still sticking in them. But very few ancient human bones have ever been found. Bones can be very important. Scientists can study bones to learn what the people looked like.

In 1996, a very old human skeleton was discovered near the town of Kennewick. It had been buried along the shore of the Columbia River. This rare find became known as Kennewick Man. It is about 9,000 years old.

Who was this ancient man? Where did he come from? How did he live? Scientists are trying to learn the answers.

Washington, Our Home

Differentiated Paths

Monitor Your Reading Rate

Explain to students that good readers monitor the rate of their reading when they have different purposes for reading. Sometimes they need to slow down and read for specific information, and sometimes they can read more quickly.

ELL and Special Needs

Have students work in pairs to reread the lesson. Tell students to stop at the end of each section and ask each other questions about what they just read. Then have partners write a sentence telling about what they read.

Gifted Learners

Have students reread this lesson to skim for important details. Tell students to write the headings of each section in the lesson. Have students skim each section for details that support the main idea of each heading and write them on a piece of paper. After reading, have students work in pairs to compare what they found.

Archaic Indians

As the land and climate changed after the Ice Age, so did the people's ways of living. Small groups of people we now call Archaic Indians lived in North America. They made a spear-throwing tool called an *atlatl*. The spears were long, thin poles with sharp stone points on the ends. The large mammoths were gone by then, and the atlatl helped hunters kill smaller, faster deer for food.

Life for these people was hard. They struggled with the forces of nature—volcanic eruptions, floods, and a cool climate.

Then, about 4,500 years ago, the climate grew warmer. Life was easier. The populations of the Indian groups grew.

Two Indian Cultures Grow

In time, two very different groups of people were living in the Northwest. Coastal Indians lived west of the Cascade Mountains. There were many groups of them, and they lived in small villages near the Pacific Ocean, Puget Sound, and other waters. East of the Cascades, there were many different groups of Plateau Indians. They lived in a dry climate, far away from the ocean.

Most of today's Native Americans are the *descendants*, or great-great-grandchildren, of the people who lived here long ago.

An atlatl helped a spear fly farther and faster.

Where Did the Word "Indian" Come From?

When Christopher Columbus first arrived in America, he thought he was near India. He called the people who lived there Indians. It soon became clear that Columbus had made a mistake, but the name stuck.

Today, we use the words "Indian," "American Indian," and "Native American." *Native* means born in a place, or being naturally from a place.

LESSON 1 What Did You Learn?

1. Who were the first people to live in the Pacific Northwest?
2. What are some examples of how the Paleo-Indians were skilled stoneworkers?
3. Why do archaeologists search for artifacts?

Native People

51

LESSON 1 What Did You Learn?

1. *The Paleo-Indians were the first people in the Pacific Northwest.*
2. *The Paleo-Indians made spear points by chipping away at small pieces of rock. They made tools from rock. They also carved petroglyphs into rocks.*
3. *Archaeologists search for artifacts to learn more about how people lived in the past.*

REFLECT

Reflect on students' understanding of the early people who lived in the Pacific Northwest, how they lived, and why their way of living changed over time. You can evaluate students' understanding through discussion. The following activity will serve as another way of assessing students' understanding of the key objectives of this lesson.

Writing Activity

Venn Diagram

Have students complete the Venn Diagram in the *Student Guide* with details about themselves and early Native Americans.

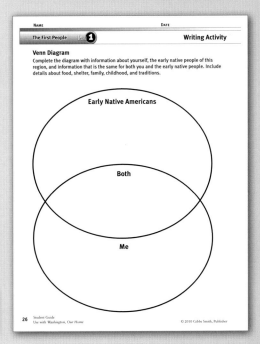

Literature Link

Archaeologists Dig for Clues

Read aloud a book such as *Archaeologists Dig for Clues* by Kate Duke to spark students' interest in archaeology and reinforce the idea that archaeological research can add to our understanding of the past. As you read, ask students to make a list of things we can learn from archaeologists. Have students share their ideas to make a class list on the board.

LESSON 2 Coastal People

Standards

GLE 4.1.2
Understands how the following theme and development help to define eras in Washington State history from time immemorial to 1889: Growth of northwest coastal and plateau tribes prior to treaties (time immemorial to 1854).

PREPARE

Activator

Details about Me

In this lesson, students learn about the life and culture of the Coastal people. Students will read about their homes, families, food, and traditions. To spark students' interest in these topics, have them complete the Details About Me activity in the *Student Guide*.

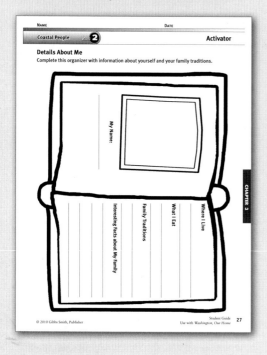

Word Study

Vocabulary Notebook

Have students start a vocabulary notebook. In a vocabulary notebook, students write the Words to Understand and other forms of the word, create a sentence that is meaningful to them, and draw a picture of the word. They also might include "tricks" for remembering the word. Obviously, you will not want students to do this with every word, but it can be helpful to reinforce the Words to Understand in the lessons.

Key Ideas

- The ocean helped the Coastal people meet their needs.
- Coastal people celebrated many traditions and passed along legends.

Words to Understand

ceremony
harpoon
legend
potlatch
totem pole
tradition
weir

In many places along the coast, the forests come near the ocean. The forests and the ocean were very important to the Coastal people. **How did they use these natural resources?**

Living Near the Sea

The land between the Pacific Ocean and the Cascade Mountains has a wet, mild climate. It is a perfect place for thick forests. In fact, forests once covered most of the western half of our state. Traveling through forests wasn't easy, so Coastal people spent most of their lives near the sea. They used canoes to travel from place to place. The sea was also a rich source of food all year long.

Childhood on the Coast

Imagine that you live in a coastal village. What is your life like? You learn by watching and listening and by helping adults. If you are a boy, you help hunt and fish. You and the other boys also learn how to make your own tools.

If you are a girl, you help gather food, dry it, and cook it. You also spend a lot of time taking care of babies. You help your mother and the other women make clothes. Most of the

Linking the Present to the Past

Even today, you may hear Coastal people say, "When the tide is out, the table is set." What does this saying mean?

52

Washington, Our Home

Words to Understand

ceremony (p. 55) *a ritual; actions done the same way each time for a special purpose*

harpoon (p. 56) *a long spear used to hunt whales*

legend (p. 58) *a story that tells about the past, or how things came to be*

potlatch (p. 54) *a ceremony of feasting and gift-giving*

totem pole (p. 60) *a carved wooden pole made by Native Americans to display family history*

tradition (p. 60) *a way of doing something the same way your ancestors did it*

weir (p. 55) *a fence built across a stream to catch fish*

A Words to Understand activity is available in the *Student Guide*.

time, you and your family don't wear many clothes because of the mild, warm weather. When it rains, however, you wear hats and capes to stay warm and dry. When it is really cold, you wear warm robes.

Food is not hard to find along the beach. You help gather clams, mussels, oysters, and crabs when the tide goes out.

Coastal Villages

Have you ever wanted to travel back in time? Pretend for a moment that you can go back hundreds of years. Imagine standing on a beach along Puget Sound. You are in a village where Coastal people live.

Along the beach is a row of wooden houses. They are made of large wooden planks held up by poles. Behind the houses is a thick forest. A stream of cold, clean water runs through the forest and down to the sandy beach. Many carved wooden canoes have been pulled up along the sand.

People are everywhere. Fathers and mothers are working and talking. Children are playing along the shore or splashing in the water. When more canoes come into sight, the children wave to welcome them.

When you go inside a house, it seems dark. There are no windows. You see rows of wide wooden shelves along the walls. These are places where the families sleep. You smell dried salmon and other meat hanging from the ceiling.

In the center of the house you see a bright fire burning in a ring of stones. The fires are important for light and cooking. You can imagine a fire keeping the family warm on cold nights.

If you lived in this plank house, your parents, brothers and sisters, aunts and uncles, and cousins might all live in the house with you. **What do you see in this house that is different from your home?**

Weavers wove yarn to make warm robes. To make the yarn, they spun plant fibers, animal hair, and wool together. They even wove in the hair from a special kind of dog.

Rain cloaks were woven from cedar bark and mountain goat fur.

Native People   53

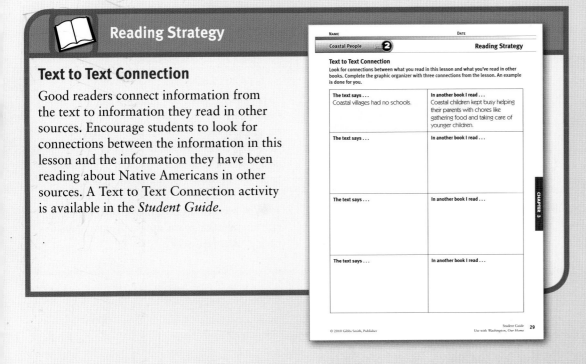

Reading Strategy

Text to Text Connection

Good readers connect information from the text to information they read in other sources. Encourage students to look for connections between the information in this lesson and the information they have been reading about Native Americans in other sources. A Text to Text Connection activity is available in the *Student Guide*.

Talk About It

Living Near the Sea *(From page 52)*
What natural resources were available for the Coastal people?
Possible answers include trees, fish, and other ocean animals.

Childhood on the Coast *(From page 52)*

In what ways was life for Coastal children different from life for children in Washington today?
Possible answers include using canoes to travel, having no schools, learning to hunt and fish, making your own tools, gathering and drying food, cooking food, spending a lot of time taking care of babies, not wearing many clothes, and gathering food from the beach.

Coastal Villages

How were coastal homes made?
The homes were made from wooded planks held up by poles.

What was it like inside the homes of a Coastal village?
The houses were dark, with no windows. There were rows of wooden shelves along the walls for beds, dried salmon and other meat hung from the ceiling, and a fire was kept in the center of the house.

Caption Answer

(From page 52) Coastal people used the natural resources to provide food, shelter, clothing, and other tools necessary for survival.

Answers may include different building materials, the roof is very high, there is a fire on the floor, the floor is dirt, there is no furniture, or people sit on the floor or on planks built around the edge of the house.

Linking the Present to the Past

(From page 52) This saying means that when the tide is out, fish are easier to catch. The fish provide food.

Talk About It

Grandmother Cedar

Why were cedar trees called Grandmother Cedar?

They were very important, just like a grandmother would be. The people had great respect for the important trees. The term grandmother was probably related to Mother Earth.

What were some of the ways that Coastal people used cedar trees?

They used cedar to make homes, furniture, and canoes. They used the bark to weave baskets, mats, hats, clothing, ropes, and even baby diapers.

What Is a Potlatch?

What sort of things were shared and celebrated at a potlatch?

Births, weddings, and the sharing of family treasures were shared and celebrated at a potlatch.

What were some of the things that went on at a potlatch?

Possible answers include songs, dances, displays of family treasures, feasts, and the sharing of gifts.

Caption Answer

Planks are made from western red cedar trees.

The Coastal people used planks like these to make their houses. **What natural resource are the planks made from?**

Grandmother Cedar

Just as important as salmon to Coastal people was the cedar tree. The people called the trees "Grandmother Cedar" because they were so important. Western red cedar is special in several ways. Its wood lasts a long time, even in a rainy climate. It can also be split fairly easily into long, straight boards.

Coastal people cut huge cedar planks to make their houses. They used smaller boards to make cradles, beds, and storage boxes. They carved cedar logs into canoes.

The bark of the cedar was also special. Its inner layer was soft and stringy. Coastal people used it to weave baskets, mats, hats, and clothing. They twisted strings of bark together to make strong ropes. They even pounded and softened bark to use for baby diapers!

What Is a Potlatch?

Today, our government keeps written records of births, weddings, and other important events. Coastal people had another way to share and remember these things. It was a special ceremony called a *potlatch*.

Suppose you are a chief. You have just received important family treasures, and you want everyone to know this. You ask members of your family to help you plan a potlatch. Together, you begin gathering food and gifts. This might take months or even years.

Finally, you are ready to invite guests. You send canoes out to other villages to tell people about the potlatch. When the guests arrive, they are dressed in their finest clothes. They are welcomed to the village with chants and dances.

Then comes the potlatch. You and your family wear special robes. You perform your songs and dances. You display the family treasures. Then you give each of your guests a gift and invite them to eat at a big feast. By accepting the gifts, each guest promises to remember the event. In this way, guests keep records for the tribe.

 Social Studies Activity

Cooperative Groups

Think Like an Archaeologist

Divide your class into groups of two or three. Photocopy two copies of a magazine advertisement for each group. For each group, cut one of the copies of the advertisement into small pieces, and leave the second copy whole to use as a reference. Put the pieces of the advertisement into separate bags, and give each group a bag. Explain to students that each piece of paper is like an artifact. It will give a clue to the whole.

Have students in each group work together to reconstruct their advertisement. After the students have worked on the project for a while, talk about the process they used to put the pieces together. Then show students the uncut advertisements. Ask students to compare the challenge they faced in reconstructing the advertisements with the challenge an archaeologist faces in reconstructing history.

Salmon, the Most Important Food

It is hard now to imagine how many salmon swam up the rivers each year. In a few weeks, people could catch enough fish to last the whole year.

The return of the salmon each spring was an important event. When the first salmon of the year was caught, there was a *ceremony,* or special event. All the people in the village thanked the salmon for giving them food. Then the fishing season began.

Native Americans knew many ways to catch salmon. One way was to build a wooden fence called a *weir* across a stream. The salmon could not swim past it. With a spear or net, a fisherman could pull out one fish after another.

Drying Food

Some of the fish were cooked over a fire and eaten fresh. The rest of the fish had to be dried so it would not go bad. The women cut each fish, cleaned it, and removed the bones. Then they hung the fish on wooden racks over smoky fires. Smoking and drying the fish kept it from spoiling. Dried fish would last until the next salmon-fishing season.

The people dried other foods, too. They spread berries in the sun. They made cakes from wild roots and dried them. Of course, dried foods are not as tasty as fresh foods, so children dipped their food in fish oil before eating it.

Coastal People

For hundreds of years, different groups of Coastal people lived apart from each other in villages. They were not organized into tribes until many years later, after the settlers came.

Here are some of the groups later called tribes:

Chinook	Muckleshoot
Hoh	Nisqually
Klallam	Nooksack
Makah	Puyallup
Ozette	Samish
Queets	Skagit
Quinault	Snoqualmie
Chehalis	Suquamish
Cowlitz	Willapa
Duwamish	
Lummi	

This is a fishing camp. **How did the people dry the fish? Why do you think they did it this way?**

Native People   55

Background Info

Salmon Life Cycle

In the spring or in the fall, salmon leave the ocean to start their difficult journey up a stream to the exact same place where they hatched from salmon eggs three to five years earlier. They cover over 10 miles a day and fight their way upstream, against the current. They brave swift rapids and rushing falls, jumping as much at 10 feet up the falls. Bruised and starved survivors reach the spawning ground. A female fish lays as many as 10,000 eggs. After the male covers the eggs with a milky substance, both adult fish float tail first downstream. In a few days they are dead. After several months, the eggs hatch and tiny fish start to grow.

Talk About It

Salmon, the Most Important Food

How did Coastal people mark the beginning of the fishing season?
They held a ceremony when the first salmon of the year were caught.

How was a weir used to catch salmon?
A weir was built across a stream like a fence to catch the salmon. Then fishermen would use a spear to kill the fish and a net to pull the fish out.

Drying Food

Why did much of the salmon caught have to be dried?
The salmon had to last until the next fishing season, so it was dried to keep it from spoiling.

What are other foods that Coastal people dried?
Possible answers include other seafood, berries, and wild roots.

Caption Answers

They hung the fish on wooden rafters above the ground.

They probably wanted to keep the fish out of reach of wild animals.

    Science Activity

Coastal People Food Pyramid

Have students think about the type of foods the Coastal people ate and the types of foods people today think are necessary for good nutrition. Have students write the foods the early people ate in a food pyramid. Ask students to compare the Coastal peoples' foods to the foods we eat today. Do the students think the Coastal people had good nutrition? Do the students think the Indians' food was more or less nutritious than the food the students eat today? Encourage students to think about how and why food has changed over time. The My Pyramid government Web site has examples of and information on the food pyramid. A link to this Web site can be found at **www.ExperienceStateHistory.com.**

Talk About It

Whale Hunters

How did the Makah prepare for the whale hunt?

They practiced the hunt over and over. Then they took time to rest and pray for a successful hunt.

A Dangerous Job

Explain the steps to hunting a whale.

First a harpoon was thrust into the whale's body. Then the canoe got out of the way. A second canoe came up on the other side, and another harpoon was thrust at the whale. Floats attached to the harpoons made it difficult for the whale to swim. When the whale slowed down, the canoes came in closer and pulled the whale to shore.

Caption Answer

The men are taking harpoons and spears to use in hunting whales.

Linking the Present to the Past

Have students work in small groups to discuss the significance of a modern whale hunt. Encourage them to discuss whether or not they think it is a good idea.

Men trained all year for a whale hunt. They had to be experts if they wanted to come home alive. **What weapons are these men taking on the boats?**

Linking the Present to the Past

Modern Makah people wanted to keep the traditions of their people by having a whale hunt. Other people did not agree with killing whales. They tried to stop the hunt.

In 1999, the Makah hunters killed one whale. They said, "It is a way to feel proud about who we are." The whale meat was shared by the tribe and their guests at a potlatch.

56

Whale Hunters

All Washington tribes had hunting skills. The Makah, however, were one of the few tribes that hunted whales. Whale hunters prepared carefully. They took time to rest and pray for a safe and successful hunt. Finally, the time of the hunt arrived. The hunters paddled out to sea in large, beautifully carved canoes. When they spotted a whale, the hunt began.

A Dangerous Job

There was no room for mistakes. One canoe came up close to the animal's left side. The chief hunter thrust his **harpoon**, or long spear, into the whale's huge body. The whale jerked wildly. This canoe had to move away quickly!

A second canoe came up from the other side. Another man thrust a harpoon into the whale. Long ropes and floats had been attached to the harpoons. The floats were seal skins filled with air. These made it hard for the animal to swim and dive. Now the whale was dragging two long ropes and many floats.

When the whale finally got tired, the canoes came in closer. The hunters killed the whale with more harpoons and pulled it to shore.

Everyone in the village came to meet the canoes. They gave thanks for a safe hunt. Whale meat and oil were favorite foods. Everyone shared in the feast.

Washington, Our Home

 Writing Activity

How to Hunt Whales

Whale hunting was a tough job. Have students create a How to Hunt Whales book. Each page should include a different step and include an illustration. Encourage students to use information from the *Student Edition* as they write their book. Have students display their books at the Early People of Washington Potlatch (See the Culminating Activity on page 44F).

i **Background Info**

A Marine Economy

Fishing was the foundation of the coastal economy. Five species of salmon ascended the rivers to spawn. The people caught them as they swam upriver. Men also trolled for salmon in the ocean, using baited hooks on kelp lines. Halibut and cod were also caught on baited hooks. The ocean also provided edible shellfish. Many kinds of clams, mussels, oysters, and crabs were harvested. Old village sites along the coast are still marked by large mounds of discarded shells. Seals, sea lions, and porpoises were also hunted by nearly all coastal tribes.

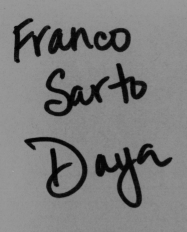

Franco
Sarto
Daya

Source

Ozette

mudslide buried their village. Whole houses were buried.

Modern archaeologists and Makah people worked together to uncover the village. They found more than 50,000 artifacts. The found tools, baskets, and other objects of everyday life.

LOOK	THINK	DECIDE
What is this artifact shaped like? What do you think it was made from?	Why do you think the people would have made something this shape?	Do you think archaeologists should dig up artifacts from places like this or leave them at their final resting place?

Native People

57

Go to the Source

🪶 Standards

GLE 5.1.2
Evaluates the accuracy of primary and secondary sources.

Study Artifacts

Use this Go to the Source Activity to spark students' interest in the Makah and in the Ozette dig. Encourage students to think like archaeologists who don't have all the clues as they complete this activity. Then complete the Technology Tie-In activity to teach students more about the Ozette dig.

🖱 Technology Tie-In

Virtual Tour of the Ozette Dig

Washington State University has an online photo gallery called Excavating Ozette 1967–1981. There are great photos with informative captions. If possible, take your class on a virtual tour of the Ozette Dig. Stop to ask students questions about the artifacts and the Makah people. A link to this site is available at **www. ExperienceStateHistory.com.**

LOOK	THINK	DECIDE
The artifact is shaped like a whale fin. It was probably made from wood, animal skin, and shells.	*The Makah are whale hunters. They probably made this as a symbol of a whale fin.*	*Students answers should provide explanation for why they feel the way they do.*

Talk About It

Learning from Legends

Why were legends important to the early people of the Pacific Northwest?

Children learned about their world through legends. Legends passed along stories of the past. Children learned important lessons through legends.

The Girl Who Lived at Lake Crescent

How were the waterfalls around Lake Crescent formed?

The waterfalls are Whik bakah's tears.

Why did Whik bakah go to live with the swans?

She felt like no one loved her where she lived.

What are some lessons that could be learned from this legend?

Possible answers include learning the importance of doing your share of chores, learning skills needed to be helpful with chores, and the good feeling that can come from working hard and learning to do new things.

 Social Studies Activity

Legend Role Play

Have students work in small groups to role play the legend, "The Girl Who Lived at Lake Crescent." Encourage students to put special emphasis on parts where the legend is teaching or explaining something. Allow students to share their role plays with the class. You may want to discuss the differences in interpretation of the legend that groups shared in their role plays.

Learning from Legends

Children learned about their world by listening to *legends*. Legends are stories that tell about the past. They often explain how things came to be. Through legends, children learned important lessons. They learned to treat all living things with respect. They learned to think of the Earth as the giving mother shared by all creatures. Imagine sitting with your family around you on a dark winter night, listening to this story.

The Girl Who Lived at Lake Crescent

There once was a girl who lived at Lake Crescent with her stepmother. Everybody in the house used to help with the work, but not this girl. She would lie down by the fire and sleep and sleep. Her dress was dirty. Her hair was tangled.

Her stepmother was tired of this. She said, "Still asleep? Whik bakah, Whik bakah. Lazy bones!" The girl was upset because all the other girls had pretty names. She walked to the lake and began to cry. She cried and cried. The waterfalls around Lake Crescent are her tears.

She heard a voice say, "Why are you crying?" The girl looked around and saw a flock of white swans. She answered, "Nobody loves me. They say I don't know how to do anything. My stepmother calls me Whik bakah."

"Why don't you stay with us?" asked the swans. "We will tell you all we know." The leader of the swans told the girl to get on his back and close her eyes. She climbed on and could feel herself going way up. When she opened her eyes, she was on the top of the Olympic Mountains.

The swans showed her how to take cedar bark from a tree. They showed her how to weave it and make a dress trimmed with duck feathers in pretty colors. They showed her how to make baskets of cedar bark and bear grass, and baskets of spruce root to carry wood. She learned what was good to eat in the woods. She was gone so long that her stepmother thought she had died.

The white swan said, "Now that you know all you need to know, you are ready to go home. You may take all the things you made." The girl climbed on the swan's back and was soon home. She thanked the swans.

The girl's stepmother didn't recognize her at first! Then she gave her a big hug. She gave a potlatch and gave the girl a good name. The girl gave each of the guests a present of something she had made herself. She was happy.

—Adapted from a legend told by Helen Peterson, published in *The History and Culture of the Indians of Washington State: A Curriculum Guide*

Writing Activity

Family Legends

Tell students that each family today has legends, even if they don't call them legends. Encourage students to think about a story their family tells of its history, to explain something, or to teach a lesson. Give examples of stories from your own family that are used to teach lessons, explain things, or share history. Some families may have stories that explain how children got their name, some stories may teach lessons that parents learned when they were young, and some stories may simply share family history.

Have students write their family legends on a piece of paper. Put the legends together to create a class book. Have one chapter called "Legends That Teach Lessons," a second chapter called "Legends That Explain Things," and a final chapter titled "Legends That Tell Stories of the Past."

Differential Paths

Expand the Legend

Remind students that legends are used to tell about the past. In this activity, students will use the legend, "The Girl Who Lived at Lake Crescent," to apply what they learned about legends.

ELL and Special Needs
Make photocopies of pages 52–53 in the *Student Edition*. Have students read the legend with a partner to look for parts of the legend that tell about the past and underline those parts in red.
Then have the students reread the legend to look for parts of the legend that teach important lessons.

Have students underline those parts in yellow. Have students read the legend a final time for parts that explain how things came to be. Tell students to underline those parts in blue.

Gifted Learners
Have students rewrite this legend in a modern-day setting. Encourage them to think about how each of the characters involved can be represented by people and things students are familiar with today. Have students share their new legends and compare the differences between them.

Talk About It

Coastal Art

What were some traditions in Coastal art?
Boys learned to carve, and girls learned to weave.

Totem Poles

How were totem poles similar to legends?
Both totem poles and legends told stories of family histories.

REFLECT

Reflect on students' understanding of how the ocean helped the Coastal people meet their needs and on the traditions of the Coastal people. You can evaluate students' understanding through discussion or evaluation of activities completed in this lesson. The following activity will serve as another way of assessing students' understanding of the key objectives of this lesson.

Writing Activity

What If . . .

Have students write a "What If . . ." story about life in a Coastal village. Encourage students to base their imaginary stories on information from the lesson. Have students complete the What If activity in the *Student Guide.*

NAME _____ DATE _____

| Coastal People Part **2** | Writing Activity |

What If . . .
Choose one of the questions and use the organizer to help you write a story using details from the chapter.

- What if you lived in a Coastal village?
- What if you discovered an ancient building from a Coastal village?
- What if people still lived in Coastal villages?
- What if you were the leader of the Coastal village?
- What if a Coastal child found himself or herself in Washington today?

☐ My Question

☐ What would happen?

☐ Details from the chapter

☐ Write your story on another sheet of paper.

30 Student Guide
Use with *Washington, Our Home*   © 2010 Gibbs Smith, Publisher

---

The Coastal people made baskets of many shapes and sizes. They created beautiful designs as they wove. Groups north of Washington made totem poles. It took a great deal of skill to carve the poles.

Coastal Art

The Coastal people had a tradition of wood carving and weaving. A **tradition** is a way of doing something the same way your ancestors did it. Boys learned how to carve, and girls learned how to weave the same way their parents did.

A good canoe carver was highly respected. So was a woman who wove fine clothes or baskets.

Totem Poles

Totem poles are the most famous examples of Coastal art. Each figure on the tall wooden pole told a story. The family treasured each story. However, totem poles were not made in Washington. In the old days, the people who made them lived farther north, in Canada and Alaska.

The people carved and painted totem poles as a way to display their family histories. This was true of many works of Coastal art, including animal designs and even songs and dances. No one else could use them. A wealthy family might own many dances, beautiful carvings, and fine baskets.

LESSON 2 What Did You Learn?

1. How did the Coastal people use the ocean as a source of food?
2. Why were "Grandmother Cedar" trees so important to Coastal people?
3. Why were legends important to Coastal people?

60   Washington, Our Home

LESSON 2 What Did You Learn?

1. Coastal people gathered clams, mussels, oysters, and crabs for food when the tide went out.
2. They used cedar to make homes, furniture, and canoes. They used the bark to weave baskets, make mats, hats, clothing, ropes, and even baby diapers.
3. Native Americans shared legends to teach lessons, explain things, or to simply share a story of the past.

LESSON 3 Plateau People

Living on the Plateau

East of the Cascades, the dry climate was very different from the wet climate of the coast. Since the people of the plateau did not have many trees to build wooden houses with, and since they could not eat seafood from the ocean, they had a different culture. There were many different groups of Plateau people. They did not all live exactly alike.

A Longhouse

Imagine that you are traveling back in time once again. Imagine yourself on the plateau in the winter. You see families living in large, snug *longhouses* all winter long. The longhouses are made from wood poles that are covered with mats made of tall, dried reeds called *tule*. The thick mats keep out the snow.

Inside the longhouse, you see children sitting and sleeping on the same kind of mats. You see and smell a fire in the center of the dirt floor. The fire keeps the children warm. In the evening, families sit around it, working, talking, and laughing.

You see that more than one family lives in the same longhouse. This means the children will always have a brother, sister, or cousin to play with. The parents will have other adults to help with the work.

Salmon Fishing

In the spring, the snow is gone. The hills and valleys are green with new plants. For the children, this is an exciting time of year. It is time for salmon fishing. It's time to travel to the fishing camps.

Each large family group has its own fishing spot. Salmon fishing days are a time for both work and play. You watch the exciting horse races and join other children in foot races and other games. In the fishing camps, adults visit and trade with people from near and far.

Key Ideas

- Plateau people used the land to meet their needs.
- Plateau people had strong spiritual beliefs.
- The people got things they wanted by trading with other groups.

Words to Understand

barter
belief
elder
longhouse
shaman
spiritual
tule

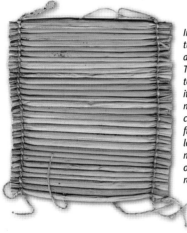

Indian women cut tall tule stems that grew along riverbanks. They laid out the tule to dry and then wove it into rectangular mats. After they covered the wooden frame of the longhouse with tule mats, the mats kept out the cold, wind, rain, and snow.

Native People

61

Words to Understand

barter (p. 65) *to trade without using money*
belief (p. 63) *something thought to be true*
elder (p. 63) *an older person*
longhouse (p. 61) *long Indian homes where several families lived together*
shaman (p. 63) *a spiritual leader who tried to heal the sick*
spiritual (p. 63) *having to do with the spirit life and not the physical*
tule (p. 61) *tall plants or reeds that grow wild in swampy places*

A Words to Understand activity for this lesson is available in the *Student Guide*.

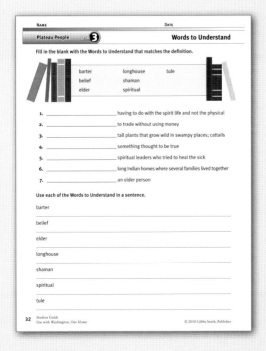

PREPARE

Activator

Differences in Cultures

The Plateau people were both similar and different from the Coastal people. Have students complete the Differences in Cultures activity in the *Student Guide* by comparing details about both groups.

Word Study

Synonyms

Write the words *barter* and *shaman* on the board. Talk about the meaning of each word. Have students think of other words that have similar meanings to these words. List all the synonyms on the board that the class can come up with. Some examples of synonyms for *barter* may include trade, bargain, exchange, and swap. Some synonyms for *shaman* may include doctor, healer, medicine man, leader.

TEACH

Living on the Plateau (From page 61)
Why was the Plateau culture so different from Coastal culture?
The people of the Plateau did not have many trees, the climate was dry, and they weren't able to eat food from the ocean.

A Longhouse (From page 61)
What was it like inside a longhouse?
Families sat and slept on mats made of tule. There was a fire in the center of the dirt floor. More than one family lived in a longhouse.

Salmon Fishing (From page 61)
Why was salmon fishing important to the Plateau people?
It was a time for both work and play. Families visited and traded with people while they fished.

Hunting and Gathering Seasons
What did the women and girls gather in the summer?
They gathered berries and nuts and dug up camas bulbs.

What animals did the men hunt in the fall?
The men hunted deer, mountain goats, sheep, rabbits, and birds.

Clothes from Animal Skins
How were everyday clothes different from clothes for ceremonies?
Everyday clothes were usually plain, but clothes for ceremonies were decorated with feathers, shells, and porcupine quills.

Camas
What are camas roots like?
They look like onions and taste somewhat like sweet potatoes.

How were camas roots prepared as food?
Women put the bulbs in large fire pits and covered each layer with moss. The bulbs were eaten whole or added to fish and meat.

After a hunt, the people might use canoes on the rivers to bring the meat to the camp. It was easier than carrying the heavy meat. **What are the people in this camp doing?**

Camas

One of the most important foods was the root of the camas plant. The camas lily has a lovely flower and a tasty root. The roots are round bulbs that look like small round onions and taste something like sweet potatoes.

To cook the bulbs, women put them in large fire pits and covered each layer with moss. Hot coals cooked the bulbs.

The families ate camas whole or added chopped camas to fish and meat.

Hunting and Gathering Seasons

When summer comes, it is time to move again. The women and girls go out to gather berries and nuts and dig up camas bulbs. Men and boys go hunting. Children learn skills by helping adults.

When fall comes, the hunting season is an exciting time. You watch the men make wooden arrows and attach sharp stone points. They make bows from wood or the horns of mountain sheep. You watch them make spears and traps. Deer, mountain goats, sheep, rabbits, and birds are not safe during hunting season!

Clothes from Animal Skins

You see women make warm clothing from animal skins. Everyday clothes are often plain, but clothes for special ceremonies are decorated with feathers, shells, and porcupine quills.

For her marriage ceremony, this young woman wears a headdress with Chinese coins, shell earrings, and strings of colored glass beads. **How can you tell this photo was taken in later years, after the traders and settlers came to the Northwest?**

62

Washington, Our Home

Reading Strategy

Text to the World Connection

Good readers are always making connections. While reading, students should try to make a connection between the text and something in the news today. As students read this lesson, ask them to look for ways they can connect the text to something in the world today. Have students complete the Text to the World Connection activity available in the *Student Guide*.

Text to the World Connection

Look for connections between the text and the world. Complete the graphic organizer with three connections that show how information in the text relates to things in the world today. An example is done for you.

The text says . . .	This reminds me of . . .
and since they could not eat sea foods from the ocean, they had a different culture.	how people who don't live near the coasts today have to have seafood flown or trucked to their state.
The text says . . .	This reminds me of . . .
The text says . . .	This reminds me of . . .
The text says . . .	This reminds me of . . .

© 2010 Gibbs Smith, Publisher

Student Guide 33
Use with *Washington, Our Home*

Wise Leaders

A group of wise adults made the rules and decided what should be done. Leaders with different skills had different duties. For example, a brave and skilled fighter might lead the group in war.

Older people, called *elders*, were treated with great respect.

I [saw] an old woman in one of the lodges. . . . She was blind . . . and had lived more than 100 winters. She [had] the best place in the house, and when she spoke, great attention was paid to what she said.

—from the diary of William Clark

Shamans

One kind of leader in both Coastal and Plateau cultures was the *shaman*. A shaman was a *spiritual* leader, or one who deals with matters relating to the spirit.

Native Americans believed that all things, including plants, rocks, and animals, had spirits. A *belief* is something thought to be true. The people believed these spirits could sometimes cause sickness. When a person was sick, they knew that both the body and the spirit needed to be healed.

Shamans were men or women with special power over spirits. They used medicines made from plants to help heal people. They also used special spiritual songs and dances.

Plateau People	
Here are some of the many different groups that lived on the plateau. In later years, the groups were called tribes by the new settlers.	
Cayuse	Nez Perce
Chelan	Okanogan
Columbia	Palouse
Colville	San Poil
Coeur d'Alene	Spokane
Kalispel	Wallula
Kittitas	Wanapam
Klickitat	Wenatchee
Kootenai	Wishram
Metho	Yakama
Nespelem	

A shaman helped heal the sick. The people believed he had special powers. **What does it look like the shaman is doing in this picture?**

Native People

63

Talk About It

Wise Leaders

How were elders treated in Plateau villages?

Elders were treated with great respect.

Shamans

What did Coastal people and Plateau people believe about spirits?

Both groups believed that all things had spirits. They believed these spirits could cause sickness, and that both the body and spirit of a person needed to be healed when the person was ill.

How did shamans help both Coastal and Plateau people?

Shamans used medicines from plants to help heal people. They also used special spiritual songs and dances.

Caption Answers

(From page 62) The people in the camp appear to be resting, working on canoes, bringing food in, and talking with one another.

(From page 62) Coins, shells, and glass beads were all items that weren't common among Plateau people. These items must have been brought by people who came to the region at a later time.

The man used ferns (green plants) to decorate his head and arms.

 Technology Activity

Plateau Art and Legends

Divide the class into two groups. Assign one group to research Plateau art and the other group to research Plateau legends. The Burke Museum of Natural History and Culture has a Web site that includes pictures of many different types of Plateau art. The British Columbia Folklore Society has a Web site that includes many different Plateau legends. Links to both of these Web sites can be found at **www. ExperienceStateHistory.com.** Have students visit these sites to find an interesting legend or piece of art to share in a small group.

Math Activity

Cooperative Groups

How Far Is a Mile?

Tell students that a mile is 5, 280 feet. Have students measure the length of one fence or the distance around the field in the school playground. Be sure to choose a distance that can be easily measured. Then have students work in groups to calculate how many times someone would have to walk the length to walk a mile. Have students walk a mile. Time the students. Talk about what it would be like to walk a mile or more each day to gather food, hunt, trade, fish, or gather natural resources needed for building. Ask students to think about how their lives would be different if they had to walk a mile or more to get food everyday.

Talk About It

Horses Come to the Plateau

How did horses make life on the Plateau easier?

Horses made traveling easier and helped Plateau people find food faster. Native Americans with horses could travel farther in search of buffalo and deer. Horses could carry heavy loads of meat back from hunting trips.

How did horses get to the Plateau?

Plateau people got horses by trading with tribes from the Great Plains who got them from Spanish explorers.

Buffalo Hunts

Why were buffalo hunts important to the Plateau people?

Buffalo meat and buffalo robes were important items to trade with people of other tribes.

Trade *(From page 65)*

Why was bartering helpful to the early Native Americans?

They were able to trade for items they needed that were not available where they lived.

Caption Answers

Teepees were portable, provided shelter for the hunters, and were easy to carry with a horse.

Horses helped the men get close to the huge buffalo. Horses made it possible for men to travel long distances to where the buffalo were and allowed them to carry buffalo meat and robes back to their village.

Plateau people strapped tall teepee poles to horses and pulled them like sleds. This was a good way to move their teepees and supplies from place to place. **Why do you think a teepee would be a good home to live in during long hunting trips?**

Horses Come to the Plateau

People in coastal villages had plenty of seafood to eat all year, but people who lived on the plateau had to travel to find food. Horses made traveling much easier.

The first horses of the kind we know today were brought to North America by Spanish explorers. The people first got horses by trading with tribes from the Great Plains. Most of the Plateau groups had at least a few horses. The Nez Perce, Palouse, and Cayuse tribes had thousands of beautiful horses. The people were very skilled at raising and riding horses.

Native Americans knew how useful horses could be. On horseback, riders could travel farther in search of buffalo and deer. Sometimes hunting trips to faraway places took months. Horses could carry heavy loads and bring the meat back home.

Buffalo Hunts

To hunt the mighty buffalo, the Plateau people traveled on horseback all the way to the Great Plains. These were large hunts. On one trip, hundreds of men took over a thousand horses. Women went along to cut and dry the meat.

Dried buffalo meat and buffalo robes were important items to trade with people in other tribes.

On the Great Plains, large herds of buffalo roamed freely. **How are horses helping the men hunt the huge animals?**

64

 Science Activity

 Cooperative Groups

Farming Could Have Helped

Early people in the Pacific Northwest didn't plant crops and farm. The Plateau people were always on the move searching for food. They ate berries and other plants they gathered. If they had farmed, they would have had a more steady supply of food, and could have stayed in one place. Ask students to think of the foods they eat that are farmed.

Challenge students to give farming a try. Divide the class into groups of four. Provide each group with paper cups, potting soil, and seeds. Over a period of two weeks, have students experiment with light, soil conditions, and water amounts. Each group should record the methods they use. At the end of two weeks, have groups compare their plants.

Then provide the groups with another cup, soil, and seeds and see if they can incorporate what they learned from other groups to improve their method of farming.

Trade

Both the people who lived near the coast and those who lived on the plateau were great traders. They brought what they had and **bartered**, or traded, for what they wanted. They might trade fish for moccasins, or camas bulbs for whale meat.

Whole families came to trade at fishing sites at Kettle Falls and the Dalles. They also set up trading sites at camas fields. Once they got horses, the people traveled as far south as California and as far east as Wyoming to trade.

In the next chapter, you will see how trading with white explorers helped the Indian people get new metal tools, weapons, and other things they never had before. Sadly, they also got diseases from the explorers. Measles and smallpox spread quickly and caused the deaths of thousands of Indians. The large groups of native people started getting smaller.

LESSON 3 What Did You Learn?

1. What are some ways that Plateau people used the land to survive?
2. What was the job of a shaman?
3. Why did the Coastal people and the Plateau people barter?

This famous fishing site is the Dalles on the Columbia River.
What is going on in this picture?

Native People

65

LESSON 3 What Did You Learn?

1. *Plateau people used natural resources to build their homes, as food, as tools, and as clothing.*
2. *The shaman healed sick people in the village with medicine from plants, along with songs, and dances.*
3. *The Coastal people and Plateau people bartered with other people to get items they needed that weren't available to them where they lived.*

REFLECT

Reflect on students' understanding of how the Plateau people used the land to meet their needs. You can evaluate students' understanding through discussion or evaluation of activities completed in this lesson. The following activity will serve as another way of assessing students' understanding of the key objectives of this lesson.

 Writing Activity

A Great Place to Live

Have students design a brochure advertising the benefits of living in a Plateau village. Have students complete the activity, A Great Place to Live in the *Student Guide*.

Caption Answer

Two people are carrying things, maybe to and from the boat. They may be setting up camp. A man in the canoe is keeping it close to the shore.

Standards

GLE 5.4.2
Prepares a list of resources, including the title, author, type of source, date published, and publisher for each source.

Washington Social Studies Skills

How to Cite Sources

Use this activity to help students prepare and cite a list of sources they can use to complete the Project Assessment available in the *Teacher Guide.*

Activate
Ask students how they can find information on early Native Americans. Make a list on the board of ideas students have to find information on the topic. Possible responses include go to the library, research on the Internet, and look in a history book.

Teach
Tell students that there are many sources of information available on the topic, as long as they go to the right places. Explain that the school or local library will have many books with information. The Internet can also provide good research information, but you need to be sure it is from a reliable source. As a class, circle items on the board that would be most helpful to students completing a research project.

As a class, read the Social Studies Skills Page. Remind student that good researchers cite a list of resources used in a research report.

Practice
Show the class a book about Native Americans from the school library and an article from the Internet. Use the sources to model how to cite each source on the board.

Apply
Have students find two sources to use to find more information on the research question they chose. Have students cite the sources they chose.

Washington Social Studies Skills

How to Cite Sources

Good researchers use more than one source to get information on a topic. When using sources to write a research report, you must cite, or tell about, the sources you used.

> To cite a source, include the author, title, type of source, publisher, and date published for each source.
> This is how you would cite information used from this textbook:
>
> Pelz, Ruth. *Washington, Our Home.* Gibbs Smith Education, 2010.

Choose a research question to guide you as you find sources for this activity.

1. **Does an archaeologist do more than just dig for artifacts?**
2. **Did Native Americans in the Southwest live like the Native Americans of the Pacific Northwest?**
3. Were Coastal people the only Native Americans to share legends?

Visit your school or local library and gather at least two additional sources for your topic. On a piece of paper, cite each of your sources. List your sources in alphabetical order by the author's last name.

How to Cite a Book:
Max, Jill. *Spider Spins a Story: Fourteen Legends from Native America.* Rising Moon, 1997.

How to Cite a Web Site:
Lynch, Tim. "The Explorers." Beyond the Map. Maritime Museum of BC. 2007 <http://beyondthemap.ca/english/>.

How to Cite an Encyclopedia:
Sturgeon, Theodore. "Science Fiction." *The Encyclopedia Americana.* International ed. 1995.

66

Washington, Our Home

Chapter Review 3

Reviewing What You Read

1. Who were the first people to live in the Pacific Northwest?
2. Explain why an archaeologist searches for artifacts.
3. Why might Native Americans in today's Washington be interested to learn about Native Americans who lived here long ago?
4. How were the homes of Coastal people different from the homes of Plateau people?
5. Explain why nature was so important to both the Coastal people and the Plateau people.
6. Do you think horses made life easier for the Plateau people? Why or why not?

Becoming a Better Reader

Making Connections

Good readers connect the text to themselves. They connect the text to things they already know or to personal experiences they have had.

Write a paragraph about a connection you have with this chapter. Perhaps you can write about how you have learned about your ancestors by studying artifacts, or about how your way of life is affected by the place where you live. Give examples of how your life has been affected.

Spotlighting Geography

Homes of Early Native Americans

In this chapter, you learned about how different groups of early Indians built their homes. What natural resources did they use? Think about how we build our homes today. Describe how our methods are the same as ancient people. How are our methods different from those of ancient people?

Native People

67

Becoming a Better Reader

Making Connections

Students should constantly be making connections when they read. This will help the students better understand what they are reading. Have students share with a partner the paragraph they wrote about a connection they had with this chapter.

Spotlighting Geography

Homes of Early Native Americans

Have students create a T-Chart by folding a piece of paper in half vertically. Tell them to label one side "Similarities" and the other side "Differences." Instruct them to write the similarities and differences between our building methods today and early Native American building methods. Allow students to share their ideas in small groups.

Reviewing What You Read

The Reviewing What You Read questions are leveled according to Bloom's Taxonomy and will help students achieve a higher level of thinking. These questions will also prepare students for the chapter assessment. The following are possible answers to the questions. Focus on students' ability to understand and apply the concepts.

1. **KNOWLEDGE** The first people to live in the Pacific Northwest were Paleo-Indians.

2. **COMPREHENSION** An archaeologist searches for artifacts to find clues about how people lived in the past.

3. **APPLICATION** They might be descendants of Native Americans who lived in this region long ago and want to learn about their personal history.

4. **ANALYSIS** The Coastal people lived in wooden houses made of large wooden planks held up by poles. Their homes had no windows. Inside, shelves around the walls served as beds for the family. Plateau people lived in longhouses made of wood poles covered with mats of tule. Family members slept on mats on the floor.

5. **SYNTHESIS** Both Coastal people and Plateau people depended on nature for survival. Their homes were made out of resources from nature. Their food came from the ocean, rivers, plants, and animals on the land. Their clothes and tools were made from resources available on land.

6. **EVALUATION** Students' answers should reflect an understanding of life of the Plateau people before and after horses were introduced to their culture. Students' responses should be supported by details from the chapter.

Interactive Chapter Review

An Interactive Chapter Review is available online at **www.ExperienceStateHistory.com.** Have students use this review to prepare for the assessments.

Chapter Assessment

Chapter Assessments are available to preview on pages 44G–44H. Assessments can be found in the *Teacher Guide* and online at **www.ExperienceStateHistory.com.**

4 Explorers and Fur Traders

CHAPTER PLANNER

CHAPTER OVERVIEW	WASHINGTON SOCIAL STUDIES GLEs
This chapter focuses on the first explorers who came to the Pacific Northwest region by sea and by land. There is a special focus on the Lewis and Clark Expedition and the days of mountain men and fur traders.	GLE 4.1.2 GLE 4.1.1 GLE 4.3.1 GLE 5.2.1 GLE 5.2.2 GLE 5.4.1 GLE 5.4.2

CHAPTER RESOURCES

ELL/Modified Chapter Plan, p. 68I

Books and Web Sites, p. 68J

CHAPTER ACTIVITIES	WASHINGTON CURRICULUM INTEGRATION
■ Explorer Portrait, p. 68E	**Writing** GLE 1.5.1
■ Explorer Interview, p. 68E	**Writing** GLE 1.1.1, GLE 1.3.1, GLE 1.4.1, GLE 1.5.1
■ Explorer Biography, p. 68F	**Reading** GLE 2.1.7, GLE 3.4.2
Explorer Math, p. 68F	**Math** GLE 4.5.E, GLE 4.5.F
Explorer Route, p. 68F	**Reading** GLE 3.2.1
Sea Otter Quiz, p. 68F	**Science** GLE 2.1.1
Compass Rose, p. 68F	**Visual Arts** GLE 2.1.1
Explorer Exhibition, p. 68F	**Writing** GLE 2.2.1, GLE 3.1.2

CHAPTER OPENER	WASHINGTON CURRICULUM INTEGRATION
We Explore, Encounter, and Trade, p. 68	**Theatre** GLE 3.2.1
What Do You See? p. 68	**Writing** GLE 2.2.1
Timeline Talk, p. 69	**Reading** GLE 3.2.2

▶Indicates an activity page located in the *Student Guide*.
■ Indicates an activity page located in the *Teacher Guide*.

The BIG Idea

How did early exploration, encounter, and trade shape our history?

CHAPTER REVIEW pp. 92–93

SOCIAL STUDIES SKILLS PAGE	WASHINGTON SOCIAL STUDIES GLEs
Create a Research Question, p. 92	**Social Studies** GLE 5.2.1 Supports **Social Studies CBA:** Dig Deep (completed in the Project Assessment for this chapter) **Writing** GLE 1.1.1, GLE 2.2.1

REVIEWING THE CHAPTER	WASHINGTON SOCIAL STUDIES GLEs
Students show what they learned by completing application activities and answering chapter review questions. Assessments for this chapter can be previewed on pages 68G-68H. Select the assessment option that best suits your goals for this chapter. Assessments are available in the *Teacher Guide* or online at **www.ExperienceStateHistory.com**.	GLE 4.1.2 GLE 4.1.1 GLE 4.3.1 GLE 5.2.1 GLE 5.2.2 GLE 5.4.1 GLE 5.4.2

CHAPTER ACTIVITIES	WASHINGTON CURRICULUM INTEGRATION
Reviewing What You Read, p. 93	**Reading** GLE 1.3.2, GLE 2.1.3
Becoming a Better Reader, p. 93	**Reading** GLE 2.1.6
Spotlighting Geography, p. 93	**Writing** GLE 3.2.1

CHAPTER ASSESSMENTS	WASHINGTON CURRICULUM INTEGRATION
■ Multiple Choice Assessment, p. 33	**Reading** GLE 1.3.2, GLE 2.1.3
■ Reading Assessment, p. 34	**Reading** GLE 2.2.1, GLE 2.2.2, GLE 2.3.3
■ Writing Assessment, p. 35	**Writing** GLE 2.2.1, GLE 3.1.2
■ Project Assessment, pp. 36–38	**Social Studies CBA:** Dig Deep **Social Studies** GLE 5.2.1, GLE 5.4.1, GLE 5.4.2 **Writing** GLE 2.2.1, GLE 3.1.2

LESSON 1
Exploring by Sea
pp. 70–77

LESSON OVERVIEW	WASHINGTON SOCIAL STUDIES GLEs
KEY IDEAS • The first explorers came to the Northwest region by sea. • Explorers wanted to claim land for their countries. • The explorers encountered Native Americans who lived here. • Explorers traded with the Indians. They also traded with China.	GLE 4.1.2

LESSON ACTIVITIES	WASHINGTON CURRICULUM INTEGRATION
▶ Exploration Storyboard, p. 70	**Visual Arts** GLE 2.3.1
Word Endings, p. 70	**Reading** GLE 1.3.1
▶ Words to Understand, p. 70	**Reading** GLE 1.3.1
Exploring the Northwest by Sea, p. 71	**Communication** GLE 3.3.1
▶ Making Mental Pictures, p. 71	**Reading** GLE 2.1.6
Sensing and Visualizing Text, p. 72	**Reading** GLE 2.1.6
Explorers' Tools, p. 73	**Science** GLE 3.2.2
Beyond the Map, p. 74	**Technology** GLE 1.3.2
So You Want to Be an Explorer?, p. 74	**Reading** GLE 2.4.1
Gray's Trade Route to China, p. 75	**Visual Arts** GLE 2.3.1
On a Sailing Ship, p. 76	**Writing** GLE 2.3.1
▶ Letter From an Explorer, p. 77	**Writing** GLE 3.1.1

LESSON 2
Exploring by Land
pp. 78–85

LESSON OVERVIEW	WASHINGTON SOCIAL STUDIES GLEs
KEY IDEAS • Other explorers came to the Northwest by land. • Lewis and Clark were the most famous explorers to reach the Northwest by land. • The explorers encountered many groups of native people. • Trade with native people helped the explorers survive.	GLE 4.1.1 GLE 4.1.2 GLE 4.3.1 GLE 5.2.2

LESSON ACTIVITIES	WASHINGTON CURRICULUM INTEGRATION
▶Packing List, p. 78	**Writing** GLE 2.2.1
Word Reports, p. 78	**Reading** GLE 1.2.2
▶Words to Understand, p. 78	**Reading** GLE 1.2.1
Lewis and Clark Route, p. 79	**Math** GLE 4.5.J
▶Using Your Senses, p. 79	**Reading** GLE 2.1.6
Adding Description, p. 80	**Reading** GLE 2.1.6, **Writing** GLE 2.2.1
Explorer Limerick, p. 81	**Writing** GLE 2.3.1, GLE 3.2.2
Lewis and Clark Timeline, p. 82	**Social Studies** GLE 4.1.1
Lewis and Clark Expedition, p. 82	**Social Studies** GLE 4.1.1
A Living Timeline, p. 83	**Theatre** GLE 3.2.1
Picture It!, p. 83	**Visual Arts** GLE 3.2.1
Go to the Source: Study Artifacts, p. 84	**Social Studies Skills** GLE 5.2.2, **Communication** GLE 1.2.1
▶My Expedition Journal, p. 85	**Writing** GLE 2.2.1, GLE 2.3.1

LESSON 3
Fur-Trading Days
pp. 86–91

LESSON OVERVIEW	WASHINGTON SOCIAL STUDIES GLEs
KEY IDEAS • Trading for furs became big business in the Northwest. • The Hudson's Bay Company built Fort Vancouver. • The fur trade brought many new settlers to our region.	GLE 4.1.2

LESSON ACTIVITIES	WASHINGTON CURRICULUM INTEGRATION
▶Anticipation Guide, p. 86	**Reading** GLE 2.1.4
Picture Cards, p. 86	**Reading** GLE 1.2.2
▶Words to Understand, p. 86	**Reading** GLE 1.2.1
▶Writing a Dialogue, p. 87	**Reading** GLE 2.1.6, **Writing** GLE 2.2.1
Fur-Trading Fort, p. 88	**Visual Arts** GLE 3.2.1
John McLoughlin, p. 89	**Technology** GLE 1.3.2
Mountain Men: The Trapping Season, p. 90	**Technology** GLE 1.3.2
David Thompson, p. 90	**Technology** GLE 1.3.2
▶You're Hired!, p. 91	**Writing** GLE 2.1.1, GLE 2.2.1

Chapter Activities

This chapter focuses on the first explorers who came to the Pacific Northwest region by sea and by land. There is a special focus on the Lewis and Clark Expedition and the days of mountain men and fur traders. Use these Chapter Activities as you work through the chapter to help students understand the key ideas.

Set the Stage

Set up a class library with books about exploration, the Lewis and Clark journey, and trappers. Some titles are suggested in the Chapter Resources. Ask your librarian for other suggestions.

Set the stage for this chapter by explaining that explorers came to this region by sea first and then by land and Lewis and Clark led one of the most famous land explorations. Tell students that many trappers came to this area in search of animal furs.

As a class, skim the chapter to preview the explorers students will be learning about in the chapter. After skimming the chapter, have pairs of students choose an explorer who had an impact on present-day Washington.

Working with a partner, students will research and complete activities to become an expert on the explorer they chose. The following are activities the pairs may complete together:

- Explorer Portrait
- Explorer Interview
- Explorer Biography
- Explorer Math
- Explorer Route
- Explorer Limerick (See page 81)

Introductory Activity

Explorer Portrait

Create a timeline to show exploration and claiming of the Pacific Northwest. A timeline can be created by writing the decades between 1540 and 1800 on pieces of paper and taping the pages together. Place the timeline around the room or down the hallway.

Next have pairs of students prepare a brief Explorer Portrait on the explorer they chose in the Set the Stage activity. The portrait should include a picture of their explorer downloaded from the Internet if possible. Have students use the Explorer Portrait form available in the *Teacher Guide*. Students should cut out their completed Explorer Portrait form and place it on the timeline in the appropriate place.

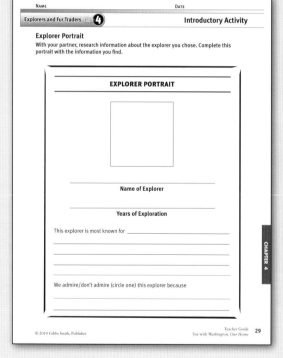

Writing Activity

Explorer Interview

Have pairs of students write an interview with the explorer they chose. Have students use the Explorer Interview checklist available in the *Teacher Guide*.

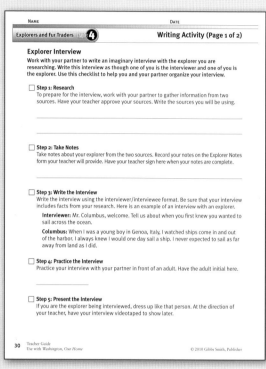

Prewriting
Students should research and gather information from two sources. An Explorer Notes form is available in the *Teacher Guide* to help students organize their information.

Drafting
Have students write a list of questions and responses based on the information gathered from their research.

Revising
Students should ask themselves if their writing is clear and based on the facts.

Editing
Have students work with an adult to edit their interview.

Publishing
Encourage students to dress the parts of the interviewer and explorer. Videotape the interviews to show later.

Reading Activity

Explorer Biography

As part of the research for their explorer report, have pairs of students read a biography about their explorer and complete the Explorer Biography book report form available in the *Teacher Guide*.

NAME _____ DATE _____

Explorers and Fur Traders 4   Reading Activity

Explorer Biography
You and your partner should read a biography about the explorer you chose and then work together to complete this form and complete the sentences that follow.

Title of the Book _____ Author _____

Biography about _____

Date of birth _____ Place of birth _____

Date of death _____ Place of death _____

This explorer is best known for . . .

_____

This explorer can best be described as . . .

_____

The most interesting fact about this explorer is . . .

_____

One question we would like to ask this explorer is . . .

_____

32   Teacher Guide
Use with *Washington, Our Home*   © 2010 Gibbs Smith, Publisher

 Math Activity

Explorer Math

As students read about their explorer, a variety of math problems will naturally arise. Math problems may relate to the distance the explorer traveled, the length of time an exploration took, or the amount of supplies the explorer took. Have students create five math problems based on factual data about their explorer. Create a bulletin board titled "Math Explorations." Post the students' math problems. Challenge students to solve the problems.

 Social Studies Activity

Explorer Route

Place a map of the world on the bulletin board. Have students use yarn to show the route of the explorer they chose to study. You can have each student use a different color of yarn. Encourage students to include a map key.

 Science Activity

Sea Otter Quiz

Have students think about how the sea otter population was affected by the trapping and trading between Indians and explorers. Explain to students that the decline of the sea otter population affected other living things in the surrounding environment.

Provide students with books on sea otters, Internet access, or other resources on sea otters. Have students work in pairs to come up with lists of other living things that may have been affected by the decline of the sea otter population.

Have students use the information they found to write a five-question quiz for their partner. Their questions should be about how the decline of the sea otter population affected other living things in the surrounding environment. Their quiz questions should be multiple choice, fill-in-the-blank, or short answer. They should also write an answer key for their quiz. Ask students to trade quizzes and answer them. Then they should discuss the answers with their partners.

 Art Activity

Compass Rose

Compasses drawn on early maps had 32 points and were very elaborate. Letters indicating north, south, east, and west were not used. North was marked with a fleur-de-lis and east with a cross. Have students use protractors, mathematical compasses, and rulers to create their own decorative compass rose.

 Culminating Activity

Explorer Exhibition

As a culminating activity, host an Explorer Exhibition. Display the students' work from this chapter. Invite parents and other classes to the exhibition. Encourage students to dress the part of their explorers and be on hand to talk about their life as an explorer in first person. Show the Explorer Interviews. Have a few students create a program "schedule" listing the interviews being shown.

Assessment Options

The Chapter Assessment options provide opportunities to evaluate students' understanding of the social studies concepts. Choose the assessment options that best meet the needs of your teaching goals. Assessments are available in the *Teacher Guide* or can be individualized at www.ExperienceStateHistory.com.

OPTION 1: MULTIPLE CHOICE ASSESSMENT

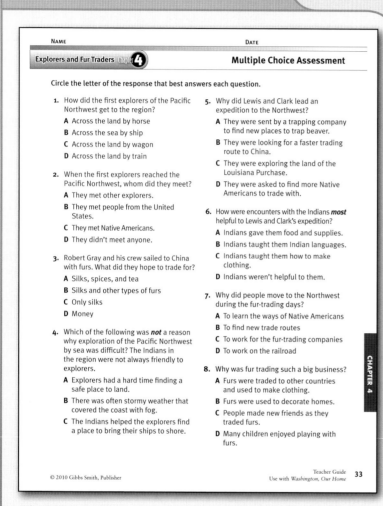

The Multiple Choice Assessment provides a quick way to assess students' understanding of the key concepts of the chapter. Have students read each question and select the best answer.

OPTION 2: READING ASSESSMENT

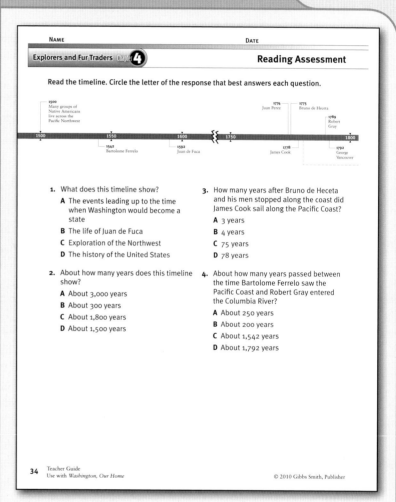

The Reading Assessment provides additional practice for the WASL Reading Test. Have students study the timeline and answer the questions that follow.

NAME _____ DATE _____

Explorers and Fur Traders Chapter **4** **Writing Assessment**

Read each question and write a short answer. Edit your response for spelling, grammar, punctuation, and capitalization.

1. Why were many of the explorations to the Pacific Northwest by sea unsuccessful?

_____

_____

_____

2. Why was the Lewis and Clark expedition so important?

_____

_____

_____

_____

3. How did early exploration, encounter, and trade shape our history?

_____

_____

_____

CHAPTER 4

© 2010 Gibbs Smith, Publisher

Teacher Guide **35**
Use with *Washington, Our Home*

The Writing Assessment provides additional practice for the WASL Writing Test. Have students read the questions and write a short answer.

NAME _____ DATE _____

Explorers and Fur Traders Chapter **4** **Project Assessment (Page 1 of 3)**

Use evidence from two different sources to draw conclusions to answer a research question.

☐ Write your research question.

_____

☐ List two resources you will use to gather information about your research question. List each resource with its title, author, type of source, date published, and publisher of the source. List your sources in alphabetical order.

_____

_____

_____

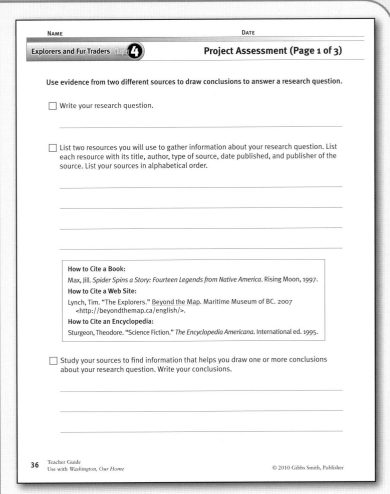

> **How to Cite a Book:**
> Max, Jill. *Spider Spins a Story: Fourteen Legends from Native America*. Rising Moon, 1997.
> **How to Cite a Web Site:**
> Lynch, Tim. "The Explorers." <u>Beyond the Map</u>. Maritime Museum of BC. 2007 <http://beyondthemap.ca/english/>.
> **How to Cite an Encyclopedia:**
> Sturgeon, Theodore. "Science Fiction." *The Encyclopedia Americana*. International ed. 1995.

☐ Study your sources to find information that helps you draw one or more conclusions about your research question. Write your conclusions.

_____

_____

_____

36 Teacher Guide
Use with *Washington, Our Home*

© 2010 Gibbs Smith, Publisher

The Project Assessment provides an alternative to the traditional assessment. This Project Assessment is designed to meet the requirement of the **Social Studies CBA:** Dig Deep.

ELL/Modified Chapter Plan

Explorers and Fur Traders

In this chapter, students learn about early exploration of the Northwest region and encounters between explorers and native people. Students will also learn about the Lewis and Clark expedition and the days of fur trapping and trading.

The following pages can be found in the ELL/Modified Chapter Guide on pages 21–25.

The ELL/Modified Chapter Plan provides a step-by-step lesson in an easy-to-use format. Lessons teach content and language objectives.

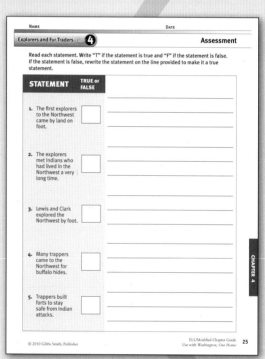

The Modified Assessment for this chapter assesses students' understanding of the key objectives of the chapter.

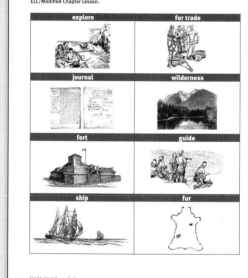

The Word Cards and Activity assist and reinforce students' learning of the chapter and prepares them for the assessment.

Books and Web Sites

Books

Ditchfield, Christin. *The Lewis and Clark Expedition.* New York: Children's Press, 2006.

Fritz, Jean and Anthony Bacon Venti. *Around the World in a Hundred Years: From Henry the Navigator to Magellan.* New York: Puffin Books, 1998.

Johmann, Carol A. and Michael P. Kline. *The Lewis & Clark Expedition: Join the Corps of Discovery to Explore Uncharted Territory.* Charlotte: Williamson Publishing Company, 2002.

Maestro, Betsy. *Exploration and Conquest: The Americas After Columbus.* New York: Harper Trophy, 1997.

Schanzer, Rosalyn. *How We Crossed the West: The Adventures of Lewis and Clark.* Washington, D.C.: National Geographic Children's Books, 2002.

St. George, Judith. *So You Want to Be an Explorer?* New York: Penguin Group, 2005.

Web Sites

The following Web sites provide resources or lesson plans for teachers and activities for students to help extend the lessons in this chapter. Go to **www.ExperienceStateHistory.com** for links to these Web sites.

Archives of Ontario

This Archives of Ontario Web site contains photos of David Thompson's maps, journals, and other artifacts from his explorations.

Beyond the Map

The Beyond the Map Web site is about the exploration of the Pacific Northwest. This site includes timelines, information on specific explorers, videos explaining ships used by explorers, and a game for students to practice their skills as explorers.

Discovering Lewis and Clark

The Discovering Lewis and Clark Web site is an excellent resource for information on Lewis and Clark.

The Mariner's Museum

The Mariner's Museum Web site includes a feature called Exploration Through the Ages that includes information on explorers from around the world. There is a great section that shows pictures of some of the early maps that were created from early explorations. There is another section with information about life at sea, including information on the struggles sailors faced as they explored.

Mountain Men: The Trapping Season

The Mountain Men: The Trapping Season Web site is designed to take students through the process of preparing to become a mountain man. There are links to other sites that have lists of supplies, maps, information on trapping, information on Indian relations, and information on the rendezvous.

National Geographic

The National Geographic Web site has a section called Lewis and Clark that includes a lots of information about the Lewis and Clark expedition including supply lists, journal entries, maps, and more.

National Geographic Kids

The National Geographic Kids Web site includes an interactive game called Go West Across America With Lewis and Clark! where students make choices along the adventure.

National Park Service

The National Park Service Web site has a section called Lewis and Clark Journey of Discovery where students can gather information and do activities to learn more about the Lewis and Clark expedition.

Oregon State Archives

The Oregon State Archives Web site provides information about John McLoughlin. There is a timeline of his life, information about his career with the Hudson's Bay Company, and copies of documents that he wrote.

PBS

The PBS Web site has a section on Lewis and Clark including an interactive timeline.

ThinkQuest

The ThinkQuest Web site has a section titled Who Goes There: European Exploration of the New World. Students can use the site to locate information about explorers. They can also play games on the site.

The BIG Idea

We Explore, Encounter, and Trade

Ask students what they have explored, encountered, or traded. Talk about the meaning of these terms. Students may have explored a forest, encountered a new friend, or traded a toy with a sibling. Divide students into small groups. Have students take turns acting out their exploration, encounter, or trade. Students who are watching will try to guess what it is that the student is acting out. Have students explain how exploration, encounter, or trade affected their history.

 Put Yourself in the Picture

What Do You See?

As a class, study the picture. Ask students who they think the people in the picture are. Ask them to think about what the Indian could be pointing at. Have students write a short journal entry from the perspective of one of the men in the picture. Have students explain who they are, what they are doing, where they are, and why they are there. Have students share their journal entries with a partner.

Caption Answer

The men on the right talking with Sacajawea are probably Lewis and Clark.

Sacajawea is probably pointing the way of where to travel next on the trail.

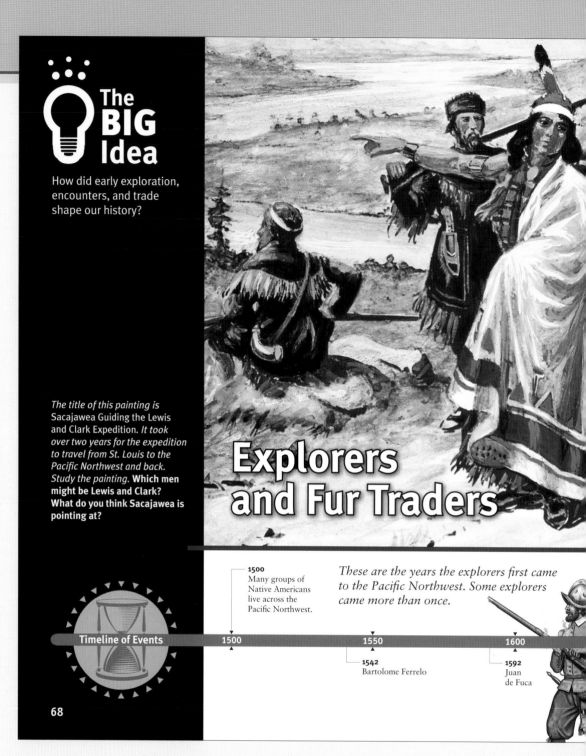

The BIG Idea

How did early exploration, encounters, and trade shape our history?

The title of this painting is Sacajawea Guiding the Lewis and Clark Expedition. *It took over two years for the expedition to travel from St. Louis to the Pacific Northwest and back. Study the painting.* **Which men might be Lewis and Clark? What do you think Sacajawea is pointing at?**

Explorers and Fur Traders

Timeline of Events

1500 Many groups of Native Americans live across the Pacific Northwest.

These are the years the explorers first came to the Pacific Northwest. Some explorers came more than once.

| 1500 | 1550 | 1600 |

1542 Bartolome Ferrelo

1592 Juan de Fuca

68

CHAPTER

4

Strong winds blew against the tall white sails of the first explorers' wooden ships. The winds pushed the ships up the foggy coast of the Pacific Northwest. The men on the ships were eager to explore and trade. They wanted the thick furs of sea otters that swam in the ocean.

After a time, Lewis and Clark led a group of explorers by land. Wide rivers carried them to the ocean in long wooden canoes. These explorers did not come to trade for furs. They came to learn about the land and people who lived here.

Timeline Activity

Timeline Talk

Direct students' attention to the timeline. Talk about the information that can be learned from the timeline. Remind students that they learned about reading timelines in their Skill Page in Chapter 1. Engage students in a discussion about the information on the timeline.

What year did the first explorer come to the Pacific Northwest?
1542

About how many years passed between the time Juan Perez explored the region and the time Robert Gray explored the region?
About 15 years

What years did Lewis and Clark explore the Northwest?
1804–1806

Who explored the Northwest region first, James Cook or Bruno de Heceta?
Bruno do Heceta

1774 Juan Perez
1775 Bruno de Heceta
1789 Robert Gray
1804–1806 Lewis and Clark

1750 — 1800 — 1850

1776–1778 James Cook
1792 George Vancouver
1825 Fort Vancouver is built.
1780s–1840s The fur trade

69

Standards

GLE 4.1.2

Understands how the following theme and development help to define eras in Washington State history from time immemorial to 1889: Maritime and overland exploration, encounter, and trade (1774-1849)

PREPARE

Activator

Exploration Storyboard

Have students complete the Exploration Storyboard in the *Student Guide* by describing an exploration they have taken. They will tell nine steps of their exploration beginning with the preparation and ending with the outcome of their exploration. Allow students to share their stories. Explain to students that they will be learning about people in history who explored the Pacific Northwest.

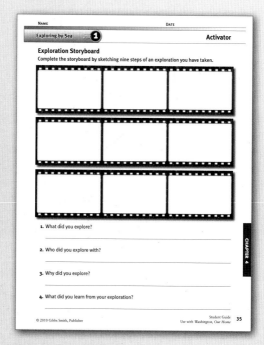

Word Study

Word Endings

As a class, make a list of suffixes that can be added to words, such as *s*, *es*, *ing*, *ed*, and *er*. Discuss how adding each suffix can change the spelling of a word. Add each of the suffixes to the Words to Understand. Before adding a suffix, have students predict whether they think the spelling of the word will change or stay the same.

LESSON 1 Exploring by Sea

Key Ideas

- The first explorers came to the Northwest region by sea.
- Explorers wanted to claim land for their countries.
- The explorers encountered Native Americans who lived here.
- Explorers traded with the Indians. They also traded with China.

Words to Understand

claim
encounter
explore
fur trade
pelt
trade route

A man from which country explored Puget Sound? Which country explored the Columbia River?

Voyages to Unknown Lands

Native Americans lived in the Pacific Northwest for thousands of years. For most of this time, they were the only people here. Other people in the world knew nothing about the region. They did not even know it existed!

The first visitors to our region came to *explore*. They were men who traveled to new places to learn about them. Each explorer hoped to find great riches. He might also find lands to claim for his country. To *claim* means to take as the owner.

Ships from Spain, England, the United States, and other countries sailed along the coasts of North and South America. Each country hoped to be the first to find new lands, new treasures, and new routes for trade.

The Spanish

Bartolome Ferrelo

The first explorer to see the Pacific Northwest from his ship was probably from Spain. Bartolome Ferrelo sailed up the Pacific Coast from Mexico. Like many of the early explorers, he did not find a safe place to land his ship, so he sailed away.

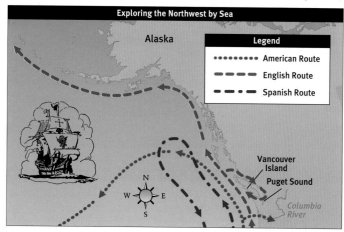

Exploring the Northwest by Sea

Alaska

Legend
········· American Route
– – – English Route
– ·· – Spanish Route

Vancouver Island
Puget Sound
Columbia River

70

Washington, Our Home

Words to Understand

claim (p. 70) *to take as a rightful owner*
encounter (p. 77) *meeting face to face*
explore (p. 70) *to travel to a new place to learn about it*
fur trade (p. 71) *a business where animal fur is traded for other things or for money*
pelt (p. 75) *the skin of an animal with the fur still attached*
trade route (p. 74) *a route over water or land that is used by traders*

A Words to Understand activity for this lesson is available in the *Student Guide*.

Juan de Fuca

It was another 50 years before Juan de Fuca headed up the Pacific Coast as captain of a Spanish ship. He told of a wide body of water that today is called the Strait of Juan de Fuca. However, he sailed on by and did not explore it.

Juan Perez

Over 180 years later, Juan Perez, another Spanish sailor, sailed north from today's Mexico. He tried to claim the land in the Pacific Northwest for Spain, but the weather was stormy, the coast was covered with fog, and his crew was sick. Instead, Perez and his crew stopped at a quiet cove called Nootka on today's Vancouver Island in Canada. Local Indians paddled out in canoes to Perez's ship and traded sea otter furs for beautiful shells. The Spanish had gathered the shells along the California coast. This might have been the beginning of the Spanish *fur trade*. The Indians traded animal skins for other items they wanted. After the short stop, Perez returned home.

Bruno de Heceta

The next year, Juan Perez again sailed up the coast. This time, he was on a ship under the command of Bruno de Heceta. Perez also took a second ship with its captain and crew.

At a place that is now called Grenville Bay in Washington, some of the crew went ashore. They put a cross for the Catholic Church into the ground and buried a bottle. Inside the bottle was a piece of paper that had writing on it. The writing said the land now belonged to Spain. After only about an hour, the men returned by a small boat to the larger ship waiting out at sea.

Then the captain of the second ship sent seven men to get fresh water and to cut firewood on the land. As their small boat went ashore, a large group of Indians came out of the forest and quickly killed all the men. Heceta watched in horror from his ship. Both ships sailed away as fast as they could.

Why Didn't Spain Settle the Northwest?

The Spanish claimed land along the coast, but they never settled there. Few Spanish explorers even went ashore. They were more interested in the fur trade. They built a fur-trading fort at Nootka and kept men there for many years.

Explorers and Fur Traders

71

Spanish explorer

The Spanish learned about sea otters from the Russians, who explored farther north. **What can you tell about sea otters by looking at this picture? Why might people want the fur?**

Talk About It

Voyages to Unknown Lands
(From page 70)

Why did explorers come to our region?
Explorers came to learn about the new land and to claim it for their countries. They also wanted to find great riches.

How did the explorers travel to the Americas?
They came by ship.

The Spanish *(From pages 70–71)*

Who was probably the first Spanish explorer to come to the Pacific Northwest?
Bartolome Ferrelo

What event may have been the beginning of the Spanish fur trade?
Juan Perez and his men anchored at today's Vancouver Island and traded sea otter furs for beautiful shells.

Caption Answers

(From page 70) An explorer from England explored Puget Sound. An explorer from America was the first to explore the Columbia River.

Sea otters live in the water and can swim. People may want the fur because it is long and soft and warm and would make great blankets, robes, and coats for cold, wet weather.

Reading Strategy

Making Mental Pictures

To help build comprehension, encourage students to engage their imaginations as they read the text. As students read the paragraph about Bruno de Heceta on page 71 in the *Student Edition,* have them imagine what it would have been like to be on the ship with Bruno de Heceta as he stopped at Grenville Bay. Encourage students think about the sights, sounds, and smells they would have experienced. Have students complete the Making Mental Pictures activity in the *Student Guide.*

NAME _____ DATE _____

Exploring by Sea — 1 — Reading Strategy

Making Mental Pictures

As you read about Bruno de Heceta's exploration, fill the chart with words to describe your mental picture. Then combine the words in the chart to write a descriptive paragraph about what you pictured.

Looks	Feels	Smells	Sounds	Tastes

Describe your mental picture.

_____
_____
_____
_____
_____
_____

© 2010 Gibbs Smith, Publisher — Student Guide 37 — Use with *Washington, Our Home*

CHAPTER 4

Map Activity

Exploring the Northwest by Sea

The Exploring the Northwest by Sea map on page 70 shows the routes that explorers followed to the Pacific Northwest region. Divide students into groups of four. Assign each student in the group a different route to study. Have students think as if they were an explorer who had followed that route. Tell students to come up with four possible reasons for taking their route. Have each student share their reasons with their group.

Talk About It

Captain James Cook

Why did Captain James Cook feel his trip to the Northwest had been a failure?
He found that the Spanish had made it to the Northwest before him, had built a fort, and were already trading with the Indians.

Why did explorers search for a Northwest Passage?
Explorers who could find a faster route between Europe and Asia could gain riches and power.

Was the Northwest Passage ever found?
No, it was not found because it did not exist.

Caption Answer

Explorers are coming to shore to trade with Indians.

 Differentiated Paths

Sensing and Visualizing Text

One of the key objectives of this lesson is to understand that explorers encountered Native Americans who already lived in the region.

ELL and Special Needs

Make photocopies of page 71 in the *Student Edition* for each student. Have students gather a different color of crayon to represent each of the five senses. Tell students to read the paragraph about Bruno de Heceta and, using the first color, highlight words that appeal to the first sense. Then have students reread the paragraph once for each remaining color, highlighting words that appeal to each of the remaining senses.

Gifted Learners

As an extension of the Making Mental Pictures activity in the *Student Guide,* have students create a picture book about the encounters between explorers and Native Americans. You may want to assign a different group of explorers to different students. Encourage them to draw pictures of what they visualize as they read the *Student Edition.* Have them summarize the encounters in their own words.

A Northwest Passage That Did Not Exist

For a long time, Europeans thought there must be a way to sail from the Atlantic Ocean to the Pacific Ocean all the way across North America. The country that found this route would have an easier way to sail between Europe and Asia. The control of this route would bring riches and power. People started to call this route the Northwest Passage.

Many explorers, including Captain Cook, tried to find a northwest passage. They searched all along the coasts of North and South America. They sailed into bays and up rivers, but the rivers always came to an end. There was no way for ships to cross North or South America. No one found the Northwest Passage because it did not exist.

*The Spanish started a fur trade with Indian people at Nootka. Captain Cook stopped there for a short time, but he never went ashore. **What activities are going on in this picture?***

The English

Captain James Cook

Other countries did not like it when Spain started claiming land in the Pacific Northwest. Each country wanted to be the most powerful by claiming the most land.

Captain James Cook was an important English explorer. Before coming to the Northwest, he had already sailed around the world twice. On one of his trips, he found the sunny islands we now call Hawaii. He called them the Sandwich Islands.

When Cook later sailed by the Northwest, he kept his ships far offshore. However, he did stop for a short time in the harbor at Nootka. He saw, to his dismay, that the Spanish were already there, trading with the Indians for sea otter furs.

Feeling that his trip had been a failure, Cook sailed once again to the Sandwich Islands. Just as he was leaving one of the islands, he was killed by native people.

Captain Cook

72   Washington, Our Home

 Background Info

Captain James Cook

Captain Cook was looking for the elusive Northwest Passage when he stopped at Nootka Island in the Pacific Northwest. Whoever discovered the passage for England was to receive a cash prize equal to nearly a million dollars today.

After Cook's death, his crew left the island and headed to China, where they were delighted to learn that the Chinese paid very high prices for the sea otter pelts Cook had brought from the Pacific Northwest. While Cook's voyage did not result in a new trade route across North America, the word about the rewarding fur trade was out, and the world hurried in.

Nootka, Vancouver Island

At Nootka, many Indians met the explorers for the first time. Nootka was on the shore of a large island. It had a quiet cove where ships could stop and put down anchors. It was different from the rest of the coast of the Northwest, where the sea was rough and ships could not land.

At Nootka, the Spanish built a fort and homes. They traded with the Indians for sea otter furs.

Later, when Vancouver visited Nootka, he met the Spanish leader. They talked and ate together. They exchanged maps they had drawn. They decided to name the large island after both of them. However, in later years, the name was shortened to Vancouver Island. Today, it is part of Canada.

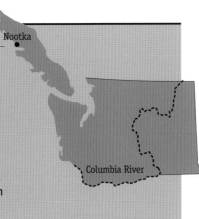

George Vancouver

An English sea captain, George Vancouver, also explored along the Northwest. Vancouver was no stranger to the region. He had already traveled to the Northwest on two other trips with Captain Cook.

This time, Vancouver left England with two ships and followed Cook's route. Vancouver was the first non-Indian to explore the many wonders of Puget Sound. He made the first maps of the region and claimed all the land around it for England. After stopping at Nootka for a short time, he sailed across the Pacific Ocean to spend the winter in the warm Sandwich Islands.

This painting shows buildings at Nootka, on Vancouver Island. George Vancouver stayed with the Spanish there for a short time. **What clues in the picture tell you the Spanish lived on the island?**

Explorers and Fur Traders   73

Talk About It

Nootka, Vancouver Island

How did Vancouver Island get its name?
The island was originally named Nootka Vancouver after George Vancouver and a Spanish leader. Over time, it was shortened to Vancouver Island.

George Vancouver

Which region of today's Washington did George Vancouver explore and map?
George Vancouver explored the wonders of Puget Sound.

Caption Answer

There are fences, homes, and other buildings on the island that are different from the homes Coastal Indians lived in.

Science Activity

Explorers' Tools

Have students research the tools explorers used to navigate their way across the oceans. The Mariners' Museum Web site has an excellent online exhibit called Exploration Through the Ages, where students can learn more about the early explorers and their tools. See www.ExperienceStateHistory.com for a link to this site.

Talk About It

The Americans
Robert Gray

Why do you think the Americans wanted Robert Gray to claim land in the Pacific Northwest?
Possible answers include to gain more land for their country, to keep enemies from living near them, and to have more land that had natural resources that could bring wealth.

Why did Robert Gray and his men have to travel all the way around South America to reach the Pacific Northwest?
There was no place where the ship could cut across the continents from the Atlantic Ocean to the Pacific Ocean.

Why were people so interested in trading with other countries?
Possible answers include getting items from other countries to resell for money.

Caption Answers

The small boat is being slammed with large ocean waves. It has tipped over in the water.

The chest is made of wood.

Technology Activity

Beyond the Map

Have students go online to the Beyond the Map Web site to learn more about the explorers in this lesson and others who explored the Pacific Northwest. Have students find information about the explorers from this lesson and gather four interesting facts that aren't mentioned in the *Student Edition*. Post the new facts on a bulletin board. A link to this Web site can be found at **www.ExperienceStateHistory.com.**

Literature Link

So You Want to Be an Explorer?

Read excerpts from Judith St. George's book *So You Want to Be an Explorer?* to the class. Encourage students to think about what it was like to be an explorer in the 1500s and 1600s and what it is like today. Have students write a paragraph telling whether or not they would like to be an explorer and why.

The Columbia River was so rough that Robert Gray saw whole trees being swept downstream. **What is happening to the small boat in this picture?**

Robert Gray used this chest on his voyage. **What is the chest made of?**

When Gray's ship arrived at Nootka on Vancouver Island, the Spanish men at the fort gave the sailors gifts of fresh vegetables. One crew member wrote, "I thought it a very handsome present."

The Americans

Robert Gray

While explorers from Spain and England were sailing along the coast of the Pacific Northwest, a new country, the United States of America, lay on the other side of the continent. George Washington was president of this new country.

George Washington and other Americans wanted Robert Gray to claim land in the Pacific Northwest for the United States. Gray was a trader. He loaded two ships with metal knives, beads, blankets, and other goods for trading with the Indian people. With a crew of sailors, the ships sailed from Boston, Massachusetts, all the way around South America and up the Pacific Coast. After finally anchoring at Nootka, the men traded with Indians and filled the ships with sea otter furs.

A Trade Route to China and Back

A *trade route* is a route of travel over water or land that is used by traders. Gray left Nootka and sailed to China. There he traded the soft furs for Chinese silks, spices, and tea. The sights and sounds of China were a new adventure for Gray.

74

Washington, Our Home

Finally, Gray left China and sailed around Asia and Africa and across the Atlantic Ocean to Boston. He sold the Chinese goods in Boston at high prices.

Gray Enters the Columbia River

After only six weeks in Boston, Gray again sailed to the Pacific Northwest. He traded up and down the coast. One day, through the fog, Gray saw what seemed to be a wide river. Could he sail into the river? His crew tried, but the water was very rough. Long sandbars blocked the way.

A month later, the men came back. They waited until the ocean tides were high enough to carry a boat over the sandbars. This time they made it! Gray sailed up the river and claimed all the land around it for the United States.

Indians took their canoes out to meet the explorers. Gray gave them nails and other metal objects in exchange for salmon, deer meat, and 450 sea otter pelts. A *pelt* is an animal skin with the fur still on it. After 10 days, Gray left and sailed to China again.

Gray was the first non-Indian to sail up the Columbia River. He was also the first American to sail around the world—twice. He started an important trade route to China. He also gave the United States a stronger claim to the Northwest.

Gray named the Columbia River after his ship, the *Columbia*.

What Do You Think ❓

What do you think the Indians thought when they first saw the explorers, who had lighter skin and hair and wore different clothes?

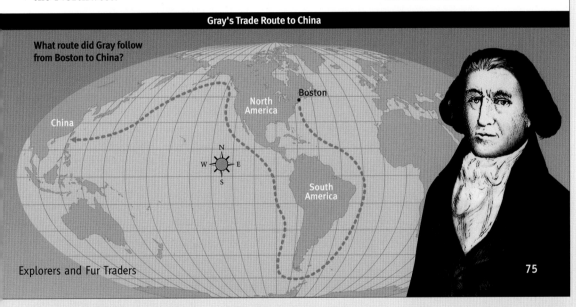

Gray's Trade Route to China

What route did Gray follow from Boston to China?

China

North America

Boston

South America

Explorers and Fur Traders

75

![Background Info icon] **Background Info**

Naming the Islands

After hearing of Gray's entrance into the Columbia River, George Vancouver returned to the area and sent a small ship to explore farther up the river.

Instead of entering the rough waters of the Columbia River, however, Vancouver spent the summer of 1792 exploring and mapping the Puget Sound region. He sailed on to Nootka and named Vancouver Island for himself and a Spanish leader. Among Vancouver's friends were the men with the last names of Baker, Rainier, Whidbey, and Puget. Find the locations named for these men.

Talk About It

Gray Enters the Columbia River

How were Robert Gray and his men finally able to enter the Columbia River after their first attempt was unsuccessful?
They waited until the ocean tides were high enough to carry the boat over the sandbars.

How did the Columbia River get its name?
It was named after Robert Gray's ship, the Columbia.

What were some of Robert Gray's greatest accomplishments?
Possible answers include that he was the first non-Indian to sail up the Columbia River, he was the first American to sail around the world twice, he started an important trade route to China, and he gave the United States a stronger claim to the Northwest.

Caption Answer

He went south, around North and South America, north to the Pacific Northwest, then on to China.

What Do You Think ❓

Encourage students to talk about how the Indians might have felt when they met Gray and his men. Encourage students to think about how they have felt when meeting people different from themselves.

![Map Activity icon] **Map Activity**

Gray's Trade Route to China

On a globe, encourage students to find the area shown on the map on this page. Talk about how, at the time of Gray's journey, there were few maps or globes that charted the lands and the oceans well. Challenge students to work in groups to draw a map of the world without referring to a map or globe. Make a list of the key places each map should include. When the students are finished, have them compare their maps to the maps of other groups and to published maps.

Talk About It

Danger on a Sailing Ship

What were some of the dangers of sailing?
Possible answers include sailing to unknown lands, getting stuck at sea with no wind to push the ship along, not being able to go ashore because of terrible storms, and running out of food and fresh water.

What were some of the dangers of sailing all the way around South America?
There were often big storms at the tip of South America. It was very cold, and some ships were lost at sea.

What were some of the dangers ships faced once they reached the Northwest?
Waves crashed into rocky cliffs, heavy fog hid the land, and ships usually stayed far from shore.

Caption Answer

The ship in this picture probably hit one of the large rocks sticking out of the water. Then it started to sink. The men on the ship probably got into the life boats, then aboard the other large ship.

Writing Activity

On a Sailing Ship

Call students' attention to the quote from a crew member's journal. Have students write a few sentences to complete the journal entry. Encourage students to make mental pictures about what else was happening on and around the ship. Tell students to describe who was on the ship, what the people on the ship were doing, where the ship was located, and why the people on the ship made the journey. Allow students to share what they wrote with other students.

Danger on a Sailing Ship

Think of sailing in a small wooden ship to lands you know little about! If the winds are not strong enough, you might be stuck in a place for days. There might also be long weeks with terrible storms and no place to land. You might run out of food and fresh water.

You sail across a large ocean and then all the way around South America. There are often big storms at the tip of South America. It is very cold. Some ships are lost at sea.

Once you get to the Northwest, waves crash into rocky cliffs. Heavy fog hides the land. Ships usually stay far from shore.

Try to imagine yourself in an explorer's ship as you read this note from an explorer's journal:

Monday, 16 April, 1792
The surf broke with great violence. . . . The nearest shore was about 2 miles distant. . . . The rain and fog [kept us from] seeing much of this part of the coast.

Ships sometimes traveled together for safety. If one ship got into trouble, the sailors could return home on the other ship. **What do you think happened to the ship in this picture?**

Background Info

Pirates!

Pirates sailed the Pacific Northwest Coast, too. Between 1572 and 1742, there were at least 25 different pirate ships preying upon ships along the West Coast of North America. Pirates came from England, Holland, and France, looking for Spanish ships to plunder. Spanish ships on their way back to New Spain were filled with expensive goods from China and the East Indies.

A Time of Encounter

Now imagine you are a young Indian boy or girl living on the coast. You watch as a huge wooden ship with wide sails gets closer to the shore. You have heard stories about men coming from other lands. You wonder who these people are and where they came from. Will they be trading partners? Will they be friends?

This was a time of great encounters. To *encounter* means to meet face to face. At Nootka, the Spanish encountered the native people and traded for furs. Later, George Vancouver encountered both the Spanish and the Indians at Nootka. They shared ideas about the land.

When Robert Gray sailed up the Columbia River, he and some Indian men met each other for the first time. The two groups traded goods before Gray sailed away.

In the coming years, more explorers would come to the Northwest. They would also encounter American Indians of the plateau and near the coast.

What Do You Think

The land the explorers claimed for Spain, England, and the United States was already the home of many groups of Native Americans. Their ancestors had lived on the land for many years.

Do you think it was right for the explorers to think they could claim the land?

LESSON 1 What Did You Learn?

1. Name an explorer who came to the Pacific Northwest region, and tell why he came.
2. What did the Indians have that the Spanish wanted to trade for?
3. How were trade routes used?

LESSON 1 What Did You Learn?

1. *Possible answers include Juan Perez, Bruno do Heceta, James Cook, and Robert Gray. They all came to this region to claim land for their home countries.*
2. *The Indians had sea otter furs the Spanish wanted.*
3. *Trade routes were used to travel quickly and easily from place to place to trade goods with other people.*

REFLECT

Reflect on students' understanding of the first explorations of this region. You can evaluate students' understanding through discussion or evaluation of activities completed in this lesson. The following activity will serve as another way of assessing students' understanding of the key objectives of this lesson.

Writing Activity

Letter From an Explorer

Have students use their visualization skills to write a letter from the point of view of one of the explorers to the king of the country that sent him. Tell students to write about what they pictured in their mind about that explorer while reading the text. Have students complete the Letter from an Explorer activity found in the *Student Guide*.

What Do You Think

Encourage students to talk about how the Native Americans and the explorers each felt about the land and how they feel when people take things from them.

GLE 4.1.2
Understands how the following themes and developments help to define eras in Washington State history from time immemorial to 1889: Maritime and overland exploration, encounter, and trade (1774-1849)

PREPARE

Activator

Packing List

Explain to students that this lesson is about the Lewis and Clark expedition. Encourage students to look at the pictures in the *Student Edition* and other books to help them compile a list of items needed to make an exploration successful. Have students complete the Packing List activity in the *Student Guide*.

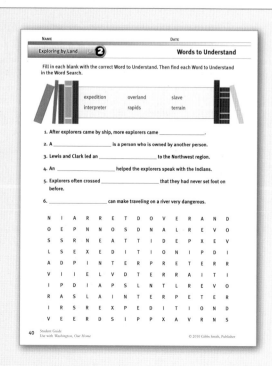

Word Study

Word Reports

Encourage students to create word reports. Word reports can be as simple as a definition and illustration of each word or as complex as a poster that illustrates each word. For example, a poster could be drawn of rapids, labeling the water, the boulders, the shore, and other details.

LESSON 2 Exploring by Land

Key Ideas

- Other explorers came to the Northwest by land.
- Lewis and Clark were the most famous explorers to reach the Northwest by land.
- The explorers encountered many groups of native people.
- Trade with native people helped the explorers survive.

Words to Understand

expedition
interpreter
overland
rapids
slave
terrain

Exploration and Trade

The first explorers to the Pacific Northwest were brave sailors. They saw the coastline of what is now Washington from their ships. The weather was so bad and the fog so thick that they rarely went ashore.

Later, explorers from Canada and the United States traveled to the Northwest. Their *overland* (across the land) travel was long and hard. To make the trip faster and easier, they traveled in boats on the rivers whenever they could. This way, they did not have to clear away trees and rocks and make trails. On their journey, the explorers encountered native people and traded with them.

Alexander Mackenzie, a fur trader from Canada, may have been the first non-Indian to cross part of the Northwest by land. He explored the rivers of British Columbia.

Lewis and Clark's Journey

The most famous explorers to reach the Northwest by land were Meriwether Lewis and William Clark. The United States had just bought a huge piece of land called the Louisiana Purchase. It went from the Mississippi River to the jagged Rocky Mountains. Many groups of Indians lived on this land.

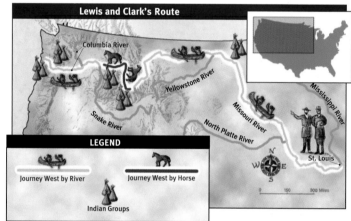

Follow the route of the expedition from St. Louis to the Pacific Ocean. Notice that at one place the men rode horses instead of traveling by canoe. **What rivers did the men follow?**

78

Washington, Our Home

Words to Understand

expedition (p. 79) *a journey taken for a specific purpose*
interpreter (p. 80) *one who translates one language into another as someone is talking*
overland (p. 78) *across land*
rapids (p. 85) *a part of the river where the current is fast and large boulders stick up of the water*
slave (p. 81) *a person owned by another*
terrain (p. 81) *a piece of land; ground*

A Words to Understand activity for this lesson is available in the *Student Guide*.

At this time, Thomas Jefferson was president of the United States. He asked Lewis and Clark to lead a large expedition to explore the land and learn about the native people they met. An *expedition* is a journey taken for a specific purpose. Jefferson also wanted the men to see if there was a water route all the way to the Pacific Ocean.

Lewis and Clark's long journey began near St. Louis, Missouri. From there, they took a large group of men up the Missouri River in boats.

Encounter with the Mandan Indians

The explorers spent their first winter in the land of the Mandan Indians who lived in today's North Dakota. The Mandan leaders welcomed Lewis and Clark's group and let them build log homes to stay in. They also let the men hunt buffalo so they would have meat for the cold winter.

The members of the expediton stopped in the evening to make camp. **What does this picture tell you about the way the men lived on their journey?**

Lewis and Clark were true to their promise to President Jefferson. They kept careful diaries of their trip. They collected samples of plants. They even sent bones, a live prairie dog, and Indian artifacts back to the president.

Explorers and Fur Traders

79

Talk About It

Exploration and Trade *(From page 78)*

Why did overland explorers travel on rivers whenever they could?
They traveled on rivers so they wouldn't have to clear away trees and rocks to make trails.

Whom did explorers encounter and trade with on their journey?
Explorers encountered native people and traded with them.

Lewis and Clark's Journey

Why were Lewis and Clark asked to lead an expedition to the Northwest?
President Thomas Jefferson had just purchased a huge piece of land and wanted the men to explore it, look for a water route all the way to the ocean, and write about the land, plants, animals, and native people they met.

Caption Answers

(From page 78) The men followed the Missouri River and the Columbia River.

The men camped. They cooked their food outdoors. In many ways, they lived like the Indians. They are dressed like Indians in leather clothes.

Reading Strategy

Using Your Senses

Teach students to use their senses to better understand and engage with the text. As students read, have them think about what they would *see, hear, smell, touch,* and *taste.* Ask students to write about what is happening in one of the pictures in this lesson as if they were in the picture. They should write a descriptive paragraph about what the people in the picture see, hear, smell, touch, and taste. Have students complete the Using Your Senses page in the *Student Guide.*

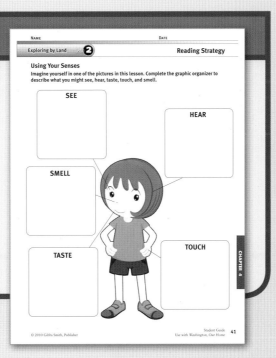

NAME _____ DATE _____

Exploring by Land ② Reading Strategy

Using Your Senses
Imagine yourself in one of the pictures in this lesson. Complete the graphic organizer to describe what you might see, hear, taste, touch, and smell.

SEE

HEAR

SMELL

TASTE

TOUCH

CHAPTER 4

© 2010 Gibbs Smith, Publisher
Student Guide 41
Use with *Washington, Our Home*

Map Activity

Lewis and Clark Route

In order to give students some idea of how far Lewis and Clark traveled, have students complete this map activity using the Lewis and Clark Route map on page 78.
Tell students to examine the map and make guesses as to how many miles the expedition covered. Using a thin string, have students lay string along each of the trails marked on the Lewis and Clark Route map. Then have students measure the length of the string used to cover the trails. Tell students to use the scale on the map to get an estimate of how far Lewis and Clark traveled.

Talk About It

Sacagawea Joins the Group

What role did Sacagawea's husband play in the Lewis and Clark expedition?
He was an interpreter between the Indians and Lewis and Clark.

How did Sacagawea help Lewis and Clark and their men?
She also served as an interpreter, and she helped them get food and horses from her own tribe.

Caption Answer

Sacagawea's clothes are made of leather, which is animal skin with the fur scrapped off. The clothes are decorated with beads and fur.

 Differentiated Paths

Adding Description

Encourage students to use their senses as they imagine the events of the Lewis and Clark expedition in this lesson.

ELL and Special Needs
Ask ELL and Special Needs students what the people on the expedition saw, smelled, felt, heard, touched, and tasted. Help students create a list of descriptive words describing their senses.

Gifted Learners
Ask Gifted Learners to rewrite the stories in this lesson by adding rich descriptions based on the five senses. Encourage students to add dialogue to the stories to show what the people in the stories may have seen, smelled, tasted, touched, or heard.

Sacagawea Joins the Group

The first winter, the explorers met a French-Canadian fur trader and his Indian wife, Sacagawea. The fur trader spoke French, English, and some Indian languages, so he worked as an interpreter for the Indians and Lewis and Clark. An *interpreter* is a person who explains as someone is speaking a different language.

The couple agreed to travel with Lewis and Clark across the Rocky Mountains and guide the group. Sacagawea carried her baby boy, Pomp, on her back the whole way.

Sacagawea was a Shoshone Indian who had been captured years earlier from her own tribe in today's Idaho. When the group reached Shoshone land, she helped the explorers get food and horses by trading with her own tribe.

Sacagawea agreed to go with Lewis and Clark. She helped as a guide and an interpreter. **What are Sacagawea's clothes made of?**

 Background Info

Sacagawea

Sacagawea's name means "Bird Woman" in the language of the Shoshone. When she was a young girl, she was captured by an enemy Indian tribe called the Hidatsas, and was sold to a Missouri Mandan Indian. Sacagawea was later sold to a French Canadian fur trader named Touissant Charbonneau. Charbonneau married Sacagawea when she was 15 or 16 years old. Her son, Pomp, grew up and became a famous guide for explorers.

Lewis and Clark met Indians all along the route. **Look at the Indian homes and the horse. What clues show that the Indians are Nez Perce who live on the plateau?**

The Hardest Part of the Journey

After the flat land of the plains, the *terrain*, or ground, changed. The trip got much harder in the tall, jagged mountains of the West. Food was running out, it often rained, and another winter was coming. Everyone was hungry and cold.

The men had to cut away thick bushes and trees to get through the mountains. Even then, the trail was barely wide enough for the horses and their packs to get through. In a few places, the trail was so steep that weaker horses fell backwards and slid down the mountainside. Some made it up again, but some did not and were left behind.

Meeting the Nez Perce

After three weeks of traveling through the steep Rocky Mountains, Clark and the others came to a Nez Perce village. The Indians were very curious to see the white people and York, Clark's black slave. A *slave* was a person owned by another person and forced to work without pay. The Indians had never seen such people before. The hungry explorers traded with the Indians for dried salmon and camas bulbs to stay alive.

Explorers and Fur Traders

81

In the Northwest, Clark was surprised to see Indians wearing sailors' jackets and carrying guns. Some had Spanish gold coins. How could this be?

For years, explorers had been trading with Coastal Indians. The items were moved from hand to hand across the land.

Background Info

Supplies for the Expedition

Lewis spent months thinking of all the supplies he would need for the trip. He thought first of bringing surveying equipment. Then he listed guns and ammunition, both for hunting and for defense. Lewis planned on the men finding and hunting food along the way, but he did take 150 pounds of portable soup, which was dried soup, for emergencies. He also took five tons of parched corn, flour, and port, more than 100 gallons of whiskey, and some coffee, sugar, and salt. This was enough food for only 40 days.

Lewis also wanted hundreds of pounds of "Indian Presents" to trade with the Indians. The presents included glass beads of many colors, metal needles, knives, and fishhooks. The Indians did not have metal objects, so these would be valuable.

Talk About It

The Hardest Part of the Journey

After crossing the plains, what factors caused the journey to become more difficult? *Possible answers include tall, rugged mountains, low food supplies, rain, the coming of winter, a trail that men had to cut their way through, and trails that were sometimes too steep for the horses to climb.*

Meeting the Nez Perce

Why do you think Lewis and Clark and their men were grateful to meet the Nez Perce after the hardest part of their journey? *Answer should mention that the explorers were hungry. They traded with the Indians for food.*

Caption Answers

There are no large mountains in the picture. Their homes are covered with the tule reeds of the Plateau Indians. The spotted horse is probably a Palouse horse common to the Nez Perce.

The Indians of the coast had probably traded with explorers for sailors' jackets, guns, and Spanish gold coins. Then those Indians traded them to other Indians farther inland.

Writing Activity

Explorer Limerick

Have pairs of students write a limerick about the explorer they have chosen to study in the Set the Stage Activity on the Chapter Activities page. (See page 68E.) Limericks are humorous poems that have 5 lines. Lines 1, 2, and 5 rhyme. Lines 3, and 4 also rhyme. Here is an example:

*There was once an explorer named Clark,
On an expedition he agreed to embark.
He explored a great land,
Lewis gave him a hand.
And on history Clark left his mark.*

Standard

GLE 4.1.1

Understands and creates timelines to show how historical events are organized into time periods and eras.

 Social Studies Activity

Lewis and Clark Timeline

Encourage students to use the information on this map to make a timeline of the expedition.

Map Activity

Lewis and Clark Expedition

The journal excerpts shown on the map are primary sources taken from the journals of Lewis and Clark. Call students' attention to the map. Encourage students to use the journal excerpts to answer the questions.

How many years do the journal entries cover? What years are they?
The timeline covers about two years, from 1804–1805.

About how many months passed between the time the expedition began and the day the men killed a grizzly bear?
About 11 months passed.

What was the first journal entry recorded entering present-day Washington?
On October 16, 1805, the expedition reached the Columbia River.

Which event happened first, Clark had to trade a pistol, a rifle, and other goods to get horses; or Sacagawea told the men they were near her people, the Shoshone Indians?
Sacagawea told the men they were near her people, the Shoshone Indians.

What happened the day after Lewis found a village of Shoshones and tried to trade for horses?
Lewis wrote in his journal that he obtained three very good horses for which he traded a coat, a pair of leggings, a few handkerchiefs, and three knives.

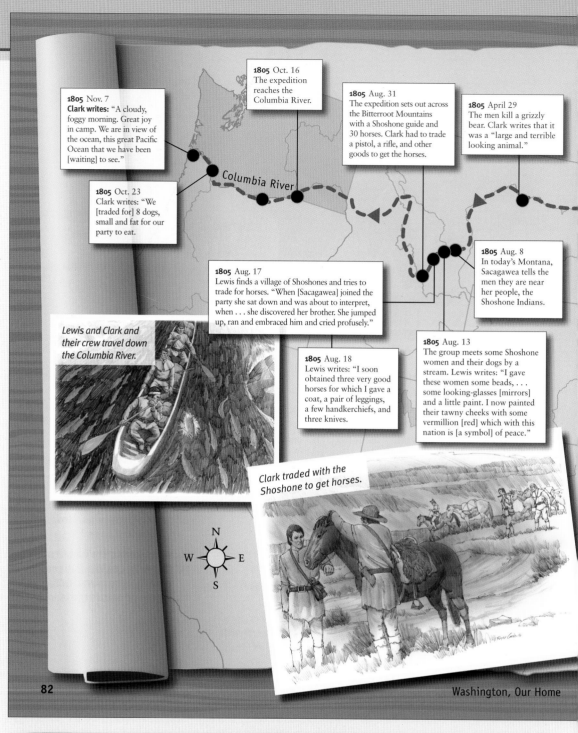

1805 Nov. 7
Clark writes: "A cloudy, foggy morning. Great joy in camp. We are in view of the ocean, this great Pacific Ocean that we have been [waiting] to see."

1805 Oct. 16
The expedition reaches the Columbia River.

1805 Aug. 31
The expedition sets out across the Bitterroot Mountains with a Shoshone guide and 30 horses. Clark had to trade a pistol, a rifle, and other goods to get the horses.

1805 April 29
The men kill a grizzly bear. Clark writes that it was a "large and terrible looking animal."

1805 Oct. 23
Clark writes: "We [traded for] 8 dogs, small and fat for our party to eat.

Columbia River

1805 Aug. 17
Lewis finds a village of Shoshones and tries to trade for horses. "When [Sacagawea] joined the party she sat down and was about to interpret, when . . . she discovered her brother. She jumped up, ran and embraced him and cried profusely."

1805 Aug. 8
In today's Montana, Sacagawea tells the men they are near her people, the Shoshone Indians.

Lewis and Clark and their crew travel down the Columbia River.

1805 Aug. 18
Lewis writes: "I soon obtained three very good horses for which I gave a coat, a pair of leggings, a few handkerchiefs, and three knives.

1805 Aug. 13
The group meets some Shoshone women and their dogs by a stream. Lewis writes: "I gave these women some beads, . . . some looking-glasses [mirrors] and a little paint. I now painted their tawny cheeks with some vermillion [red] which with this nation is [a symbol] of peace."

N W E S

Clark traded with the Shoshone to get horses.

82

i **Background Info**

The Men of the Expedition

Meriwether Lewis and William Clark were co-captains of the expedition. They took 31 other men. One was John Colter, who became a famous mountain man and explorer. The expedition was a military mission, and most of the men were enlisted in the U.S. Army. On the way to the winter camp in the Mandan Village, however, Lewis hired three French trappers who spoke Indian languages.

Lewis & Clark
EXPEDITION

Follow the route of Lewis and Clark as they make their way to the Pacific Ocean. Read their diary accounts and the dates they wrote them.

1805 Feb. 11
Sacagawea gives birth to Pomp, a baby boy.

1804 Nov. 4
Clark hires Charbonneau as an interpreter. His wife, Sacagawea, agrees to come along on the trip.

1804 Oct. 1
The men get ready to spend the winter with the Mandan Indians. Clark writes: "The [Indians]are brave . . . and [friendly]."

Mississippi River

Missouri River

1804 Sept. 7
On the Great Plains, the men capture a prairie dog to send back to President Jefferson.

Lewis's dog, Seaman, traveled all the way to the ocean and back.

1804 May 14
The expedition begins.

**St. Louis
START**

 Standard

GLE 4.3.1
Understands that there are multiple perspectives regarding the interpretation of historical events and creates an historical account using multiple sources.

Social Studies Activity

A Living Timeline

After studying the timeline map of the Lewis and Clark expedition, break students into small groups. Assign each group a few events from the map to act out. Encourage students to make and use props to act out each event. Read the journal entries as students act out the events.

 Art Activity

Picture It!

Assign students events from the journal entries. Have students create an illustration for their event, including the date. Use string to create a timeline. Have students organize their pictures chronologically and hang them on the timeline.

 Background Info

The End of the Journey

When the men reached the small community of St. Charles a short distance from St. Louis, they were warmly welcomed by the townspeople, who were "excessively polite" but "could hardly believe that it was us, for they had heard and had believed that we were all dead and were forgotten." The men were honored by a dinner and a ball. They gave speeches.

Early the next morning, the men wrote two letters. One was to the president, and the other was a letter to Clark's brother. They knew the letters would be published throughout the country, and they wanted them to reflect well on the journey. Lewis, who was more educated and a better writer, wrote for both men.

83

Go to the Source

Standards

GLE 5.2.2
Understands the main ideas from an artifact, primary source, or secondary source describing an issue or event.

Study Artifacts

The branding iron belonged to Captain Meriwether Lewis. The details of this artifact's manufacture have been lost over time, but historians have speculated that it might have been produced in 1804 in the armory at Harpers Ferry, Virginia, or perhaps by Private John Shields, a member of the expedition known for his iron-working skills. Lewis probably traded the iron in spring of 1806 near The Dalles. In the 1890s, Hood River resident Linnaeus Winans found the iron on the north shore of the Columbia River near Memaloose Island.

Too large for branding livestock, this iron was probably used to mark wooden packing crates, barrels, and leather bags. Lewis's iron was also used to mark trees as the expedition made its way slowly across the continent.

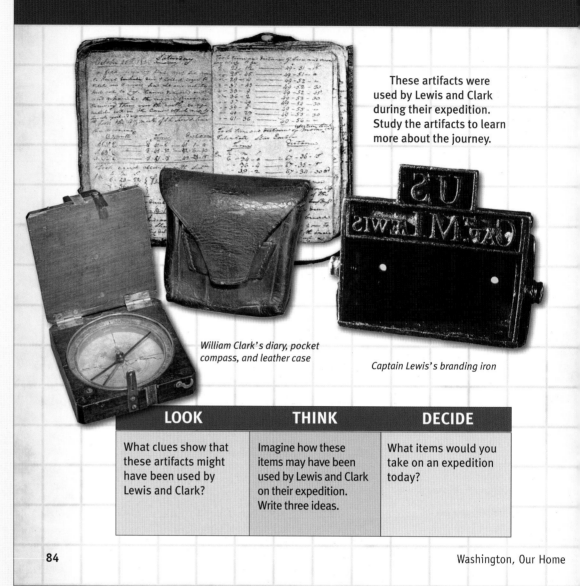

Go to the Source

Study Artifacts

These artifacts were used by Lewis and Clark during their expedition. Study the artifacts to learn more about the journey.

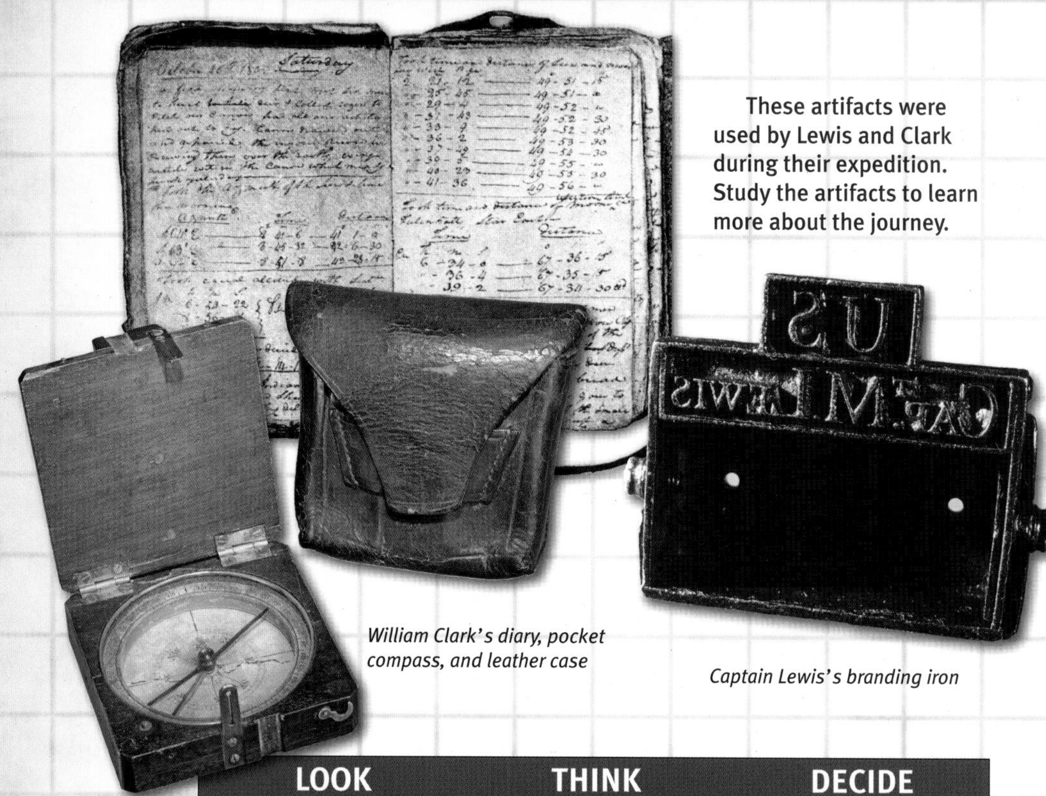

William Clark's diary, pocket compass, and leather case

Captain Lewis's branding iron

LOOK	THINK	DECIDE
What clues show that these artifacts might have been used by Lewis and Clark?	Imagine how these items may have been used by Lewis and Clark on their expedition. Write three ideas.	What items would you take on an expedition today?

LOOK	THINK	DECIDE
Possible answers include journal writing about an expedition, a compass used to help explorers find their way, and the words "Captain M. Lewis" written on the branding iron.	*Answers should mention details of the Lewis and Clark expedition and how each of these artifacts might have been used.*	*Possible answers may include food, water, clothing, medicine, clothes, toys, and books.*

The Northwest at Last

In October, the whole group traveled down the Snake River to the Columbia River. The weather was better, but the rivers had hundreds of *rapids,* where the current was fast and large boulders stuck up out of the water. Rapids could sink a boat quickly. During the last three weeks on the river, the men were constantly unloading and loading the canoes so they could carry them on land around the most dangerous rapids.

On this last part of the trip, the men saw Indian camps every day. They traded for salmon and dog meat to stay alive.

After 18 months of travel, the group reached the Pacific Ocean. They crossed the Columbia River and made their winter camp near where Astoria, Oregon, is today. They built a small fort and called it Fort Clatsop. In the spring, the men, Sacagawea, and two-year-old Pomp began the long trip home.

The group traveled hundreds of miles in canoes. **What landforms does this painting show?**

A Successful Trip

After 28 months of traveling, the group finally arrived home. The people in St. Louis were surprised to see them. They thought the explorers had died on the journey.

Lewis and Clark's trip was a huge success. They went on to see President Jefferson in Washington, D.C. They brought gifts with them, including Indian artifacts from the Northwest.

LESSON 2 What Did You Learn?

1. Why did Lewis and Clark lead an expedition to the Northwest?
2. How were encounters with the Indians helpful to Lewis and Clark?
3. How did Lewis and Clark's meeting with the Nez Perce Indians help the explorers survive?

Explorers and Fur Traders

85

REFLECT

Reflect on students' understanding of the importance of the Lewis and Clark expedition and whether it was a successful expedition or not. You can evaluate students' understanding through discussion or evaluation of activities completed in this lesson. The following activity will serve as another way of assessing students' understanding of the key objectives of this lesson.

Writing Activity

My Expedition Journal

Have students think about what it would have been like to travel with Lewis and Clark. Encourage students to think about what they may have seen, smelled, tasted, touched, or heard during a day on the expedition. Have students complete My Expedition Journal in the *Student Guide* by writing a journal entry about a day on the expedition with Lewis and Clark.

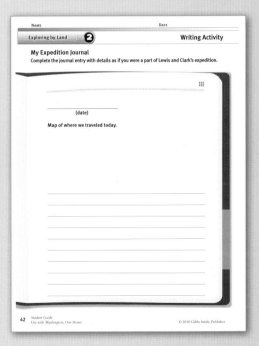

LESSON 2 What Did You Learn?

1. *President Thomas Jefferson asked Lewis and Clark to lead an exploration of the large piece of land the United States had purchased.*
2. *Possible answers include the Indians provided Lewis and Clark with food, shelter, and information as they traveled.*
3. *The Nez Perce traded with Lewis and Clark, giving them food.*

Caption Answer

The painting shows mountains and a river.

🔲 **Standards**

GLE 4.1.2
Understands how the following themes and developments help to define eras in Washington State history from time immemorial to 1889: Maritime and overland exploration, encounter, and trade (1774-1849)

PREPARE

Activator

Anticipation Guide

Tell students that this lesson will be about the fur-trading days in the Northwest. To activate prior knowledge, ask students to share what they know about the fur-trading days. Have students complete the Anticipation Guide in the *Student Guide* to find out more about what they will be learning in this lesson.

NAME		DATE
Fur-Trading Days 🔳		**Activator**

Anticipation Guide
Read each statement. Write a "T" if you think the statement is true or an "F" if you think the statement is false. After reading the lesson, correct any incorrect ideas you may have had.

STATEMENT	TRUE or FALSE	Did you change your answer after reading? Explain.
1. Sea otters were the first animals the explorers wanted.		
2. Beaver furs were used to make tools.		
3. Forts were built to give trappers a place to play games and eat.		
4. The Hudson's Bay Company was the largest trapping and trading company.		
5. Fort Vancouver was a very quiet, peaceful place.		
6. People came from all over the world to work at forts.		
7. John McLoughlin was a great leader of the Hudson's Bay Company.		
8. Mountain men lived in beautiful homes and didn't travel very often.		

© 2010 Gibbs Smith, Publisher — Student Guide 43 — Use with *Washington, Our Home*

Word Study

Picture Cards

Have students create picture cards for the Words to Understand in this lesson. Encourage students to write the word on one side of the card and an illustration that represents the meaning of the word on the other side. Allow students to work with partners, to quiz each other on the Words to Understand by showing either side of the cards.

Key Ideas

- Trading for furs became big business in the Northwest.
- The Hudson's Bay Company built Fort Vancouver.
- The fur trade brought many new settlers to our region.

Words to Understand

brigade
felt
immigrate
sawmill
stockade
survey
wilderness

Big Business in Oregon Country

Wild animals roamed the land and waters of the Pacific Northwest. One explorer saw "bears, wolves, foxes, deer, river otters, sea otters, raccoons, brown minks, beavers, wild cats, gray rabbits, squirrels, mice, and seals."

Many of the animals had thick fur. Fur trading became big business in the region traders called Oregon Country. Oregon Country was most of the land that is now Oregon, Washington, Idaho, and part of British Columbia, Canada. It was a big place.

Sea otters were the first animals the explorers wanted. These animals were also the first that almost became extinct. The next important animals to be hunted for their furs were beavers.

From Beaver Fur to Top Hats

In the 1800s, tall black hats made of beaver fur were very popular for men. To make the hats, beaver fur and wool were soaked and pressed to make *felt*. This firm, shiny felt was shaped to make the hats. Women also wanted beaver fur collars on their coats. Men and women wanted fur gloves.

After the explorers and fur traders came, Indians killed beavers so they could trade with the white men. They exchanged the thick furs for metal pots, knives, guns, cloth, clothes, blankets, and other things the white trappers had.

Top hats were made of beaver fur.

Beavers—Nature's Engineers

Beavers are fascinating animals. They have long, sharp teeth for cutting down trees. Tree bark is their favorite food. Beavers cut down small trees and drag them to the center of a stream. They add more trees and shorter branches. Then they pile on dirt and stones to hold the wood in place. This large pile becomes a dam that blocks a stream and forms a pond.

On the edge of the pond, the beavers pile up more branches and dirt to build a strong, safe home. They enter the home through an underwater tunnel.

86

Washington, Our Home

Words to Understand

brigade (p. 89) *a large group of trappers or soldiers organized for a special activity*

felt (p. 86) *a thick cloth made by pressing and heating fur and wool together*

immigrate (p. 89) *to move into a new country or place to live*

sawmill (p. 88) *a building where logs are sawed into boards*

stockade (p. 87) *a strong, tall fence made from logs*

survey (p. 91) *to measure the land*

wilderness (p. 89) *a place in its natural state, where few people live*

A Words to Understand activity for this lesson is available in the *Student Guide*.

NAME		DATE
Fur-Trading Days 🔳		**Words to Understand**

Draw a line to match each Word to Understand with its correct definition.

immigrate	a large group of trappers or soldiers organized for a special activity
survey	a thick cloth made by pressing and heating fur and wool together
sawmill	to move into a new country or place to live
felt	a building where logs are sawed into boards
brigade	a strong, tall fence made from logs
wilderness	to measure the land
stockade	a place in its natural state, where few people live

Use each of the Words to Understand in a sentence that shows the correct meaning of the word.

brigade

felt

immigrate

sawmill

stockade

survey

wilderness

44 Student Guide — Use with *Washington, Our Home* — © 2010 Gibbs Smith, Publisher

This is Fort Walla Walla on the Columbia River. **What are the men carrying to the fort?**

Fur-Trading Forts

There were many forts in the Northwest. A fort was a group of buildings with a tall fence around them. The tall fence, or *stockade,* was made of thick logs.

Forts were built to protect traders and settlers from Indian attacks, but they were used mostly as trading centers. Much of the work of trading for furs went on in forts. Read this list of furs taken in during one year at one fort:

- 1,038 large beavers
- 700 rats
- 190 racoons
- 33 large black bears
- 13 small black bears
- 2 elk
- other animals

Explorers and Fur Traders

87

Talk About It

Big Business in Oregon Country
(From page 86)
For which part of animals did many traders come to the Oregon Country?
Many traders came for the fur of animals.

From Beaver Fur to Top Hats
(From page 86)

How were beaver furs used during this time period?
Beaver fur was pressed to make felt that was used for top hats and other articles of clothing.

Why did Indians begin trapping beaver?
Indians trapped beaver because the white men wanted beaver fur.

Fur-Trading Forts

Why were many forts built in the Northwest during this time period?
Forts were built to protect traders and settlers from Indian attacks and as places for trading.

Caption Answer

The men are carrying large bundles of animal pelts to trade.

Reading Strategy

Writing a Dialogue

After reading this lesson, have students use their visualization skills to write a dialogue between two people during the fur-trading days. Writing a dialogue requires students to think about who is talking and where the conversation is taking place. Have students complete the Writing a Dialogue activity found in the *Student Guide.*

NAME _____ DATE _____

Fur-Trading Days Lesson **3** **Reading Strategy**

Writing a Dialogue
Creating an imaginary dialogue helps you understand the information you read in a nonfiction text. Write a dialogue or conversation that may have occurred between two mountain men during the fur-trading days. Give your dialogue a title.

Title: _____

Who Is Speaking   Speaker's Words

CHAPTER 4

© 2010 Gibbs Smith, Publisher   Student Guide **45**   Use with *Washington, Our Home*

Talk About It

The Hudson's Bay Company

How was Fort Vancouver like a small city?
Inside and outside of the fort there were stores, workshops, a small school, farms, and all kinds of work going on.

Why do you think sawmills and flour mills were sometimes built around forts?
Answer should mention something about a lot of people living in and around forts and needing wood and flour for shelter and food.

Caption Answers

The stockade is in the upper, right corner of the drawing, and the farms are found outside the fort.

Men traveled from Washington to China and back to trade. This vase was probably brought back on a trade route from China.

Social Studies Activity

Fur-Trading Fort

Life in a fur-trading fort was very busy. After reading about forts in this lesson, allow students to create a 3D model of a fur-trading fort. Have students use a shoebox or other small box and cut one of the sides off, leaving an open diorama box. Encourage students to create details of a fort. Students can use play dough, construction paper, and objects from home to create a model of a fort.

Fort Vancouver started as a fort surrounded by a strong stockade. It grew to a be a small town with buildings, farms, and orchards. **In this drawing of Fort Vancouver, can you find the stockade and the farms?**

Fort Vancouver

Pieces of this vase were found at the site of Fort Vancouver. The vase was from China. **How do you think it got to the fort?**

The Hudson's Bay Company

There was a lot of money to be made by trapping and trading furs. The furs were sent to the big cities of America and across the ocean to Europe. American and English companies all wanted to control the fur trade. The biggest company was the Hudson's Bay Company. This English company played an important part in the settlement of Washington.

Fort Vancouver

The Hudson's Bay Company had forts in many places. Its main fort was Fort Vancouver. It stood where Vancouver, Washington, stands today.

The officers of the company and their families lived inside the fort. Other workers lived outside. Many of the traders had Native American wives, but most of the people at the fort were men.

The fort was almost like a small city, with all kinds of work going on. Inside were stores, workshops, and a small school. Outside was a building called a *sawmill*. Inside it were large saws used for cutting logs into flat boards. There was also a flour mill for grinding wheat into flour. Fields of wheat, oats, and barley produced food. There were fruit trees and vegetable gardens. Hundreds of farm animals grazed nearby.

Washington, Our Home

88

Background Info

Fort Vancouver

There were very few women at Fort Vancouver. John McLoughlin's daughter, Eloisa, was treated as the princess of the fort. Her father was in charge of all operations. Her mother was a Native American. Like many other children of the day who had white fathers and Indian mothers, Eloisa grew up as a child of two cultures.

Fort Vancouver was a trading post, not a military fort. It was the main source of supplies and information for early trappers, missionaries, and settlers. Today you can visit Fort Vancouver and see things almost as they were more than 200 years ago.

In a Hudson's Bay trading post, both Indians and trappers traded pelts for other items they wanted. **How are the Indians in this painting keeping warm?**

Immigrants from Many Countries

People *immigrated* to Fort Vancouver from many places. They came from England, Scotland, Canada, and the United States to work in the fur trade. Native Americans also worked at the fort.

Hawaiians came, too. Some found work on fur-trading ships that stopped in Hawaii. Others worked at forts in the Northwest.

John McLoughlin

The leader of the Hudson's Bay Company activities in Oregon Country was John McLoughlin. He ran the business of the company. He decided where the traders would go and how many goods to trade for furs.

McLoughlin made sure Native Americans were treated fairly. He helped people in need. He was also a medical doctor. He became a powerful person in the Pacific Northwest.

The Brigades

Each year, McLoughlin sent a large group of traders into the wilderness to get furs. A **wilderness** is a place in its natural state, where few people live. The group of traders was known as a **brigade**. The men trapped and traded as they went.

Traders from several countries and Native Americans of many tribes were part of the brigades. Some men took their Indian wives along. The brigade leader wore a tall fur hat, fancy shirt, and long coat with gold buttons. The men often sang songs as they traveled.

Explorers and Fur Traders

John McLoughlin

When the Hudson's Bay Company needed a leader in Oregon Country, it chose an excellent trapper and medical doctor who had worked with Indian people before. Dr. McLoughlin was a tall man with long, white hair. Indians called him the "White-Headed Eagle." His wife was half Indian and half French.

McLoughlin was from Quebec, Canada. He traveled by canoe and horseback across Canada for four months to get to his new home. He built a new fort near the mouth of the Willamette River and called it Fort Vancouver. It became a busy settlement where trappers and Indians lived and worked. Settlers stopped at the fort to rest and get new supplies.

Today, Dr. McLoughlin's statue stands in the capitol building in Washington, D.C. The statue was placed there by the state of Oregon.

89

Talk About It

Immigrants from Many Countries

Where were some of the places that immigrants came from to work for the Hudson's Bay Company?
Possible answers include England, Scotland, Canada, the United States, and Hawaii.

John McLoughlin

What were some of John McLoughlin's responsibilities as the leader of the Hudson's Bay Company?
He ran the business of the company. He decided where traders would go and how many goods to trade for furs. He made sure Native Americans were treated fairly. He served as a medical doctor.

The Brigades

What did the brigade do?
The brigade was sent into the wilderness to trap and trade.

Caption Answer

The Indians are keeping warm by wearing robes made of animal skins and colorful blankets they got from the traders.

John McLoughlin

Oregon State Archives has a Web site about John McLoughlin. The site includes information on McLoughlin's career with the Hudson's Bay Company. The site also includes a timeline of major events from McLoughlin's life. Have students visit this Web site to learn more about McLoughlin. Encourage students to find and write five interesting facts about McLoughlin. A link to this site can be found at **www.ExperienceStateHistory.com**.

Talk About It

Mountain Men

How were mountain men different from other men who worked for the Hudson's Bay Company?
Mountain men didn't work for the Hudson's Bay Company. They worked for themselves or smaller fur companies.

What was life like for a mountain man?
Answers should include spending time trapping, working, and sleeping outside in all kinds of weather; there were no stores for food; there were no doctors if men got sick; and the men walked and rode horses through the mountains.

Why did many mountain men leave Oregon Country to trap in other places in the West?
It was not easy for mountain men to compete with the powerful Hudson's Bay Company.

Opening the Way for New Settlers
(From page 91)
About how long did the fur trade last?
The fur trade lasted about 60 years.

What are some of the benefits to Americans that came from the fur-trading years?
Possible answers include learning a lot about Oregon Country, including getting to know the Native Americans, learning about climate and natural resources, and making the first maps of the Pacific Northwest.

How do you think the fur-trading days set the stage for many future settlers to come to the Pacific Northwest?
Answer should include that the trappers and traders opened up the land to white settlement by sharing information and maps.

Caption Answer

The trappers are using horses to travel through the mountains and to carry furs and supplies.

Mountain Men

The most famous fur traders in United States history were called mountain men. They walked and rode horses through the Rocky Mountains. These men did not work for the Hudson's Bay Company. They worked for themselves or for other fur companies.

Mountain men spent their time in the mountain valleys, trapping animals for their fur. They worked and slept outside in all kinds of weather. There were no stores to go to if they ran out of food and no doctors if they got sick.

Work began in the fall, when the animals' fur was thick enough to keep them warm through the winter. Every day, the men set their traps. Sometimes they traveled many miles in one day to check them. If they found a dead animal in a trap, they took it out of the trap and cleaned and dried the skin.

Mountain men were fur trappers. They trapped in mountain valleys all over the West. **How are these trappers using horses?**

90

 Technology Activity

Mountain Men: The Trapping Season
Have your students learn what it was like to be a mountain man. At the Mountain Men: The Trapping Season Web site, students are taken through the many tasks required to be prepared for the work of a mountain man. Students are shown maps they can use for trapping, lists of supplies they will need, and much more. A link to this Web site can be found at www.ExperienceStateHistory.com.

WASHINGTON PORTRAIT

David Thompson

The Archives of Ontario has a Web site all about David Thompson and his explorations of North America. Have students explore this site and take notes of six places David Thompson explored. Have students share their lists in small groups and locate each place on a map. A link to this Web site can be found at www.ExperienceStateHistory.com.

The title of this painting is Uninvited Visitors. **Who do you think the uninvited visitors are—the mountain men or the Indians riding up on horseback?**

Some of the trappers worked alone. Others worked in groups. Many married Native American women, and the whole family worked together. Often, trappers spent the winter in an Indian village. Then they moved on in the spring.

Some mountain men stayed in Oregon Country. However, it was not easy for them to compete with the powerful Hudson's Bay Company. Many left to trap in other places in the West.

Opening the Way for New Settlers

The fur trade was important to Washington history for about 60 years. During that time, trappers and traders learned a lot about Oregon Country. They got to know the native people, and the native people got to know the new settlers.

Trappers learned about the climate and natural resources. They explored the land and made some of the first maps of the Pacific Northwest. All these things would be important to the settlers who would soon come to live in the Northwest.

WASHINGTON PORTRAIT

David Thompson

David Thompson was born to a poor family in England. At age 14, he was sent by his family to work for the Hudson's Bay Company. He went to Canada and worked at fur-trading forts.

While trapping, Thompson broke his leg and could not walk for a year. The broken leg turned out to be a good thing, because instead of trapping animals, Thompson spent that time learning how to *survey* (measure) the land and make maps. When he got older, Thompson mapped large regions of the Northwest and the whole Columbia River. He also set up trading posts.

Thompson married Charlotte Small, an Indian woman. They had 13 children.

LESSON 3 What Did You Learn?

1. What caused more people to move to the Northwest during the fur-trading days?
2. Why was fur trading a big business during this time period?
3. Describe life at a fur-trading fort.

Explorers and Fur Traders

LESSON 3 What Did You Learn?

1. *People came to the Northwest to work for the Hudson's Bay Company and other trapping companies.*
2. *Many furs were sold to Europe, where the fur was used to make top hats and other articles of clothing.*
3. *Life in a fur-trading fort was very busy, much like in a small city. There were workshops, stores, and even small schools.*

REFLECT

Reflect on students' understanding of the impact the fur-trading days had on the Northwest. You can evaluate students' understanding through discussion or evaluation of activities completed in this lesson and by having students complete the last column in the Anticipation Guide for this lesson in the *Student Guide*. The following activity will serve as another way of assessing students' understanding of the key objectives of this lesson.

Writing Activity

You're Hired!

Have students imagine they are John McLoughlin or a leader of another fur-trading company. Tell students they will be writing instructions that will be given to new trappers and traders who come to work with the company. Encourage students to think about what they learned from this lesson to write instructions that will help trappers and traders survive and be successful at their job. Have students complete the You're Hired! activity in the *Student Guide*.

Caption Answer

The Indians are riding up to the mountain men, who appear to be guarding their location, and probably their furs.

Standards

GLE 5.2.1
Creates and uses a research question to conduct research on an issue or event.

Create a Research Question

Use this activity to help students learn how to write a good research question. After this activity is complete, students will use the question they came up with to complete the Project Assessment available in the *Teacher Guide*.

Activate

As a class, come up with a list of questions that students have about the Lewis and Clark expedition. Encourage students to think about what they learned about the expedition in this chapter and what they want to learn more about. Write the questions on the board.

Teach

Tell students that good researchers often use questions they have about a topic to guide their research. Explain to students that some of the questions on the board would be easy to research and some would be very difficult to research. Explain to students that questions that are too small or too big cannot be researched. Talk about the examples found on the Washington Social Studies Skill Page.

Practice

Go through the list of questions written on the board. As a class, cross off questions that are too big or too small. Generate some more questions that are just right.

Apply

Have students complete the Create a Research Question activity.

Create a Research Question

The Lewis and Clark expedition was very important in helping the people in the United States learn about the Northwest. Lewis and Clark shared information about the land and people that would help future settlers.

Think about some part of the expedition you have a question about. Maybe you would like to learn more about a person on the expedition, a place the explorers went, or an event that happened on the trip.

Write your question on a piece of paper. The answer to the question should also fit on the paper.

Use the items below to be sure your question is a good one to research.

1. Is your question just the right size—neither too big nor too small?
   - Too big: "What did Lewis and Clark learn on their expedition?" (It would be impossible to answer this question in a one-page paper.)
   - Too small: "What state was Lewis from?" (This could be answered in one word.)
   - Just right: "What kinds of food did Lewis and Clark take on their expedition?"

2. Can the question be researched?
   - "Who was smarter, Lewis or Clark?" (This cannot be researched. The answer cannot be found.)

3. What sources will you use to answer your question?

Washington, Our Home

Chapter Review 4

Reviewing What You Read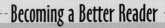

1. Why did the first explorers come to the Pacific Northwest?
2. What were some of the problems the Spanish explorers faced?
3. Draw a conclusion about why you think Robert Gray was determined to sail up the Columbia River.
4. Explain what you think were the hardest and the easiest parts of the Lewis and Clark expedition.
5. How do you think exploring the Pacific Northwest would be different if it were explored today?
6. Would you like to explore a new land? Why or why not?

Becoming a Better Reader

Visualize the Text

Good readers "see" the story in their heads as they read. It's like watching a movie in your head every time you open a book. Picturing the story helps you make connections so you can understand what you are reading. We call this reading strategy "visualizing the text."

This chapter is full of stories of exciting people and events. Choose one person or one event from this chapter to describe or retell in your own words.

Spotlighting Geography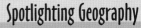

Map Your Neighborhood

Take a walk with a family member or with your entire class to a safe location nearby. You could go to a friend's house, store, office building, or church. Make a map of the route you travel. Be sure to include important landmarks on your map, such as streets, parking lots, parks, or buildings you pass along the way.

Compare your mapmaking experience to that of the early explorers. Write a paragraph about your mapmaking experience. Was it hard? Why or why not?

Explorers and Fur Traders 93

Reviewing What You Read

The Reviewing What You Read questions are leveled according to Bloom's Taxonomy and will help students achieve a higher level of thinking. These questions will also prepare students for the chapter assessments. The following are possible answers to the questions. Focus on students' ability to understand and apply the concepts.

1. **KNOWLEDGE** Explorers came to the Pacific Northwest to explore and claim new lands, to find great riches, and to find new trade routes.

2. **COMPREHENSION** The Spanish explorers had a hard time finding a safe place to land ships. They faced stormy weather, sickness, and Indian attacks.

3. **APPLICATION** Students' conclusions should mention details about what Robert Gray encountered once he sailed up the river.

4. **ANALYSIS** Possible answers may include traveling in the mountains as the hardest part and staying in the Indian villages as the easiest part.

5. **SYNTHESIS** Exploring would be easier today because we have maps, automobiles, and better tools.

6. **EVALUATION** Students' reasons for their answers should reflect what they learned from this chapter.

Interactive Chapter Review

An Interactive Chapter Review is available online at **www.ExperienceStateHistory.com**. Have students use this review to prepare for the assessments.

Chapter Assessment

Chapter Assessments are available to preview on pages 68G–68H. Assessments can be found in the *Teacher Guide* and online at **www.ExperienceStateHistory.com**.

Becoming a Better Reader

Visualize the Text

In preparation for this activity, read a short picture book to the class without showing them the pictures. Have them take notes, using their five senses as you read. After reading the book, have students compare what they pictured with a neighbor. Read the book again, showing the pictures. Discuss with the class how important it is to tell a story with details that use the senses, so readers and listeners can visualize the text.

Spotlighting Geography

Map Your Neighborhood

Before beginning this activity, share various maps with students and discuss what features good maps include. Also discuss items that aren't necessary to include on a map. You may want to model for the class by drawing a map on the board of the route to the lunchroom or some place all students will be familiar with. Have students share their completed maps and see if other students can tell where the map is leading.

CHAPTER

5 Early Immigration and Settlement

CHAPTER PLANNER

CHAPTER OVERVIEW	WASHINGTON SOCIAL STUDIES GLEs
This chapter focuses on the first non-native groups to settle in Oregon Country. Attention is given to missionaries and to settlers who came on the Oregon Trail.	GLE 2.1.1 GLE 3.1.1 GLE 3.2.3 GLE 4.1.2 GLE 4.2.1 GLE 4.3.1 GLE 5.1.2 GLE 5.2.2 GLE 5.4.1

CHAPTER RESOURCES

ELL/Modified Chapter Plan, p. 94I

Books and Web Sites, p. 94J

CHAPTER ACTIVITIES	WASHINGTON CURRICULUM INTEGRATION
Go West!, p. 94E	**Communication** GLE 2.2.2
Along the Trails West, p. 94E	**Reading** GLE 3.4.3
My Journey West, p. 94E	**Writing** GLE 1.1.1, GLE 1.2.1, GLE 1.3.1, GLE 1.4.1, GLE 1.5.1, GLE 1.6.1
The Trail West, p. 94E	**Visual Arts** GLE 3.2.1
■ Math for the Journey West, p. 94F	**Math** GLE 4.5.E
■ Jerky for the Journey, p. 94F	**Science** GLE 2.1.5
■ Party Like a Pioneer, p. 94F	**Reading** GLE 3.4.3

CHAPTER OPENER	WASHINGTON CURRICULUM INTEGRATION
Settlers Presentation, p. 94	**Communication** GLE 1.2.1
Settle a Town, p. 94	**Theatre** GLE 2.2.1
Timeline Talk, p. 95	**Reading** GLE 3.2.2

▶Indicates an activity page located in the *Student Guide*
■ Indicates an activity page located in the *Teacher Guide*

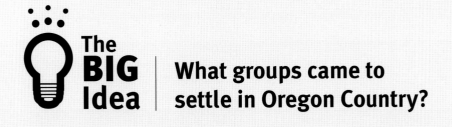

The BIG Idea | What groups came to settle in Oregon Country?

CHAPTER REVIEW   pp. 114–115

SOCIAL STUDIES SKILLS PAGE	WASHINGTON SOCIAL STUDIES GLEs
Draw a Conclusion, p. 114	**Social Studies** GLE 5.4.1 Prepares students for **Social Studies CBA:** People on the Move (completed in the Project Assessment for this chapter)

REVIEWING THE CHAPTER	WASHINGTON SOCIAL STUDIES GLEs
Students show what they have learned by completing application activities and answering chapter review questions. Assessments for this chapter can be previewed on pages 94G–94H. Select the assessment option that best suits your goals for this chapter. Assessments are available in the *Teacher Guide* or online at **www.ExperienceStateHistory.com**.	GLE 2.1.1 GLE 3.1.1 GLE 3.2.3 GLE 4.1.2 GLE 4.2.1 GLE 4.3.1 GLE 5.1.2 GLE 5.2.2 GLE 5.4.1

CHAPTER ACTIVITIES	WASHINGTON CURRICULUM INTEGRATION
Reviewing What You Read, p. 115	**Reading** GLE 1.3.2, GLE 2.1.3
Becoming a Better Reader, p. 115	**Reading** GLE 2.1.3
Spotlighting Geography, p. 115	**Social Studies** GLE 3.1.1, **Writing** GLE 2.2.1

CHAPTER ASSESSMENTS	WASHINGTON CURRICULUM INTEGRATION
■ Multiple Choice Assessment, p. 45	**Reading** GLE 1.3.2, GLE 2.1.3
■ Reading Assessment, p. 46	**Reading** GLE 2.2.6
■ Writing Assessment, p. 47	**Writing** GLE 3.1.1, GLE 3.1.2
■ Project Assessment, pp. 48-49	**Social Studies CBA:** People on the Move **Writing** GLE 2.2.1, GLE 3.1.1, GLE 3.1.2

LESSON 1
The Missionaries   pp. 96–103

LESSON OVERVIEW	WASHINGTON SOCIAL STUDIES GLEs
KEY IDEAS • Missionaries came to the Northwest to teach their religion to the Indians. • Missionaries also built schools and orphanages.	GLE 4.1.2 GLE 4.2.1 GLE 4.3.1 GLE 5.1.2

LESSON ACTIVITIES	WASHINGTON CURRICULUM INTEGRATION
▶Word Splash, p. 96	**Writing** GLE 2.2.1
Parts of Speech, p.96	**Reading** GLE 1.3.2
▶Words to Understand, p. 96	**Reading** GLE 1.3.1
▶Using Heads to Find Main Ideas, p. 97	**Reading** GLE 2.1.3
Summarizing Using Main Ideas, p. 98	**Reading** GLE 2.1.7
The Stout-Hearted Seven, p. 99	**Communication** GLE 2.1.6
Jack's Math, p. 100	**Math** GLE 4.3.B
Two Points of View Interview, p. 101	**Writing** GLE 3.2.2
Mother Joseph, p. 102	**Writing** GLE 2.3.1, GLE 2.2.1
Missions in Oregon Country, p. 102	**Communication** GLE 2.2.2
▶Diamante Poem, p. 103	**Writing** GLE 2.3.1, GLE 2.2.1

LESSON 2
The Oregon Trail   pp. 104–113

LESSON OVERVIEW	WASHINGTON SOCIAL STUDIES GLEs
KEY IDEAS • The pioneers made a hard trek across the Oregon Trail to get free land. • They made a new life in Oregon Country. • The movement west changed life for the Native Americans.	GLE 2.1.1 GLE 3.1.1 GLE 3.2.3 GLE 4.2.1 GLE 5.2.2

LESSON ACTIVITIES	WASHINGTON CURRICULUM INTEGRATION
▶ Packing List, p. 104	**Writing** GLE 2.2.1
Compound Words, p. 104	**Reading** GLE 1.2.1
▶ Words to Understand, p. 104	**Reading** GLE 1.3.1
▶ Making an Outline, p. 105	**Reading** GLE 2.1.7
The Oregon Trail, p. 106	**Communication** GLE 2.1.6, **Social Studies** GLE 3.1.1
Go to the Source: Examine a Secondary Source, p. 108	**Social Studies** GLE 5.2.2.
Web of Main Ideas, p. 108	**Reading** GLE 2.1.3, **Social Studies** GLE 5.2.2
George Washington Bush, p. 109	**Writing** GLE 2.2.1
Is It Worth the Cost?, p. 110	**Communication** GLE 2.2.1
Compare Two Journals, p. 111	**Writing** GLE 2.2.1
Oregon Trail Jeopardy, p. 111	**Communication** GLE 1.1.2
Wagons, Ho! A Diary of the Oregon Trail, p. 112	**Writing** GLE 2.3.1, **Reading** GLE 3.2.1
Picture the Clothes, p. 112	**Visual Arts** GLE 2.2.1
▶ Writing a Summary, p. 113	**Writing** GLE 3.1.1, **Reading** GLE 2.1.7

Chapter Activities

This chapter focuses on missionaries who came to the Northwest and on the first groups that traveled along the Oregon Trail and settled in Oregon Country. Use the Chapter Activities to help students understand how the missionaries and pioneers shaped the history of the land that would one day become the state of Washington.

 Set the Stage

Set up a class library with books about the Oregon Trail. Some titles are suggested on page 94J. Ask your librarian for other suggestions. Consider displaying a map that shows the Oregon Trail and some of the other routes to the West.

 Introductory Activity

Go West!

Ask students to make a list of the 10 things they would pack if they were moving today. Talk about the transportation mode they would use for their move. Once students have completed their lists, have them get into groups of four and compile one list of the things they would bring. Groups should then negotiate down to a list of the 10 most important things from the combined list.

Now tell students that through the study of this chapter they will be moving with their families from Missouri to Oregon Country during the mid-1800s. Have students cross off anything on their list that requires electricity or wasn't invented until after 1900. Talk with students about what is left on their lists. Ask students if the things on their lists would make survival possible for a move from Missouri to Oregon Country. Have groups rewrite their lists with the 10 most important things to bring for a trip west. Explain to students there are no moving vans, no cars, and no airplanes. The primary method of transportation available is the covered wagon train.

 Reading Activity

Along the Trails West

Many of the pioneers moving west along the Oregon Trail in the 1800s wrote about their experiences in personal journals. Some of those diaries and journals have been preserved, and excerpts are available at The Oregon Trail and The Historic Oregon Web sites. Select a few journal entries to read together as a class or in small groups. These journal entries will serve as a model for the journal writing called for in the Writing Activity. Go to **www.ExperienceStateHistory. com** for links to these sites.

 Writing Activity

My Journey West

Have students keep a journal of their imaginary journey along the Oregon Trail with their family in the mid-1800s. Provide students with journals or have students make their own using brown paper grocery sacks for the cover. Cut the sacks to the appropriate size. Wad the sacks into a ball, and then press them flat. Paint the sacks lightly with black watercolor paint to give them a look of weathered leather. To make the journal, staple writing paper together using the sacks as the cover. Instead of staples, you may want students to tie the book together with leather straps for a more authentic look.

Prewriting

Have students think about their real families living in Independence, Missouri (the Gateway to the West) in the mid- to late-1800s. Then using the information from this chapter and the journal read together in the Reading Activity, have students write about the preparation for the journey, the actual journey (including the mode of transportation), and their arrival in the Oregon Country.

Drafting

Provide time for students to write in their journals. Encourage students to use detailed descriptions about what they see, hear, and experience along the way. You may want to provide daily prompts or suggestions for writing, including some of the following:

- Tell the reasons your family moved west.
- Describe your covered wagon and the supplies your family packed.
- Describe what you saw on your journey.
- Write about others you met along the trail.
- Describe what you saw as you entered into Oregon Country.

Revising

Have students choose one entry from their journals to revise. They should revise it to include more detail and facts from the chapter.

Editing

Have students work in pairs to edit their journal entries for spelling, grammar, capitalization, and punctuation.

Publishing

Have students read their journal entries in small groups.

 Art Activity

The Trail West

Share the book *The Trail West: Exploring History Through Art* by Ellen Galford with the class. Have each student choose one of the pictures in the book to write a story about. If possible, make color copies of the art for students to use as covers for their stories or display the art and stories on the bulletin board.

Math for the Journey West

Have students use their math skills to calculate some of the information that the early pioneers would need in order to plan for their journeys west. Math for the Journey West is available in the *Teacher Guide*. You may want to make a bulletin board using the information from this page and encourage students to write their own math problems for others to solve.

Jerky for the Journey

There were no fast food restaurants along the Oregon Trail. Nor were there coolers to keep foods fresh without refrigeration. Travelers heading west had to think of other ways to preserve food for the long journey. One common food was jerky. Jerky is a meat that has been preserved through a process of drying. A recipe is provided in the *Teacher Guide*. Do the activity as a class or have volunteers do the activity at home. Talk about how removing moisture from food helps to preserve the food longer.

Party Like a Pioneer

As a culminating activity, host a Pioneer Party for all the "folks" who have made the move to Oregon Country. The Pioneer Party is a celebration of surviving the long and hard journey west. It will include food, games, music, and other activities common to the early pioneers. Invite parents to the party. Display the students' projects completed through this chapter. Suggestions for hosting a Pioneer Party are available in the *Teacher Guide*.

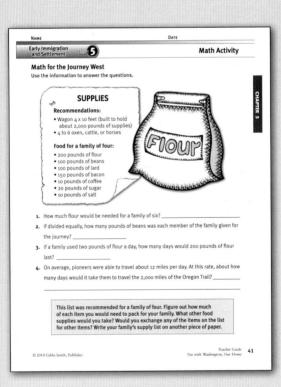

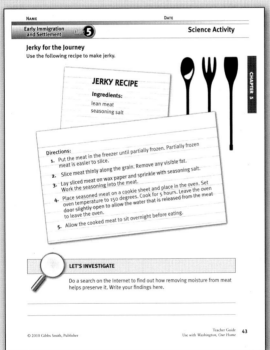

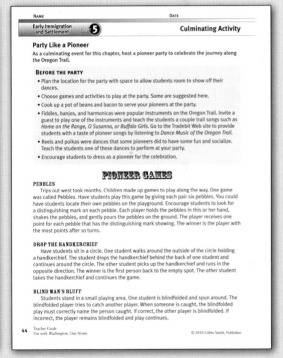

Assessment Options

The Chapter Assessment options provide opportunities to evaluate students' understanding of the social studies concepts. Choose the assessment options that best meet the needs of your teaching goals. Assessments are available in the *Teacher Guide* or can be individualized at **www.ExperienceStateHistory.com.**

OPTION 1: MULTIPLE CHOICE ASSESSMENT

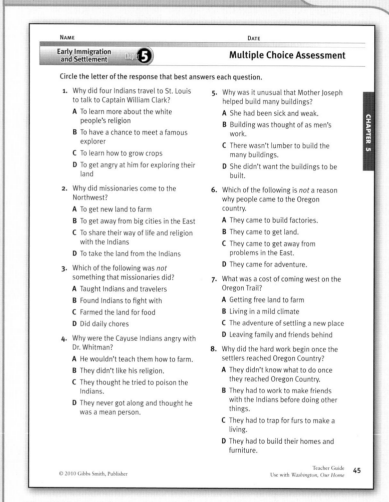

The Multiple Choice Assessment provides a quick way to assess students' understanding of the key concepts of the chapter. Have students read each question and select the best answer.

OPTION 2: READING ASSESSMENT

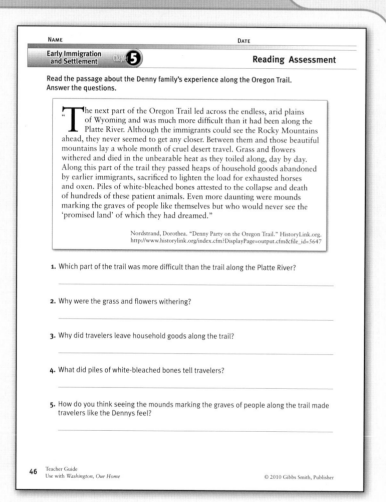

The Reading Assessment provides additional practice for the WASL Reading Test. Have students read the passage and answer the questions that follow.

NAME   DATE

Early Immigration and Settlement Chapter **5**   **Writing Assessment**

CHAPTER 5

Answer the prompt. Use this checklist to help organize your writing. Write your final copy on another piece of paper.

In what ways did the movement west change life for Native Americans?

WRITING CHECKLIST

❑ Think about your response. Write some of your ideas.

_____

_____

_____

❑ Write a sentence stating the main idea of your answer.

_____

_____

❑ Write three to six sentences providing details about your answer with facts you learned in this chapter.

_____

_____

_____

_____

_____

❑ Write one sentence restating the main idea of your answer.

_____

_____

❑ Review your writing. Check for correct grammar, spelling, capitalization, and punctuation. Make sure you used facts to support your answer.

❑ Rewrite your paragraph on another piece of paper. Use your neatest writing. Staple this page to your final copy.

© 2010 Gibbs Smith, Publisher   Teacher Guide
                                   Use with *Washington, Our Home*   47

The Writing Assessment provides additional practice for the WASL Writing Test. Have students use the checklist to write a paragraph in response to the writing prompt about this chapter.

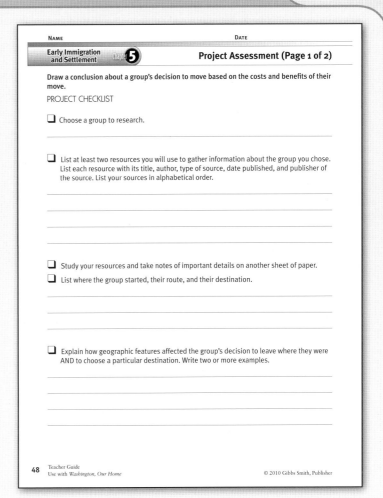

NAME   DATE

Early Immigration and Settlement Chapter **5**   **Project Assessment (Page 1 of 2)**

Draw a conclusion about a group's decision to move based on the costs and benefits of their move.

PROJECT CHECKLIST

❑ Choose a group to research.

_____

❑ List at least two resources you will use to gather information about the group you chose. List each resource with its title, author, type of source, date published, and publisher of the source. List your sources in alphabetical order.

_____

_____

_____

❑ Study your resources and take notes of important details on another sheet of paper.

❑ List where the group started, their route, and their destination.

_____

_____

_____

❑ Explain how geographic features affected the group's decision to leave where they were AND to choose a particular destination. Write two or more examples.

_____

_____

_____

_____

48 Teacher Guide
    Use with *Washington, Our Home*   © 2010 Gibbs Smith, Publisher

The Project Assessment provides an alternative to the traditional assessment. This Project Assessment is designed to meet the requirement of the **Social Studies CBA:** People on the Move.

ELL/Modified Chapter Plan

Early Immigration and Settlement

Students will learn how the early pioneers traveled along the Oregon Trail and how they settled in Oregon Country. In this lesson, students will connect their own immigration experiences or the immigration experiences of their families with that of the pioneers moving west.

The following pages can be found in the ELL/Modified Chapter Guide on pages 27–33.

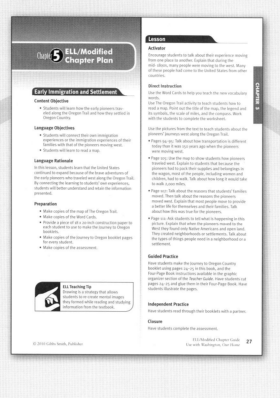

The ELL/Modified Chapter Plan provides a step-by-step lesson in an easy-to-use format. Lessons teach content and language objectives.

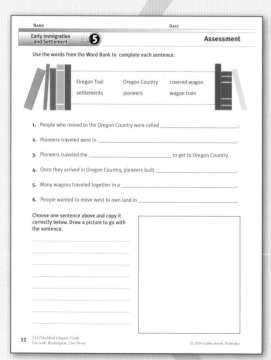

The Modified Assessment for this chapter assesses students' understanding of the key objectives of the chapter.

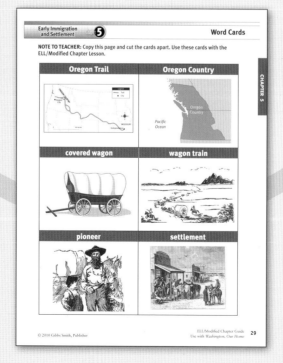

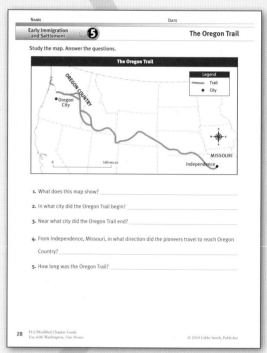

The Word Cards and Activity assist and reinforce students' learning of the chapter and prepares them for the assessment.

Books and Web Sites

Books

Frazier, Neta Lohnes. *Stout Hearted Seven.* New York City: Sterling Children's Books, 2006.

Galford, Ellen. *The Trail West: Exploring History Through Art.* Toucan Publishing, 2004.

Harness, Cheryl. *The Tragic Tale of Narcissa Whitman and a Faithful History of the Oregon Trail.* A Cheryl Harness History Series. Washington, D.C.: National Geographic, 2006.

Hermes, Patricia. *Westward to Home: Joshua's Oregon Trail Diary.* My America Series. New York: Scholastic, 2001.

Huntington, Karen. *Chief Timothy.* Kenmore, Washington: Education Resource Network, 1996.

Jeffrey, Julie Roy. *Converting the West: A Biography of Narcissa Whitman.* Oklahoma City: Norman Publishing, 1991.

Landau, Elaine. *The Oregon Trail.* True Books Series. New York: Children's Press, 2006.

Levine, Ellen. *If You Traveled West in a Covered Wagon.* New York: Scholastic, 1992.

Mercati, Cynthia. *Wagons, Ho! A Diary of the Oregon Trail.* Logan, Iowa: Perfection Learning Corp., 2000.

Olsen, Tod. *How to Get Rich on the Oregon Trail.* National Geographic Children's Books, 2009.

Wagner, Tricia Martineau. *It Happened on the Oregon Trail.* Guilford, CN: 2005.

Web Sites

The following Web sites provide resources or lesson plans for teachers and activities for students to help extend the lessons in this chapter. Go to **www.ExperienceStateHistory.com** for links to these Web sites.

Bureau of Land Management

Bureau of Land Management Web site has a 158-page resource booklet about the Oregon Trail. It was designed to be used to prepare students for a field trip to the Oregon Trail Interpretive Center in Baker City, Oregon. It is filled with interesting facts and activities about the Oregon Trail.

Historic Oregon City

The Historic Oregon City Web site has a feature on the End of the Oregon Trail Interpretive Center. This site provides lots of information about the end of the Oregon Trail.

The Oregon Trail

The Oregon Trail Web site provides information about the trail, historic sites along the trail, diaries and memoirs, and facts about the trail.

PBS

The PBS Web site has a feature, New Perspectives on the West, that provides many interesting stories about settling the West. Written for adults, this Web site provides perspectives that many other sites do not.

Serra School

The Serra School Web site provides a PowerPoint presentation that can be used to introduce this chapter or as a follow up to provide additional information on the Oregon Trail.

ThinkQuest

The ThinkQuest Web site has an interesting, kid-friendly site where students can read more about the supplies, hardships, and pioneers traveling on the Oregon Trail. In addition, the ThinkQuest Web site has a feature on pioneers that will help students learn more about the people who journeyed west.

Washing State Historical Society

Washington State Historical Society has a feature on the Web site titled Columbia Kids: Exploring Time and Place in the Pacific Northwest. This site provides interesting facts and stories about Washington and the Pacific Northwest.

The BIG Idea

Settlers Presentation

If the technology at your school is available, have students work in pairs to create a PowerPoint presentations about the settlers who came to Oregon Country. Allow students to use the Internet to find pictures and information about the different groups that settled in Oregon Country. When the projects are complete, allow students to share their presentations with the class.

If your school does not have the technology available for students to create PowerPoint presentations, have students create presentations on posterboards to hang around the classroom. Allow students to use the Internet, if possible, or find pictures and information in books from the library to copy and include on their posters.

Put Yourself in the Picture

Settle a Town

Tell students that the people in the painting on this page were pioneers coming to settle in the Northwest. Explain that during this time many people came to this area for different reasons.

Have students work in small groups to talk about why their town or city might have been settled. Tell students to discuss why people came to this area, why they stayed, and who they were. Have each group come up with one possible story to role play of why their city or town was settled.

Caption Answer

The people probably felt sad to leave their homes behind and tired from traveling on the trail.

There are oxen pulling the wagons and horses that men are riding.

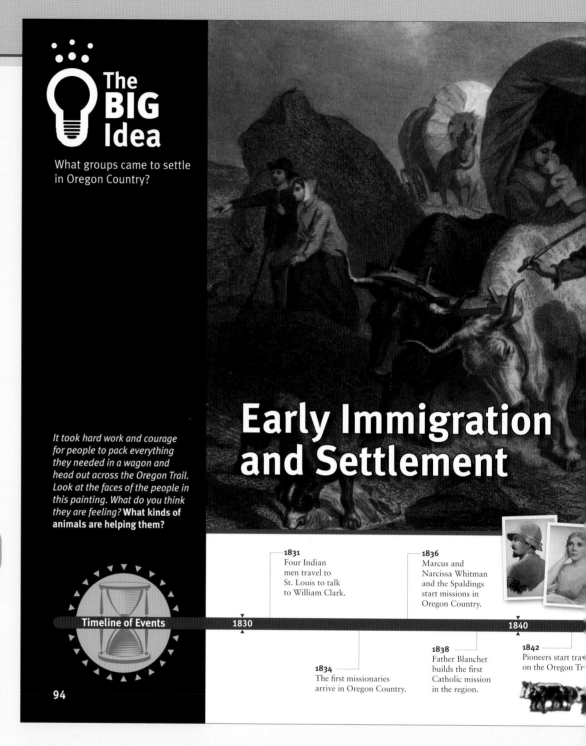

The BIG Idea

What groups came to settle in Oregon Country?

It took hard work and courage for people to pack everything they needed in a wagon and head out across the Oregon Trail. Look at the faces of the people in this painting. What do you think they are feeling? **What kinds of animals are helping them?**

Early Immigration and Settlement

Timeline of Events

94

1830

1831
Four Indian men travel to St. Louis to talk to William Clark.

1834
The first missionaries arrive in Oregon Country.

1836
Marcus and Narcissa Whitman and the Spaldings start missions in Oregon Country.

1838
Father Blanchet builds the first Catholic mission in the region.

1840

1842
Pioneers start trav on the Oregon Tr

CHAPTER 5

A new era of immigration and settlement began in Oregon Country. The first settlers to arrive, build homes, and stay were missionaries. They brought change to the people who lived here.

After the missionaries came a steady stream of pioneers on the Oregon Trail. They built cabins and farmed. Some of the towns and cities we know today started as small groups of log cabins next to a river. Was your town one of them?

1844
The George Washington Bush family settles in Bush Prairie.

1847
The Whitmans are killed by Indians. Many Protestant missions close.

1856
Mother Joseph comes to Vancouver.

1851
The first white settlers build homes in what is now Seattle.

1862
Walla Walla officially becomes a town. Tacoma starts with the building of a sawmill.

1850

1860

1846
Tumwater (formerly Bush Prairie) becomes the first American settlement along Puget Sound.

Olympia begins as a small settlement of log cabins.

95

Timeline Activity

Timeline Talk

Look at the first two events on the timeline. How might these two events have been related? What do you think the four Indian men said to William Clark?
Allow students to discuss how the two events might be related with a partner. Tell students that they will learn how these two events are related through their study of this chapter.

When were the first missions started in Oregon Country?
The first missions were started in 1836 by Marcus and Narcissa Whitman.

How many years passed between the time that the first missions began and when pioneers started traveling on the Oregon Trail?
Six years pass between the time the first missions began and the time pioneers started traveling on the Oregon Trail.

For how many years was the settlement Bush Prairie known by that name?
Bush Prairie was known by that name for two years. In 1846, Bush Prairie became Tumwater.

List the following towns in the order that they were settled, earliest to latest: Walla Walla, Olympia, Tacoma, and Seattle.
1846 Olympia; 1851 Seattle; 1862 Walla Walla & Tacoma

How long was the Whitman Mission in operation?
The Whitman Mission existed for about 11 years, from 1836 to 1847.

Standards

GLE 4.1.2

Understands how the following themes and developments help to define eras in Washington State history from time immemorial to 1889: Immigration and settlement (1811–1889)

PREPARE

Activator

Word Splash

A word splash is a great way to activate students' prior knowledge on a topic. Have students use each of the words and phrases provided from the lesson in a paragraph. Reading the paragraphs will give an idea about the students' prior knowledge.

Word Study

Parts of Speech

On the board, share an example of a dictionary entry with the class. Talk about the information dictionary entries provide, including the parts of speech for each word. Give students dictionaries and have them look up each of the Words to Understand. Instruct them to create a two-column chart to organize the words into nouns and verbs. Remind students that some words can be both a noun and a verb, depending on how they are used. Have students write a sentence to demonstrate how to use each Word to Understand for its parts of speech.

LESSON 1 The Missionaries

Key Ideas

- Missionaries came to the Northwest to teach their religion to the Indians.
- Missionaries also built schools and orphanages.

Words to Understand

convert
disease
massacre
missionary
orphanage
religion
tragedy

A Request for Missionaries

When the fur traders came to the Northwest, life for native people began to change. Hunting was no longer just a way of getting food. Some Indian hunters began killing animals to get their furs. They traded the furs for metal tools and other new things. With metal knives and axes, Native Americans could carve wood more easily. The wool blankets they got were colorful and warm.

Some Indians believed that these things the fur traders owned were gifts from powerful spirits or gods. They began to wonder about the traders' religion. They thought learning about it would help them understand the white people's ways.

Three Nez Perce and one Flathead Indian went all the way to St. Louis to talk to Captain William Clark. They had heard about him when Lewis and Clark visited the Northwest. The Indians told Clark they would like to learn about the white people's religion.

A missionary speaks to a group of Indians. **Who else besides Indians is pictured in this group?**

Washington, Our Home

Words to Understand

convert (p. 98) *to change another person's religious beliefs*

disease (p. 100) *sickness*

massacre (p. 101) *the violent murder of a large group of people*

missionary (p. 97) *a person who tries to teach his or her religion to others*

orphanage (p. 103) *a home for children who have no parents*

religion (p. 97) *beliefs, practices, and worship of God or the supernatural*

tragedy (p. 100) *a horrible event*

A Words to Understand activity for this lesson is available in the *Student Guide.*

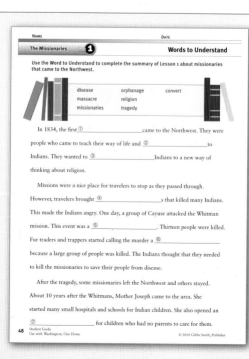

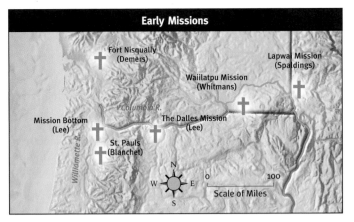

Early Missions

Fort Nisqually (Demers)
Lapwai Mission (Spaldings)
Waiilatpu Mission (Whitmans)
Columbia R.
Mission Bottom (Lee)
The Dalles Mission (Lee)
St. Pauls (Blanchet)
Willamette R.

Scale of Miles
0   100

Both Catholics and Protestants opened missions in Oregon Country. **Along what rivers did the missionaries settle?**

Missionaries Come to the Indians

Newspapers printed the story of the Indians' visit to Clark. Churches heard about this request. Before long, missionaries headed to Oregon Country. These **missionaries** were men and women who came to teach their way of life and religion to Native Americans. **Religion** has to do with beliefs about God. The missionaries were the first Americans to build homes and stay in the Northwest.

"Hear! Hear! Who will respond to the call from beyond the Rocky Mountains? . . . Let two . . . men, [without] families, . . . live with them and teach Christ to them."

—Written in the journal of the Methodist Missionary Society

Jason Lee and Daniel Lee were the first to answer the request of the Nez Perce. The Lees were Methodist ministers. Instead of settling with the Nez Perce, they decided to settle in the Willamette Valley. The Indian people there did not take to the white people's ways. Their children did not like the strict rules of the mission school. Jason Lee went back east but later returned with more settlers.

Some members of the Hudson's Bay Company were Catholics. They wanted priests. Father Francis Blanchet answered the call. He spent most of his time with trappers, not the Indians. But soon other Catholic missionaries came.

Some missionaries were Protestant. Others were Catholic. Both groups were Christian.

Early Immigration and Settlement

97

GLE 4.2.1 — STANDARDS block

STANDARDS

GLE 4.2.1
Understands and analyzes how individuals caused change in Washington State history.

TEACH

Talk About It

A Request for Missionaries
(From page 96)

How did hunting change for native people when fur traders came to the Northwest?
Native people began hunting to get furs for trading.

Why did four Indians travel to St. Louis to talk to Captain William Clark?
They told him they would like to learn about the white people's religion.

Missionaries Come to the Indians

Why did missionaries come to Oregon Country?
Men and women heard about the Indians' visit to Captain William Clark and came to teach their way of life and religion to the Native Americans.

Caption Answers

(From page 96) There is a missionary teaching a group of Indians, mountain men, and explorers.

Missionaries settled along the Willamette and Columbia Rivers.

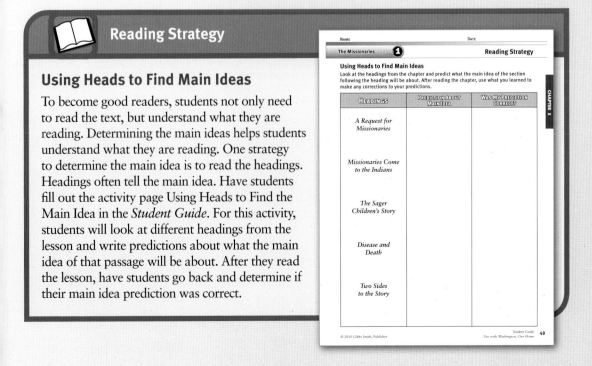

Reading Strategy

Using Heads to Find Main Ideas

To become good readers, students not only need to read the text, but understand what they are reading. Determining the main ideas helps students understand what they are reading. One strategy to determine the main idea is to read the headings. Headings often tell the main idea. Have students fill out the activity page Using Heads to Find the Main Idea in the *Student Guide*. For this activity, students will look at different headings from the lesson and write predictions about what the main idea of that passage will be about. After they read the lesson, have students go back and determine if their main idea prediction was correct.

NAME _____ **DATE** _____

The Missionaries   Lesson 1   **Reading Strategy**

Using Heads to Find Main Ideas
Look at the headings from the chapter and predict what the main idea of the section following the heading will be about. After reading the chapter, use what you learned to make any corrections to your predictions.

HEADINGS	PREDICTION ABOUT MAIN IDEA	WAS MY PREDICTION CORRECT?
A Request for Missionaries		
Missionaries Come to the Indians		
The Sager Children's Story		
Disease and Death		
Two Sides to the Story		

CHAPTER 5

© 2010 Gibbs Smith, Publisher   Student Guide 49   Use with *Washington, Our Home*

Talk About It

Protestant Missionaries— The Whitmans and the Spaldings

Where did the Whitmans and Spaldings stop to spend time before traveling on to Walla Walla?
They stopped at Fort Vancouver and spent time with Dr. Vancouver and the other people there.

Where did the Whitmans and the Spaldings end up staying and building missions?
The Whitmans stayed in a place near today's Walla Walla, and the Spaldings went to a place near the Nez Perce in today's Idaho.

What was the day in the life of a missionary like?
Missionaries worked hard. Their days were filled with praying, teaching and doing many chores. Life was often lonely, far away from relatives and friends.

Caption Answer

There are buildings that look like homes where travelers could stop to rest.

Differentiated Paths

Summarizing Using Main Ideas

The Reading Strategy for this lesson teaches students to use the heads in the text to learn about the main ideas of reading passages. Heads often tell the main idea.

ELL and Special Needs

Have ELL and special needs students summarize the lesson using the heads as a guide. You may choose to have students with limited writing skills verbally summarize the lesson's main ideas by looking at the heads in the book. For students with more advanced English skills, have them use the main heads in the lesson in a short paragraph summarizing the lesson.

Gifted Learners

Have students use headings from chapters 3, 4, and 5 to write a summary of what they have learned about Washington's history so far this year. Encourage students to include many headings in order to include many details about what they have learned.

Protestant Missionaries— The Whitmans and the Spaldings

Marcus and Narcissa Whitman

Among the early missionaries were a doctor named Marcus Whitman and his wife, Narcissa. They came west with another couple, Henry and Eliza Spalding, and some fur traders.

For seven long months, across plains and mountains, they made their journey. Finally, the group reached Fort Vancouver. They stayed there and rested. Dr. McLoughlin was very kind to them. He gave them food and a place to stay. He asked Narcissa to help teach music to his daughter and the other children. Narcissa wrote in her diary:

"This morning I visited the school to hear the children sing. There were about fifty-one children, who have French fathers and Indian mothers. . . . English is spoken by only a few."

After a time, the Whitmans left Fort Vancouver. They traveled to a place near what is now Walla Walla. The Cayuse Indians lived in villages there. The Spaldings went to a place near the Nez Perce tribe in what is now Idaho.

Missionaries tried to convert the Indians to a new way of thinking about religion. To **convert** a person means to change that person's beliefs.

The missionaries worked hard. Their days were filled with praying, teaching, farming, and doing many chores. Life was often lonely so far away from relatives and friends.

The Whitman Mission grew to become a busy community near the river. The Whitmans hoped other settlers would come. In one year, over 5,000 travelers stopped at the mission to rest and get supplies. **What do you see in the picture that shows the mission was a resting place?**

98   *Washington, Our Home*

Mission Life

A mission was a small religious community where the missionaries and others lived. Each mission had homes, farms, a church, and a school.

The missionaries held religious meetings. They also taught the Indians to raise animals, grow crops, grind wheat to make flour, and weave wool into cloth.

Most missionaries learned Indian languages. They also taught English so the Indians could read the Bible. Indian people sometimes lived and worked at the missions, but usually they came to attend church or school.

The Sager Children's Story

Catherine Sager was just nine years old when her family decided to go west. She had two older brothers and three younger sisters. Another baby sister was born on the trip.

Travel with a wagon train was pleasant for a while. Then one day, Catherine got caught under the wagon and broke her leg. Then her parents got sick. First her father died, and later her mother died. The seven Sager children were alone.

Other adults took care of the children until they reached the Whitman Mission. There the children received a warm welcome and a happy surprise. Dr. and Mrs. Whitman adopted the whole family. The Whitmans' only daughter had drowned at age two, so they were happy to have a family again.

The children studied at the mission school and helped with chores. They had three peaceful years. Then trouble struck again. The Whitmans and some of the other people at the mission were killed. Four of the Sager sisters survived. When they grew up, they gave speeches and wrote about their lives. Here is part of what Catherine wrote about mission life:

Mrs. Whitman and the girls did the work in the summer. Each of us had her tasks. When the work was done, we all sat in a large room at our sewing, save one of us, who read aloud.

In the spring, the evenings were spent in the garden putting in seeds. Sometimes the boys would bring horses for us to ride. At times we would go with the doctor to visit the lodges where the Indians were sick.

Catherine Sager Pringle, Elizabeth Sager Helm, and Matilda Sager

This doll once belonged to Catherine Sager. **How is it different from dolls today?**

Early Immigration and Settlement

99

Literature Link

The Stout-Hearted Seven

The Stout-Hearted Seven: Orphaned on the Trail by Neta Lohnes Frazier is based on a true story originally written by one of the Sager survivors. This book makes a great read-aloud. Have students keep a journal and write their responses to the book every few pages. You may wish to have them write details of the Oregon Trail talked about in the book, or connect parts of the book to themselves, for example. Reading the story about the children will make the time period come alive for your class. Having students keep a response journal while listening to the book will support listening comprehension.

Talk About It

Mission Life

What types of buildings were found at missions?
Missions had homes, farms, churches, and schools.

What things did Indians learn at missions?
They learned about the religions of the settlers. They also learned to raise animals, grow crops, grind wheat to make flour, and weave wool into cloth. They learned English so that they could read the Bible.

The Sager Children's Story

What was the first unlucky thing that happened to the Sager family?
Catherine Sager got caught under the wagon and broke her leg.

What surprise did the Sager children receive when they reached the Whitman Mission?
All of the Sager children were adopted by the Whitmans.

What was the final tragedy to come upon the Sager children?
The Whitmans and some of the Sager children were killed in the attack on the Whitman Mission.

How was life for the Sager children at the Whitman Mission different from your life today? How is it the same?
Encourage students to reread the excerpt from Catherine Sager on this page to find similarities and differences.

Caption Answer

The doll appears to be made out of leather or animal skin. Most dolls today have movable arms and legs.

Talk About It

Disease and Death

Why were the Cayuse unhappy with people who came to stay at the Whitman Mission?
Fur traders and travelers from the East were sick with measles or smallpox and spread the diseases to the Indians. Many Indians died from horrible diseases.

Why were the Indians angry at Dr. Whitman when they got sick?
They blamed Dr. Whitman for not making the people well. Some thought he tried to poison the Indians so the settlers could have Indian land and animals.

The Whitman Massacre

What were some of the frustrations the Indians felt that lead to the Whitman Massacre?
Indians had been frustrated with settlers and travelers bringing disease to the region. They were angry with Dr. Whitman for not making them well when they were sick.

Why were the 47 women and children who were taken captive finally released?
Fur traders in other settlements heard what had happened. The traders gave the Indians 62 blankets, 63 cotton shirts, 37 pounds of tobacco, 600 loads of ammunition, and 12 guns to get the captives back.

What happened to many other missions after news of the attack on the Whitman Mission spread?
Many other missions closed. Mission families were afraid.

Caption Answers

The might show the Indians as the victims.

This picture shows the Indian point of view. The Indian is very sick.

Linking the Present to the Past

Encourage students to do research to find the answer to this question. Explain to students that vaccines were created to prevent these diseases, but sometimes people who haven't been vaccinated still get these diseases today.

Pictures can tell a story. What story does this picture tell about the Whitman Massacre? **How might the picture be different if an Indian artist had made it?**

The Indians had not been around diseases like measles and smallpox before. When the Cayuse came down with measles, about half of the tribe died. **Which point of view does this picture represent?**

Disease and Death

At first, the Cayuse Indians and the Whitmans got along. Some Cayuse men, women, and children often visited the mission. However, as time went by, the Cayuse were not happy to have so many new settlers cross their land. Even worse, some fur traders and travelers from the East were sick with measles or smallpox. Many Indians died when they got these horrible *diseases*. Most were older people and young children. Families cried for the loss of their children. It was a horrible time.

The Cayuse were angry. Almost half of their tribe had died of measles. Dr. Whitman had tried to help the Indians, but his simple medicines could not save them. The Indians blamed Dr. Whitman for not making the people well. Some thought he had tried to poison the Indians so the settlers could have Indian land and animals.

The Whitman Massacre

One day, a group of Cayuse attacked the Whitman Mission. They broke into homes and other buildings and killed 13 people, including the Whitmans and the two Sager boys. Then the Indians carried away 47 women and children and took them to an Indian village. The children and their mothers were scared. What would happen to them?

As soon as fur traders in other settlements heard what happened, the traders went to Indian villages to find the captives. After a meeting with Indian leaders, the traders gave the Indians 62 blankets, 63 cotton shirts, 37 pounds of tobacco, 600 loads of ammunition, and 12 guns to get the captives back.

For both sides, it was a time of *tragedy*, or great suffering. After the killings, many of the other missions closed. Mission families were too afraid to stay.

Linking the Present to the Past

Measles and smallpox killed thousands of people. Do people today still get these diseases? What has been done to prevent them?

 Math Activity

Jack's Math

The National Park Service has a Web site called Jack's Math. Jack was a ranger at Whitman Mission for nearly 30 years. He knew about the out-of-doors, including how to measure trees, rivers, and ponds. This site includes instructions on how to use the same techniques he used to measure trees or ponds at your home or school playground. A link to the Jack's Math site can be found at **www.ExperienceStateHistory.com**.

Two Sides to the Story

A *massacre* is the violent killing of a large group of people. After the Whitmans were killed, other missionaries and fur trappers started calling the murders a massacre. The Indians, on the other hand, said they had to kill the Whitmans to save their people from Dr. Whitman's poison.

An Oregon newspaper published many articles about the event. The first article here describes a meeting of Cayuse chiefs. The second is a letter from a girl who saw what happened. Read the two documents, and think about the different points of view.

A young Indian who understands English and slept in Dr. Whitman's room heard the Doctor, his wife, and Mr. Spalding [who was visiting] express their desire of possessing the Indians' lands and animals.

He also states that Mr. Spalding said to the Doctor: "Hurry and give medicines to the Indians, that they may soon die."

That for several years they had to [suffer] the deaths of their children and that . . . they were led to believe, that the whites had undertaken to kill them all.

. . . these are the motives [reasons], which made them . . . kill the Americans.

The principal chiefs of the Cayuse,
Printed in *The Oregon Spectator*
December 20, 1847

Dr. was sitting in the sitting room talking with Mrs. W. how gloomy things were, & things he had heard which were causing much anxiety, when there was some Indians came & sayed they wished medicine. He stepped into the kitchen where they were and were talking to them about their sickness & so on, when one of the Indians steped behind the Dr. and struck him on the head with a tomahock. That seemed to be the signal for the slaughter. One of the Sager boys was in the room with the Dr., he was struck down and his throat cut. Some men that were butchering a beef were shot and cut down. The miller at the mill was shot; a tailor working in his room was shot in his bowels and died that night. . . . Mrs. Whitman steped [sic] to the door window and was shot in the breast by a half breed that had stoped at the Dr. with the intention of staying all winter there.

Eliza Spalding Warren, 10-year-old witness

What Do You Think

- Do you think "massacre" is the right word for what happened at the Whitman Mission?

- Why do you think it is important to remember the sad, terrible parts of history as well as the good parts?

Early Immigration and Settlement   101

Writing Activity

Two Points of View Interview

Tell students to think as though they are newscasters who travel back in time to interview witnesses of the attack on the Whitman Mission. The first witness will be a Cayuse Indian and the second will be one of the Sager children. Have students write a dialogue of questions to ask the witnesses along with responses from both witnesses. Encourage students to think as if they were a Cayuse Indian, or a Sager child as they write their responses. Have students share their dialogues in small groups to compare their responses.

Standards

GLE 4.3.1
Understands that there are multiple perspectives regarding the interpretations of historical events and creates an historical account using multiple sources.

GLE 5.1.2
Evaluates the accuracy of primary and secondary sources.

Talk About It

Two Sides to the Story

After reading what the principal chiefs of the Cayuses said, what do you think about the reasons why the Indians attacked the Whitman Mission?
Encourage students to think about how they would have felt if they were a Cayuse Indian.

How did the 10-year-old girl describe the events?
She described them as very violent, scary events. She described how different people at the mission were killed.

How do you think the Indians felt at the time of the attack on the mission?
The Indians were probably very angry and wanted to attack the mission so their people could live in peace and health.

How do you think the girl and other people at the mission felt at the time of the attack?
They were probably afraid, and surprised about what was happening.

What Do You Think

After students read about the attack on the Whitman Mission, break the class into small groups to share their opinion. Tell students to support their opinion with facts from the chapter.

It is important to remember the sad, terrible parts so that we can learn from them. If we don't know about the sad parts of history, we might make the same mistakes again.

Talk About It

Catholic Missions

How were Catholic missions different from Protestant missions?

Catholic missions were built to serve traders who were already Catholic. They did not try to make big changes in the Indians' way of life.

How did the Indians feel about the Catholic missions?

The Indians felt that the Catholic missions were easier to accept. They were built primarily for traders so the Indians didn't feel like they were trying to change their way of life.

Linking the Present to the Past

Ask students why they think the Whitmans and Mother Joseph were chosen to represent our state in our nation's capitol.

Caption Answer

There is a cross on top of the building. It was probably put there to let people know that this building was a mission, or part of a mission.

Mother Joseph
(from page 103)

Mother Joseph was a hard-working woman who did a lot of good things and helped many people. Have students complete a Cause and Effect chart with things that Mother Joseph did for others, and the effects that her acts had on peoples' lives or the history of Washington. A Cause and Effect Chart can be found in the *Teacher Guide*.

Catholic Missions

After the Whitmans were killed, many Protestant missions closed. However, some Catholic missions stayed open.

Catholic missions were different. Catholic priests had come to Fort Vancouver to serve the fur traders who were already Catholic. They did not try to make big changes in the Indians' way of life. Instead, they taught Bible stories and prayers. As a result, Catholic missions were easier for the Indians to accept.

The best-known Catholic missionary in the Northwest came to Washington about 10 years after the Whitmans. Her name was Mother Joseph.

Linking the Present to the Past

In our nation's capitol building, each state has two statues of important people. Washington's statues are of Dr. Whitman and Mother Joseph.

St. Paul's Indian Mission was built near Kettle Falls. **What do you see on top of the building? Why do you think it was put there?**

Washington, Our Home

 Social Studies Activity

Missions in Oregon Country

We learned in this lesson that there were groups of Catholic and Protestant missionaries who came to Oregon Country. Missions were busy places with lots of activities going on. Missions made an impact on the history of Oregon Country. Have students work in groups to create a poster presentation on one of the missions or groups of missionaries. Encourage students to use books and resources from the Internet to find more information. Have students present any information on the missions or groups of missionaries that wasn't mentioned in the lesson. Tell students to include pictures, maps, and facts on their poster.

Mother Joseph

If you ever think one person can't cause change, think of the story of Mother Joseph.

Esther Pariseau was a very talented young woman living in Canada. At age 20, she was already skilled in building and working with tools. When a new community for Catholic women opened, Esther joined and became a nun. She learned many skills, from nursing and gardening to running a business.

Later, Esther led four other nuns to a new Catholic mission in Vancouver, Washington. She willingly made the difficult trip, which took more than a month, "to care for the poor and the sick, educate the children, and bring the light of Christ into the lives of all we met." She also received a new name—Mother Joseph.

Mother Joseph started many small hospitals and schools for Indian children. She also opened *orphanages*, or homes for children who had no parents to care for them.

Although it was unusual at the time for a woman to do men's work, Mother Joseph helped build many of the buildings herself. She drew up the plans, checked the men's work, laid bricks, and carved beautiful woodwork. She raised money for her projects by traveling around the country on horseback and riverboats with other nuns. In the rough towns and mining camps of the Northwest, the gentle woman in a black robe asked for money. The miners often gave it to her.

Mother Joseph worked all over the Northwest until she was almost 80 years old. One of her finest buildings, Providence Academy in Vancouver, built in 1873, is still there today.

LESSON 1 What Did You Learn?

1. Why did missionaries come to the Northwest?
2. Why did the Cayuse Indians become angry with the Whitmans and other settlers?
3. In what ways did missionaries help with the settlement of the Northwest?

Early Immigration and Settlement   103

LESSON 1 What Did You Learn?

1. *Missionaries came to the Northwest to teach their way of life and religion to the Indians. Three Nez Perce and one Flathead Indian went all the way to St. Louis to talk to Captain William Clark about the white people's religion.*
2. *The Indians blamed Dr. Whitman for not making the people well. They thought he had tried to poison the Indians so the settlers could have Indian land and animals. The Indians were angry with settlers and travelers for bringing disease.*
3. *Missionaries helped build relationships with the Indians, and they built missions that served as stopping places for settlers and travelers coming to the Northwest.*

Reflect on students' understanding of the early missions in Oregon Country and the effects missionaries had on the history of Washington. You can evaluate students' understanding through discussion or evaluation of activities completed in this lesson. The following activities will serve as another way of assessing students' understanding of the key objectives of this lesson.

Writing Activity

Diamante Poem

Have students write a diamante poem about the early missions in Oregon Country. Encourage students to use information from this lesson to write their poem. A Diamante Poem activity is available in the *Student Guide*.

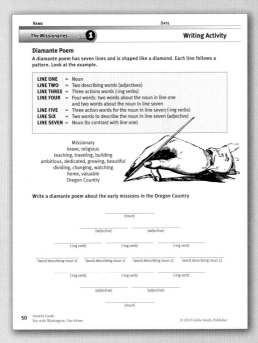

 Standards

GLE 2.1.1
Understands and analyzes the costs and benefits of people's decisions to move and relocate to meet their needs and wants.

GLE 3.2.3
Understands that the geographic features of the Pacific Northwest have influenced the movement of people.

PREPARE

Activator

Packing List

Ask students to imagine what it might have been like to live in the 1850s. Tell them their family has been living in the Northeast but has decided to leave the busy city to move to the Northwest where they can get free land. Explain that they will have to leave or sell many of their belongings. Have students complete the Packing List activity in the *Student Guide*.

Word Study

Compound Words

Explain to students that a compound word is made up of more than one word. Write the words *hardship* and *homestead* on the board. Ask students to think of other compound words. Explain that the meaning of the compound word is usually very different from the meanings of the individual words.

LESSON 2 | The Oregon Trail

Key Ideas

- The pioneers made a hard trek across the Oregon Trail to get free land.
- They made new lives in Oregon Country.
- The movement west changed life for Native Americans.

Words to Understand

benefit
cost
frontier
hardship
homestead
immigrant
pioneer
slavery

Wagons Head West

Long ago, there were no roads or railroads leading to the Pacific Northwest. Missionaries and other settlers who wanted to move to Oregon Country had only one choice. They would have to make their own trail across America. The route became known as the Oregon Trail.

The trail started in Missouri. Few people lived west of the frontier towns there. A *frontier* is the edge of settled land.

Most of the settlers who started on the trail came from cities east of Missouri. Some were immigrants from Europe and other countries. An *immigrant* is a person who comes to live in a new country.

The trail followed rivers most of the way. Travelers on the trail crossed the flat plains, then went on through the steep Rocky Mountains. Once they got to Oregon Country, they were happy to stop and rest at the Whitman Mission. Most of the settlers then followed the trail on to Fort Vancouver. After another rest, they spread out and started farms and towns.

Elijah White, a former missionary, brought 100 settlers from Missouri to Oregon's Willamette Valley. Their route became known as the Oregon Trail. **What landforms do you see in this picture? Do you think they were easier to cross than rivers and mountains?**

Washington, Our Home

Words to Understand

benefit (p. 110) *what you get in return for paying the cost*

cost (p. 110) *what you give up to get what you want*

frontier (p. 104) *a region on the edge of settled land*

hardship (p. 106) *suffering*

homestead (p. 107) *to claim, farm, and improve land*

immigrant (p. 104) *a person who moves into a country*

pioneer (p. 105) *a person who is among the first settlers to move to a new place*

slavery (p. 107) *when people are bought and sold and forced to work for their owners without pay*

A Words to Understand activity for this lesson is available in the *Student Guide*.

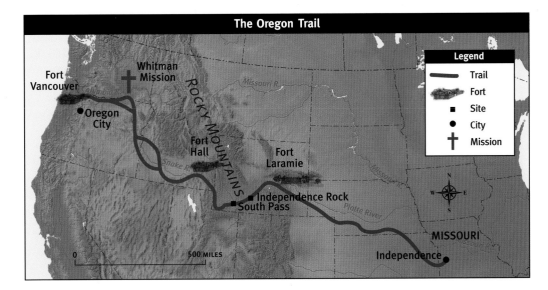

The Oregon Trail

Legend
- Trail
- Fort
- ■ Site
- ● City
- ✝ Mission

Pioneers

The early settlers are called *pioneers* because they were among the first people to move to a new place and start settlements or towns. Large groups of pioneers traveled along the trail. They carried their things in wooden wagons pulled by oxen or mules. One group followed another, making a long line called a wagon train. The settlers' horses and cattle walked behind. The group moved very slowly, often just 12 miles a day. (Today, you can travel 12 miles in 12 minutes by car!)

Day and Night

During the day, there was work to do. Children gathered firewood as the wagons moved slowly along. Some of the men rode off on horseback to hunt. If they were lucky, they might shoot a deer or a buffalo for everyone to eat. On other days, food, firewood, and water were hard to find.

At night, the wagons formed a large circle. In the center of the circle, each family built a fire and cooked dinner. People often sang songs and shared stories. They slept in the wagons or on the ground. Early the next morning, after breakfast, they started walking again. This went on day after day for many months.

Follow the trail to see where the pioneers traveled. **Where did the trail start? Where did it end? What rivers did the trail follow?**

"Sometimes the dust is so great that the drivers cannot see their teams of animals, though the sun is shining brightly."

—Elizabeth Wood, 1851

Early Immigration and Settlement

105

Reading Strategy

Making an Outline

Making an outline is a useful tool for all readers. Outlines give readers an overview of the main idea and key ideas of a chapter. Lesson outlines generally have two parts, the main topic and the subtopics. Have students look at Lesson 1 of this chapter and find the headings and subheadings. As a class, create an outline for Lesson 1 on the board. Ask students to complete the Making an Outline activity for Lesson 2 in the *Student Guide*. Have students check their outline with a partner.

NAME _____ DATE _____

The Oregon Trail Lesson **2**   **Reading Strategy**

Making An Outline
Use headings and subheadings from Lesson 2 to complete the outline.

Title: The Oregon Trail

I. Wagons Head West
   A. _____
   B. Day and Night
   C. _____

II. Why Did They Come?
   A. _____

III. Go to the Source
   A. _____

IV. George Washington Bush
   A. _____
   B. _____

V. Costs and Benefits of Making the Trip
   A. _____
   B. _____

VI. At the End of the Trail

VII. Made By Hand
   A. _____

VIII. Changes for Native Americans

© 2010 Gibbs Smith, Publisher   Student Guide **53**
Use with *Washington, Our Home*

TEACH

Talk About It

Wagons Head West *(From page 104)*

Why was the Oregon Trail created?
Missionaries and other settlers who wanted to move to Oregon Country had no roads to travel on, so they created the Oregon Trail.

Why do you think the trail followed rivers most of the time?
Encourage students to think about what resources the rivers provided to travelers as they traveled through the wilderness.

Why do you think it was helpful to have a marked trail for all travelers to follow?
Encourage students to think about the benefits of following a marked trail instead of traveling into the unknown.

Pioneers

How did pioneers travel on the Oregon Trail?
Pioneers traveled in wooden wagons and followed one another to create a wagon train. The group traveled very slowly.

Day and Night

What were some of the chores that pioneers had to do during the day as they traveled?
Possible answers include gathering firewood, hunting, and finding food and water.

What were nights like for pioneers traveling west?
All of the wagons formed a circle and families often built fires in the middle. People sometimes sang and shared stories after eating dinner. Pioneers slept in their wagons or on the ground.

Caption Answers

(From page 104) There are hills in this part of the trail. They were much easier to cross than steep mountains and rushing rivers.

The trail started in Missouri and ended in Oregon Country. The trail followed the Platte, Snake, and Columbia Rivers. Encourage students to study and discuss the physical features along the trail.

 **Standards**

GLE 3.1.1
Constructs and uses maps to explain the movement of people.

Talk About It

Danger on the Trail

What were some of the hardships travelers on the Oregon Trail faced?

There were hot and dusty weeks of walking under the burning sun. On other days it rained, and the wagons got stuck in the mud. Sometimes there was fighting with the Indians. Crossing rivers could be hard. Crossing steep mountains was even harder.

Pioneer Diaries

Describe some of the experiences that Lydia Rudd wrote about in her journal.

Encourage students to look back at the journal entries and discuss some of Lydia Rudd's experiences with a partner.

Caption Answer

There are small islands in the river to help pioneers cross the river more easily. They could stop and rest on the small islands, and the water probably wasn't as deep in this part of the river.

Pioneer Diaries

Some women in the wagon trains kept diaries of their trips. Lydia Allen Rudd wrote these notes:

June 2. We have had a [hard] day. Our road has been sand hills. The sand is six inches deep in places.

August 14. Bought a salmon fish from an Indian today, weighing 7 or 8 pounds. Gave him an old shirt, some bread, and a sewing needle.

September 1. Traveled 14 miles today on the Blue Mountains. Climbed up and down the highest hills that I ever saw a person pass over. Very steep and rocky. No water for our [animals].

Danger on the Trail

The trip across the Oregon Trail was a brave adventure. But it was not easy. Every day, it seemed, there were problems and dangers to face. It was a time of great *hardship*, or suffering.

There were hot and dusty weeks of walking under the burning sun. On other days it rained, and the wagons got stuck in the mud.

The land the pioneers crossed was home to different Indian tribes. With so many pioneers hunting wild animals for food and so many cattle eating the wild grass, the Indian people worried that there would not be enough for everyone. Sometimes this led to fighting.

Crossing rivers could be hard. There were no bridges. Sometimes the travelers found a shallow place to walk across the river. At other times, they had to build wooden rafts to carry the wagons across the swift river. Sometimes animals and people drowned.

Crossing steep mountains was even harder. There were trees and bushes that had to be chopped down to make a trail. The travelers and their tired animals did the best they could. They tried to find open routes, called passes, through the mountains. But with no roads, these mountain crossings were always hard.

In this painting, the artist shows a wagon train crossing a river. **Why do you think the people chose to cross here instead of at another place in the river?**

106

Washington, Our Home

 Map Activity

Cooperative Groups

The Oregon Trail

(From page 105)

Divide the class into small groups. Have each group come up with their own creative way to create a map of the Oregon Trail. Students may choose to make a salt dough relief map, a map on a poster board with yarn, or a map using a computer program. Each map should include the following items:

- Starting location
- The destination
- The route
- Tribes along the route
- Geographic features (physical characteristics) that affected the route
- A title
- Captions or symbols that describe the movement of the settlers
- A legend
- A compass

Ahead in the distance lay open land as far as the eye could see. **What do you think the people thought when they saw the land spread out before them?**

Why Did They Come?

Why did so many people move so far and make such a long trip? There were many reasons.

Some people came for adventure. They wanted a chance to explore a beautiful new place and start a new life.

Some wanted to get away from problems in the East. One of those problems was *slavery*. African people were bought and sold and forced to work for their owners for the rest of their lives. Many settlers wanted to put slavery far behind them. But the main reason they came was for land.

The Promise of Land

At the end of the Oregon Trail there was a great deal of good land. In Oregon Country, families could *homestead*. That means they could claim a piece of land, farm it for a certain number of years, and then own it for free or at a very low cost.

At first, every family that came to Oregon Country got a large piece of land to homestead. Later, when the best farmland was gone, settlers came to start stores, hotels, or maybe even doctors' offices.

Early Immigration and Settlement

107

Background Info

Animals of Choice

Oxen were the best choice for pulling wagons. They ate prairie grass, could pull heavy loads, and were not as likely to be stolen by Indians as horses were. Those who could afford it took an extra team in case anything happened to the animals on the trip. Cows were taken along to provide milk. Families took horses for riding and exploring and to have in the new home. Chickens, goats, and dogs also walked the thousands of miles to Oregon Country.

Go to the Source

GLE 5.2.2

Understands the main ideas from an artifact, primary source, or secondary source describing an issue or event.

Examine a Secondary Source

The book that this excerpt is taken from is a book written especially for kids. There are many books written on the topic of the Oregon Trail. See the Books and Web Sites section for this chapter. If possible, gather some of these books or see your librarian for other books about the Oregon Trail. Create a small classroom library with books on the topic. Encourage students to find books to add to the classroom library. Tell students that books written about the Oregon Trail that give facts can be a great primary or secondary source.

Social Studies Activity

Web of Main Ideas

After studying the information on this page, have students choose at least two main ideas from the excerpt of *Westward Ho!* Have students complete a web with details from the excerpt that support each main idea. The main idea should be at the center of the web, surrounded by details that support the main idea. A web graphic organizer is available in the graphic organizer section of the *Teacher Guide*.

✖ Go to the Source
Examine a Secondary Source

A book about the Oregon Trail can be a wonderful secondary source. Reading the book will help you learn about the long trip along the trail. One great book is *Westward Ho! An Activity Guide to the Wild West*, by Laurie Carlson. The book has a lot of interesting facts about travel on the trail. It also has many crafts you can make. Read this piece from the book and answers the questions.

As the trip wore on, the oxen and horses grew tired and weak. People began to toss out heavy items such as furniture, clothing, and tools to lighten the load for the weak animals. By the middle of the trip the trail was scattered with people's clothing and blankets, wooden barrels, chests, stoves, tools, and mirrors.

Then supplies gave out. People started to barter with each other. Precious dishes and fancy items were of no value—everyone wanted a sack full of beans instead!

No matter the hardship, people still had fun on the way. They marveled at the towering Rocky Mountains and the herds of buffalo that carpeted the plains. They saw bubbling springs of soda water, hot springs, and ice caves. They saw more country than they had ever seen in their lives. It was a time of excitement and wonder.

(From *Westward Ho! An Activity Guide to the Wild West*, by Laurie Carlson. Reprinted by permission of the publisher.)

LOOK	THINK	DECIDE
What words describe the Oregon Trail?	What were some of the supplies travelers were running out of?	What would you have packed to take with you on the Oregon Trail? What would you have thrown out to lighten your load?

108

Washington, Our Home

LOOK	THINK	DECIDE
Possible answers include hardship, fun, Rocky Mountains, herds of buffalo, springs of water, hot springs, ice caves, excitement, and wonder.	*Possible answers could include food, beans, or other items necessary for survival.*	*Students' answers should reflect knowledge of items necessary to survive on the trail. Encourage students to think about what they would need the most and what they could do without.*

George Washington Bush

George Washington Bush was a tall, strong man. He fought in two wars. Then he worked in Oregon Country as a trapper for the Hudson's Bay Company. He left and traveled to Missouri, where he farmed and raised cattle. Bush was a free African American, but Missouri was a state that allowed slavery. It was a hard place for a free black man to make a life.

Bush married a white woman named Isabelle. She had worked as a nurse. She also helped on the farm. When the couple had children, the children were not allowed to go to public schools. George and Isabelle and their five sons decided to go west on the Oregon Trail. They hoped to find a better life in the Northwest.

A Sad Surprise

When the family arrived at Fort Vancouver after seven long months of travel, they got a sad surprise. Black settlers were not welcome in the Willamette Valley. Leaders there had just voted to keep out blacks.

Disappointed and angry at being turned away, Bush and other settlers headed north. Near today's Olympia, the group built one large house where all the families lived until they could build their own log homes. They plowed the ground and farmed.

Nisqually Indians taught the new settlers to gather oysters, dig clams, and fish for trout and salmon. They showed the settlers how to weave grass mats to sleep on and to place over the walls of their homes. The mats kept out cold winter winds.

A Good Neighbor

Bush was known as a good farmer and a kind neighbor. When other settlers moved to the region, he gave them seeds and helped them start farms.

The Bushes were the first African American settlers in the Puget Sound region of Washington. Others came to join them. Bush and his settlement also helped give the United States a stronger claim to the land.

P O R T R A I T

Bush Prairie

The town of Bush Prairie was named for George Washington Bush.

Turned away by other settlers, George and Isabelle Bush started their own settlement.

GLE 4.2.1
Understands and analyzes how individuals caused change in Washington State history.

Talk About It

George Washington Bush

Why did George Washington Bush and his wife decide to come west on the Oregon Trail?
They hoped to make a better life for their children. They had been living in Missouri where slavery was allowed and their children weren't allowed to go to a public school.

What did George Washington Bush discover when he reached Fort Vancouver?
He got a sad surprise. Black settlers were not welcome in the Willamette Valley.

How were Indians near today's Olympia helpful to George Washington Bush and other settlers?
Indian neighbors taught the new settlers to gather oysters, dig clams, and fish for trout and salmon. They showed the settlers how to weave grass mats to sleep on and to place over the walls of their homes.

Why was the Bush family so important to Washington's history?
The Bush family were the first African American settlers in the Puget Sound region of Washington State. Bush and his settlement also helped give the United States a stronger claim to the land.

P O R T R A I T

George Washington Bush

George Washington Bush promoted the movement of African American people to Washington State. Bush was known as a good farmer and a kind, helpful neighbor. Tell students to find details mentioned on this page and in other books that support the idea that George Washington Bush was important to the history of Washington. After gathering details about Bush, have students write a persuasive essay about Bush. Encourage students to persuade the readers of their essays that George Washington Bush is one of the most important people from the history of Washington State.

Talk About It

Costs and Benefits of Making the Trip

What are some things in your life that have costs and benefits?
Possible answers include learning to play a sport, working on a school project, making a new friend, and learning to play an instrument.

With a partner, have students discuss what other costs and benefits there might be for traveling on the Oregon Trail. After giving students time to discuss, ask students to share what they talked about with the whole class.

At the End of the Trail

What happened once travelers reached the end of the Oregon Trail?
Leaders of the Hudson's Bay Company directed travelers where to settle. They were told to go south of the Columbia River.

Why did other travelers want to settle north of the Columbia River?
They had heard about the land north of the Columbia River. They knew of the excellent harbors of Puget Sound, where ships could anchor and bring in supplies.

Costs and Benefits of Making the Trip

When you really want something, you often have to give up something to get it.

- What you give up is the **cost**.
- What you get in return is the **benefit**.

When people decided to move west, they had to weigh the costs and benefits. Look at the chart to see some of the costs and benefits of coming to Oregon Country. Can you think of any others?

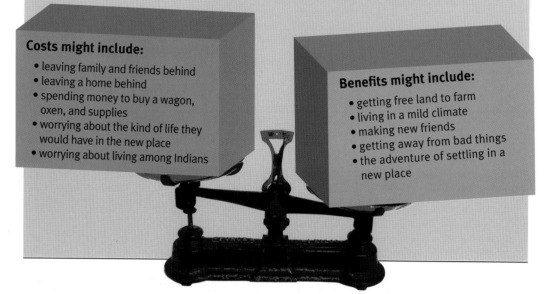

Costs might include:
- leaving family and friends behind
- leaving a home behind
- spending money to buy a wagon, oxen, and supplies
- worrying about the kind of life they would have in the new place
- worrying about living among Indians

Benefits might include:
- getting free land to farm
- living in a mild climate
- making new friends
- getting away from bad things
- the adventure of settling in a new place

At the End of the Trail

As the pioneers arrived in Oregon Country, leaders of the Hudson's Bay Company at Fort Vancouver directed them where to settle. They told them to go south of the Columbia River, to what is now Oregon. Most of the settlers started farms and towns in the Willamette Valley there.

The rich land, clear rivers, and fresh air seemed like a great reward for the long journey to the West. There were animals to hunt and trees to cut for timber. The ocean provided seafood. The climate was mild, and the soil was rich.

However, other settlers had heard about the land north of the Columbia River. They knew of the excellent harbors of Puget

---

 Social Studies Activity

Is It Worth the Cost?

Organize students into small groups to discuss the costs and benefits of traveling on the Oregon Trail. Once students are in groups, tell students to decide if they think the benefits of the trip were worth the cost. Encourage students to take turns sharing their opinions with the group. After allowing students time to discuss their opinions, ask the class if anyone changed their mind after hearing other student's reasons. Explain that there is no right answer and that students may feel differently about the same topic. Tell students that historians often have different opinions on topics, even after being presented with the same facts.

Sound, where ships could anchor and bring in supplies. Settlers started building homes around Puget Sound and in the Cowlitz River Valley. Towns such as Tumwater, Tacoma, Olympia, Centralia, Alki Point (Seattle), and Port Townsend started small. They grew larger as more and more settlers moved in.

Made by Hand

The trip across the Oregon Trail had been hard. It was only the beginning of the hard work. Once they got their land, families had to build their own homes and furniture. They cut down trees with simple tools. Then they split the logs into rough boards. The first houses they made were small wooden cabins. These often had no windows because there was no place to buy glass in Oregon Country.

In fact, there was no place to buy most of the things the settlers needed. They could not buy stoves, so they built stone fireplaces for heating and cooking. They could not buy oil lamps, so they made candles. They made their own soap, too.

The first homes were built log by log. **What jobs are people doing in this picture? What natural features do you see in the background?**

Early Immigration and Settlement

111

Memories of Childhood Homes

I was brought to Washington . . . by my parents in 1877. We came by train to San Francisco and by boat to Neah Bay. My father . . . thought [this country] was the garden spot of the world. He built a log house, and I grew up there. I listened to wolves howling. They sometimes caught our sheep.

We rode horseback over trails, or walked, or rode in Indian canoes on the ocean. Once when I was sick, I was hauled out over the trail on a sled across the mountains.

— Jennie S. Tyler
in *Told by the Pioneers*

[My first cabin] was a small log house . . . one room. My father had gotten some sacks of wheat. . . . My sister Annie and I slept on those sacks. They were cold. . . . [My father] got a load of lumber . . . and he made some chairs. He just took a piece of board and made them, and then he cut down some birch trees and made the back and legs.

— Elsie Koehler Johnson
in *Homestead Girlhoods*

Talk About It

Made by Hand

Why was reaching the end of the Oregon Trail only the beginning of the hard work?
Once settlers reached the new land, they had to build their own homes and furniture. There was no place to buy many of the supplies settlers needed to build these things.

Memories of Childhood Homes

How was Jennie S. Tyler's journey to Washington different than the journey taken by pioneers on the Oregon Trail?
She came by train to San Francisco. Her family traveled much faster and without the many dangers. She then traveled by boat to Neah Bay. This was also faster than traveling by wagon. There were dangers, but they were fewer and much different from traveling on the Oregon Trail.

What was it like in Elsie Koehler Johnsons's first cabin?
It was a one room log house. Elsie and her sister slept on sacks of wheat. Their father made chairs out of lumber and birch trees.

Caption Answers

People are either working in the garden, dragging logs to build with, stacking the logs to build the house, bringing water from the river, or cooking something over a fire.

There is a river and many trees in the background that people are using as resources for food and shelter.

Technology Activity

Oregon Trail Jeopardy

The Historic Oregon City has a Web site with a Teacher Resources link. On this page of resources, there is a Jeopardy Game download where you can download a PowerPoint file with a Jeopardy game. There are also instructions included for how to play the game. A link to the Historic Oregon City Web site can be found at **www.ExperienceStateHistory.com**.

Writing Activity

Compare Two Journals

Students can learn a lot about what life was like for new settlers in Oregon Country from the two journal excerpts on this page. The people who wrote these journals had very different experiences. Have students compare the experiences of these two girls using a Venn diagram. After students have completed their diagram, have them share what they wrote with a partner. A Venn diagram is available in the graphic organizer section of the *Teacher Guide*.

Talk About It

Made by Hand
(Continued from page 112)

What work did settlers have to do to get their own food?
They had to clear trees and rocks from the land so they could plant crops. They raised cows and made cheese and butter from the milk. They caught fish and killed ducks, deer, and rabbits for meat.

How was clothing made?
The women made all the clothes for the family from wool and made shoes from animal skins.

What did settlers do for fun?
At night they told stories and played games. Children played games outside.

Pioneer Schools

What was school like for settler children?
Students of all ages shared a single room with one teacher. There were only a few books and very little paper. Students wrote on slates or even the dirt outside.

Why was the school year often only a few months long?
The rest of the time, children were needed to work at home and on the farm.

Changes for Native Americans
(From page 113)

What were some of the negative effects that came from many settlers moving west?
Settlers cleared a lot of land for farming and animals had to find new homes. This meant Indians had to find new hunting grounds. Settlers killed buffalo that Indians needed for survival.

How did Indians react to the many changes brought by settlers?
Some Indians began to dress, hunt, and live like the settlers. Some Indians held on to their way of life and got used to the changes around them.

Caption Answers

There are 20 school children in the picture.

Compare the number of students in your school and class today to the number of children in this early schoolhouse.

Fun and Games

Here is what one girl wrote about two games she played:

Hide and seek in a jungle of young Douglas firs was most delightful; the great fir and cedar trees, logs and stumps, [gave] cover for any number of players.

The teeter-board was available when the neighbor's children came.... The longest board that could be found was placed across a large log. A huge stone rested in the middle, and the children, boys and girls, little and big, crowded on the board, almost filling it. Then we carefully 'waggled' it up and down.

—Emily Inez Denny
in *Blazing the Way*

This early schoolhouse was made of logs. **How many students can you count in the picture? About how many students are in your school today? In your class?**

112

The families provided their own food. This meant clearing the land so they could plant crops. Day after day, from morning until dark, the men, women, and children worked. They raised cows and made cheese and butter from the milk. They caught fish and killed ducks, deer, and rabbits for meat.

The women made all the clothes for the family. They raised sheep, cut their wool, spun it into thread or yarn, and wove or knitted it into clothes. They even made shoes from animal skins.

After dark, by the light of a lamp, the settlers liked to tell stories. They also played guessing games and checkers.

Children had few toys, but they still had fun. In good weather, they played games outside with their brothers and sisters. If they lived near other children, they played together after their chores were done.

Pioneer Schools

One of the first things the settlers wanted was a school for their children. Students of all ages shared a single room with one teacher. There were only a few books and very little paper. Students wrote on slates or even in the dirt outside.

Often the school year was only a few months long. The rest of the time, children were needed for work at home and on the farm.

On weekends, the schoolhouse became a meeting place. Church meetings were held there. So were dances, plays, spelling bees, singing classes, and town meetings.

Washington, Our Home

 Literature Link

Wagons, Ho!
A Diary of the Oregon Trail

Wagons, Ho! A Diary of the Oregon Trail, tells the story of the hardships a young girl and her family faced on the Oregon Trail. It shares insight about what life was like as part of a wagon train during the trek west. Read the book aloud to your class. Have students write a journal entry as if they were traveling along the Oregon Trail. Encourage students to include information they have learned about the Oregon Trail from this lesson and the book.

 Art Activity

Picture the Clothes

Clothing for the settlers of Oregon Country was very different from what we wear today. The pioneers made their own clothing from resources that were available to them from nature. Have students draw pictures of clothing the settlers wore. Tell students to include detail in their drawings that show the clothing was handmade from natural resources. Encourage students to think about what the settlers' clothes looked like in the different seasons as they make their drawings.

Changes for Native Americans

You have learned about some of the changes brought by the missionaries and fur traders. The movement west on the Oregon Trail changed life even more for the Native Americans. Now thousands of settlers were coming. They took more land. When they cleared the trees to build farms, the animals had to find new homes. That meant the Indians had to find new hunting grounds.

On the plains, along the trail, more and more settlers were shooting buffalo. Sometimes they shot them just for sport. The plains tribes relied on buffalo to meet many of their needs. Their way of life had to change as the buffalo began to disappear.

Some Indians began to dress more like the settlers and live more like they did. Many Indians had traded for guns, so they had new weapons and ways of hunting. Those who held on to their ways of life had to adapt to the changes around them.

New towns and businesses brought even more people. In the next chapter, you will read how the land was divided to make territories and states. You will learn how the Indians and pioneers faced the challenge of sharing the land.

As more settlers came west, more change came west. By the time trains were bringing settlers across the plains, hunters were shooting millions of buffalo just for their hides. The Plains Indians' way of life was disappearing along with the buffalo. **How did the movement west change life for the Indians of Oregon Country?**

"I first tasted potatoes, bread, vegetables, and other white men's food when I was ten years of age. Indian food is mostly fish, whale meat, sea lion, elk, deer, and bear. Cornflakes and fruit are the only food of the white man I like. "

—William Mason
in *Told by the Pioneers*

LESSON 2 What Did You Learn?

1. Why was traveling along the Oregon Trail so difficult?
2. Why did so many travelers make the hard trek along the Oregon Trail?
3. How did settlers change Oregon Country?

Early Immigration and Settlement

113

REFLECT

Reflect on students' understanding of the history of the Oregon Trail, and what life was like once settlers reached Oregon Country for the new settlers and the Native Americans. You can evaluate students' understanding through discussion or evaluation of activities completed in this lesson. The following activity will serve as another way of assessing students' understanding of the key objectives of this lesson.

✏ Writing Activity

Writing a Summary

Students will write a summary of the lesson using the outline from the Reading Strategy activity, Making an Outline. The summary should include at least three of the main ideas covered in the lesson with supporting details for each main idea. Have students complete the activity, Writing a Summary, in the *Student Guide*.

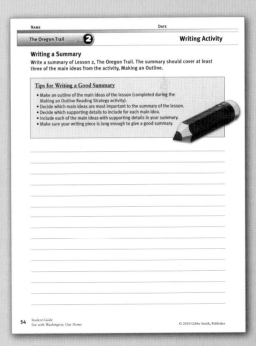

The Oregon Trail 2   Writing Activity

Writing a Summary
Write a summary of Lesson 2, The Oregon Trail. The summary should cover at least three of the main ideas from the activity, Making an Outline.

Tips for Writing a Good Summary
• Make an outline of the main ideas of the lesson (completed during the Making an Outline Reading Strategy activity).
• Decide which main ideas are most important to the summary of the lesson.
• Decide which supporting details to include for each main idea.
• Include each of the main ideas with supporting details in your summary.
• Make sure your writing piece is long enough to give a good summary.

54 Student Guide
Use with Washington, Our Home   © 2010 Gibbs Smith, Publisher

Caption Answer

Possible answers include they began to dress and live more like settlers, they used guns for hunting, they had to adapt to new lands, and they caught diseases from the newcomers.

LESSON 2 What Did You Learn?

1. *Possible answers may include hot and dusty weeks of walking under the burning sun, rainy days, wagons got stuck in the mud, fights with the Indians, crossing rivers, and crossing mountains.*
2. *Some people came for adventure. They wanted a chance to explore a beautiful new place and start a new life. Some wanted to get away from problems in the East, including slavery. Others came to get land to farm and live on.*
3. *Settlers changed the land by clearing the land for trails, building homes on it, planting crops, and hunting animals.*

Standards

GLE 5.4.1

Draws clear, well-reasoned conclusions and provides explanations that are supported by artifacts and/or primary sources in a paper or presentation.

Washington Social Studies Skills

Draw a Conclusion

Use this activity to help students learn how to draw good conclusions. Complete this activity to prepare students for the Project Assessment available in the *Teacher Guide*.

Activate

Share these riddles with your students. Give one clue at a time, allowing students to make guesses after each clue.

> I come in many colors
> I'm faster than a bicycle
> You can buy me new or used
> I have a trunk
> I have four wheels
> I have a license plate
> I am a CAR

> My mother is a queen
> I live in a colony
> I help flowers reproduce
> I can sting
> I am an insect
> I am a BEE

> I am round
> My favorite number is one
> I am made by the government
> I am made of copper
> A president's face is on me
> I am a kind of money
> I am a PENNY

Washington Social Studies Skills

Draw a Conclusion

Sometimes we read things that don't give us all the facts about a topic. Some authors leave clues in their writing and then let us come to our own conclusions.

History is like a good book that doesn't give us all the facts. It gives us only some of the facts so we can draw our own conclusions. Good historians don't jump to conclusions about why and how things happened in history. They carefully study their topic before coming to a conclusion. They support their conclusion with facts.

Use the facts from this chapter to write a clear conclusion about the challenges pioneers faced when moving west.

1. On a sheet of paper, write words from the chapter that describe the challenges faced by pioneers moving west.
2. Study the facts you gathered, and write a conclusion about the challenges pioneers faced.
3. Revise your conclusion so it is well-supported by the facts you have gathered. Your conclusion should state an idea that the textbook does not already share.
4. On another sheet of paper, write a paragraph with your conclusion as the topic sentence. Support your topic sentence with facts from the chapter.

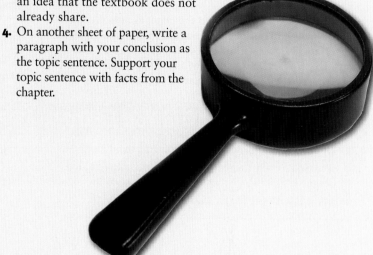

Washington, Our Home

Teach

Explain to students that when you draw conclusions, you use the information you already know, the information given to you, and put them together to make a decision. Just like with the riddles. You already know some things about bees, cars, and pennies. You used your knowledge and the clues you were given to make a decision about what was being described.

Practice

Have students work in pairs to think of an item most students would be familiar with. Have the pairs write riddles for the item they chose. Tell them to start with clues that cover big, general topics and then give final clues that are more specific. Give students a chance to share their

riddles with the class or with other pairs of students. Tell students to try to guess what the item is in as few clues as possible. Explain that by doing this, they are drawing conclusions.

Apply

Have students draw a conclusion, following the directions on the Social Studies Skills Page. Tell students to use what they know in their head and what they know from the textbook to draw their conclusion.

Chapter Review 5

Reviewing What You Read

1. Tell why settlers and missionaries moved to the Northwest.
2. Describe why Indians were unhappy with Dr. Whitman.
3. Choose one of the stories of missionaries from the chapter, and tell why the mission was successful or unsuccessful.
4. Use what you learned from the chapter to tell why you think so many settlers came west during this time period.
5. What if an Oregon Trail were created today? How would it be different?
6. Think about what you learned in this chapter to decide if you think settlers were more helpful or harmful to Native Americans. Write your answer.

Becoming a Better Reader

Find the Main Idea

When reading nonfiction information, good readers always keep in mind the main idea of what they are reading. Thinking about the main idea helps good readers organize the new information they read about. Main ideas can be found in chapter titles and lesson titles and in headings.

What is the main idea of this chapter? Write a paragraph stating the main idea and three supporting ideas. Use the titles of the chapter and lessons to help you.

Spotlighting Geography

Terrain of the Oregon Trail

Different kinds of maps show different things. Geographers use physical maps to study the terrain of the land. The Oregon Trail map on page 105 is a physical map that shows the terrain along the Oregon Trail.

Use the Oregon Trail map to write a paragraph describing the terrain along the trail. Describe how the terrain changes from the beginning to the end of the trail.

Early Immigration and Settlement

115

Reviewing What You Read

The Reviewing What You Read questions are leveled according to Bloom's Taxonomy and will help students achieve a higher level of thinking. These questions will also prepare students for the chapter assessment. The following are possible answers to the questions. Focus on students' ability to understand and apply the concepts.

1. **KNOWLEDGE** Missionaries came to share their religion and way of life with the Indians. Settlers came for many reasons. Some came for adventure, some to escape the troubles in the East, and others came for land.

2. **COMPREHENSION** Indians thought Dr. Whitman tried to poison them and that he wasn't helping them get well because he wanted their land.

3. **APPLICATION** Students' answers should include details about the missionaries talked about in this chapter.

4. **ANALYSIS** Students' conclusions should be supported by facts from the chapter and should explain why settlers came to Oregon Country.

5. **SYNTHESIS** Students' answers should display an understanding of what would be necessary to travel to the Northwest today.

6. **EVALUATION** Students' opinions should be supported by details from the chapter.

Interactive Chapter Review

An Interactive Chapter Review is available online at www.ExperienceStateHistory.com. Have students use this review to prepare for the assessments.

Chapter Assessment

Chapter Assessments are available to preview on pages 94G–94H. Assessments can be found in the *Teacher Guide*. They can also be found online at www.ExperienceStateHistory.com.

Becoming a Better Reader

Find the Main Idea

After students write their paragraph, have them exchange papers with a partner, read their paragraph, and highlight the main idea with a green crayon or colored pencil. Then have students read to find each of the supporting details and highlight them with a yellow crayon or colored pencil. Once all the main ideas and their supporting details have been highlighted, have students determine if any remaining sentences support the main idea. If they do not, have them circle those sentences. Have students return their papers to their partner. Have students revise their summaries of the chapter as necessary.

Spotlighting Geography

Terrain of the Oregon Trail

Have students research to come up with a list of other types of maps people use. Tell them to write a short description of what each type of map is and what it is used for. Have students share their lists in small groups and compare what they found.

CHAPTER

6 Territories and Treaties

CHAPTER PLANNER

CHAPTER OVERVIEW	WASHINGTON SOCIAL STUDIES GLEs
This chapter focuses on the territories and treaties that were made prior to statehood. Attention is given to the growth and change in the region that lead to statehood.	GLE 3.2.3 GLE 4.1.2 GLE 4.2.1 GLE 4.3.1 GLE 5.2.2 GLE 5.4.1 GLE 5.4.2

CHAPTER RESOURCES
ELL/Modified Chapter Plan, p. 116I
Books and Web Sites, p. 116J

CHAPTER ACTIVITIES	WASHINGTON CURRICULUM INTEGRATION
Writing a Class Treaty, p. 116E	**Communication** GLE 2.2.1, GLE 2.2.2
■ Reading a Treaty, p. 116E	**Reading** GLE 3.4.3
Writing an Argument, p. 116E	**Writing** GLE 1.1.1, GLE 1.2.1, GLE 1.3.1, GLE 1.4.1, GLE 1.5.1, GLE 1.6.1, GLE 2.3.1
■ Along the Nez Perce Trail, p. 116F	**Math** GLE 4.5.E
■ Comparing Maps, p. 116F	**Social Studies** GLE 3.1.1, GLE 3.1.2
■ Minerals at Home, p. 116F	**Science** GLE 1.1.5
Sign on the Dotted Line, p. 116F	**Visual Arts** GLE 2.1.1
The Great Debate, p. 116F	Communication GLE 2.2.1

CHAPTER OPENER	WASHINGTON CURRICULUM INTEGRATION
Conflict and Resolution, p. 116	**Communication** GLE 2.2.2
Before and After, p. 116	**Visual Arts** GLE 3.2.1
Timeline Talk, p. 117	**Reading** GLE 3.2.2

▶ Indicates an activity page located in the *Student Guide*
■ Indicates an activity page located in the *Teacher Guide*

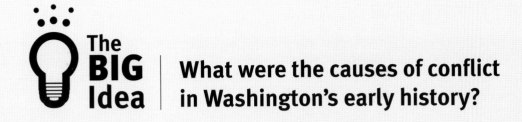

The BIG Idea | What were the causes of conflict in Washington's early history?

CHAPTER REVIEW	pp. 146–147
SOCIAL STUDIES SKILLS PAGE	**WASHINGTON SOCIAL STUDIES GLEs**
Write About a Historical Event From Multiple Perspectives, p. 146	**Social Studies** GLE4.3.1, GLE 5.4.1, GLE 5.4.2
REVIEWING THE CHAPTER	**WASHINGTON SOCIAL STUDIES GLEs**
Students show what they have learned by completing application activities and answering chapter review questions. Assessments for this chapter can be previewed on pages 116G-116H. Select the assessment option that best suits your goals for this chapter. Assessments are available in the *Teacher Guide* or online at **www.ExperienceStateHistory.com.**	GLE 3.2.3 GLE 4.1.2 GLE 4.2.1 GLE 4.3.1 GLE 5.2.2 GLE 5.4.1 GLE 5.4.2
CHAPTER ACTIVITIES	**WASHINGTON CURRICULUM INTEGRATION**
Reviewing What You Read, p. 147	**Reading** GLE 1.3.2, GLE 2.1.3
Becoming a Better Reader, p. 147	**Reading** GLE 2.2.1
Spotlighting Geography, p. 147	**Social Studies** GLE 3.2.3
CHAPTER ASSESSMENTS	**WASHINGTON CURRICULUM INTEGRATION**
■ Multiple Choice Assessment, p. 57	**Reading** GLE 1.3.2, GLE 2.1.3
■ Reading Assessment, p. 58	**Reading** GLE 1.3.2, GLE 2.1.3, GLE 3.4.3
■ Writing Assessment, p. 59	**Writing** GLE 2.2.1, GLE 2.3.1
■ Project Assessment, pp. 60–61	**Social Studies** GLE 4.3.1 **Writing** GLE 2.1.1

LESSON 1
Two New Territories pp. 118–123

LESSON OVERVIEW	WASHINGTON SOCIAL STUDIES GLEs
KEY IDEAS • The United States gained control of land in the Northwest. • Oregon Country became Oregon Territory. • Oregon Territory was divided and Washington Territory was formed.	GLE 4.1.2 GLE 5.2.2

LESSON ACTIVITIES	WASHINGTON CURRICULUM INTEGRATION
▶Pacific Northwest in 1859, p. 118	**Social Studies** GLE 3.1.1
Multiple Meaning Words, p.118	**Reading** GLE 1.3.1
▶Words to Understand, p. 118	**Reading** GLE 1.3.1
▶Recognizing Sequence, p. 119	**Reading** GLE 2.2.1
Oregon Territory, 1848–1853, p. 120	**Social Studies** GLE 3.1.1
Washington Territory, 1853–1863, p. 121	**Social Studies** GLE 3.1.1
Go to the Source: Study a Map of the Pig War, p. 122	**Social Studies** GLE 5.2.2
Conflict Resolution, p. 122	**Social Studies** GLE 5.2.2, GLE 4.4.1
▶This Land is My Land, p. 123	**Writing** GLE 3.1.1

LESSON 2
The Treaty-Making Era pp. 124–133

LESSON OVERVIEW	WASHINGTON SOCIAL STUDIES GLEs
KEY IDEAS • The Indians and the U.S. government leaders had different points of view about the land. • Treaties created Indian reservations. • Some Indians fought to defend their lands.	GLE 3.2.3 GLE 4.1.2 GLE 4.2.1

LESSON ACTIVITIES	WASHINGTON CURRICULUM INTEGRATION
▶Making Promises, p. 124	**Writing** GLE 2.2.1
More Multiple Meaning Words, p. 124	**Reading** GLE 1.3.1
▶Words to Understand, p. 124	**Reading** GLE 1.3.1
▶Recognizing Point of View, p. 125	**Reading** GLE 2.4.1
Isaac Stevens, p. 126	**Technology** GLE 1.3.2
Where In Time is Isaac Stevens?, p. 126	**Social Studies** GLE 5.2.2 **Technology** GLE 1.3.2
Instant Transcriber, p. 126	**Reading** GLE 3.4.3 **Technology** GLE 1.3.2
Write a Treaty, p. 127	**Writing** GLE 2.2.1
Clothing of Indian Groups, p. 128	**Communication** GLE 2.2.2, **Visual Art** GLE 2.1.1
Indian Reservations in the 1800s, p. 129	**Social Studies** GLE 5.2.1
Chief Sealth's Speech, p. 129	**Social Studies** GLE 4.3.1
Reservation Report, p. 130	**Writing** GLE 3.1.1
Pan for Gold, p. 131	**Science** GLE 1.1.1
Native Americans in the Gold Rush, p. 131	**Technology** GLE 1.3.3
Thunder Rolling in the Mountains, p. 132	**Reading** GLE 3.4.3
Nez Perce Summer, 1877, p. 132	**Technology** GLE 1.3.2
Chief Joseph, p. 132	**Technology** GLE 1.3.2, GLE 1.3.3
▶Letter of Opinion , p. 133	**Writing** GLE 2.1.1

LESSON 3

Becoming a State
pp. 134–145

LESSON OVERVIEW	WASHINGTON SOCIAL STUDIES GLEs
KEY IDEAS • New industries brought immigrants to the territory. • New towns and cities grew. • Washington became a state.	GLE 4.1.2

LESSON ACTIVITIES	WASHINGTON CURRICULUM INTEGRATION
▶Anticipation Guide, p. 134	**Reading** GLE 2.1.4
Word Reports, p.134	**Reading** GLE 1.3.2
▶Words to Understand, p. 134	**Reading** GLE 1.3.1
▶Recognizing Cause and Effect, p. 135	**Reading** GLE 2.1.7
May Arkwright Hutton, p. 136	**Writing** GLE 2.3.1
How a Steam Engine Works, p. 137	**Science** GLE 2.1.3
Across the Continent, p. 137	**Social Studies** GLE 3.1.1
James J. Hill, p. 138	**Writing** GLE 2.2.1
Railroads Bring Change, p. 138	**Math** GLE 4.5.E
I Am, p. 140	**Writing** GLE 3.2.2
Immigrants in Your Family, p. 141	**Social Studies** GLE 3.2.3
Immigrant Groups, p. 142	**Writing** GLE 2.2.1
John Nordstrom, p. 143	**Technology** GLE 1.3.2
Washington's Population Today, p. 143	**Technology** GLE 1.3.2, GLE 1.3.3
Washington State, p. 144	**Visual Arts** GLE 2.1.1
▶Front Page News!, p. 145	**Writing** GLE 2.3.1

Chapter Activities

This chapter focuses on the causes of conflict in Washington's early history as the land changed from Oregon Country to the Washington Territory, and the events that led to Washington's statehood. Students learn about the treaties the U.S. government entered into with the Indians in order to take control of the land. Use the Chapter Activities to help students understand how this treaty-making period shaped the land that would later become the state of Washington.

 Set the Stage

Set up a class library with books about the Washington Territory, Chief Joseph and the Nez Perce, Governor Isaac Stevens, and the treaty-making time. Some titles are suggested on page 116J. Ask your librarian for other suggestions. Consider displaying different maps that show how the boundaries changed during this time.

 Introductory Activity

Writing a Class Treaty

Choose an issue on which your class faces disagreements. This could be anything from how to complete a class project to who should line up first to go to lunch. After choosing your topic, have the class brainstorm possible solutions. Make a list on the board. Have students work in groups of four to write a treaty. Explain that a treaty is an agreement made between two or more parties. Encourage students to write a treaty that is fair to all parties involved. Have each group share their treaty with the class. As a class, vote for a treaty that solves the problem in a fair way.

 Reading Activity

Reading a Treaty

Many treaties were written during this period of Washington's history. Use this activity to give students an opportunity to read an excerpt from an actual treaty written by Governor Isaac Stevens. After reading the selection, have students answer the questions about the treaty. You may choose to have students complete this activity in pairs, groups, or as a class because of the more difficult wording used in the treaty.

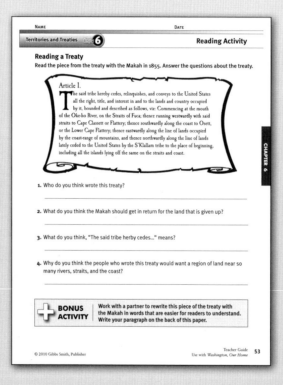

 Writing Activity

Writing an Argument

Persuasive writing is an important skill that cannot be taught too early. But writing an argument can seem intimidating to elementary students. Use this activity to introduce students to the basic concepts of lobbying for something that is important to them (or that they want) and making persuasive arguments. Start by explaining persuasive arguments and when they are used. Discuss topics that would be good for writing a persuasive argument. Tell students that they will be writing a persuasive argument about whether or not they think the United States government should have taken land from Native Americans.

Prewriting

Have students fill out the Persuasion Map available in the graphic organizers section of the *Teacher Guide*.

Drafting

Have students write a five-paragraph persuasive essay using the Persuasion Map as a guide. Tell students to introduce the goal in their introductory paragraph, use each main reason as a topic sentence for paragraphs 2–4, and restate the goal in the concluding paragraph.

Revising

Have students revise their essay to make sure they include facts in their reasons for their argument.

Editing

Have students work with a partner to edit their essay for spelling, grammar, punctuation, and capitalization errors.

Publishing

Encourage students to type their essays using a word processing program. Have students share their essays with the class.

Math Activity

Along the Nez Perce Trail

Have students calculate math problems along the trail of the Nez Perce. An Along the Nez Perce Trail activity, including a map and questions, is available in the *Teacher Guide*. You may want to have students write their own questions as well.

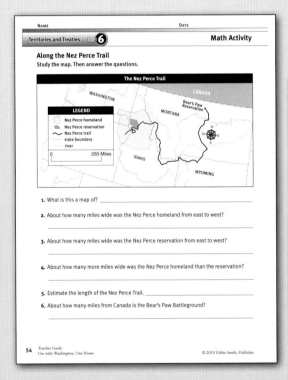

Science Activity

Minerals at Home

Many immigrants and settlers wanted the land in this region because of the valuable rocks and minerals that were discovered. Land was taken away from Native Americans to be mined by others who wanted to make money. Explain that many useful and valuable minerals are still mined in Washington today. A Minerals at Home activity is available in the *Teacher Guide* to help students discover how minerals are used in their daily lives.

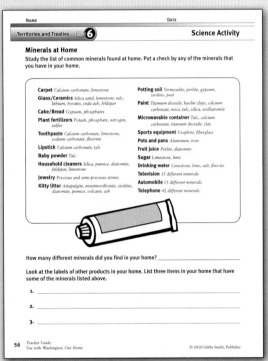

Social Studies Activity

Comparing Maps

Have students compare a map of Washington and Oregon in 1853 to a map of Washington and Oregon in 1863. These maps are available in the *Teacher Guide*. Have students answer the questions.

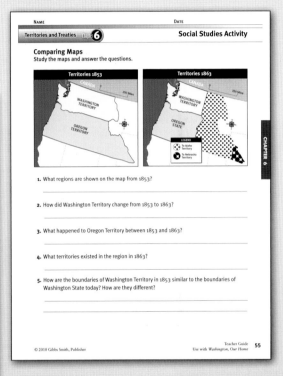

CHAPTER 6

Culminating Activity

The Great Debate

As a culminating activity, organize a debate in your classroom. Have students represent either the U.S. government or the Indians and research the perspective of their group on the treaty-making era. You may want to start the debate by introducing an event from the chapter and allowing some students from both sides of the debate to respond with how they feel about the event. Remind students to support their statements with facts from the chapter or other sources. Continue to introduce more events from the chapter until all students have had a chance to respond.

Art Activity

Sign on the Dotted Line

Tell students that many Indians used to sign treaties using an "X." The "X"s provide information about differences in the ways the Indians and U.S. government viewed the treaties. An "X" also indicated their inability to read or write. Talk about what signatures mean. Encourage students to look at some famous signatures and come up with their own signature. Have students create their signature on an 8 ½" by 11" piece of white paper. Display the signatures around the classroom.

Assessment Options

The Chapter Assessment options provide opportunities to evaluate students' understanding of the social studies concepts. Choose the assessment options that best meet the needs of your teaching goals. Assessments are available in the *Teacher Guide* or can be individualized at **www.ExperienceStateHistory.com.**

OPTION 1: MULTIPLE CHOICE ASSESSMENT

The Multiple Choice Assessment provides a quick way to assess students' understanding of the key concepts of the chapter. Have students read each question and select the best answer.

OPTION 2: READING ASSESSMENT

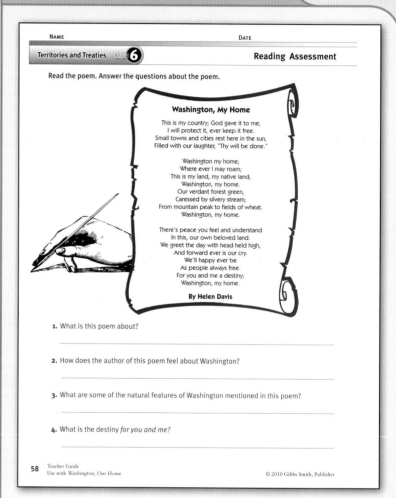

The Reading Assessment provides additional practice for the WASL Reading Test. Have students read the passage and answer the questions that follow.

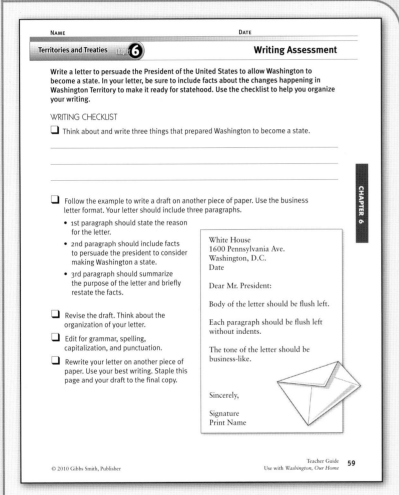

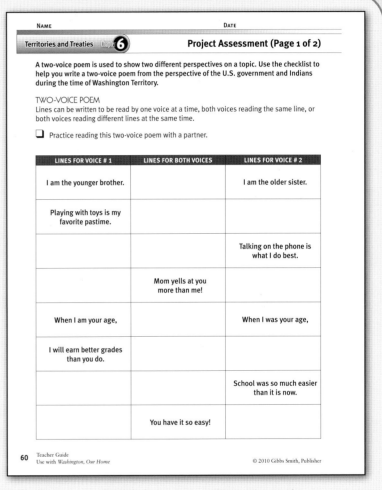

The Writing Assessment provides additional practice for the WASL Writing Test. Have students use the checklist to write a letter persuading the president of the United States to allow Washington to become a state.

The Project Assessment provides an alternative to the traditional assessment. Have students use the checklist to write a two-voice poem from the perspective of the U.S. government and the Indians in Washington Territory.

ELL/Modified Chapter Plan

Territories and Treaties

Students will learn how the early pioneers traveled along the Oregon Trail and how they settled in the Oregon Country. In this lesson, students will connect their own immigration experiences or the immigration experiences of their families with that of the pioneers moving west.

The following pages can be found in the ELL/Modified Chapter Guide on pages 35–39.

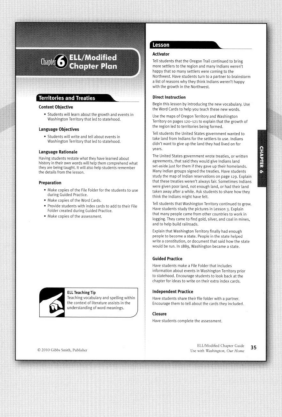

The ELL/Modified Chapter Plan provides a step-by-step lesson in an easy-to-use format. Lessons teach content and language objectives.

The Modified Assessment for this chapter assesses students' understanding of the key objectives of the chapter.

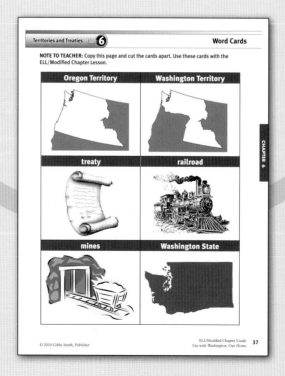

The Word Cards and Activity assist and reinforce students' learning of the chapter and prepares them for the assessment.

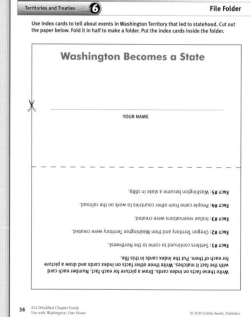

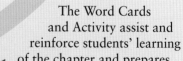

Books and Web Sites

Books

Chief Joseph. *That All People May Be One People, Send Rain to Wash the Face of the Earth*. Missoula, Montana: Mountain Meadow Press, 1995.

Grey, Alan E. *The Life of Chief Joseph*. Wasatch Press, 2008.

McAuliffe, Bill. *Chief Joseph of the Nez Perce: A Photo-illustrated Biography*. Mankato, Minnesota: Capstone Press, 1999.

Nelson, Charlene and Ted. *The Nez Perce*. New York: Scholastic, 2003.

O'Dell, Scott and Elizabeth Hall. *Thunder Rolling in the Mountains*. New York: Dell Yearling, 1992.

Sutcliffe, Jane. *Chief Joseph*. History Maker Bios. Lerner Publications, 2004.

Web Sites

The following Web sites provide resources or lesson plans for teachers and activities for students to help extend the lessons in this chapter. Go to **www.ExperienceStateHistory.com** for links to these Web sites.

Animated Engines

The Animated Engines Web site has animated examples of how different types of steam engines work.

Nez Perce Summer, 1877

The Nez Perce Summer 1877 Web site by the National Park Service is a great resource of background information on the Nez Perce War. The history of the war is broken down into events and themes with related information for each. There are a number of useful maps included in this site that would be helpful when teaching about the Nez Perce War.

Native Americans in the Gold Rush

This PBS site, Native Americans in the Gold Rush, contains a map, timeline, interactive activities, and a teaching guide for teachers.

NCES Kids' Zone

Students can use this Kids' Zone Web site to create professional-looking graphs for a more creative way to present information.

Nordstrom

The Nordstrom Web site shares a history of the company. There are images and great details on the history of a man who came to the Northwest for the gold rush and started what would become one of the most successful fashion specialty stores.

U.S. Census Bureau

The U.S. Census Bureau Web site contains information on the population of each state. Use this site to help students understand the diverse population of our state.

The Treaty Trail

The Washington State Historical Society has a Web site called The Treaty Trail: U.S.-Indian Treaty Councils in the Northwest. This site has four excellent interactive activities for students. The Instant Transcriber allows students to read a primary source personal letter about Washington Territory. The In Their Own Words activity shares excerpts of speeches from multiple people at the Walla Walla Council. The Spin Gallery gives a 360° view of artifacts from the treaty-making era. Where In Time Is Isaac Stevens is a primary source-based activitiy that encourages students to use critical thinking.

Washington History

The Washington History Web site has a featured titled The Treaty Trail filled with primary and secondary source documents, information, and lesson plans about the treaty-making period in Washington's history.

Wikimedia Commons

Wikimedia Commons is a Web site that houses millions of media files that anyone can use. From this site you can access many helpful images from the territory and treaty-making era.

The BIG Idea

Conflict and Resolution

Tell students that a conflict is a fight. Ask students to think about times when they have or might have conflict in their lives. Tell students that conflict might occur when they're deciding what game to play or how to play it, when they're competing in sports, or when someone tells them to do something they don't want to do. Explain to students that conflicts have occurred all throughout history. The most important part of a conflict is how it is resolved. Have students fill a T-chart with conflicts that students have and a good way to resolve each conflict.

Put Yourself in the Picture

Before and After

Ask students to describe what is happening in the picture. Have students imagine what the land in this painting looked like 100 years before this treaty council. Have students imagine what the land in this painting looked like 100 years after the council, in the late 1900s. Have students draw or paint what they imagined. Hang the pictures on the wall with the before and after images grouped together.

Caption Answer

The United States flag is raised and blowing in the wind.

The BIG Idea

What were the causes of conflict in Washington's early history?

Flathead Indians meet with Governor Isaac Stevens. These meetings were called treaty councils. **Can you see the men signing a treaty? What symbol of the United States do you see?**

Timeline of Events

1846 Oregon Country is ruled by the United States. Vancouver Island and British Columbia become part of Canada.

1848 Oregon Country becomes the Oregon Territory.

1850

1853 Washington Territory is created. Isaac Stevens is the first governor.

1854-1856 Governor Stevens signs 10 treaties with the Indians. The Indians give up tribal lands and move to reservations.

1855 The Yakama War

1860

116

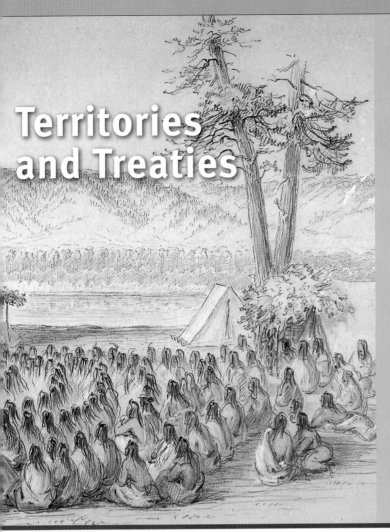

Territories and Treaties

CHAPTER 6

At one time, only American Indians lived in what is now Washington. Then the Spanish came to trade and explore. Americans came on the Oregon Trail.

Everyone agreed that the land and climate were wonderful. However, no one could agree who owned the land.

In this chapter, you will learn how Indians were forced to leave their land. You will learn how the United States finally came to own the Northwest. You will learn how Washington became a state.

Timeline Activity

Timeline Talk

When were the first treaties signed in the Washington Territory?
The first treaties were signed in 1854, in western Washington.

What happened to the San Juan Island as a result of the Pig War?
The San Juan Islands become part of the Washington Territory.

How many years after the first treaties were signed did Washington become a state?
Forty-five years passed between the time the first treaties in Washington Territory were signed and the time Washington became a state.

What happened the same year that Washington became a state?
There were large fires in Seattle, Spokane, and Ellensburg.

What event took place in 1877?
The Nez Perce war was in 1877.

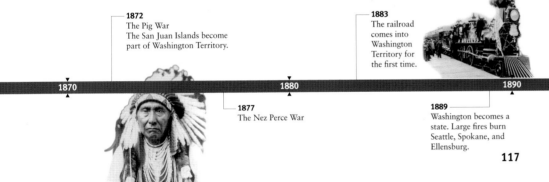

1872
The Pig War
The San Juan Islands become part of Washington Territory.

1883
The railroad comes into Washington Territory for the first time.

1870 — **1880** — **1890**

1877
The Nez Perce War

1889
Washington becomes a state. Large fires burn Seattle, Spokane, and Ellensburg.

117

LESSON 1 Two New Territories

PREPARE

Activator

Pacific Northwest in 1859

Show students a map of Washington State today. Tell students that Washington has only been a state with these boundaries since 1889. Explain that in this chapter they will be learning about many events that led to statehood. Have students complete the map with important locations to the history of our state for the activity, Pacific Northwest in 1859, available in the *Student Guide*.

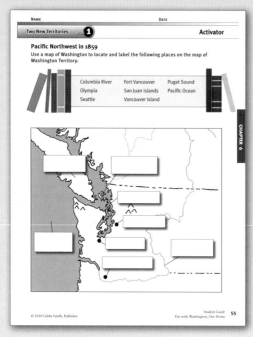

Word Study

Multiple Meaning Words

Have students research the meaning of each of the Words to Understand. Encourage them to look up the definition in the glossary in this book, in different dictionaries, and through dictionaries online. Tell them to look for multiple meanings of each word as it is used for different parts of speech (noun, verb, etc.). Have students compare the different definitions for the same part of speech but from different sources. Have students share what they found with the class.

118

Key Ideas

- The United States gained control of land in the Northwest.
- Oregon Country became Oregon Territory.
- Oregon Territory was divided, and Washington Territory was formed.

Words to Understand

compromise
governor
negotiate
ownership
territory
treaty

This picture shows a British camp in 1868. **Why did so many people want to claim the land?**

Who Claimed the Northwest?

Before the fur traders came, all the Northwest was Indian land. Later, the Hudson's Bay Company came to the region. The British owned that company, so they thought they should also own Oregon Country.

Remember, Oregon Country was a very large land region. It included today's Oregon, Washington, Idaho, and parts of Montana and Wyoming. It also included the San Juan Islands, Vancouver Island, and parts of British Columbia, Canada.

You learned in the last chapter that thousands of American pioneers walked to Oregon Country on the Oregon Trail. They settled on the rich farmland. They started towns and opened businesses.

Soon there were more American settlers than fur traders in Oregon Country. They wanted the land to become part of the United States. However, Britain still claimed all the land around Puget Sound. Both countries wanted *ownership* of the beautiful land. Each wanted to be the only owner.

118

Washington, Our Home

Words to Understand

compromise (p. 119) *an agreement that is reached by each side giving up something it wants*

governor (p. 121) *the top government leader of a territory or state*

negotiate (p. 119) *to talk back and forth to reach an agreement*

ownership (p. 118) *the fact of being an owner*

territory (p. 120) *a land region owned and ruled by a country; a region that is not a state*

treaty (p. 119) *a written agreement between two groups*

A Words to Understand activity for this lesson is available in the *Student Guide*.

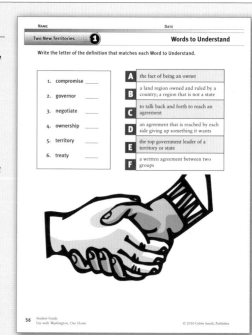

The Oregon Treaty

The United States also wanted Puget Sound, and the president said he would go to war against Britain to get it. However, neither country really wanted to fight. They decided to *negotiate*, or talk back and forth until they could agree.

Finally, leaders from both countries reached a *compromise*. They agreed that both countries would get part of the land. A line at 49 degrees north latitude would be the dividing line.

The men signed the Oregon Treaty. A *treaty* is a written agreement between two groups.

The treaty said:

- Great Britain would keep Vancouver Island and the land north of the line.
- The United States would keep the land south of the line.

This is the region we now call the Pacific Northwest. In those days, it was called Oregon Country.

In the Oregon Treaty, the British gave up their claim to the land we call the Pacific Northwest. **Which president's name is at the top of the treaty?**

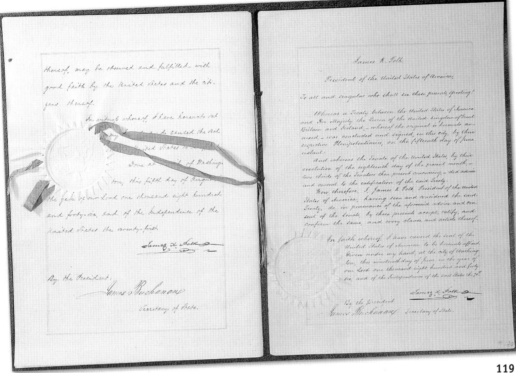

119

TEACH

Talk About It

Who Claimed the Northwest?
(From page 118)

Why did Britain think they should own Oregon Country?
Britain owned the Hudson's Bay Company in the region, so they thought they should own the land.

Which of today's states made up Oregon Country?
Oregon Country included today's Oregon, Washington, Idaho, and parts of Montana and Wyoming.

Why do you think both America and Britain wanted to be the only owner of Oregon Country?
Encourage students to think about what resources Oregon Country had to offer and what benefits come to a country when they gain more land.

The Oregon Treaty

How did the United States and Britain solve the problem when both countries wanted ownership of Puget Sound?
They decided to negotiate so that they wouldn't have to go to war. They decided both countries would get part of the land. They divided the land at 49 degrees north latitude.

Caption Answers

(From page 118) There were many natural resources from the land that people could use to live or to make money.

President Polk's name is at the top of the treaty.

Reading Strategy

Recognizing Sequence

Explain to students that to understand some events or actions, good readers must recognize the order in which things occur. Tell students that the order in which things occur is also called sequence. Talk with students about the sequence of events that led to the creation of Oregon Territory. Refer back to Chapter 5 to talk about the missions, the Oregon Trail, and the first settlers to come to this region. Explain that good readers and writers use clue words such as *first, then, after, next, before, last,* and *finally* when sequencing events. Have students complete the Recognizing Sequence activity available in the *Student Guide*.

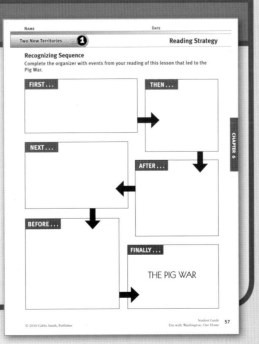

Talk About It

Oregon Territory

What were the benefits of Oregon Country becoming Oregon Territory?
The territory was ruled by the United States government and settlers could ask the government for help to get things like roads, schools, and an army.

Who made the rules for Oregon Territory?
The United States government set up the rules and laws for the people in the new territory.

Caption Answer

Having a representative at the U.S. capital meant that people in the territory could have a say in decisions that were made about the country. Territories could also receive funding, or money, from the government to help with projects in the territory.

Map Activity

Oregon Territory, 1848–1853

Call students' attention to the map on this page. Have students study this map to answer these questions. You may want to have students compare the map on this page to a map of the Northwest today.

• What present day states were part of Oregon Territory?

Washington, Oregon, Idaho, and parts of Montana and Wyoming made up Oregon Territory.

• What landforms and natural resources were found in Oregon Territory?

Possible answers include the Cascade mountains, the Pacific coastline, the Columbia River, timber, fish, and soil.

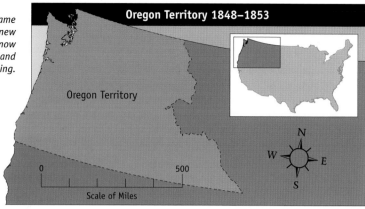

Oregon Country became Oregon Territory. The new territory included what is now Washington, Oregon, Idaho, and parts of Montana and Wyoming.

Oregon Territory

The little pioneer towns in Oregon Country were slowly starting to grow. Families wanted things like roads and schools. They wanted an army to help keep them safe. They wanted the United States government to help with these things.

The settlers sent letters to U.S. leaders, asking for help. The leaders listened. They decided to make Oregon Country into Oregon Territory. A **territory** is a land region owned and ruled by a country. It is not yet a state. The U.S. government set up rules and laws for the people in the new territory.

At first, Oregon Territory was huge! All of Oregon Country was part of it.

Becoming a territory meant settlers had help from the government. They could send someone to the U.S. capital to represent them. **How would this make life easier for the settlers?**

Washington, Our Home

Background Info

Making Boundaries

When territories were being formed and boundaries were being established, there was a detailed system that had to be followed. In order to plot and map the land holdings for legal title, the land was surveyed, then marked on a grid pattern. That pattern was based on latitude and longitude, and was divided into townships and sections.

• A township was a square six miles in each direction.
• A township was divided into 36 sections.
• Each section was one mile each direction, or 640 acres.
• Each section was numbered.
• Sections were divided into quarter sections of 160 acres each.

A homesteader checked with the land office in the nearest town and located on a map a quarter section he wanted to claim.

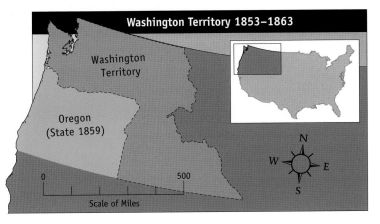

Washington Territory 1853–1863

Washington
Territory

Oregon
(State 1859)

0   500

Scale of Miles

Washington Territory included parts of what are now Idaho and Montana. Compare this map with the map on page 120. What had changed?

Washington Territory

It wasn't long before settlers living north of the Columbia River wanted to separate from Oregon Territory. They wanted their own government. They wanted it to be closer to home. Congress voted to create a new territory.

The new territory was called Washington Territory. At first, the people wanted to name it Columbia, but it was named Washington after George Washington, the first president of the United States.

Each territory was ruled by leaders chosen by the U.S. government. Each territory also had its own capital city where leaders made some of the rules.

Olympia was made the capital city of the new territory. It is still our capital city today.

The First Governor

Isaac Stevens was made the first governor of the territory. A ***governor*** is the top leader of a territory or a state. Governor Stevens traveled all across the country to get to Washington. He helped govern, or rule, the territory.

The new governor's wife also came to the new territory, but she came by ship. She sailed around South America and up the coast to her new home. After her long trip, she expected a larger town with nice homes. She wrote: "Below us, in a deep mud, were a few low wooden houses at the head of Puget Sound. My heart sank."

Territories and Treaties   121

Talk About It

Washington Territory

Why do you think settlers wanted to name Washington Territory *Columbia*?
The Columbia River forms part of the boundary of the territory and was an important natural resource for many people in the region.

How did the Washington Territory get its name?
It was named after George Washington, the first president of the United States.

The First Governor

Who was the first governor of the territory and how was he chosen?
The first governor was Isaac Stevens and he was chosen by the United States government.

How did the governor's wife get to the territory and what did she think about it when she arrived?
She traveled to the territory by ship. She was not happy to see the territory was deep in mud with a few low wooden houses.

Caption Answer

Oregon is a state. The remaining land from Oregon Territory because Washington Territory.

 Map Activity

Washington Territory, 1853–1863

Call students' attention to the map on this page. Have students study the map to answer these questions. You may want to have students compare the map on this page to a map of the Northwest today.

• What present day states were once part of Oregon Territory, but were separated to make Washington Territory?

   Washington, Idaho, and parts of Montana and Wyoming were once part of Oregon Territory.

• What landforms and natural resources were found in Washington Territory?

   Have students study a physical map of the Northwest to find landforms and natural resources that would have been found in Washington Territory.

121

Go to the Source

Standards

GLE 5.2.2
Understands the main ideas from an artifact, primary source, or secondary source describing an issue or event.

Study a Map of the Pig War

This map shows the proposed boundaries for the San Juan Islands during the Pig War. The National Park Service has a Web site all about the Pig War. The site is connected with the San Juan National Historic Park and also has a link to general information about the islands. A link to this site can be found at **www.ExperienceStateHistory.com**. Have students visit this site to see pictures of the men involved in the incident and to find more information about the history of the Pig War.

Social Studies Activity

Conflict Resolution

The Pig War is an important part of the history of the Northwest because it celebrates how individuals and nations can resolve conflicts without resorting to violence. Write the phrase *Conflict Resolution* on the board. Explain to students that conflict resolution is problem-solving between people. Write the following four steps to resolving conflict on the board. Talk about each step.

1. Define the problem.
2. Recognize point of view.
3. Discuss possible solutions.
4. Choose a solution and act it out.

Have students work in groups to write a possible conflict resolution for the problems between the Americans and the Indians who lived on the same land in Washington Territory. For step 4, have students write about how they think the solution may have changed the relationship between Americans and Indians.

Go to the Source
Study a Map of the Pig War

This map shows the San Juan Islands that both the British and the Americans wanted to own. The lines show different ways the countries thought the islands should be divided. Study the map and answer the questions.

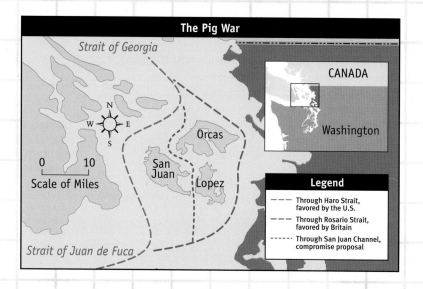

LOOK	THINK	DECIDE
What is shown on this map?	Why do you think the United States favored the boundary line through the Haro Strait?	Do you agree with the idea of settling the argument by dividing the islands through the San Juan Channel? Why or why not?

122

Washington, Our Home

LOOK	THINK	DECIDE
Possible answers include the San Juan Islands during the Pig War, and the region where the Pig War took place.	The boundary through the Haro Strait included all of the San Juan Islands as part of the United States of America.	Students' answers should show insight on conflict resolution and compromise. Answers may mention details from the chapter supporting answers about the Americans having a stronger hold on the land.

U.S. soldiers study where to place guns at San Juan Island. **What are the soldiers in the background doing?**

Pigs, Potatoes, and Talk of War

Great Britain and the United States had signed a treaty. But one question still had to be answered. Who owned the San Juan Islands? Both British and American settlers lived on the islands. Both countries thought the islands should be theirs.

One day, a British neighbor's pig walked onto a farm owned by an American. The pig ate some of the American's potatoes. The farmer was angry. "Keep your pig on your own land!" he shouted. The British man refused.

The American farmer shot the pig. Anger between the English and Americans grew stronger. Both countries sent soldiers to the islands. There was talk of war.

Instead of fighting, however, the countries asked the ruler of Germany to decide who should own the islands. The German man listened to both sides. He decided that the United States had a stronger claim. Ever since then, the San Juan Islands have been part of Washington. The "Pig War" was settled. The only life lost was one pig.

LESSON 1 What Did You Learn?

1. What did the British and Americans decide about who got ownership of the land in the Northwest?
2. Why was Oregon Country made Oregon Territory?
3. How did Great Britain and the United States decide who got ownership of the San Juan Islands?

Territories and Treaties

123

LESSON 1 What Did You Learn?

1. *The British and the Americans wrote the Oregon Treaty to solve the disagreement. Both sides got part of the land.*
2. *The settlers in Oregon Country wanted things like roads, schools, and an army. They wanted the United States government to help. The United States made Oregon Country into Oregon Territory so they could help with these things.*
3. *The British and the Americans asked the ruler of Germany to decide who should own the San Juan Islands. The United States got ownership of the San Juan Islands.*

REFLECT

Reflect on students' understanding of the events that led to the forming of the two territories in the Northwest, changes that occurred in the Washington Territory, and the details of the Pig War. You can evaluate students' understanding through discussion or evaluation of activities completed in this lesson. The following activity will serve as another way of assessing students' understanding of the key objectives of this lesson.

Writing Activity

This Land is My Land

It seemed like everyone wanted to own land in the Northwest. The Indians, Americans, and British all wanted to own all or part of the land. Each group had reasons that were important to them. Have students complete the organizer with reasons why each group wanted to own land in the Northwest. A This Land is My Land activity can be found in the *Student Guide*.

Caption Answer

The men in the background are digging and building things. They are preparing for war.

Standards

GLE 4.1.2
Understands how the following themes and developments help to define eras in Washington State history from time immemorial to 1889: Territory and treaty-making (1854–1889)

PREPARE

Activator

Making Promises

Tell students the Native Americans and early settlers made promises to each other called *treaties*. Explain that today business people make promises to each other called *contracts*. Tell students that people their age make promises, too. Have students complete the Making Promises activity, available in the *Student Guide*.

NAME	DATE

The Treaty-Making Era 2 — Activator

Making Promises
Look up these words in a dictionary and write the meanings.

promise: _____

contract: _____

treaty: _____

Look at the cartoons. Each of these people are making promises to each other. Write what you think each person is saying.

© 2010 Gibbs Smith, Publisher — Student Guide Use with *Washington, Our Home* **59**

Word Study

More Multiple Meaning Words

Remind students that some words have multiple meanings. Pete's PowerPoint Station has a free PowerPoint presentation you can use to teach this concept. For a link to this site, go to **www.ExperienceStateHistory.com**. Talk about the word *reservation*. Ask students to look the word up in the dictionary. Have students write sentences showing the three different meanings of the word.

Key Ideas

- Indians and U.S. government leaders had different points of view about the land.
- Treaties created Indian reservations.
- Some Indians fought to defend their lands.

Words to Understand

civilize
conflict
council
defend
fertile
lumber
perspective
profitable
reservation
surrender

Native Americans and Settlers

When traders, trappers, and missionaries came, the Indians traded with them. The Indians worked for the fur companies. They helped them build homes and churches. However, things changed as thousands of settlers came west on the Oregon Trail.

Different Points of View About the Land

The Indians and settlers thought about the land in different ways. They had different *perspectives*, or points of view.

The settlers claimed land, put fences around it, and kept other people away. They wanted to start large farms and grow crops on the land. They also wanted to make money by cutting down trees to sell and raising cattle to sell to other people. The settlers changed the land by building roads and buildings.

Indian lands, however, were thought to be for their whole group. No one in the group owned his own land. Indians had hunting and fishing grounds for everyone to use. They used the

Settlers fished and hunted wild animals that Indian people needed for food. They wanted to live on land where Indian families had lived for a long time. **What clues in the picture tell you how settlers used the land?**

124

Washington, Our Home

Words to Understand

civilize (p. 127) *to bring to a higher stage of education and culture*
conflict (p. 127) *problems between two people or groups*
council (p. 127) *a meeting where a group of people makes decisions*
defend (p. 131) *to drive away danger or attack*
fertile (p. 127) *good for growing crops*
lumber (p. 127) *logs sawed into boards*
perspective (p. 126) *point of view*
profitable (p. 127) *to make money*
reservation (p. 127) *land set aside for Native Americans*
surrender (p. 133) *to give up*

A Words to Understand activity for this lesson is available in the *Student Guide*.

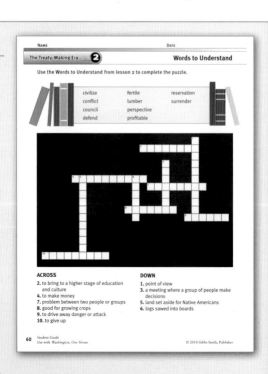

NAME	DATE

The Treaty-Making Era 2 — **Words to Understand**

Use the Words to Understand from lesson 2 to complete the puzzle.

civilize	fertile	reservation
conflict	lumber	surrender
council	perspective	
defend	profitable	

ACROSS
2. to bring to a higher stage of education and culture
4. to make money
7. problem between two people or groups
8. good for growing crops
9. to drive away danger or attack
10. to give up

DOWN
1. point of view
3. a meeting where a group of people make decisions
5. land set aside for Native Americans
6. logs sawed into boards

60 Student Guide Use with *Washington, Our Home* © 2010 Gibbs Smith, Publisher

natural resources to provide food, shelter, and clothes. Without their lands, the Indians could not live.

As more and more settlers came to the territories, these different points of view about the land caused *conflict*, or problems, between the groups of people. Sometimes the conflicts ended in war.

Governor Stevens and Indian Treaties

Governor Stevens traveled around the territory. He invited Indian leaders to councils. A *council* is a meeting where a group of people try to decide what to do. They try to solve a problem. At the large outdoor meetings, interpreters changed English into Indian languages. In this way, Indians could understand more of what Governor Stevens was telling them.

Indian Reservations

The governor thought problems between Indians and settlers would be better if the Indians lived only on land set aside just for them. The places were called *reservations* because the land was reserved for Indians. No one else could live there.

Governor Stevens promised Indian leaders that the U.S. government would give them blankets, clothes, flour, tools, and money in exchange for their land. Stevens promised that the Indians could leave the reservations to hunt and fish for food. He promised that Indians and settlers could live in peace.

Realizing they had little choice, many Indian leaders signed the treaties. In just over a year, the governor had made 10 treaties with Indians. Life changed for Indians in the territory.

This picture shows the Blackfeet Treaty Council. Governor Stevens stands at the center under a canvas tent. **How is this picture similar to the one on page 116-117?**

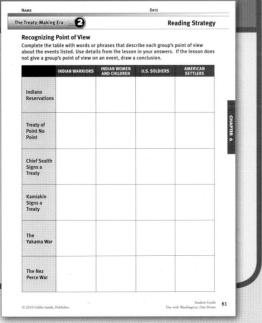

The first council ended with the signing of the Treaty of Medicine Creek. Medicine Creek is now named McAllister Creek. It is near Olympia.

Why Did Settlers Want Indian Lands?

Settlers wanted land that was *profitable*. This means they wanted to make a profit, or money, from the land. They wanted to sell *lumber* (logs sawed into boards) from forests. They wanted to sell crops they could grow on Indian land.

Often, the reservations were on land that was not as fertile as the land the Indians were forced to leave. *Fertile* means good for growing crops. The reservation land did not always have as many natural resources as Indian homelands.

125

Reading Strategy

Recognizing Point of View

Remind students that point of view is the way a person thinks about something that happened. (Point of view was discussed on page 15 in Chapter 1.) As students read this lesson, encourage them to think about the different points of view in each event. Tell students to consider how four different groups of people felt about each event: Indian warriors, Indians women and children, U.S. soldiers, and American settlers. Have students complete the Recognizing Point of View activity available in the *Student Guide*.

NAME _____ DATE _____

The Treaty-Making Era **②**   **Reading Strategy**

Recognizing Point of View

Complete the table with words or phrases that describe each group's point of view about the events listed. Use details from the lesson in your answers. If the lesson does not give a group's point of view on an event, draw a conclusion.

	INDIAN WARRIORS	INDIAN WOMEN AND CHILDREN	U.S. SOLDIERS	AMERICAN SETTLERS
Indians Reservations				
Treaty of Point No Point				
Chief Sealth Signs a Treaty				
Kamiakin Signs a Treaty				
The Yakama War				
The Nez Perce War				

© 2010 Gibbs Smith, Publisher   Student Guide **61** Use with Washington, *Our Home*

Standards

GLE 3.2.3
Understands that the geographic features of the Pacific Northwest have influenced the movement of people.

TEACH

Talk About It

Native Americans and Settlers
(From page 126)

What problems did settlers bring?
Settlers wanted to live on Indian land, they fished and hunted animals Indians needed for food, and they brought diseases.

Different Points of View About the Land *(From page 126)*

How did settlers feel about the land?
The settlers felt that land was something to be claimed and used to make money.

How did Indians feel about the land?
Indians felt the lands were to be for their whole group. No one in the group owned his own land.

Governor Stevens and Indian Treaties

What happened at a *council*?
A council is a meeting where a group of people try to decide what to do. These councils were large outdoor meetings where Indians and settlers met to try to solve the problem of sharing land.

Indian Reservations

What was the purpose of creating reservations?
The governor thought having Indians living on land set aside just for them would solve problems between settlers and Indians.

Why do you think Indians signed treaties even though they didn't want to?
Encourage students to consider how the Indians felt watching more and more settlers come to the region over the years.

Why Did Settlers Want Indian Lands?

Why did settlers want Indian Lands?
They wanted to sell lumber from the forests, and to sell crops they could grow on the land.

What were some of the problems with the reservations?
The reservations were often on land that was not fertile. There was no access to fishing on some reservations.

Talk About It

Issac Stevens

What kind of student was Isaac Stevens when he was young?

He was a whiz at math problems and always tried to learn as much as he could and do as much as he could. He graduated from West Point Military Academy with the best grades of the class.

Why did it take Stevens a year to travel to the new Washington Territory?

He worked as a surveyor as he traveled, trying to find the best railroad route from the East to Puget Sound.

Why were people in Olympia surprised when Stevens arrived?

He didn't look like the people thought the new governor would look. He was short, had long hair, and his clothes were wrinkled.

What were some of the goals Stevens wanted to achieve while in office?

He wanted a better way to deliver mail, better roads, and a library. His main goal was to have Indians in the area give up their land to the United States government.

Isaac Stevens

The Washington State Historical Society has a feature on their Web site called The Treaty Trail: U.S.- Indian Treaty Councils in the Northwest. This site includes lots of information about Isaac Stevens as well as activities that allow students to study primary and secondary sources. Have students visit this site and explore the activities. A link to this site can be found at **www.ExperienceStateHistory.com.**

Isaac Stevens

How did Isaac Stevens, born in the state of Massachusetts, end up as the first governor of Washington Territory? The story started when Stevens was a boy. At school, he was a whiz at math problems. He always tried to learn as much as he could and do as much as he could do. At age 16, he left home to learn how to be a soldier. A few years later, he graduated from West Point, a military academy, with the best grades of the class. Stevens fought in a war with Mexico. Then he learned to survey land.

Governor of the Territory

At age 35, Stevens was appointed as the first governor of the new Washington Territory. On his year-long trip across the country, he worked as a surveyor to find the best railroad route from the East to Puget Sound.

When he finally arrived at a hotel in Olympia, he didn't look like the people thought the new governor would look. A short man, Stevens' hair was long and his clothes were wrinkled. Men at the hotel told him he would have to stand outside until the new governor arrived!

Once in office, Stevens went right to work. He wanted a better way to deliver mail. He wanted better roads than the muddy trails used at the time. He wanted to create schools and a library.

Indian Treaties

Stevens was also put in charge of Indian affairs. He spent the next two years traveling and meeting Indians from many groups. He wanted the Indians to give up their land to the U.S. government. Many of the treaties he negotiated are still in effect today.

The city of Lake Stevens and Stevens Elementary School in Seattle are named for Isaac Stevens.

 Technology Tie-In

Where in Time is Isaac Stevens?

From the Washington State Historical Society Web site, have students learn about Isaac Stevens from primary and secondary sources. This activity encourages them to think like a historian and choose which sources they would use to find information about various Stevens artifacts. Have students list which primary and secondary sources they studied during the activity and what information they gathered from each source. A link to this site can be found at **www.ExperienceStateHistory.com.**

Social Studies Activity

Instant Transcriber

From the Washington State Historical Society Web site, have students study the letter in the Instant Transcriber online activity. Encourage students to study the letter to find out who wrote the letter, who it was written to, why it was written, and what the letter was about. A link to this site can be found at **www.ExperienceStateHistory.com.**

The Stevens Treaties

1855 — Dec. | Jan. | Feb. | Mar. | Apr. | May | Jun. | Jul. | Aug. | Sep. | Oct. | Nov. | Dec. | Jan. — 1856

December 1854
Medicine Creek Treaty

January 1855
Treaty of Point Elliot

Treaty of Point No Point

Treaty of Neah Bay

June 1855
Treaty with the Walla Walla, Cayuse, and Umatilla

Treaty with the Yakama

Nez Perce Treaty

July 1855
Treaty of Hell Gate

October 1855
Treaty with the Blackfeet

January 1856
Quinault Treaty

Understanding Each Other

Often the groups did not communicate well because they spoke different languages. When Governor Stevens got Indian leaders to make their marks on a treaty, the words on the treaty were not always understood by the Indians. The Indians could not read the printed words. After they signed the treaties, they were forced to leave their homes and move to smaller land regions.

The treaties promised much to the Indian peoples. However, sometimes the promises were not kept. The treaties were sometimes changed when the needs of the settlers changed.

Many white people believed the Indians should become like them. They saw them as wild people who needed to be taught. They wanted to *civilize* them, or make them more educated and cultured. They thought the Indians should become part of white society.

What Do You Think ?

Do you think it was good or bad to make so many treaties in a short amount of time?

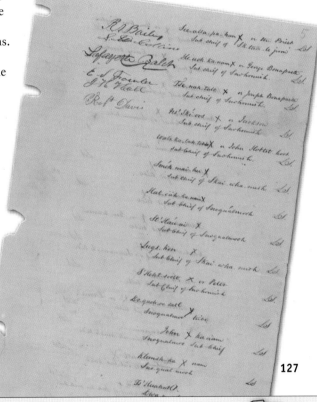

The Treaty of Point Elliott was one of the treaties Governor Stevens signed with the Indians. **Can you see the "X" marks? Why do you think some of the chiefs signed with an "X?"**

Territories and Treaties

127

Talk About It

Understanding Each Other

Why did the groups sometimes have a hard time communicating?
The groups spoke different languages.

What was unfair about having Indians sign a treaty when they couldn't always read the printed words?
The Indians did not always understand what the treaties were and sometimes signed them without knowing what was going to happen.

What happened after treaties were signed?
Sometimes promises made in the treaties were kept, and sometimes they weren't. The treaties were sometimes changed when the needs of the settlers changed.

Caption Answer

As a class, discuss possible reasons why some of the chiefs signed with an "X." Explain that some of the chiefs might not have known how to write and some showed how they were feeling by only signing an "X."

What Do You Think ?

Have students write their opinions in a journal and explain why they feel that way. Explain that there is no right or wrong answer, people will have different opinions.

 Writing Activity

Cooperative Groups

Write a Treaty

Have students work in small groups to write a treaty of trade with another small group. Before writing the treaty, have each group decide what item they want from the other group. Encourage students to work together to write a treaty of what they think would be a fair trade with the other group. Have each group exchange their treaties and hold a council to discuss what they will and will not accept from the treaty.

Standards

GLE 4.2.1
Understands and analyzes how individuals caused change in Washington State history.

Talk About It

Treaty of Point No Point

Why did Governor Isaac Stevens hold a council on the Kitsap Peninsula?
He wanted the Indians who lived there to give up the peninsula.

After reading the Indians' words about the council, how do you think they felt about giving up their land?
They didn't want to leave their land. The natural resources on the peninsula provided their food; they were worried that they wouldn't have enough food to eat if they gave up their land.

Why do you think the Indians gave up their land even though they didn't want to?
The number of settlers in the area had grown so fast, the Indians probably felt outnumbered.

Art Activity
Cooperative Groups

Clothing of Indian Groups

Because each Indian group is its own nation with its own government, many groups dress differently. Go to the Wikimedia Commons Web site to view images of several Washington Indian groups, including the Skokomish, Suquamish, Nez Perce, Cayuse, Walla Walla, Umatilla, and Yakama. Download images of their clothing. Divide the students into seven groups, one for each of the Indians groups represented. Have students write about what they see in the images and what the clothing tells about the Indian group. Have students recreate the clothing of the Indian group they studied. They may choose to draw, paint, or use other materials to create the clothing. See **www.ExperienceStateHistory.com** for a link to this site.

Indian Leaders Speak Out

Indian leaders signed the treaties, but they had strong feelings about giving up their land.

They talked about it over and over again. Translators wrote down some of the things the Indian leaders said. Their words are important to the history of our state.

Treaty of Point No Point

On the northern tip of the Kitsap Peninsula, Governor Stevens held a council. He wanted the Indians who lived there to give up the peninsula. He promised that the Indians could still hunt and fish on the land.

Over 1,200 Indian men showed up at the council. Translators explained to them what Stevens wanted. A newspaper, the *Pacific Northwest Quarterly*, published these words from Indian leaders. *Hool-hol-tan*, a Skokomish leader, said:

I wish to speak my mind as to selling the land. Great chief! What shall we eat if we do so? Our only food is berries, deer, and salmon. Where then shall we find these? I don't want to sign away my right to the land. Take half of it and let us keep the rest . . . I don't like the place you have chosen for us to live on. I am not ready to sign the paper.

L'Hau-at-scha-uk said:

I do not want to leave the mouth of the river. I do not want to leave my old home, and my burying ground. I am afraid I shall die if I do.

Chief Sealth

After talking all day, the Indians asked if they could think about the treaties overnight. The next morning they came to the site carrying white flags of peace. They marked the document and gave up their land.

Background Info

Chief Sealth

At a young age, Sealth earned the reputation of a leader and a warrior. He ambushed and defeated groups of enemy raiders and attacked other tribes that lived on the Olympic Peninsula. He owned slaves that he captured during his raids. He was tall and broad at nearly six feet; this earned him the nickname Le Gros (The Big One) from the Hudson's Bay Company traders. Chief Sealth was also known as a great public speaker. It is said that when he addressed his audiences, his voice carried from his camp to the Stevens Hotel at First and Marion (3/4 of a mile distance). Although Sealth was a very skilled warrior and leader, he started losing ground to the more powerful Patkanim of the Snohomish when white settlers started showing up in large numbers. Sealth and other Indian chiefs in the area made friendly relationships to keep peace among the tribes. The city of Seattle is named after him.

Chief Moses Moves His People

Chief Moses was a leader of the Columbia-Sinkiuse tribe. After he signed a treaty, he took his people to the Yakama Reservation. He told how the settlers created problems for the Indian people:

There are white men living in my country. Some can stay forever and some must go. . . . People who raise hogs in my country [white people] must go with their hogs, because they kill out the young camas [bulbs] and to kill that is to starve us. It is our bread and we cannot eat earth. . . .

—From a letter from Chief Moses, 1879

Chief Sealth Signs a Treaty

Chief Sealth was a leader of the Suquamish and Duwamish groups. He was known as a friend of the settlers.

Like most of the coastal leaders, Chief Sealth decided to sign a treaty. It allowed his people to leave the reservations each year and go fishing as they always had. For them, it seemed that their old way of life could still go on.

Chief Sealth gave a speech at the treaty ceremony that later became famous. He said:

The settlers are many. They are like the grass that covers vast prairies. My people are few. You say you will buy our lands and give us enough to live on. We will accept your offer. But to us, the land of our ancestors will always be special. Every hillside, every plain and forest is filled with their spirits. The white man will never be alone. Our spirits will always be here.

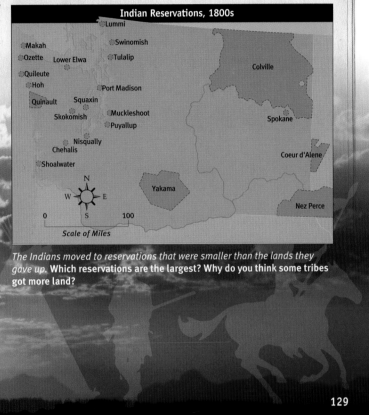

Indian Reservations, 1800s

Lummi, Makah, Ozette, Lower Elwa, Swinomish, Tulalip, Quileute, Hoh, Quinault, Squaxin, Skokomish, Muckleshoot, Puyallup, Port Madison, Colville, Spokane, Nisqually, Chehalis, Shoalwater, Coeur d'Alene, Yakama, Nez Perce

Scale of Miles 0 100

The Indians moved to reservations that were smaller than the lands they gave up. Which reservations are the largest? Why do you think some tribes got more land?

Territories and Treaties

129

Talk About It

Chief Moses Moves His People

What problems were settlers causing for Chief Moses and his people?
The hogs that settlers were raising were killing camas bulbs that the Columbia-Sinkiuse people ate.

Chief Sealth Signs a Treaty

What was Chief Sealth known as?
He was known as a friend of the settlers.

What did the treaty that Chief Sealth signed say his people could still do?
The treaty said his people could leave the reservations each year and go fishing as they always had.

 Map Activity

Indian Reservations in the 1800s

As a class, discuss the map of Indian reservations in the 1800s. Talk about the size and location of each reservation. Have students research Washington Indian reservations on the Internet and in books from the school and city libraries to answer these questions:

- How many Indian reservations are in use in Washington today?
- Which reservation in Washington has the most people living on it today?
- Which reservation in Washington had the most people living on it in the 1800s?

Allow students to share their findings with the class.

 Differentiated Paths

Chief Sealth's Speech

One of the key objectives of this lesson is to understand that the Indians and the U.S. government had different points of view about the land.

ELL and Special Needs

As a class, read Chief Sealth's speech. Stop at the end of each sentence to talk about the meaning of the speech. Explain that men in the U.S. government wrote the treaties. Tell students that the Indians and the U.S. government had different points of view about the land. Have students work in pairs to complete a Venn diagram with words or phrases describing how each group felt about the land. A Venn diagram is available in the graphic organizer section of the *Teacher Guide.*

Gifted Learners

Have students read Chief Sealth's speech on this page. Discuss what Chief Sealth's point of view was about the treaty and the land. Encourage students to think about how the Indian women and children, U.S. soldiers, and American settlers felt at the time the treaty was signed. Have students write a short speech from the point of view of the other three groups of people in response to Chief Sealth's speech. Hold a council and allow students to share their speeches with the class.

129

Talk About It

The Yakama People

Describe the group of people who met at a council with Governor Stevens at Walla Walla.

The Indian men were Nez Perce, Cayuse, Walla Walla, Umatilla, and Yakama. The Yakama people were not a tribe. They were 14 groups who spoke the same language and shared hunting grounds.

At the council, what did Kamiakin say he wanted?

He wished for a good government agent who would pity the good and bad of the group and take care of them. He wanted to get back to his garden.

Caption Answer

Encourage students to think about the setting and meaning of the council and discuss how they would feel.

Have students consider the perspectives of the United States government and the Indians.

 Writing Activity

Reservation Report

Have students choose an Indian reservation from the map on page 129. Tell them to research information about the reservation. Tell students to be sure to cover the following topics in their report:

- Reservation name
- Location (include a map)
- Name of the Indian group
- Date reservation was established
- History of the reservation
- The reservation today

130

The Yakama People

During one of Governor Stevens' councils, he met with 5,000 Indians at Walla Walla. They were Nez Perce, Cayuse, Walla Walla, Umatilla, and Yakama people. Until the meeting, the Yakama people were not a tribe. They were 14 groups that spoke the same language and shared hunting grounds. Governor Stevens grouped them into one tribe. He named Kamiakin, a respected Indian, as "head chief" of the whole group. Kamiakin was a proud but quiet man. He had not wanted to come to the council at all. He said:

The forest knows me; he knows my heart. He knows I do not desire a great many goods. All that I wish for is a good [government] agent who will pity the good and bad of us and take care of us. I have nothing to talk about. I am tired. I am anxious to get back to my garden. That is all I have to say.

Since the Nez Perce and Yakama were larger tribes, Stevens agreed to give them large reservations in their homelands. The smaller tribes had to agree to this.

The Nez Perce arrive for the Walla Walla Treaty Council. **How might you feel if you were one of them? How might you feel if you were standing with Governor Stevens as the Indians arrived?**

130

Washington, Our Home

This painting shows the Battle of Seattle during the Yakama War. The artist, Emily Inez Denny, was three years old at the time of the battle. **How would you describe what is happening in the painting?**

The Yakama War

Only a few years after the treaties were signed, something happened that changed everything. Gold was found near the upper Columbia River. Men rushed onto the Yakama Indian Reservation to find gold and get rich.

Stevens told the whites not to enter the Yakama lands, but they came anyway. The Indians who lived on the reservation were angry. They wanted to *defend* their land. They started killing the gold-seekers.

Then soldiers from the U.S. Army rode in on horses. They captured Chief Kamiakin and his people. This ended the fighting for a short time.

At the same time, Seattle was attacked by Indians. It seemed as if the whole region was at war. Again U.S. soldiers came. This time, they were surrounded by Indians. The Indians killed some of the soldiers. During the dark night, however, the rest of the soldiers escaped. They had to leave their guns and horses behind.

The army sent a group of 600 more soldiers to punish the Indians. They killed 700 Indian horses. They killed 24 Indian leaders. They also forced the Indians to sign peace treaties, ending the Yakama War.

Chief Kamiakin was told he could return to the reservation in peace, but he would not go. He spent the rest of his life alone in the wilderness.

Territories and Treaties

131

Talk About It

The Yakama War

Why were American settlers rushing onto Indian reservations?
Gold was found near the upper Columbia River. Men wanted to find gold and get rich.

How did Indians react to white people coming onto their reservations?
The Indians on the reservations were angry. They started killing the gold-seekers to defend their land.

Why did the fighting stop for a short time?
Soldiers from the U.S. Army captured Chief Kamiakin and his people.

Encourage students to think about how the Indians and the Americans felt about gold being found on the Indian reservation.
Have students journal their feelings about this event.

Caption Answer

There is a battle taking place near the coast. Women and children are running for safety.

Science Activity

Pan for Gold

Tell students that gold is a mineral, not a rock. Minerals are the building blocks that make up rocks. Gold can be found in different kinds of rock. Because gold is heavier than most sediments and gravel in a stream, it and other heavy minerals can be collected in a pan. Have your students participate in a gold panning experience. Mix small rocks painted gold in a large tub with dirt and water. Have students take turns scooping up dirt from the "river bottom" using a pie pan with netting of some kind along the bottom of the pan. After scooping up the dirt, have students lift the netting and gently shake the contents of the river bottom until the lighter rocks and minerals have been sifted out and the gold nuggets are left in the netting.

Technology Tie-In

Native Americans in the Gold Rush

Much like the famous gold rush of 1849 in California, the discovery of gold in Washington caused many problems for Indians. PBS has a Web site titled The Gold Rush that contains stories from Native Americans about the gold rush in California. Indians in both California and Washington experienced some of the same horrible experiences of having their land taken away and poor treatment by gold-seekers. You may want to choose a few of the stories from this site to share with the class. Have students compare the experiences of the Indians in California to the experiences of Indians in Washington. Have students play the game Strike It Rich! found on this Web site. This game has students choose a character from history and role play to see if they can strike it rich in their search for gold.

Talk About It

The Nez Perce War

What was the problem the Nez Perce faced when they gave up land?
They didn't have a lot of land where they could hunt, fish, and gather food.

Chief Joseph

Why did the army tell Chief Joseph's people that they had to go?
Gold was discovered on the Nez Perce land and more settlers were coming who wanted land.

What did Chief Joseph decide to do when the army told his people they had to go?
(From page 133)
He wanted only peace. He decided he would help his people escape to Canada.

What happened after Chief Joseph decided to lead his people to Canada?
(From page 133)
The U.S. Army followed and there were many battles. For 105 days the group walked toward Canada. The weather turned cold and there was little food. Just before they reached the border, the army attacked. Many Indians died in the battle.

Chief Joseph Surrenders
(From page 133)

How did Chief Joseph feel when he surrendered?
He was sad, cold, and hungry. He surrendered to save his people.

Caption Answer

The families lived close to each other and spent a lot of time together. They used resources from the land for their homes, food, and clothing.

Technology Tie-In

Nez Perce Summer, 1877

The National Park Service has a Web site with information about the Nez Perce War. The information is a great source of information for teachers. There are also maps of different stages of the Nez Perce War that would be helpful to show students. A link to this site can be found at **www.ExperienceStateHistory.com.**

The Nez Perce War

The Nez Perce were a large Plateau tribe. They were peaceful people. In earlier years, they had helped Lewis and Clark and some of the missionaries.

After treaties were made, the Indians gave up their land. This was hard on the people. On the dry plateau, food was hard to find. The people had to have a lot of land where they could hunt, fish, and gather food. Without their hunting lands, they could not survive.

Chief Joseph

Chief Joseph's father, also called Chief Joseph, had signed Governor Stevens' first treaty at Walla Walla. After the older chief died, his son took his place as leader of the Nez Perce.

Then gold was found on Nez Perce land. More settlers and miners were coming every day, and they wanted the Nez Perce to leave. The army told Chief Joseph's people they had to move again.

Chief Joseph still wanted peace, but some of the young men in the tribe did not. They did not want to move to a reservation far from where they lived. They wanted to fight or escape.

The Nez Perce lived peacefully on the reservation until gold was discovered there. **What does this picture tell you about their lives?**

132   Washington, Our Home

Literature Link

Thunder Rolling in the Mountains

Thunder Rolling in the Mountains by Scott O'Dell makes an excellent read-aloud. This short chapter book about a young Nez Perce girl tells how her people were driven off their land by the U.S. Army and forced to retreat north. Chief Joseph is one of the main characters in this book. As you read the book, have students write down things the book mentions that they learned through their study of Washington State history this school year. Go to **www.ExperienceStateHistory.com** for a link to this site.

Chief Joseph (From page 133)

Chief Joseph was a proud leader who did not want to surrender. Explain to students that there were many other Indian chiefs in the history of the United States who felt the same way that Chief Joseph felt. Have students work in small groups to research other famous Indian chiefs on the Internet. Have students compare and contrast details about Chief Joseph and the Indian chief they chose to research. A Venn diagram, for comparing and contrasting, is available in the graphic organizers section of the *Teacher Guide.*

Chief Joseph and his warriors surrender. **What is Chief Joseph handing over?**

Chief Joseph made his decision. He wanted only peace, but he would help his people escape to Canada. About 700 men, women, and children walked north with the young men. The U.S. Army followed, and there were many battles. The Nez Perce won many of them. They used bows and arrows, shotguns, and rifles. They outshot and outrode the army.

For 105 days the group walked toward Canada. Then October came with bad weather. The people were cold, and there was little food. Just before they reached the border, the army attacked. Many Indians died in the battle.

Chief Joseph Surrenders

The next day, a snowstorm blew in. Heartsick, freezing, and hungry, Chief Joseph had no choice but to **surrender**, or give up. He said:

It is cold and we have no blankets. The little children are freezing to death. . . . My heart is sick and sad. From where the sun now stands, I will fight no more forever.

LESSON 2 What Did You Learn?

1. How did the Indians feel about the land? How did the U.S. government feel about the land?
2. What were the purposes of the many treaties signed?
3. What were some of the problems caused by moving Indians to reservations?

Territories and Treaties

Chief Joseph

The leader of the Nez Perce was *Hin-maton-Yal-a-kit*, which meant Thunder Traveling to Lofty Mountain Heights. The white settlers called him Chief Joseph.

Chief Joseph lived part of his childhood at a Christian mission. Many of his people had become Christians. Chief Joseph was helpful to the settlers.

The peaceful life changed for the Nez Perce when gold was found on their land and they were told to leave. Chief Joseph led his people away. After fighting many battles and facing cold weather, he knew his people could stand no more. He surrendered.

The army moved the people to a reservation in faraway Oklahoma. Many died there. Later, the government brought the people back to Washington. Chief Joseph, the proud leader, died there.

133

Reflect on students' understanding of the history of the treaty-making era in Washington Territory and the effect it had on the Indians and the American settlers. You can evaluate students' understanding through discussion or evaluation of activities completed in this lesson. The following activity will serve as another way of assessing students' understanding of the key objectives of this lesson.

Writing Activity

Letter of Opinion

Have students write a letter to the United States Bureau of Indian Affairs (BIA) presenting their opinion about the treatment of the Indians. Encourage students to use facts to support their opinion. Have students complete the Letter of Opinion activity available in the *Student Guide.*

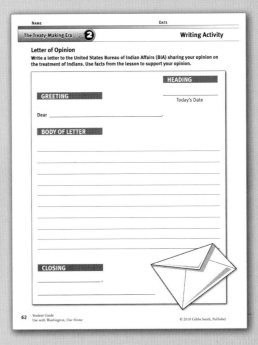

Caption Answer

Chief Joseph is handing over a gun to the army. This was a symbol of his surrender.

LESSON 2 What Did You Learn?

1. *Indian lands were thought to be for their whole group. No one in the group owned his own land. Indians had hunting and fishing grounds for everyone to use. The settlers claimed land, put fences around it, and kept other people away. They wanted to use natural resources to make a profit.*
2. *Many of the treaties were signed to remove Indians from lands that settlers wanted and put them on reservations.*
3. *Many Indians were moved to reservations were they didn't have the resources they needed for food, clothing, and shelter.*

LESSON 3 Becoming a State

Standards

GLE 4.1.2
Understands how the following themes and developments help to define eras in Washington State history from time immemorial to 1889: Immigration and settlement

PREPARE

Activator

Anticipation Guide

To activate students' prior knowledge and build interest before reading, have students complete the Anticipation Guide activity available in the *Student Guide*. Have students answer yes or no to each question before reading and correct any mistakes after reading.

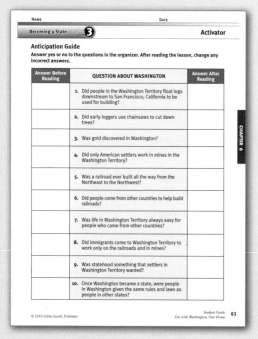

Key Ideas

- New industries brought immigrants to the territory.
- New towns and cities grew.
- Washington became a state.

Words to Understand

community
discrimination
ethnic
gold rush
opportunity
spike

Lumber companies found plenty of trees in Washington Territory. These loggers are at work in Bellingham.

134

Lumber, Gold, and Growth

The year was 1849. Gold had been found in California the year before. Thousands of people called "forty-niners" were heading there, hoping to become rich. The *gold rush* had begun. California was booming. Its population was growing fast.

At the same time, Washington's towns were still very small. But all the people living in California helped the Northwest grow. How did this happen?

Logging

The city of San Francisco, California, was a shipping port. The people there needed wood to make shipping docks and buildings. They even built wooden sidewalks. Where would the people get all the wood they needed?

Washington Territory had plenty of forests with big, tall trees. Workers cut down trees near the water. They floated the logs downstream, then tied them together. Ships pulled the piles of logs to San Francisco. Logging was big business.

Little by little, lumber and shipping towns sprang up around Puget Sound. The small towns of Olympia, Seattle, Port Townsend, and Tacoma grew.

Timber!

Early loggers had no machines to help them. All the power came from people and animals.

Two men worked on each tree. They started the cut with axes. Then one man stood on each side of a tree. Each man pulled his end of a giant saw. Back and forth they sawed until the tree fell.

After the tree crashed to the ground, teams of oxen hauled the logs out of the forest. Here is how one logger described the work.

"This is how we worked, Rud and Me. I chopped from the left, Rud from the right. Then each swung from the hips with the axe. Shunk-shink! Shunk-shink! Then we began to saw timber."

Washington, Our Home

Word Study

Word Reports

Have students create word reports about words from the Washington Territory. A word report can be as simple as an illustration and definition of a new word or as complex as a poster illustrating many new words.

Words to Understand

community (p. 139) *a group of people living near each other in a place*

discrimination (p. 139) *to treat other people badly just because they are different*

ethnic (p. 143) *referring to a minority race*

gold rush (p. 134) *a rush to a new gold field in hopes of getting rich*

opportunity (p. 141) *a good chance for progress or advancement*

spike (p. 138) *a very long, thick nail*

A Words to Understand activity for this lesson is available in the *Student Guide*.

Logging was hard work. After cutting the trees down, the men had to get them ready to be moved. "Buckers" had to cut off the branches. They had to make sure the trunks weren't too long for the sawmill. Logging was also dangerous work. On a steep hill or mountain, a huge log might roll down and crush someone. **What tools do the men in this picture have?**

Territories and Treaties   135

TEACH

Talk About It

Lumber, Gold, and Growth
(From page 134)

Why were many people rushing to California?
Gold had been found in California and many people wanted to find gold to get rich.

Logging *(From page 134)*

How did the growth in California help Washington Territory grow?
San Francisco needed lumber from Washington Territory for building. Many people worked to cut lumber and send it downstream to California.

Which Washington Territory towns grew a lot because of logging?
Olympia, Seattle, Port Townsend, and Tacoma all grew because of logging.

Timber! *(From page 134)*

Why was early logging so difficult?
Early loggers had no machines to help them. All the power came from people and animals.

Caption Answer

The men are using axes and long saws to cut the trees down.

 Reading Strategy

Recognizing Cause and Effect

Tell students that good readers use several strategies to help them understand new information. One of these strategies is recognizing cause and effect. Almost every event has a cause or reason behind it. Take an event from the lesson, such as the growth in immigration from other countries. Ask students what the cause of the event was. From the reading, students should understand that the cause of the immigration was the need for workers in mines and on the railroads. After reading the lesson, have students complete the Cause and Effect activity available in the *Student Guide*.

NAME _____ DATE _____

Becoming a State   Lesson **3**   **Reading Strategy**

Cause and Effect
After reading lesson 3, complete the Cause and Effect chart.

CAUSE	EFFECT
San Francisco, California needed lumber for building.	
	All logging had to be done by people and animals.
Gold and silver were discovered in Washington Territory.	
	The Great Northern railroad was built and ended in Seattle.
Building a railroad was hard work. Many men were needed to finish the job.	
	Many bosses in America looked for workers in Japan.
Washington finally had enough people to become a state!	

© 2010 Gibbs Smith, Publisher   Student Guide **65**
                                       Use with *Washington, Our Home*

135

Talk About It

Gold and Silver

What was the exciting news from the Washington Territory?
Gold and silver had been found in the Washington Territory.

Why did many miners stop in the little town of Walla Walla?
Many miners stopped in Walla Walla to buy supplies for mining.

Coal Mining

Why was coal needed in the Washington Territory?
Coal was needed to heat homes in the territory.

What invention made coal even more important?
Steam engines needed coal. As coal burned, it heated up water in the tank. When the water boiled, steam shot up and made the engines turn.

Caption Answer

There are buildings where the men ate and slept. The camp is busy with people coming to and from the mines.

May Arkwright Hutton

Have students create a Shutter Fold book to display details about May Arkwright Hutton's many accomplishments. First, have students do further research about May Arkwright Hutton on the Internet or in books from the school and city library. After gathering information for the book, instruct students how to create this book, following the diagram provided. Tell students to decorate the front with an image that represents May Arkwright Hutton. On the inside, have students choose a creative way to display the information they found.

May Arkwright Hutton

May Arkwright was one of thousands of people who hurried west to start a new life in mining towns. Life in the mining areas was rough and wild. May was not afraid, though. She knew what she wanted to do. She would make money by fixing food for miners.

May cooked in a saloon and then opened a boarding house for men. She married Al Hutton, a railroad worker. With some partners, the Huttons bought a mine in Idaho. May kept cooking, and Al kept his railroad job.

The partners dug for four years. Then, one day, they found silver! May said, "The Lord gave me money to serve." The Huttons moved to Spokane. They helped orphans, miners, and others in need. May worked for women's voting rights.

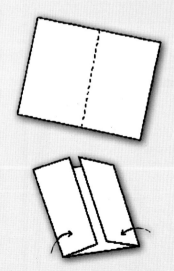

Gold and Silver

Gold was being mined in California. About six years later, exciting news arrived from eastern Washington Territory. Gold and silver had been found there, too! Hopeful miners hurried to places that are now in eastern Washington, Idaho, and Montana.

Many miners stopped in the little town of Walla Walla to buy supplies. It became the largest town in the region.

Coal Mining

Gold and silver were not the only minerals people wanted. People needed a lot of coal. They burned black lumps of coal in furnaces to heat their homes.

Men worked in coal mines under the ground. The miners came from many countries.

Coal became even more important after steam engines were invented. As coal burned, it heated up water in a tank. When the water boiled, steam shot up and made the engines turn. This kind of engine turned the wheels on steamships and trains.

Many mining camps looked like this one. **What buildings and activities do you see?**

Railroads Across the Nation

There were already many railroads in the East, but people wanted to travel by train all the way across the country. After many years of hard work, the first railroad from Nebraska all the way to California was built. Settlers could take a train to California and then take a ship to Puget Sound. This was much easier and faster than the trip by wagon across the Oregon Trail.

Still, Northwest settlers wanted their own railroad. Trains would bring new settlers to the region. The railroads would also bring things the settlers needed, such as cooking stoves, window glass, and cloth.

The Northern Pacific Comes to Washington

Finally, a railroad was built to the Northwest. It was called the Northern Pacific. The tracks ran from Minnesota to Portland, Oregon, and then north to Tacoma.

The other towns on Puget Sound wanted a railroad, too. The people of Seattle were angry that the tracks ended at Tacoma. They decided to build their own tracks. However, they soon found that this was hard work. They gave up after building just a small part.

Ten years later, the people in Seattle got their wish. A new railroad, the Great Northern, came to Seattle.

This was the first train headed to Oregon on the Northern Pacific Railway. **Why do you think people decorated the train?**

Across the Continent

- Seattle
- Tacoma
- Spokane
- Portland
- St. Paul
- Omaha
- Sacramento
    0   500 MILES

Legend
- Northern Pacific
- Great Northern
- Central Pacific
- Union Pacific

Territories and Treaties

Talk About It

Railroad Across the Nation

What was the new, easier way to travel to the Washington Territory?
Travelers could take the train from Nebraska to San Francisco and then travel by ship to Puget Sound.

Why did the settlers in the Northwest want their own railroad?
Trains would bring new settlers to the region. The trains could also bring things the settlers needed, such as cooking stoves, window glass, and cloth.

The Northern Pacific Comes to Washington

Did the railroad ever reach Puget Sound?
Yes, ten years after people in Seattle tried to build their own tracks and gave up.

Caption Answer

They had waited so long for a train and were so excited to finally have one. They decorated the train to show their excitement.

Map Activity

Across the Continent

Using the scale on the map, have students work in pairs to estimate the length of each of the railroads. Tell students to rank them from longest to shortest. Have students write a few sentences to describe the terrain that each railroad crossed.

Science Activity

How a Steam Engine Works

Visit the Animated Engines Web site to show students animated diagrams of how steam engines work. After sharing the site, have students write the steps of how a steam engine works. Ask students to list what machines may had been powered by steam engines in the Washington Territory. A link to this site can be found at **www.ExperienceStateHistory.com.**

Talk About It

Working on the Railroad

What was it like working on the railroad?
Railroad workers worked 10 hours a day in the burning heat of summer and the freezing cold of winter. Everything had to be done by hand. Work was hard. The work was dangerous. Many men got hurt.

Caption Answer

The crew cut through the hill to make way for the railroad track.

James J. Hill

James Hill learned skills in English, geometry, and surveying land at a young age. These skills helped him as an adult in his future business. Explain to students that they are learning things in their young age that will help them in their future career choices. Have students make a list of skills they have learned in school and how that skill could help them in a future career.

James J. Hill

As a boy in Canada, James Hill was an excellent student, but he had to quit school when his father died. He was already very good at English, geometry, and surveying land. These skills were valuable once Hill got interested in railroads.

When he was old enough, Hill went to work in a store to earn money for his family. Later, he moved to Minnesota and worked on a steamboat. Soon he owned his own shipping business.

Hill began buying railroads and building his own trains. He went on to run the Great Northern Railway Company. The railroad helped bring settlers to the Northwest. It helped industry grow.

138

Working on the Railroad

Thousands of workers helped build the great railroads of the West. They came from Europe, Asia, and many parts of the United States. They worked 10 hours a day in the burning heat of summer and the freezing cold of winter.

Building a railroad was hard work. Everything had to be done by hand. Railroad workers used picks, shovels, and plows to make a flat path. They built bridges over rivers and blasted tunnels through the mountains with dynamite. The work was dangerous. Many men got hurt.

Next, workers laid the ties. Ties were heavy bars of wood, eight feet long. Across these, the men placed heavy iron rails. Finally, they pounded long thick nails called *spikes* into the rails to keep them on the ties. Think of pounding spikes with heavy hammers for 10 hours!

It took a lot of muscle power to lay the tracks.
How has this crew changed the land?

Washington, Our Home

 Math Activity

Railroads Bring Change

The railroads made travel easier. The trip across the country could now be done in almost a week. More people moved here to work. Draw this chart on the board and have students study the information to answer the questions.

- By how much did the population of each town grow from 1880 to 1890? *Seattle: 39,304; Tacoma 34,908; Spokane 19,642*
- Which town was the largest in 1880? 1890? *Seattle*
- Which town was the smallest in 1880? 1890? *Spokane*
- What changes happened between 1880 and 1890 that made these towns grow quickly? *Railroads were built connecting the East to the West. This made it easier for people to travel to the West.*

CITY	SEATTLE	TACOMA	SPOKANE
POPULATION IN 1880	3,533	1,098	350
POPULATION IN 1890	42,837	36,006	19,992

About 1,500 Chinese workers helped finish the Northern Pacific Railroad. **What clues in the picture tell you about the challenges they faced?**

Chinese Workers

One of the largest groups of railroad workers came from China. Many people in China were very poor. News of the California gold rush caused great excitement in China. "There's a mountain of gold in America!" people said.

Thousands of Chinese men came to the United States. They hoped to earn money to take home to their families in China.

The first men to arrive from China went to look for gold. However, Chinese workers were not treated fairly. The best gold mining areas were closed to them. So were good jobs. Other people called them bad names. This kind of *discrimination* hurt the Chinese.

Chinese men had to find other ways to earn money. Some started small businesses. Some cooked food or washed and ironed clothes for other people. Many more went to work for the railroads.

After laying the tracks to California, many Chinese workers helped build the railroads of the Northwest. Others worked in mines. Some worked in fish canneries. They cleaned the fish and put them into cans. It was cold, smelly work.

Each year, new workers came. While they were here, most lived in "Chinatowns." These were *communities* where people could share their Chinese culture.

New Laws Keep the Chinese Out

The Chinese worked long hours for low pay. Other workers saw this. They were afraid that the bosses would want more Chinese workers, and white workers would lose their jobs.

When times were bad and there were few jobs, many white people felt angry at the Chinese. A law was passed. It said that no more Chinese workers could come to the United States. The law was later cancelled.

Chinese workers were paid less than other workers even if they did the same job.

Territories and Treaties

139

Talk About It

Chinese Workers

Why did many railroad workers come from China?
Many people in China were very poor. Thousands of Chinese men came to the United States hoping to earn money. Many men came from China to work in mines. When they had problems with discrimination, many men began working on the railroads.

Why do you think many Chinese immigrants chose to live in "Chinatowns?"
When immigrants came to a country that was different from theirs, it was hard. They lived near people who shared their same culture and traditions so that they felt more at home.

New Laws Keep the Chinese Out

Why were laws made to prevent more Chinese workers from coming to America?
Chinese workers worked long hours for low pay. White workers were afraid bosses would want more Chinese workers and white workers would lose their jobs.

Caption Answer

The men are working outside despite the snow and cold weather. They are working in the mountains, so they probably had to climb to get there.

 Background Info

Anti-Chinese Laws

Congress passed the Chinese Exclusion Act, which stopped Chinese laborers from entering the country. A few years later, when many white workers were jobless, they turned their anger against Chinese residents. Violent riots erupted in Issaquah, Tacoma, and Seattle. Over a thousand Chinese people were expelled from Washington Territory. Their homes and businesses were burned. Chinese men in Walla Walla and Pasco were attacked by white residents. Like many other times in history, racial prejudice made life miserable for immigrants. It was many years before laws were passed that made it illegal to hire or pay a person differently because of race.

Talk About It

Japanese Workers

Why did many Japanese immigrants start coming to America?

After laws stopped the Chinese from coming, bosses looked for workers in Japan. Japanese men filled many of the jobs that Chinese workers had done.

Were things any better for Japanese workers?

No, Japanese workers got low pay for hard work.

Picture Brides

Why were Japanese brides that came to America called picture brides?

It was common for families in Japan to choose husbands or wives for their older children. Parents would send pictures to America of the bride they chose for their sons. When the bride's ship came from Japan, the man picked his new wife out of the crowd from the photo.

Caption Answer

Encourage students to find similarities and differences between the clothes they wear and the clothes the family in the picture is wearing.

Japanese Workers

After laws stopped the Chinese from coming to the United States, bosses looked for workers in Japan. Japanese men filled many of the jobs that Chinese workers had done for the mines, railroads, and fish canneries.

Like the Chinese, Japanese workers got low pay for hard work. One young man wrote:

> My work was to cut down trees or to build the railroads, digging and filling land in the mountains. It was hard work. I was only a boy of a little more than 15.
>
> I had never done hard labor before. When I worked 10 or 12 hours a day, the next morning, I couldn't open my hands. For two or three months, I dipped them in hot water to stretch the fingers, and sometimes I secretly cried.
>
> I had good reason to work my hardest . . . for when I left Japan, I had promised my mother, 'I'll surely come back to Japan in a year.'

A Japanese family sits for a photo in their new country. **How do their clothes compare to the clothes you wear?**

Picture Brides

After they had saved a little money, many Japanese men began to think about getting married. At that time, it was common for families in Japan to choose husbands or wives for their older children. The young men in America wrote home and asked their families to arrange a marriage.

When girls were chosen, they sent the men a photo. Then they came across the ocean on ships. When the ship came from Japan, the man picked out his new wife from the photo.

These "picture brides" worked as hard in America as their husbands did. Many Japanese families started farms. They planted and picked fruits and vegetables to sell in the cities. Strawberries were one of their most important crops. Japanese Americans were also the first to grow oysters in Washington's bays.

140

Washington, Our Home

Differentiated Paths

I Am

An important reason to differentiate learning is to build students' self-esteem. Recognizing that we all learn in different ways and at different rates is a fact, not an evaluation. Have students think about who they are—what their strengths are as well as their weaknesses. Also, have students think about events in their lives that have had an impact on who they are. For immigrants that came to Washington Territory, it was life-changing to move to a new country.

ELL and Special Needs

Encourage ELL and Special Needs learners to draw an "I Am" picture showing their strengths and weaknesses or perhaps illustrating a life-changing event in their lives. Ask them to tell you about what they drew. If they are able, have them write a few words or phrases describing the pictures.

Gifted Learners

Encourage Gifted Learners to write an "I Am" poem or essay describing who they are.

Three years before Washington became a state, the Statue of Liberty welcomed immigrants in New York Harbor. Some of the people came to work in Washington. **How do you think this family felt when they saw the statue for the first time?**

A Land of Opportunity

An **opportunity** can provide a good chance to live a better life. There were many opportunities in Washington. There were plenty of jobs. A family could start a new business. They could get good farmland for a low price. The climate was mild, and Washington was a pleasant place to live.

Most of the new settlers came from the United States and Canada. Many also came from Europe. Many people in Europe were poor. They couldn't find jobs or good land for farming. They often faced discrimination. Millions of immigrants came to America. It was a place of land and jobs and freedom.

A Polish immigrant boards a ship with his belongings.

Linking the Present to the Past

Today, immigrants still come to Washington. Are there immigrants in your school? Learn something about the countries they left. Learn how they feel about their lives in a new country.

Territories and Treaties

141

Social Studies Activity

Immigrants in Your Family

Tell students to learn as much as they can about where their family's ancestors lived. Have students locate the places on a world map. On the board, make two lists: "Washington in the 1800s" and "Our Class." Under the heading "Washington in the 1800s," list the countries people came from to settle in Washington Territory. Under the heading "Our Class," write the countries where students' ancestors have come from. Encourage students to share the stories of how and why their ancestors came to this region.

Talk About It

A Land of Opportunity

What were some of the opportunities that brought people to Washington Territory?
There were plenty of jobs, a family could start a new business, they could get good farmland for a low price, the climate was mild, and Washington was a pleasant place to live.

Where were the new settlers coming from?
Most were coming from the United States and Canada. Many also came from Europe.

Why did settlers come from Europe?
Many people in Europe were poor. They couldn't find jobs or good land for farming. They often faced discrimination. America was a land of jobs and freedom.

Caption Answer

Students' answers should reflect an understanding of the difficulty of the trip to America. The family was probably excited and relieved to see that they were almost to America.

Linking the Present to the Past

Challenge students to talk to immigrant students at the school to learn more about the country they came from and their feelings about life in America. Allow students to share what they learned with the class.

Talk About It

More People to Come

Why did so many immigrants from Norway, Sweden, and Denmark settle around Puget Sound?
The land around Puget Sound reminded the immigrants of home.

What were some of the countries immigrants came from and the jobs they worked?
Encourage students to look back at this page to find a country immigrants came from and jobs that they worked.

An Italian Boy's Story

What was the trip to America like for this boy from Italy?
He road a mule to board the train which took him to an old ship. The ship was crowded and filthy. They were crowded with all their things. The food was awful.

Making a New Home

Why was making a new home in America difficult?
Most of the immigrants did not speak English. They had little money and knew little about American life.

Caption Answer

Their lives were probably difficult, living in a country different than their homeland. However, it was probably exciting to learn things about their new country.

Writing Activity

Immigrants Groups

Have students make a three-column chart, or make copies of the Three-Column Chart available in the graphic organizers section of the *Teacher Guide*. Tell students to choose three immigrant groups. Students may choose Chinese workers, African immigrants, European immigrants, Japanese workers, or other groups. Tell them to find information in this book and in other books from the school and city library on the three groups of immigrants they chose. Tell students to fill the chart with information about why each group came, problems they faced, and how they helped the state grow.

142

---

*Ole and Anna Moen were both immigrants from Norway. They met while working in a hotel in Minnesota. Anna was a waitress, and Ole played in the hotel band. They moved to Washington, got married, and had seven children. **Look at the faces of the children. What do you think their lives were like?***

Edward Saloman was an early governor of Washington Territory. He was from a Jewish immigrant family.

An Italian Boy's Story

The trip to America was not easy, as this boy wrote:

We had no idea what was in store for us. We were loaded onto a mule and taken to the train. We went aboard an [old ship]. We had left the Old Country. We were moving slowly toward a New World.

We were packed in filthy bunks like herring [fish] in a barrel. All our things were crowded in there with us—even the tin dishes in which we ate the awful food we were served.

More People Come

The largest group of European immigrants to Washington came from Norway, Sweden, and Denmark. The land around Puget Sound reminded the people of home. Many settled in the fishing town of Ballard, which later became part of Seattle.

The next largest group of immigrants had people from Ireland, England, Scotland, and Wales. The people found jobs in cities and mines. They named some of the cities. For example, Aberdeen is named for a city in Scotland. Conway is a name from Wales.

Germans were the third largest group to arrive. Some became bankers and business leaders in cities. Some farmed in eastern Washington. Other families came from Russia, Italy, France, Greece, and Croatia.

The first large group of African Americans came to Washington by train. They came to work in the mines in the Cascade Mountains. Some helped build railroads. Others worked on the ships that sailed up and down the Columbia River and along the coast.

Making a New Home

Making a new home in America was not easy. Most of the immigrants did not speak English. They had little money and knew little about American life.

Background Info

Irish Immigrants

In the 1840s a terrible disaster hit Ireland, where most people existed on a diet of potatoes. A fungus infected the potato crop, causing them to turn black and shrivel up. Men and women took their starving children and moved away to the "Promised Land" of America. Most Irish immigrants settled in the cities along America's Eastern Coast, where they usually lived in poverty. Irish men had come to Washington Territory from California in the wake of that state's gold rush. They settled first in Walla Walla. Some of the Walla Walla Irish moved north, where they started the first agricultural communities in the Columbia Basin. Other Irish came as laborers on the transcontinental railroads.

142

Immigrants who spoke the same language and had the same culture helped each other. They often lived near each other. These neighborhoods are called *ethnic* neighborhoods. Many groups built churches, temples, or other gathering places.

After a time, most of the people learned English. They became Americans. But they did not want to forget the good things about their homelands. They kept their foods, religion, songs, and art. They shared them with family and friends.

Let's Play!

Immigrant children learned English much faster than their parents did. They also learned American games. When they were not working or going to school, boys played baseball. If they didn't have a ball and bat, they played stickball. Knowledge of baseball heroes and rules was the badge of a true American.

One woman later wrote:

Sometimes we girls watched the boys play their games. We girls played only girls' games. We played hopscotch, only it was called "potsy." Mama didn't like me to play potsy. Hopping on one foot and pushing the thick piece of tin, I wore out a pair of shoes in a few weeks!

Many immigrants came to work at the Port Blakely mill. Before long, the Port Blakely schools had students from many ethnic backgrounds.

WASHINGTON PORTRAIT

John Nordstrom

John Nordstrom came to America from Sweden at the age of 16. He traveled through many states, working in mines, forests, and farms. Then he spent two hard years in Alaska looking for gold. He didn't find any.

Nordstrom was tired of hard work for low pay. He decided to go to business college. After that, he and a friend opened a shoe store in Seattle. The little store grew slowly, but finally made money. Nordstrom and his partner opened more stores in other cities. Today, Nordstrom department stores can be found in cities around the United States.

Chapter 6 Lesson 3

Talk About It

Making a New Home
(Continued from page 142)

Why did many immigrants who spoke the same language stay together?
They stayed together to help each other and to keep their culture alive.

Let's Play!

What were some games immigrant children played?
Possible answers include baseball, stickball, hopscotch, and potsy.

How do games the immigrant children played compare to games you play today?
Encourage student to compare and contrast the games with a partner. Ask some students to share what they discussed with the class.

WASHINGTON PORTRAIT

John Nordstrom

The store that John Nordstrom and his friend opened was a small shoe store. Today, the Nordstrom Company sells everything from shoes to blankets. Have students visit the Nordstrom Web site to find at least five ways that the company has grown and changed since it was first opened. A link to this Web site can be found at **www.ExperienceStateHistory. com.**

Technology Tie-In

Washington's Population Today

Have students visit the U.S. Census Bureau Web site to explore facts about Washington's population today. Use the Population Finder feature to find information about Washington State. Tell students to find five facts about the population of Washington. Then have them make predictions about how those numbers have changed since the last time the census information was taken. A link to this Web site can be found at **www.ExperienceStateHistory.com.**

Talk About It

Statehood at Last, 1889

What did the people in Washington Territory have to do before they could become a state?
They had to write a state constitution. The constitution said how the state's government must be run.

How did people in Washington celebrate when they got the news that their territory was a state?
They dressed in their best clothes, marched in parades, held dances, gave speeches, and hung flags and banners on buildings.

Why do you think people in Washington wanted statehood so badly?
As a state, the representatives in Washington, D.C., have a vote. The people of Washington get to choose their governor and officials.

Fire! *(From page 145)*

How was the fire in Seattle started?
A cabinet maker was heating glue in his basement shop. The pot boiled over and the glue caught fire.

What were some of the effects of the fires in Washington?
People lost their homes and workplaces. Some people worked in tents until new brick and stone buildings were made.

Caption Answers

Our country is made up of 50 states.

The telegram is addressed to Governor Elisha P. Ferry.

The telegram says the president signed the proclamation declaring Washington to be a state.

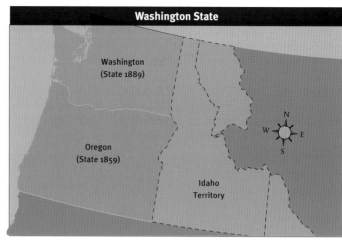

Washington State

Washington was the 42nd state. **How many states do we have now?**

Washington (State 1889)

Oregon (State 1859)

Idaho Territory

Statehood at Last, 1889

Washington finally had enough people to become a state! It was something the settlers had wanted for a long time. First, however, the people had to write a state constitution. This document said how the state's government would be run.

It was a great day when the people got the news that their territory was a state. They dressed in their best clothes. They marched in parades. At night, there were dances. People gave speeches. In cities all over the state, people hung banners and flags on buildings.

What did it mean to be a state? It meant that the leaders Washington sent to Congress would now have a vote there. It meant that instead of the president choosing the governor and other officials, the people of Washington could vote for these leaders. We will learn more about our state government in the next chapter.

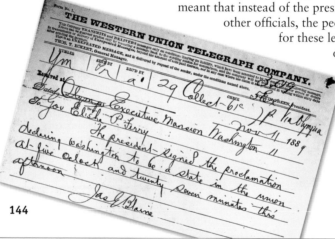

On November 11, 1889, Washington officials got this telegram. It was from the president of the United States. **To whom is it addressed? What does it say?**

Washington, Our Home

144

 Map Activity

Washington State

Now that Washington is a state, it has boundaries and can develop its own identity to set it apart from other states. Divide the class into small groups. Provide each group with a large poster board. Tell each group to use the poster board to create a map of Washington. The map should include symbols that show why Washington is unique. For instance, students might draw apples in the regions of our state that are known for growing apples. Allow students to use the Internet and other books to find more details about our state.

Fire!

The year Washington became a state was also a year of fires. Huge fires burned down the wooden buildings in Seattle, Spokane Falls (as Spokane was called then), and Ellensburg.

How did the fires start in Seattle? On a hot, dry afternoon, a cabinet maker was heating glue in his basement shop. The pot boiled over, and the glue caught fire. Flames spread quickly through the shop. Winds carried it from one wooden building to the next. The fire jumped across the street. Soon entire blocks were on fire.

It was a sad time for the people who lost their homes and workplaces. Some people worked in tents until new brick and stone buildings were made.

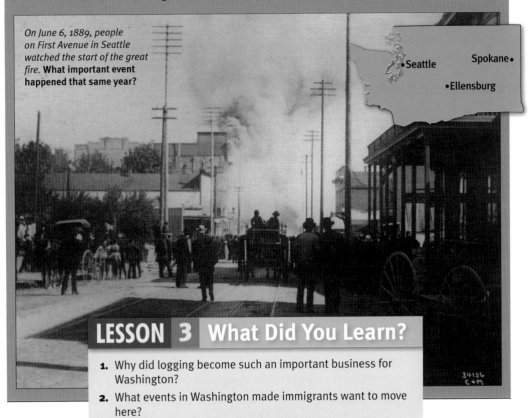

On June 6, 1889, people on First Avenue in Seattle watched the start of the great fire. **What important event happened that same year?**

LESSON 3 What Did You Learn?

1. Why did logging become such an important business for Washington?
2. What events in Washington made immigrants want to move here?
3. List some of the countries immigrants came from and the reasons they came to Washington.

Territories and Treaties

145

REFLECT

Reflect on students' understanding of the growth Washington Territory experienced prior to statehood and how the growth led to statehood. You can evaluate students' understanding through discussion or evaluation of activities completed in this lesson. The following activity will serve as another way of assessing students' understanding of the key objectives of this lesson.

✏️ Writing Activity

Front Page News!

Newspapers across the country told the news of the newest state. Have students write a newspaper article sharing the exciting news of Washington's statehood.

Tell students to use details from the chapter to explain the events leading up to statehood. A Front Page News! activity is available in the *Teacher Guide*.

NAME _____ DATE _____
Becoming a State ③ Writing Activity

Front Page News!
Write a newspaper article telling the exciting news of Washington's statehood. Use details from the chapter to tell about events that led to statehood.

Washington Times   November 11, 1889

HEADLINE: _____

66 Student Guide
Use with *Washington, Our Home*   © 2010 Gibbs Smith, Publisher

LESSON 3 What Did You Learn?

1. *People were moving to California for the gold rush and wood was needed to make shipping docks and buildings there.*
2. *Some people came to work as loggers, some came to mine for gold, silver, or coal, some came to work for the railroad, and others came for land and business opportunities.*
3. *A large group of Chinese immigrants came to work on the railroad, but also worked in mines and fish canneries. Japanese immigrants came to fill many of the jobs Chinese workers had done. Many people came from Europe and Canada to work various jobs in cities and mines. Immigrants came from Africa to work mines in the Cascade Mountains, help build railroads, and to work on ships.*

Caption Answer

The fires happened the same year Washington became a state.

Standards

GLE 4.3.1
Understands that there are multiple perspectives regarding the interpretation of historical events and creates an historical account using multiple sources.

GLE 5.4.1
Draws clear, well-reasoned conclusions and provides explanations that are supported by artifacts and/or primary sources in a paper or presentation.

GLE 5.4.2
Prepares a list of resources, including title, author, type of source, date published, and publisher for each source.

Washington Social Studies Skills

Write About An Historical Event from Multiple Perspectives

Activate

Ask your students the question, *What was your favorite part of the school day yesterday?* Allow different students to share which part of the day was their favorite and why. Ask students why they don't all have the same opinion about what the best part of the day was. Explain to students that everyone experienced the day from their own perspectives, or point of view. Tell them that each student is right in feeling the way that they do about they day because they each had very different experiences.

Teach

Tell students that much like their different perspectives on yesterday's school day, people have different perspectives on events from history. Explain that it is important for historians to study events in history from multiple perspectives before drawing conclusions. They gather as many facts as they can so they can understand even more about history.

Ask students what events from this chapter require historians to study many perspectives. Make a list on the board. Ask students to discuss with a partner why it is important to study each of the events from multiple perspectives. Ask some students to share what they discussed with the class.

Write About a Historical Event from Multiple Perspectives

Historians study many perspectives to form opinions and draw conclusions about history.

The Battle of the Big Hole was a costly battle in the Montana Territory between the Nez Perce and U.S. Army during the Nez Perce War. Study the comments made about the Battle of the Big Hole by a Nez Perce chief and a soldier in the U.S. Army.

"What made Joseph so hostile was the killing of some of their women and children by accident as we were told not to shoot the squaws and I honestly can say it was not done on purpose."

—Private Homer Coon, 7th Infantry

"The Nez Perce never make war on women and children; we could have killed a great many women and children while war lasted, but we would feel ashamed to do so cowardly an act."

—Chief Joseph, Nez Perce

❑ Visit your school or city library, or research on the Internet to find at least two more accounts of the Battle of the Big Hole.

❑ Study your sources and the sources on this page. Look for details about how the Indians and the U.S. Army felt about the Battle of the Big Hole and why each group felt that way. Take notes as you study your sources.

❑ Draw conclusions about how the Indians and the Americans felt about the Battle of the Big Hole. Write down your conclusions.

❑ Write a paper describing your conclusions. Use details from your sources to support your conclusions.

❑ List the sources you found. Include title, author, type of source, date published, and publisher for each source. Attach your list of sources to your finished paper.

146

Practice

Write the following groups on the board:

- U.S. government
- Indians
- Settlers

Have students work in small groups to discuss how each group felt about the growth and expansion of the Pacific Northwest and why they felt that way. Have each group assign a writer to take notes during the discussion. Have a presenter from each group share what the group discussed about how the groups felt. Explain to the class that each of these groups had very different perspectives about this time in history because they were experiencing it from different points of view.

Apply

Have students write about the Battle of Big Hole from multiple perspectives, following the directions on the Social Studies Skill Page.

Chapter Review 6

Reviewing What You Read

1. Name the groups of people who wanted to claim the Northwest.
2. Describe what the Oregon Treaty was and the changes it made.
3. Complete the sentence using details from the chapter. Explain why you completed the sentence that way:
   Indian reservations were _____ places.
4. Compare the Yakama War to the Nez Perce War.
5. Imagine that gold and silver had never been discovered in Washington. How might our state's history have been different?
6. Do you think immigrants were happy to call Washington their new home? Why or why not?

Becoming a Better Reader

Understanding the Text

All writers place events in a story in a certain order, or sequence. They also have their own point of view on the topic. All events you read about have a cause or reason behind them.

Choose an event from this chapter. Write a paragraph explaining the sequence of things leading up to the event, the different points of view people have about the event, and the causes or reasons for the event.

Spotlighting Geography

Gold Fever!

Gold was an important natural resource in Washington Territory. Where was gold found in the territory? Are there any gold mines in Washington today? Do you know how much gold has actually been found in Washington? Research these three questions in an encyclopedia or on Web sites your teacher recommends. Then make a pie graph to show where gold has been found in Washington. The biggest slice of the pie should show the place where the most gold has been found.

Territories and Treaties

147

Becoming a Better Reader

Understand the Text

Group students according to which event they wrote about. Have students who wrote about the same events share their paragraphs with each other. Within their groups, encourage students to talk about the differences in what they wrote about and why each person wrote what they did. As a whole class, invite some students to share how their writing was different. Explain to students that readers each make their own opinions about what they read.

Spotlighting Geography

Gold Fever!

After students have gathered information for this activity, you may want to have students go to the Kids' Zone Web site where they can create a graph online. This Web site allows students to make professional-looking pie graphs, bar graphs, line graphs, and area graphs. See www.ExperienceStateHistory.com for a link to this site.

Reviewing What You Read

The Reviewing What You Read questions are leveled according to Bloom's Taxonomy and will help students achieve a higher level of thinking. These questions will also prepare students for the chapter assessment. The following are possible answers to the questions. Focus on students' ability to understand and apply the concepts.

1. **KNOWLEDGE** England thought they should own the land because the Hudson's Bay Company was there. More and more American settlers were moving to the region and wanted the land to be part of the United States. The Indians did not want anyone to claim the land. They wanted it to be available for everyone to use.

2. **COMPREHENSION** The Oregon Treaty was an agreement between America and Britain. It said the countries would each get part of the land in the Pacific Northwest. A line at 49 degrees north latitude would be the dividing line.

3. **APPLICATION** Students' answers should show an understanding of what life on reservations was like. Answer should be supported by details from the chapter.

4. **ANALYSIS** Students' answers should include details from the chapter and tell how the wars were similar and how they were different.

5. **SYNTHESIS** Students' answers should include details and events from our state's history and describe how they would be different if gold and silver had never been discovered.

6. **EVALUATION** Students' opinions should be supported by details from the chapter.

Interactive Chapter Review

An Interactive Chapter Review is available online at **www.ExperienceStateHistory. com**. Have students use this review to prepare for the assessments.

Chapter Assessment

Chapter Assessments are available to preview on pages 116G–116H. Assessments can be found in the Teacher Guide. They can also be found online at **www.ExperienceStateHistory.com**.

CHAPTER

7 Our Government

CHAPTER PLANNER

CHAPTER OVERVIEW	WASHINGTON SOCIAL STUDIES GLEs
This chapter focuses on our national, state, tribal, and local governments. It also talks about our responsibilities as citizens. The chapter activities provide you with a unifying theme to tie the learning of the chapter together.	GLE 1.1.1 GLE 1.1.2 GLE 1.2.1 GLE 1.2.2 GLE 1.4.1 GLE 4.4.1 GLE 5.1.1 GLE 5.4.1 GLE 5.4.2

CHAPTER RESOURCES	
ELL/Modified Chapter Plan, p. 148I	
Books and Web Sites, p. 148J	

CHAPTER ACTIVITIES	WASHINGTON CURRICULUM INTEGRATION
Rights and Rules, p. 148E	**Writing** GLE 2.1.1
Government in the News, p. 148E	**Reading** GLE 3.4.3
■ Representatives Per State, p. 148E	**Math** GLE 4.5.E
■ Political Portrait, p. 148E	**Writing** GLE 1.1.1, GLE 1.2.1, GLE 1.3.1, GLE 1.4.1, GLE 1.5.1, GLE 1.6.1
■ Historic Document, p. 148F	**Social Studies** GLE 5.1.1, GLE 5.2.2
USDA Web site, p. 148F	**Science** GLE 2.2.5
Washington Interstate Signs, p. 148F	**Visual Arts** GLE 2.1.1
Constitution Day Celebration, p. 148F	**Reading** GLE 3.2.1

CHAPTER OPENER	WASHINGTON CURRICULUM INTEGRATION
Cause and Effect of Government, p. 150	**Communication** GLE 2.2.1
Visit the Washington Legislative Building, p. 150	**Technology** GLE 1.3.2

▶Indicates an activity page located in the *Student Guide*
■ Indicates an activity page located in the *Teacher Guide*

The BIG Idea | How does government affect our lives?

CHAPTER REVIEW pp.174–175

SOCIAL STUDIES SKILLS PAGE	WASHINGTON SOCIAL STUDIES GLEs
Identify a Problem and Solve It, p. 174	**Social Studies** GLE 5.4.1

REVIEWING THE CHAPTER	WASHINGTON SOCIAL STUDIES GLEs
Students show what they have learned by completing application activities and answering chapter review questions. Assessments for this chapter can be previewed on pages 148G–148H. Select the assessment option that best suits your goals for this chapter. Assessments are available in the *Teacher Guide* or online at **www.ExperienceStateHistory.com.**	GLE 1.1.1 GLE 1.1.2 GLE 1.2.1 GLE 1.2.2 GLE 1.4.1 GLE 4.4.1 GLE 5.1.1 GLE 5.4.1 GLE 5.4.2

CHAPTER ACTIVITIES	WASHINGTON CURRICULUM INTEGRATION
Reviewing the Chapter, p. 147	**Reading** GLE 1.3.2, GLE 2.1.3
Becoming a Better Reader, p. 147	**Reading** GLE 2.3.2
Spotlighting Geography, p. 147	**Social Studies** GLE 3.1.1

CHAPTER ASSESSMENTS	WASHINGTON CURRICULUM INTEGRATION
■ Multiple Choice Assessment, p. 68	**Reading** GLE 1.3.2, GLE 2.1.3
■ Reading Assessment, p. 69	**Reading** GLE 1.3.2, GLE 2.1.3
■ Writing Assessment, p. 70	**Writing** GLE 2.3.1, GLE 3.1.1, GLE 3.1.2
■ Project Assessment, pp. 71–72	**Social Studies CBA:** Whose Rules? **Social Studies** GLE 1.1.2, GLE 1.2.2, GLE 5.4.2

LESSON 1
Levels of Government   pp. 152–161

LESSON OVERVIEW	WASHINGTON SOCIAL STUDIES GLEs
KEY IDEAS • Governments provide order and protect the people. • There are levels of government to meet the needs of the people. • Governments create and carry out laws.	GLE 1.2.1 GLE 1.2.2

LESSON ACTIVITIES	WASHINGTON CURRICULUM INTEGRATION
▶Our National Anthem, p. 152	**Reading** GLE 3.4.2
Picture Dictionary, p. 152	**Reading** GLE 1.3.1
▶Words to Understand, p. 152	**Reading** GLE 1.3.1
▶Using a Web, p. 153	**Reading** GLE 2.1.7
Lend a Hand, p. 154	**Communication** GLE 2.2.2
How Does Government Affect Me?, p. 154	**Technology** GLE 1.3.2
Washington Counties and County Seats, p. 155	**Writing** GLE 3.1.1, GLE 3.1.2
Tic Tac Taxes, p. 156	**Technology** GLE 1.3.2
Take Me to Your Leader, p. 156	**Writing** GLE 2.2.1
Washington State Symbols, p. 157	**Visual Arts** GLE 2.1.1
Our Government from A to Z, p. 157	**Reading** GLE 3.2.1
Sticky Notes Reading and Discussion, p. 157	**Reading** GLE 2.1.6
Washington Tribal Reservations, p. 158	**Communication** GLE 2.2.2
A Presidential Moment, p. 159	**Communication** GLE 3.1.1
President for a Day, p. 159	**Technology** GLE 1.3.2
History of Our Flag, p. 159	**Technology** GLE 1.3.3
Government Mobile, p. 160	**Visual Arts** GLE 2.1.1
Court's in Session, p. 160	**Theatre** GLE 2.1.1
▶School Rules, p. 161	**Writing** GLE 2.2.1

LESSON 2
Our Rights, Our Laws — pp. 162–169

LESSON OVERVIEW	WASHINGTON SOCIAL STUDIES GLEs
KEY IDEAS • Our state constitution supports freedom and rights. • Our laws protect our rights.	GLE 1.1.1 GLE 1.1.2 GLE 1.2.2 GLE 4.4.1 GLE 5.1.1

LESSON ACTIVITIES	WASHINGTON CURRICULUM INTEGRATION
▶Washington Rights, p. 162	**Writing** GLE 2.2.1
Picture Dictionary Part 2, p. 162	**Reading** GLE 1.3.1
▶Words to Understand, p. 162	**Reading** GLE 1.3.1
▶Using Two-Column Notes, p. 163	**Reading** GLE 2.1.7
Crazy But True Laws, p. 164	**Reading** GLE 3.4.2
Evaluate a Law or Policy, p. 164	**Social Studies** GLE 1.1.2 **Communication** GLE 2.2.2
Go to the Source: Analyze a Political Cartoon, p. 166	**Social Studies** GLE 5.2.2
Make a Political Cartoon, p. 166	**Social Studies** GLE 5.2.2 **Visual Arts** GLE 2.1.1
Boldt Decision History, p. 167	**Reading** GLE 3.4.3
Who's Who in State Government, p. 168	**Technology** GLE 1.3.2
Legislative Bills, p. 168	**Reading** GLE 3.4.3
▶Laws to Protect My Rights, p. 169	**Writing** GLE 2.2.1

LESSON 3
Our Responsibilities — pp. 170–173

LESSON OVERVIEW	WASHINGTON SOCIAL STUDIES GLEs
KEY IDEAS • Citizens have responsibilities. • Citizens can work together to make a difference.	GLE 1.4.1

LESSON ACTIVITIES	WASHINGTON CURRICULUM INTEGRATION
▶A Helpful Town, p. 170	**Writing** GLE 2.2.1
A Picture Dictionary Part 3, p. 170	**Reading** GLE 1.3.1
▶Words to Understand, p. 170	**Reading** GLE 1.3.1
Character Traits, p. 171	**Writing** GLE 3.1.1
▶Use Note-Taking, p. 171	**Reading** GLE 2.1.7
Being a Good Citizen, p. 172	**Reading** GLE 3.4.2
Reading Buddies, p. 172	**Communication** GLE 2.2.2
Lend a Hand, p. 172	**Communication** GLE 2.2.1, GLE 2.2.2
▶Responsibility—What's That?, p. 173	**Writing** GLE 2.2.1, GLE 3.1.1

Chapter Activities

The focus of this chapter is on our national, state, tribal, and local government. Use the Chapter Activities to help students understand how the government is organized and how it works to keep its citizens safe.

 Set the Stage

Decorate your room in red, white, and blue. Place government pictures and posters on the bulletin boards. Set up a class library with books about our national, state, tribal, and local governments. Some titles are suggested in the Chapter Resources on page 148J. Ask your librarian for other suggestions. If possible, schedule a state or local politician or person who works in a government office to talk with your class about what he or she does.

 Introductory Activity

Rights and Rules

To make the idea of the constitution real for students, take pictures of several different areas, such as the cafeteria, library, bus area, and playground. Have students choose one area and answer the following questions:

- What is the place in the picture?
- What rights do students have in this place?
- What rules does this place have?
- Why are these rules important?

Have students create a poster using the pictures and the answers. The posters can be displayed in the particular area so other students can read about their rights and rules.

 Reading Activity

Government in the News

Create a bulletin board with four sections: national, state, tribal, and local. Have students read articles in the newspaper and news magazines relating to government at the national, state, tribal, and local levels. Have students clip the headlines or titles of the articles and place them on the bulletin board. Students should also write a brief summary of the articles on an index card. The summaries should include *who, what, when, where,* and *why* about the articles.

 Math Activity

Representatives Per State

Have students study the map showing the representatives from each state to Congress. The Representatives Per State map along with questions is available in the *Teacher Guide.*

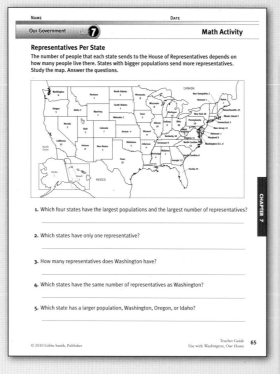

 Writing Activity

Political Portrait

Throughout the *Student Edition*, students have read portraits about people in Washington. Have students use these portraits as models for their own writing.

Prewriting
Have students choose and research someone past or present who served or is serving Washington at the national, state, tribal, or local level.

Drafting
Have students write a portrait about the person they chose.

Revising
Have students read their portraits with a partner to help clarify their writing.

Editing
Students should reread their portraits to check for correct spelling, grammar, punctuation, and capitalization.

Publishing
Have students write their final copies on the Political Portrait form available in the *Teacher Guide.*

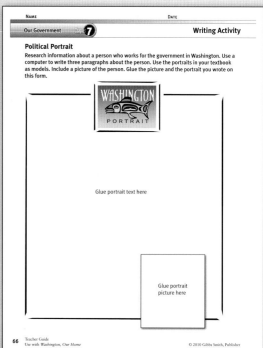

Social Studies Activity

Historic Document

Divide students into groups. Provide each group with a different historic document to view and answer questions about. Some documents students may analyze include:

- The Declaration of Independence
- The Preamble to the U.S. Constitution
- The U.S. Constitution
- The Bill of Rights
- The Washington State Constitution

Have groups complete the document analysis page and present their findings to the class. Links to Web sites where these documents can be found are available at **www.ExperienceStateHistory.com.** A Historic Document activity page is available in the *Teacher Guide.*

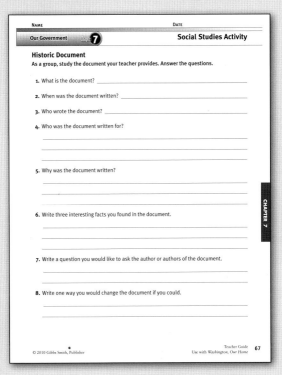

 ## Science Activity

USDA Web Site

The United States Department of Agriculture serves under the president of the United States. The department advises the president about food, agriculture, and natural resources. Have students go online to the USDA Web site and find out more about what this department does and the jobs available within the department. Have students write five facts they learn from this Web site. For a link to this site see **www.ExperienceStateHistory.com.**

 ## Art Activity

Washington Interstate Signs

The signs on the Interstate Highway System in Washington look the same as Interstate signs in other states. It is important to have common Interstate signs so travelers can easily find information as they go from state to state. The national government provides 90% of the funding for the Interstate Highway, but state governments build and maintain the highways. Ask students to imagine that the national government has just decided that each state can design their own Interstate Highway signs. Tell them to design a sign that would represent Washington State and include information that is important to travelers. Provide students with drawing and construction paper on which to design their signs.

 ## Culminating Activity

Constitution Day Celebration

As a Culminating Activity to this chapter, have students plan a Constitution Day Celebration. Host a parade. Encourage students to dress in red, white, and blue or as symbols of the country. Have students display their political portraits completed for the Writing Activity.

Assessment Options

The Chapter Assessment options provide opportunities to evaluate students' understanding of the social studies concepts. Choose the assessment options that best meet the needs of your teaching goals. Assessments are available in the *Teacher Guide* or can be individualized at www.ExperienceStateHistory.com.

OPTION 1: MULTIPLE CHOICE ASSESSMENT

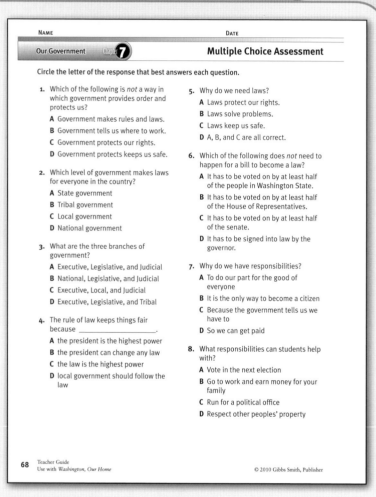

The Multiple Choice Assessment provides a quick way to assess students' understanding of the key concepts of the chapter. Have students read each question and select the best answer.

OPTION 2: READING ASSESSMENT

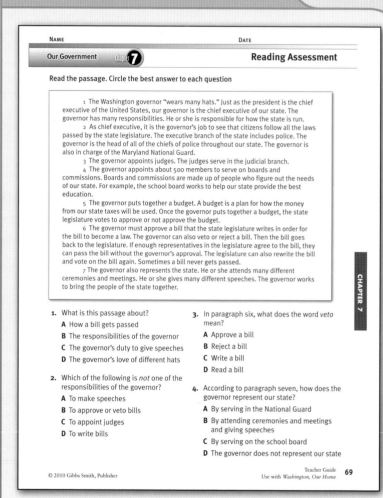

The Reading Assessment provides additional practice for the WASL Reading Test. Have students read the passage and answer the questions that follow.

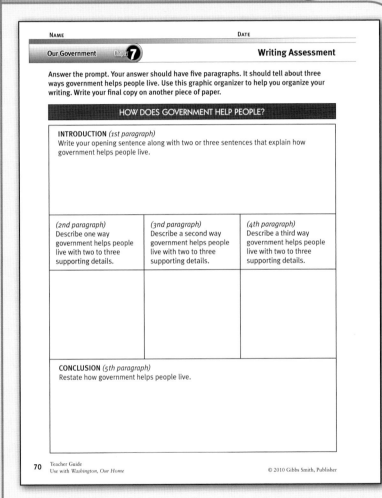

NAME _____ DATE _____

Our Government Chapter 7   **Writing Assessment**

Answer the prompt. Your answer should have five paragraphs. It should tell about three ways government helps people live. Use this graphic organizer to help you organize your writing. Write your final copy on another piece of paper.

HOW DOES GOVERNMENT HELP PEOPLE?

INTRODUCTION (1st paragraph)
Write your opening sentence along with two or three sentences that explain how government helps people live.

(2nd paragraph) Describe one way government helps people live with two to three supporting details.	(3rd paragraph) Describe a second way government helps people live with two to three supporting details.	(4th paragraph) Describe a third way government helps people live with two to three supporting details.

CONCLUSION (5th paragraph)
Restate how government helps people live.

The Writing Assessment provides additional practice for the WASL Writing Test. Have students use the organizer to write a five-paragraph essay in response to the writing prompt about this chapter.

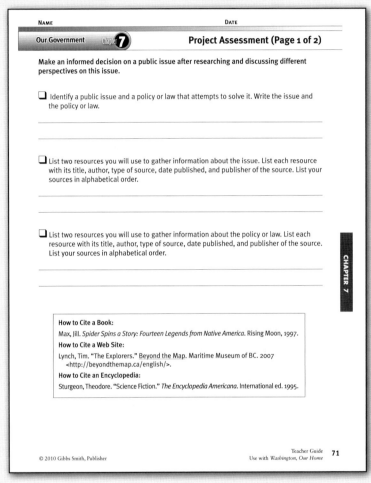

NAME _____ DATE _____

Our Government Chapter 7   **Project Assessment (Page 1 of 2)**

Make an informed decision on a public issue after researching and discussing different perspectives on this issue.

❑ Identify a public issue and a policy or law that attempts to solve it. Write the issue and the policy or law.

_____

❑ List two resources you will use to gather information about the issue. List each resource with its title, author, type of source, date published, and publisher of the source. List your sources in alphabetical order.

_____

❑ List two resources you will use to gather information about the policy or law. List each resource with its title, author, type of source, date published, and publisher of the source. List your sources in alphabetical order.

_____

How to Cite a Book:
Max, Jill. *Spider Spins a Story: Fourteen Legends from Native America*. Rising Moon, 1997.
How to Cite a Web Site:
Lynch, Tim. "The Explorers." Beyond the Map. Maritime Museum of BC. 2007
        <http://beyondthemap.ca/english/>.
How to Cite an Encyclopedia:
Sturgeon, Theodore. "Science Fiction." *The Encyclopedia Americana*. International ed. 1995.

CHAPTER 7

The Project Assessment provides an alternative to the traditional assessment. This Project Assessment is designed to meet the requirement of the **Social Studies CBA:** Whose Rules?

ELL/Modified Chapter Plan

Our Government

Students will learn about the different levels and branches of government. They will also learn about the roles of each level and branch of government.

The following pages can be found in the ELL/Modified Chapter Guide on pages 41–45.

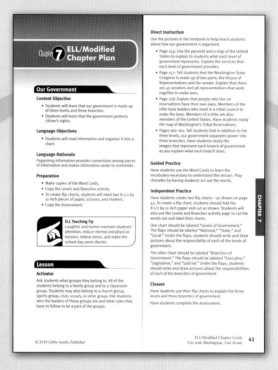

The ELL/Modified Chapter Plan provides a step-by-step lesson in an easy-to-use format. Lessons teach content and language objectives.

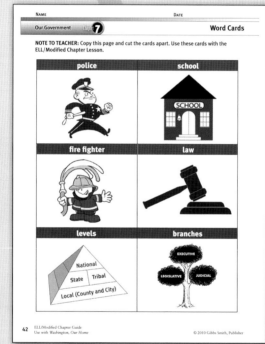

The Word Cards and Activity assist and reinforce students' learning of the chapter and prepares them for the assessment.

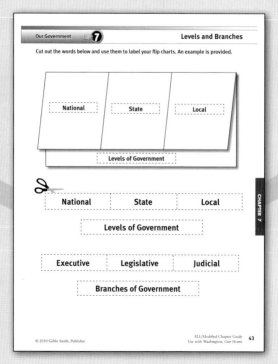

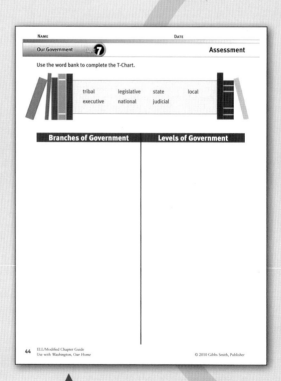

The Modified Assessment for this chapter assesses students' understanding of the key objectives of the chapter.

Books and Web Sites

Books

De Capua, Sarah. *Being a Governor.* New York: Children's Press, 2003.

———. *Making a Law.* New York: Children's Press, 2004.

———. *Paying Taxes.* New York: Children's Press, 2002.

———. *Serving on a Jury.* New York: Children's Press, 2001.

———. *Voting.* New York: Children's Press, 2002.

Hamilton, John. *Branches of Government.* Edina: ABDO Publisher, 2005.

Kroll, Virginia L. *Good Citizen Sarah.* Morton Grove: Albert Whitman & Company, 2007.

Linz, Kathi and Tony Griego. *Chickens May Not Cross the Road: And Other Crazy (But True) Laws.* Boston: Houghton Mifflin, 2002.

Martin, Bill, and Michael Sampson. *I Pledge Allegiance.* Somerville: Candlewick Press, 2004.

Murdico, Suzanne J. *Volunteering to Help the Environment.* New York: High Interest Books, 2000.

Pearl, Norman. *The Bill of Rights.* Minneapolis: Picture Window Books, 2007.

Scillian, Devin. *A is for America.* Chelsea: Sleeping Bear Press, 2001.

Swain, Gwenyth. *Declaring Freedom: A Look at the Declaration of Independence, the Bill of Rights, and the Constitution.* Minneapolis: Lerner Publications, 2003

Web Sites

The following web sites provide resources or lesson plans for teachers and activities for students to help extend the lessons in this chapter. Go to **www.ExperienceStateHistory.com** for links to these Web sites.

The Charters of Freedom

The Charters of Freedom is a feature within the National Archives Web site. This site contains links to some of the most important government documents of our country. Students can view the Declaration of Independence, the U.S. Constitution, and the Bill of Rights. Images of the actual documents are available, as well as transcripts to make them easier to read.

EconEdLink

The EconEdLink Web site provides information about economics and government for kids. This site is centered on curriculum standards and based on the essential principles of economics.

Flag Picture Gallery

The UShistory.org Web site contains images and information on the history of America's flag.

Governor's Office of Indians Affairs

This Washington government Web site contains information on the American Indian tribes in Washington.

HistoryLink.org

This Washington State-based history site contains articles on the Boldt Decision and other topics mentioned in this chapter.

How Does Government Affect Me?

This PBS Kids Web site provides excellent information on the services that communities provide for their citizens. Students can also learn about voting and other government topics. Have students complete the President for a Day activity to learn more about the role of the President of the United States.

Presidential Timeline

The Presidential Timeline contains pictures and information on U.S. presidents from the twentieth century.

United States Department of Agriculture

The USDA Web site is a government site that provides information about food, agriculture, and natural resources in our country. Students can use this site to find information about this government organization.

Washington State Capitol

The General Administration of the state of Washington site has a virtual tour of the state capital. You can take students on a guided tour, or simply explore the capitol.

Washington State Constitution

The Washington Secretary of State Web site contains a link to the Washington State Constitution. The document is available to download as a pdf.

Washington State Legislative Building

The Washington Secretary of State Web site has pictures and information detailing the history of our state's legislative building. Use this site to take your class on a virtual field trip of the building.

Washington State Legislature

This Washington State government site shows the agenda of the legislature and information on current bills and current issues in the state legislature.

White House Kids

The White House Kids Web site provides educational information for the children about the president, the White House, and more.

Unit Opener Activity

Living in Washington

Tell students that the last few chapters have been about the history of Washington leading to statehood. Explain that the next two chapters will be about life in Washington today. These chapters will be about topics that affect students directly.

To activate prior knowledge and peak interest in the topics of the next chapters, have students work in groups to create a list of topics they think they need to know about in order to live in Washington today. Have each group write their list on a poster board. Hang all the finished poster boards in the front of the classroom and discuss the lists as a class. Look for topics that are repeated on posters and topics that are unique to posters.

 Put Yourself in the Picture

Skyline of Seattle

Seattle is a busy town with many places to see and things to do. Ask students if they recognize any famous buildings from the skyline of Seattle. Discuss the buildings students recognize. Have students create a brochure of places to see and things to do in Seattle. If possible, encourage students to visit places in Seattle to gather information for their brochure. Students can also gather information online. Have students illustrate their brochures to make them exciting.

Caption Answers

There are many tall buildings and mountains in the background. Encourage students to think about the last few chapters as they discuss what they might see if they could look into the past. Students may want to look back at images in chapters 3–6.

Have students discuss how the buildings and physical features might change if they could look into the future.

UNIT 3

Living in Washington

You have learned about Washington's land and history. You have learned how we became a state. Let's jump forward now and learn about our state today. Let's learn about our government. Laws affect everyone! Let's learn how people work and earn money in our great state.

Look out across the skyline of Seattle. What do you see? If you could look through the lens into the past, what might you see? If you could look into the future, what might you see?

148

149

The BIG Idea

Cause and Effect of Government

Have students create or complete a cause and effect chart about government organizations. The organizations should be the cause and students should research the organizations to find the effect they have on citizens. You may want to brainstorm a list of government organizations as a class, or have students ask their families to help them list some as a homework assignment.

This activity will help set the stage for this chapter by encouraging students to think about services the government provides. A Cause and Effect chart is available in the graphic organizers section of the *Teacher Guide*.

Put Yourself in the Picture

Visit the Washington State Legislative Building

If you are unable to schedule a field trip to the state legislative building, take students on an online tour at the Washington Secretary of State Web site. This site provides a look at the history of the building, dating back to 1928. Have students describe the most interesting part of the tour. A link to this site can be found at **www.ExperienceStateHistory.com**.

Caption Answer

Allow students to share what they think happens inside this building. Listening closely to their answers will give you an idea of the background knowledge students have of government.

The BIG Idea

How does government affect our lives?

If you want to see our state government in action, visit the State Legislative Building in Olympia. Leaders from all around the state meet there to make laws for the people of Washington. **What do you think you might hear inside these walls? What might you see?**

150

Our Government

7

You might think that government is just for adults, but rules and laws affect your life in many ways. Children, as well as adults, have rights. They have responsibilities. They follow rules and laws.

If you play ball in a park, ride in a car on a road, or fill up your bathtub with clean water, you are using services provided by the government. Government is for all of us.

151

 Background Info

Washington State Legislative Building

Approximate Costs of Principal Finish Materials:	
Marble	$840,000
Plastering	$187,000
Ornamental Iron	$45,000
Ornamental Bronze	$320,000
Stone Carving	$180,000
Interior Wood Trim	$84,000
Rubber Tile	$65,000
Painting	$122,000
Elevators	$96,000
Plumbing, Heating, and Ventilating	$383,000
Total Cost of Building in 1928	$6,791,595.88
Cost of Furnishings in 1928	$594,172.33
TOTAL	$7,385,768.21

FOR SOME COMPARISONS: To reconstruct the Legislative Building with the same materials and workmanship today, it would cost over $1 billion. That is 135 times more!

More fun facts like these can be found online at the State of Washington General Administration Web site. A link to this site can be found at **www.ExperienceStateHistory.com.**

PREPARE

Activator

Our National Anthem

Have students listen to a recording of "The Star Spangled Banner." Encourage students to learn the song. Ask students if this song represents their feelings about our country. Have students complete the Our National Anthem activity available in the *Student Guide*.

Levels of Government | **1** | Activator

Our National Anthem

Read the first verse of our national anthem, "The Star Spangled Banner." Use the Internet to research more information about the anthem and find answers to the questions.

Oh, say can you see, by the dawn's early light,
What so proudly we hailed at the twilight's last gleaming?
Whose broad stripes and bright stars, through the perilous fight,
O'er the ramparts we watched, were so gallantly streaming?
And the rockets' red glare, the bombs bursting in air,
Gave proof through the night that our flag was still there.
O say, does the star-spangled banner yet wave
O'er the land of the free and the home of the brave?

1. Look up these words in the dictionary. Write the definitions on the back of this page.
   twilight   gleaming   perilous   rampart   gallantly   glare   spangled

2. What is the title of the national anthem? _____

3. Who wrote this song? _____

4. This song was written during a war. Which war was it? _____

5. What is the main message of this song? _____

6. Write a new verse for this song.
   _____

© 2010 Gibbs Smith, Publisher | Student Guide **67** | Use with *Washington, Our Home*

Word Study

Picture Dictionary

Have the class work together to create a picture dictionary. Have each student choose one of the words in this lesson, write its definition, draw a picture illustrating the word, and write a sentence using the word. Students will be doing this throughout the whole chapter. At the end of the chapter, bind the pages together to form a book. Share the book with the class.

Caption Answer

This badge is a symbol of law and order in the United States. It is worn by men and women who work to keep people safe.

152

Key Ideas

- Governments provide order and protect the people.
- There are levels of government to meet the needs of the people.
- Governments create and carry out laws.

Words to Understand

constitution
county
enforce
representative
sovereignty
tax
tribal council

LESSON 1 Levels of Government

Law and Order

A long time ago, a miner found a gold nugget at the edge of a river. Soon hundreds of men crowded around the place, searching for gold. One man wearing a dirty hat put up a sign that said, "Welcome to the town of Get Rich."

People quickly put up shacks, tents, and a few wooden buildings to live in. Someone opened a store to sell food, boots, and tools. Outside every shack was thick mud. There were no real roads. People threw their garbage out behind their homes, so flies and wasps swarmed everywhere. People dumped waste into the river.

Then things got even worse in the town of Get Rich. When men argued, they settled the matter with fists and guns. The meanest people got their way. Every so often, a miner stole someone else's gold. Nothing or no one was safe.

One evening, after a quick dinner of beans and bread, the people in Get Rich got together to decide what to do about their town. They wanted law and order. They wanted their rights to be protected. They wanted a government to make laws and **enforce**, or make people obey, those laws. They needed a sheriff to arrest bullies and put them in jail.

If you were at that town meeting, what changes would you make so Get Rich would be a better place to live? What laws would you want? What services would you suggest? What rights would you want? Who would make the laws and provide the services?

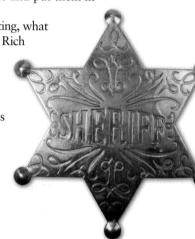

This is a sheriff's badge. A sheriff's job is to keep the peace and enforce the laws. **What do you think of when you see one of these badges?**

152

Washington, Our Home

Words to Understand

constitution (p. 156) *a written plan for government*
county (p. 155) *a government region within a state*
enforce (p. 152) *to make sure people obey (a law or rule)*
representative (p. 156) *a person elected to vote for other people*
sovereignty (p. 158) *self-rule; supreme power or authority*
tax (p. 156) *money people must pay to the government*
tribal council (p. 158) *a group that makes laws for an Indian tribe on Indian lands*

A Words to Understand activity for this lesson is available in the *Student Guide*.

Levels of Government | **1** | Words to Understand

Use the definitions to help you unscramble each Word to Understand.

1. ntyvosereig _____
   self-rule; supreme power or authority

2. xta _____
   money people must pay to the government

3. niotcontusti _____
   a written plan for government

4. sentpreretiveta _____
   a person elected to vote for other people

5. tynouc _____
   a government region within a state

6. blairt nccouil _____
   a group that makes laws for an Indian tribe on Indian lands

7. nfoecer _____
   to make sure people obey (a law or rule)

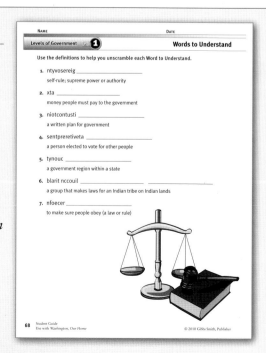

68 | Student Guide
Use with *Washington, Our Home* | © 2010 Gibbs Smith, Publisher

Government Is for All of Us

Governments help people just like you. Government workers make laws and rules. They provide protection. They offer many services. Let's read more about what they do for us.

Making Rules and Laws

What if there were no traffic lights or stop signs, and three cars came to an intersection at the same time? If none of the cars stopped, there would be an accident. How do we know whose turn it is to go through the intersection? We know because we have rules. Rules tell us who should go and who should stop. Rules make things run smoothly. They make things safer.

People in a community and in our nation agree to follow certain rules or laws. If someone breaks the law, he or she might have to pay a fine, provide community service, or go to jail.

Protecting Our Rights

One of the most important things our government does is protect our rights. Let's say you park your new bike outside. While you are inside playing, someone steals your bike. You are angry because you know that is not fair. That bike was your property. What can you do?

You can go to the police. They will try to find your bike and the person who stole it. We have laws against stealing. These laws protect your property rights.

You also have personal rights. These are things like your right to state your opinion without being arrested. You have a right to belong to the religion of your choice. Our laws protect these important rights.

Providing Services

The government pays workers who build and staff our public schools, police and fire departments, and public libraries. They build and maintain public parks and swimming pools, roads, and sidewalks. They plow the snowy streets and collect the garbage every week.

Our Government

What Do You Think ?

Have you seen someone break a rule or law? What happened?

POLICE

153

Reading Strategy

Using a Web

Good readers know how to find details. Explain to students that as they read this chapter they will be focusing on the details that support the main idea. To better explain how to find details in a passage, have students complete the Using a Web to Locate Details activity, available in the *Student Guide*. Have students complete the web with the main idea and details that support the main idea of the lesson. Use a large piece of butcher paper to draw a large web for the class. Have each student place a detail from their web on the class web. Spend time discussing how students determined what were the important details in relation to the main idea.

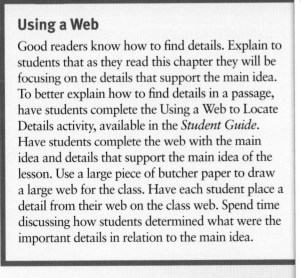

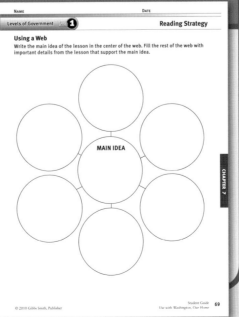

NAME _____ DATE _____

Levels of Government **1** Reading Strategy

Using a Web
Write the main idea of the lesson in the center of the web. Fill the rest of the web with important details from the lesson that support the main idea.

MAIN IDEA

CHAPTER 7

© 2010 Gibbs Smith, Publisher

Student Guide **69**
Use with *Washington, Our Home*

Standards

GLE 1.2.2
Understands how and why state and tribal governments make, interpret, and carry out policies, rules, and laws.

TEACH

Talk About It

Law and Order (*From page 152*)

How is the town of Get Rich similar to the town in which you live?
Possible answers include the town has buildings, stores, it needed roads, people have garbage, and people make decisions together.

How is the town of Get Rich different from the town in which you live?
Possible answers include there were no real roads, people threw garbage out behind their homes, they dumped waste into the river, men settled fights with fists and guns, and no one was safe.

Have students discuss the changes they would make to Get Rich with a partner.
Encourage students to answer the questions in the last paragraph on page 152

Making Rules and Laws

Why is it important to have rules?
Rules make things run smoothly and they make things safe.

Protecting Our Rights

What are some ways that government can protect our rights?
Police and other groups have the job of protecting us. They help us when we have problems and make sure other people don't get in the way of our rights.

Provides Services

What are some services provided by the government?
Possible answers include public schools, police, fire departments, libraries, public parks, swimming pools, roads, sidewalks, they plow streets, and collect garbage.

What Do You Think ?

Discuss what can happen to people who break laws. Explain that these consequences help stop people from breaking rules or laws. This helps keep people safe.

153

Talk About It

Levels of Government

What are the different levels of government and what does each level do?

Local governments make laws and rules for people in towns, cities, and counties. State governments make laws for people who live in each state. Tribal governments make laws for American Indians on tribal lands. The national government makes laws for everyone in the country.

Local Government

Why is it important to have government close to home?

Towns all over our state are so different, we want government close to us who understands how life is where we live.

Cities and Towns

What are some of the services provided by local government?

Water for homes and businesses, sidewalks, streets, streetlights, parks, libraries, police officers, and Fourth of July fireworks are all services provided by the local government.

Caption Answer

There wouldn't be people to help put fires out. People wouldn't feel safe without police officers.

 Social Studies Activity

Lend a Hand

As a class, talk about some of the ways students can volunteer in the school or community. Make a list of some of the ideas students come up with. Choose one of the ideas and have the class do it. This may be as simple as picking up trash on the playground to involvement in a community-wide program.

Levels of Government

You already know that our country is the United States of America. It is made up of 50 states that work together. We are united under one government. But did you know that there are other levels of government? Wherever you live in our country, you live under several levels. Each level does a different job. Each level has certain powers.

Local governments make laws and rules for the people in towns, cities, and counties.

State governments make laws for the people who live in each state.

Tribal governments make laws for American Indians on tribal lands.

The national government makes laws for everyone in the country.

Local Government

Local government is government closest to home. Why do we want government close to home? In some parts of our state, tall buildings are everywhere. The streets are crowded with cars and people. There are many businesses. In other parts of our state, farms spread over the land. There are fewer people, and life is quieter. Small farming towns might need different laws than large cities. They might need different services.

Cities and Towns

Cities and towns are part of local government. City leaders make rules and laws about what kinds of buildings can be built in a town and how high the buildings can be. They make laws about how fast drivers can go on city streets. They decide how to spend city money.

Have you ever thought about what it takes to keep your town or city running? We all need water for our homes and businesses. We need sidewalks, streets, and streetlights. We want parks, libraries, and police officers. We want to watch fireworks on the Fourth of July. City governments provide all of these services.

*People such as firefighters and police officers work for local governments. **What do you think would happen if local governments did not provide these services?***

Washington, Our Home

Technology Tie-In

How Does Government Affect Me?

Have students visit the PBS Kids Web site for excellent information on the services that communities provide for their citizens. Students can take a tour around town by clicking on different places that provide services for their citizens. For a link to the Web site, go to **www.ExperienceStateHistory.com.**

Counties

Counties are another form of local government. States are divided into government regions called *counties*. Washington has 39 counties. Each has its own county government offices at a town called the county seat. All the people in the county, no matter what town they live in, have to live by the rules of the county.

Besides making rules for the county, county governments provide services. They run police and fire stations. They provide clean water. They hire people to collect the garbage. If your parents are driving too fast on a road, they might get stopped by a county police officer. If you are in the car, you might see bright lights flashing from the top of the police car!

The city or town where county government offices are located is called the county seat. **Find your county on the map. What is your county seat? Have you ever been there?**

This is the Lincoln County Courthouse in Davenport. County judges work there. Courthouses also hold records, such as birth and marriage certificates.

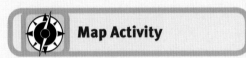

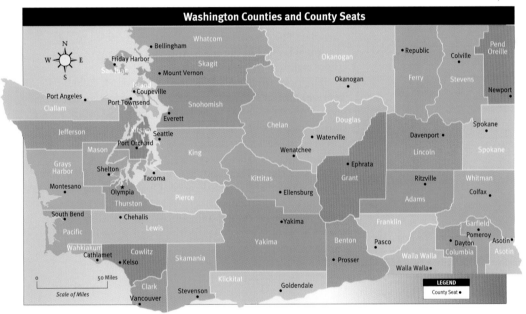

Washington Counties and County Seats

LEGEND
County Seat •

Our Government

155

Talk About It

Counties

How many counties does Washington have?
Washington has 39 counties.

What is the town called where the county government offices are located?
The county seat is the town where the county government has its offices.

What are services that a county provides?
The county makes rules, runs police and fire stations, provides clean water, and hires people to collect garbage.

Caption Answer

Have students work with a partner to find their county and county seat.

Encourage students to share experiences they have had visiting the county seat.

🧭 Map Activity

Washington Counties and County Seats

Have each student choose a county and research its county seat, important cities and towns, landforms, the population of the county, and two or three interesting places in the county. After students have collected all the information, have them write a report of their county on the computer. Their report should include a map of the county. You may want students to write the office of the county seat to request information about the county.

Talk About It

State Government

What document was written years ago that is still the plan for how our state government should run?
The state constitution was written in 1889 and is still used today.

Who makes the laws for people who live in our state?
Representatives make laws for people in our state.

What are taxes used for?
Taxes are used to help pay for services people need.

What are some topics covered in articles in the state constitution?
Articles talk about rights given to people who live in the state, how leaders should be chosen, taxes, and the boundaries of our state.

Caption Answers

The seal of the state of Washington; 1889; Washington became a state in 1889.

There weren't computers or typewriters when the constitution was written.

Article 1 is titled Declaration of Rights.

Technology Tie-In

Tic Tac Taxes

Go online to the EconEdLink Web site and play the Tic Tac Taxes game with your class. Divide the class into two teams, "X"s and "O"s. Have students answer the questions. If they are correct, their team is awarded an "X" or "O" to play. For a link to this site, see **www.ExperienceStateHistory.com.**

Our state seal is the official seal of our government. It is used on important documents. **What do the words say? What is the date on the seal? What happened that year?**

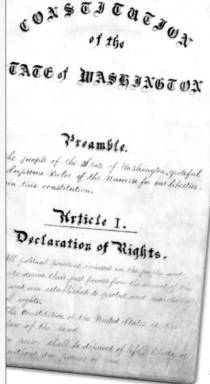

The state constitution is the plan for how our government works. **Why do you think it was written by hand? What does the title of Article 1 say?**

State Government

State government is government for the whole state. No matter what city, town, or county you live in, you follow the rules and laws of our state government.

You have learned that a long time ago the people in Washington Territory had to write a *constitution* before Washington could become a state. Today, this important document is still the plan for how our state government should run.

Our state constitution is divided into parts called articles. The first article lists all the rights given to the people who live in the state. You will learn more about these rights in the next lesson.

The next articles tell how men and women called *representatives* make the laws for the people who live in the state. Other articles have to do with crime. Some are about state roads, schools, and other services. Another article says how leaders should be chosen.

Do you know what *taxes* are? Taxes are money the people must pay to the government. The government uses the taxes to pay for services the people need. Our state constitution has an article all about taxes.

The boundaries of our state are also described in the constitution. One article states the location of each boundary line.

Washington, Our Home

Writing Activity

Take Me to your Leader

List many different groups the students may be a part of. Some possible groups include family, scouts, school, church, choir, student council, soccer teams, and so on. Have students respond with who the leader of the group is. Follow this with a discussion about the need for leaders. Have students write a paragraph about the qualities of a good leader.

"Let's work together. Let's be bold and courageous."

—Chris Gregoire,
Our twenty-second governor

The people of Washington get to choose their leaders. We choose state senators, who serve for four years. This picture shows the state senate in action.

Washington State Legislature

Senate	**House of Representatives**
49 senators	98 representatives

Two groups, or houses, of lawmakers work together to make laws.

We also choose men and women to send to the House of Representatives. They serve for two years. You can send them letters or e-mail to tell them what you think. Together, the senators and representatives make the laws for our state.

Our Government

157

 Art Activity

Washington State Symbols

Washington has a lot of state symbols. Each symbol means something important to our state. Many of the symbols can be found around the state capital. Have students choose a state symbol to research. Tell students to record their information on a piece of paper. Then have students create the symbol in a creative way. Students may paint the symbol, or create the symbol with clay, for example. Allow students to share their symbol and its information with the class

 Literature Link

Our Government from A to Z

Share Devin Scillian's book, *A Is for America*, with students. Have students use this book as a model for a class book about our government. As a class, brainstorm a list of topics related to our government that start with each letter of the alphabet. Then have students create pages for the class book.

Differentiated Paths

Sticky Notes Reading and Discussion

ELL and Special Needs
Provide each student with five small sticky notes. Ask students to read the lesson with a partner and place the sticky notes on anything they find interesting, or anything they don't understand. Once students have finished reading the lesson, talk about the things they marked as a whole group.

Gifted Learners
Provide each student with five small sticky notes. Ask students to read the lesson and place the sticky notes on anything they find interesting, or want to learn more about. Once students have finished reading the lesson, talk about the things they marked as a whole group. Have students choose one topic they marked which they would like to learn more about. Have students find books, magazines, newspaper articles, and Web sites on their topic. After studying the sources, have students share five interesting things they learned about their topic.

Tribal Government

Ask students why they think tribal governments are able to have tribal sovereignty.

Remind students that in Chapter 6 they learned about treaties and reservations that the United States government made when they settled on Indian land. Encourage students to draw conclusions and support their answers with facts.

What is the group of leaders called who meet to make laws?

The tribal council meets to make laws. These laws may or may not be the same as the laws of the Washington State government.

How is tribal government similar to kinds of local government of Washington State?

Tribal government can tax citizens. They can manage activities on tribal lands. They can build schools, have police forces, and issue license plates.

How many tribes in Washington are recognized by the U.S. government?

There are 29 recognized tribes in Washington.

Caption Answer

The tribes need more money to meet the needs of the people on the reservations. They are able to make their own laws to allow gambling and casinos.

The Spokane, Coeur d' Alene, Tulalip, and other tribes have opened gambling casinos. Gambling is against the law in the rest of Washington. The tribal leaders opened the casinos to make money and provide jobs for the people of the tribes. **How is this an example of tribal government meeting the needs of the tribe?**

Tribal Government

Some places in Washington have their own special kind of government. American Indians who live on reservations have tribal **sovereignty,** or self-rule. That means tribal governments are separate from state and local governments. Tribal governments can make their own laws.

Members of the tribe vote to elect their leaders and decide how the tribal government will be run. Then, the leaders meet in a **tribal council** to make the laws. These laws may or may not be the same as the laws and rules of the Washington State government.

Tribal governments can also tax citizens. They can manage activities on tribal lands. They can build schools, have police forces, and issue license plates.

While American Indians can be citizens of a tribe, they are also citizens of the United States. They are protected by the U.S. Constitution, like everyone else. Today, there are 29 tribes in Washington that are recognized by the U.S. government.

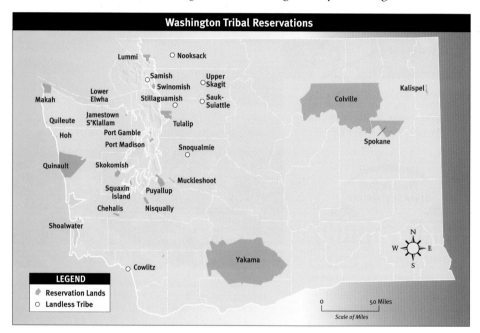

Washington Tribal Reservations

LEGEND
- Reservation Lands
- Landless Tribe

158

 Map Activity

Cooperative Groups

Washington Tribal Reservations

Have students work in small groups and choose an American Indian tribe to research. The Governors Office of Indian Affairs has a Web site with information on each of the tribes in Washington State. Have students visit this site and others to learn more about the tribe they chose to research. Have groups choose at least five interesting facts about the tribe they chose. Groups should work together and use the facts to write a song to a well-known tune, such as Twinkle, Twinkle Little Star. Encourage students to come up with actions to their song as well. Have each group share their song with the class. A link to this site can be found at **www.ExperienceStateHistory.com.**

National Government

National government is government for the whole country. It is the highest level of government.

Our national government is set up by the U.S. Constitution. The Constitution states how leaders should be elected and how they should make laws for the country. It also sets out rules about education, a militia, and taxes.

The Constitution has a Bill of Rights that protects our most important rights. We will read more about rights in the next lesson.

A Capital City

The capital of our national government is Washington, D.C. Representatives from each state meet at the U.S. Capitol Building to make the laws. The White House is also in the city. That is where the president and his family live. There are hundreds of government buildings in Washington, D.C.

LEVEL	PLACE	EXAMPLES OF POWER
NATIONAL	UNITED STATES	• relations with other countries • protection of our country • money printing • interstate roads
STATE	WASHINGTON	• state lands and resources • state roads • sales tax collection • driver's licenses
LOCAL	COUNTIES, CITIES, TOWNS	• city police and firefighters • county roads and bridges • water and sewer • public schools

Our Founding Fathers did not want the national government to have all the power. They thought it was important for the states to have some power, too. Look at the chart to review the levels of government and their powers.

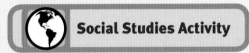

Washington State: Olympia

CAPITAL CITIES

United States: Washington, D.C.

Washington, D.C., is all the way across the nation from Washington State.

Our Government

This is the U.S. Capitol Building in Washington, D.C. No matter what state, county, or town you live in, you must follow the laws made here by our national government.

159

Talk About It

National Government

How is national government similar to local government? How is it different?
National government is set up by a constitution, has elected leaders, and makes laws. It is different because it is government for the whole country.

A Capital City

What important things are in Washington, D.C.?
The U.S. Capitol is there where representatives meet from each state to make laws. The White House is also in the city. That is where the president and his family live. There are hundreds of government buildings in Washington, D.C.

 Social Studies Activity

A Presidential Moment

Have students research one or two presidents so that all the presidents are covered. Students should compile the information into a two-minute speech highlighting the important points of each president's life. Daily before the Pledge of Allegiance, have a few students present their speech about one president. The White House Kids of the Presidential timeline Web sites are good online sources for biographical information about U.S. presidents. See www.ExperienceStateHistory.com for links to these sites.

 Reading Activity

History of Our Flag

Have students research the ways our nation's flag has changed since Betsy Ross's first version in 1876. Go to www.ExperienceStateHistory.com for a link to a site with information about our nation's flag

Technology Tie-In

President for a Day

Have students go online to the PBS Kids Web site to get a glimpse into a day in the life of a president. The White House Kids Web site also has some fun games and quizzes about the role of the president and the executive branch of our government. Go to www.ExperienceStateHistory.com for a link to the Web site.

Talk About It

Executive Branch

Who is the leader of the executive branch?
The president of the United States is the leader of the executive branch.

Legislative Branch

What is the role of the legislative branch?
The legislative branch makes the laws.

What is the name for the legislative branch?
Congress is the name for the legislative branch.

How many senators does each state send to Washington, D.C.?
Each state sends two senators to Washington, D.C., to help make laws.

How many people does each state send to the House of Representatives in Washington, D.C.?
The number of people sent from each state to the House of Representatives depends on how many people live in the state.

How many representatives does Washington State have in the House of Representatives?
Washington State has nine representatives.

Judicial Branch *(From page 161)*

What does the judicial branch do?
The judicial branch decides what laws mean and what the punishment should be for people who break the laws. It decides if laws are fair and follow the constitution.

Art Activity

Government Mobile

Have students create a mobile illustration of the branches of government. On a wire hanger, have students hang three circles labeled Executive Branch, Legislative Branch, and Judicial Branch. Then from each of these circles, students should hang circles that show the different groups that fit under those branches.

★★ Creating and ★★ Carrying Out Laws

Branches of Government

In addition to the three levels, our government separates power among three branches of government. Each branch has its own responsibilities. Each branch limits the power of the other two. This system of checks and balances makes sure that no single branch becomes too powerful.

Executive Branch

The executive branch carries out the laws. The president of our country is the leader of the executive branch. The president suggests new laws, meets with leaders of other countries, and is in charge of the military.

In the branches of government tree, find the reporters asking the president questions. What would you ask the president if you had the chance?

Legislative Branch

The legislative branch makes the laws. Congress is the name for the legislative branch. There are two houses in Congress—the Senate and the House of Representatives.

Each state sends representatives to Washington, D.C., to help make laws. Every state sends two senators. The number of people that each state sends to the House of Representatives depends on how many people live there. States with bigger populations send more representatives. Washington has nine representatives in the U.S. House of Representatives.

In the tree, find the people giving speeches about the laws they want passed.

Washington, Our Home

Social Studies Activity

Court's in Session

Have students hold a mock trial to solve a real problem at school. Ask the students to talk about the problem that is happening at school. Assign roles for each student. Roles include judge, jury members, court recorder, plaintiff, defendant, the lawyers for both sides, and the witnesses. You could also have students play the role of the media.

Have the two sides prepare their cases and submit a list of witnesses to the court. Set a court date. On the day of the court session, set up your classroom as a courtroom. Encourage students to dress appropriately for a day in court. Have each side present their arguments and call their witnesses. Then have the jury deliberate and reach a verdict. Once the verdict has been read, the two sides must abide by the decision of the court.

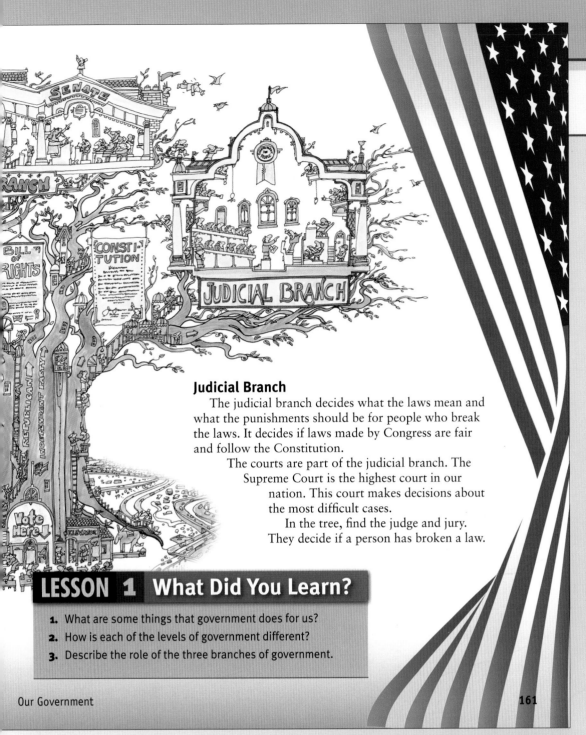

Judicial Branch

The judicial branch decides what the laws mean and what the punishments should be for people who break the laws. It decides if laws made by Congress are fair and follow the Constitution.

The courts are part of the judicial branch. The Supreme Court is the highest court in our nation. This court makes decisions about the most difficult cases.

In the tree, find the judge and jury. They decide if a person has broken a law.

LESSON 1 What Did You Learn?

1. What are some things that government does for us?
2. How is each of the levels of government different?
3. Describe the role of the three branches of government.

Our Government

161

REFLECT

Reflect on students' understanding of the role of government to provide order, and to create and carry out laws. Students should also understand the different levels of government and how they help meet the needs of people. You can evaluate students' understanding through discussion or evaluation of activities completed in this lesson. The following activities will serve as another way of assessing students' understanding of the key objectives of this lesson.

 Writing Activity

School Rules

Remind students that it is the government's role to create and carry out laws. Explain that smaller organizations such as schools have people in charge who create and carry out rules. Encourage students to think about their school and classroom rules as they complete the School Rules activity available in the *Student Guide*.

NAME   DATE

Levels of Government **1**   **Writing Activity**

School Rules

Make a list of school and classroom rules you must follow. Next to each rule, write how that rule protects your rights. Decide which rules you would like to get rid of and tell why. For each rule you would like to get rid of, write another rule to replace it.

School and Classroom Rules	How the Rule Protects My Rights

The Rules I Would Like to Get Rid Of and Why

Rules I Would Add

70   Student Guide
Use with *Washington, Our Home*   © 2010 Gibbs Smith, Publisher

---

LESSON 1 What Did You Learn?

1. *Government makes laws, keeps us safe, and provides many services such as public education, libraries, police officers, roads, and garbage removal.*
2. *National government makes laws for everyone in the country, tribal government makes laws for American Indians on tribal lands, state government makes laws for people who live in each state, and local government makes rules and laws for people who live in towns, cities, and counties.*
3. *The executive branch carries out the laws, the legislative branch makes the laws, and the judicial branch decides what laws mean and what the punishment should be for people who break the laws.*

Standards

GLE 1.1.1
Understands the key ideal rights set forth in Article 1 of the Washington State Constitution.

GLE 1.1.2
Evaluates the effectiveness of a law or policy by explaining how it promotes ideals.

PREPARE

Activator

Washington Rights

Explain to students that rights are privileges that we have. Encourage students to think about the rights that they have in Washington. Have students complete the organizer with words or pictures that start with each letter in Washington. A Washington Rights activity is available in the *Student Guide*.

Word Study

Picture Dictionary Part 2

Have students add the Words to Understand for this lesson to the picture dictionary created in Lesson 1 (see page 152). Encourage students to think of other words having to do with our rights and laws.

LESSON 2 — Our Rights, Our Laws

Key Ideas

- Our state constitution supports freedom and rights.
- Our laws protect our rights.

Words to Understand

bill
ideal
liberty
rights
rule of law
veto

What Are Rights?

One of the jobs of our government is protecting our rights. **Rights** are the privileges we are entitled to. They are things we believe we all have a claim to. Our country was founded on the idea that there are certain rights no government can take away. That is why rights hold an important place in our constitution.

Article 1 of our state constitution lists these rights. It is about our ideals. **Ideals** are our beliefs about the way things should be. Look at the chart to learn some examples of the rights and ideals in our state constitution.

YOUR RIGHTS	WORDS IN THE CONSTITUTION	WHAT IT MEANS
Life, *liberty* (freedom), and property (land or things you own)	"No person shall be deprived of life, liberty, or property, without due process of law."	No person can have their life, liberty, or property taken away without good reason and fair treatment by the courts.
Free speech and ideas	"Every person may freely speak, write and publish on all subjects, being responsible for the abuse of that right."	The government cannot tell you what you can or can't say, write, or print. However, you can't spread lies about people or break the laws.
Religious freedom	"Absolute freedom . . . in all matters of religious . . . belief and worship, shall be guaranteed to every individual, and no one shall be [harmed] in person or property on account of religion."	You can choose to accept and follow any religious ideas. No one can harm you or your property because of your religious beliefs or actions.

162   Washington, Our Home

Words to Understand

bill (p. 168) *a written proposal for a law*
ideal (p. 162) *an idea about the way things should be; something that is believed to be perfect or best*
liberty (p. 162) *freedom; the state of being free*
rights (p. 162) *the privileges citizens are entitled to*
rule of law (p. 163) *the idea that no one is above the law; the law is the highest power*
veto (p. 169) *to say no to a bill; to prevent a bill from becoming a law*

A Words to Understand activity for this lesson is available in the *Student Guide*.

How Laws Protect Our Rights

How do laws protect our rights? We will learn about some examples from everyday life. But first, there is an important rule to understand. It is called the rule of law.

The Rule of Law

In our country, there is no king. The law is king! Our Founding Fathers set it up this way so that no one person could get too powerful. If one person had all the power, he could make everyone do whatever he wanted. Things might not be fair.

The *rule of law* means that the law is the highest power. No person, not even the president, is above the law. Everyone must obey it. That's how things stay fair.

Because we get to choose the people who make the laws, we have a say in them. If we don't like how a leader represents us, we can vote for someone else next time. We can vote for someone who will make the kinds of laws and decisions we want.

Our Government

Our Founding Fathers thought hard about how to make the best government. They wanted it to be based on liberty, justice, and laws. This painting shows them writing the U.S. Constitution. **John Adams (a leader who was not at this meeting) said we should have "a government of laws and not of men." What do you think he meant by that? Do you recognize any of the men in the painting? What are they doing?**

What Do You Think ?

Does freedom of speech mean you can say false things that bring harm to other people? How can we use our rights so they don't get in the way of other people's rights?

163

Standards

GLE 1.2.2
Understands how and why state and tribal governments make, interpret, and carry out policies, rules, and laws.

TEACH

Talk About It

What Are Rights? (*From page 162*)

Why do rights hold an important place in our constitution?
Our country was founded on the idea that there are certain rights no government can take away.

What are some of the ideals from Article 1 of our state constitution?
Possible answers include life, liberty, property, free speech and ideas, and religious freedom.

The Rule of Law

How does the rule of law protect our rights?
The rule of law prevents any one person from getting too powerful. It means that the law is the highest power. No one is above the law. That's how things stay fair.

Caption Answer

He meant that laws should be the highest power so that no man could get too powerful.

The Founding Fathers of our country are in a meeting, writing the U.S. Constitution.

What Do You Think ?

No, you cannot spread lies about people. You can say, write, or print anything you want as long as it doesn't bring harm to other people.

As long as we use our rights responsibly and don't harm other people, we won't get in the way of other people's rights.

Reading Strategy

Using Two-Column Notes

Good readers take notes as they read. This helps them pay attention as they read. It also gives readers something to look back to when they need to remember the details of what they read. Using two-column notes is a great tool to aid readers in finding details that support the main idea. Have students use the Using Two-Column Notes activity available in the *Student Guide* to find the details within each heading of this lesson.

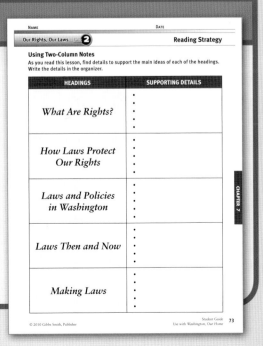

NAME _____ DATE _____

Our Rights, Our Laws | Lesson **2**   **Reading Strategy**

Using Two-Column Notes
As you read this lesson, find details to support the main ideas of each of the headings. Write the details in the organizer.

HEADINGS	SUPPORTING DETAILS
What Are Rights?	• • •
How Laws Protect Our Rights	• • •
Laws and Policies in Washington	• • •
Laws Then and Now	• • •
Making Laws	• • •

© 2010 Gibbs Smith, Publisher   Student Guide   Use with *Washington, Our Home*   73

Standards

GLE 5.1.1
Understands the concepts used in documents and sources.

Talk About It

Laws that Solve Problems

Why was a seat belt law made?
Too many people were getting hurt in car accidents.

Do you think it is a good idea for the government to make laws that protect people?
Have students share what they think with a partner and explain why they feel that way.

Laws that Protect the Environment

Why did lawmakers pass a bill limiting fishing in some areas?
The salmon were in danger of becoming extinct.

Do you think it is a good idea for the government to make laws that protect the environment?
Have students share what they think with a partner and explain why they feel that way.

 **Literature Link**

Crazy But True Laws

Just for fun, read Kathi Linz's book *Chickens May Not Cross the Road: And Other Crazy (But True) Laws* to the class. As the title suggests, the book is filled with crazy but true state laws. Talk about each state's right to create laws that apply to the people of the state. You may want to use this book as inspiration for writing some new classroom rules.

★★★ Laws and Policies ★★★
in Washington

Washington leaders make all kinds of laws. Some laws protect our personal rights. Other laws protect our environment. Some were made to solve problems. Here are some everyday examples of the many kinds of laws we have.

Laws That Solve Problems

Whenever you get into a car or truck, the first thing you do is put on your seat belt. Do you know that there is a law that says you must always wear a seat belt in a car? Do you know why?

Too many people were getting hurt in car accidents. To solve this problem, lawmakers passed a law saying everyone must buckle up. Children younger than eight years old must either sit in a child's car seat or in a booster seat. Children's seat belts must cross in front and not under the arm or behind the back. Washington was the first state in the nation to pass this type of law.

Laws That Protect the Environment

Salmon fishing is a big industry. So many fishermen were catching salmon that there weren't enough salmon left. The salmon were in danger of becoming extinct. In 2005, lawmakers voted to bring things back into balance in our waters. They passed Senate Bill 5610. It had a plan to limit fishing in some areas and put more salmon into some of the regions.

Washington, Our Home

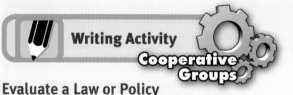 **Writing Activity**

Cooperative Groups

Evaluate a Law or Policy

Have students work in groups to evaluate the effectiveness of a law or policy. Have each group choose a law or policy from this lesson, or another law with your approval. Tell students to study the law or policy and write ways that it promotes ideals. After students have evaluated the law or policy, have students write suggestions for how the law could better promote ideals. Encourage each group to present their information in a PowerPoint presentation.

No Smoking Beyond this Point

Laws That Protect Our Right to Life

We have learned that cigarette smoke is harmful not only to the people smoking but to the people around them. Many voters in Washington wanted to ban smoking in public places. To ban means to make it against the law. They wanted the law to protect their right to live a healthy life. From now on, you won't smell cigarette smoke in restaurants, bowling alleys, or parks.

Laws for Public Safety

A new Washington law says it is against the law to talk on a cell phone or tap out a text message while driving a car. If caught by the police, a person doing this will receive a ticket and be fined $101.

Many people had wanted this law for a long time. Others did not. Then Billy Williams, age 12, was walking to the school bus when he was hit by a car. He had brain injuries and was taken to a hospital. The driver of the car was not paying enough attention to driving while he was talking on a cell phone.

"Every time I see a person on a cell phone," said Billy, "I say, 'A person on a cell phone!' I just scream it out." Can you see how this law helps make people feel safer?

Personal Freedom or Public Safety?

Sometimes people think laws take away their rights to do what they want to do. They think these laws take away their personal liberty. Other people think the laws are important for the safety of everyone.

What Do You Think ❓

How do you think our state's seat belt, cell phone, and smoking laws protect a person's right to life? Do you agree or disagree with the laws? Why?

Our Government

Talk About It

Laws that Protect Our Right to Life

Why did people vote to ban smoking in public places?
Smoking is not only harmful to the people smoking but to the people around them.

Do you think it is a good idea for the government to make laws that protect our right to life?
Have students share what they think with a partner and explain why they feel that way.

Laws for Public Safety

Why did people in Washington want a law for it to be against the law to talk on a cell phone or tap out a text message while driving a car?
People using a cell phone while driving can be distracted and bring harm to others.

Do you think it is a good idea for the government to make laws for public safety?
Have students share what they think with a partner and explain why they feel that way.

What Do You Think ❓

Have students work in small groups to discuss how our state's seat belt, cell phone, and smoking laws protect a person's right to life. Have a member from each group share what the group talked about with the whole class.

Standards

GLE 5.2.2
Understands the main ideas from an artifact, primary source, or secondary source describing an issue or event.

Analyze a Political Cartoon

Use this activity to follow the information studied on page 165.

Art Activity

Make a Political Cartoon

Tell students that political cartoons are used to persuade people to see from the point of view of the artist. Tell students to think of an issue or event in which there are multiple points of view. After choosing a topic, have students draw a cartoon to persuade people to see from their point of view. Tell students that political cartoons usually exaggerate, or overdo, the physical characteristics of people or things to make a point. Encourage students to be creative. Hang the finished cartoons on a bulletin board to share them with the class.

✖ Go to the Source
Analyze a Political Cartoon

Salmon have always been important to people in Washington. As Washington has grown, more and more people have fished for salmon. They have built dams across the rivers. This changed the path that salmon travel to lay their eggs. It changed the natural places where they live and breed.

In time, the number of salmon dropped. Many people were concerned. They wanted to make sure wild salmon would not disappear forever.

In 2005, lawmakers passed Senate Bill 5610. It limited fishing in certain areas and put more salmon into some of the regions. People hoped it would bring back, or recover, the salmon.

LOOK	THINK	DECIDE
What do you notice about the river in this political cartoon?	How might this cartoon relate to the bill that was passed in 2005?	Do you think the artist of the cartoon thinks it is important to protect salmon? Why or why not?

Washington, Our Home

LOOK	THINK	DECIDE
The river the fish are swimming in is crossing a road that a car is driving on.	*Possible answers include the salmon are now back in places where they hadn't been in some time.*	*Students' answers should be supported by details from the cartoon.*

Laws Then and Now

The Boldt Decision

Do you know that rules and laws made over a hundred years ago affect decisions made much later? Do you remember the Indian treaties Governor Stevens made? Long ago, the treaties promised American Indians that if they moved to reservations, they could still fish in their usual places in their usual ways.

As Washington grew, more and more people were catching fish to sell or for sport. Soon there weren't many fish left. The state government said the tribes could no longer fish in certain places. They could only fish for certain kinds of fish. They would have to follow the same fishing laws as everyone else.

Indians said the new laws went against their treaty rights. They wanted to be able to fish just as their ancestors had. The tribes asked a judge to decide.

In 1974, the decision came. Judge George Boldt said the Indian fishing rights stand. Indians could continue to catch salmon as they always had. They were pleased. Tribal members continue their fishing traditions today.

Linking the Present to the Past

Today, people work together to bring back larger fish populations. They make rules about fishing for salmon and steelhead. They work to keep the water clean so fish can live in it. They make rules for dams so the fish can still swim through the rivers.

The Boldt Decision supported Native American fishing rights. **Why do you think it is important to Native Americans to keep their ways of fishing as well as their fishing rights?**

Reading Activity

History of Our Flag

HistoryLink.org has an article about Native Americans who protested the denial of treaty tights in 1964 that led to the Boldt Decision. Print this article and have students read it to understand the Native American perspective on the issue. After reading the article, ask students to come up with three details that describe the Native American perspective and the U.S. government perspective on the issue. A link to this site can be found at **www. ExperienceStateHistory.com.**

Standards

GLE 4.4.1
Understands that significant historical events in Washington State have implications for current decisions.

Talk About It

Laws Then and Now

Why are tribal members allowed to continue fishing traditions today, even if the state government said other people can't fish in certain areas?

The first governor of Washington, Isaac Stevens, made a treaty with Indians long ago that said they could continue their fishing traditions.

Can you think of any other decisions or events in the history of Washington that might affect how things are done today?

Encourage students to look back at chapters 3–6 for ideas of decisions or events from Washington's past that might affect how things are done today.

Linking the Present to the Past

Write the words *Cause and Effect* on the board. Under *Effect* write the phrases *people work together to bring back larger fish, rules about fishing salmon and steelhead, keep water clean,* and *rules for dams.* Explain that these actions people are taking are a result or effect of things that have happened in the past. As a class, come up with the causes that led to the effects on the board.

Caption Answer

Traditions of the Native American culture have existed for hundreds of years. Fishing is part of their culture. It is important to keep their culture alive.

Talk About It

From a Bill to a Law

How can people who don't work for the government have a say in bills that go to the House of Representatives?

People can call or write to their representatives to share their ideas.

The Representatives Meet

What two groups make up the legislature?

The senate and the House of Representatives make up the legislature.

The Representatives Vote

(From page 169)

How many representatives have to vote on a bill for it to get passed on to the other group in the legislature?

A majority, or more than half, of the representatives must vote for a bill for it to be passed on to the other group in the legislature.

The Governor Signs the Bill into a Law

What happens to a bill after it is voted on by more than half of the senate and the House of Representatives?

The bill goes to the governor, where he decides whether to pass or to veto the bill.

 Technology Tie-In

Who's Who in State Government

Have students research and download pictures from the Internet showing who's who in our state government. This information could be made into a bulletin board or into a class book.

★★★ Making Laws ★★★

Leaders at each level of government make laws and rules. Does your school have a student council? If it does, each class elects a person or two to be part of the council. The council members from all of the classes meet together. They might vote for rules that all the children in the school will have to obey. The council member from your class is your representative.

Just like in a student council, the adults of Washington State vote for representatives. The representatives vote for laws that all the people in the state have to obey.

Tribal councils are also made up of representatives. They make laws and decisions for the tribe.

From a Bill to a Law

A lot of people have ideas about what laws they think should be made. The people can call or write to their representatives and explain what they want. If a representative thinks the idea is a good one, he or she can write up the idea. The written idea for a law is called a *bill*. Here's how it works in our state government.

The Representatives Meet

The representatives of our state meet in two different groups. One is called the senate. The other is called the house of representatives. Together, both groups are called the legislature.

A bill starts out in either the senate or the house. Representatives talk about it. Some might like the bill, and some might not. They invite other people who are interested in the bill to tell what they think about it.

 Differentiated Paths

Legislative Bills

Learning about our state legislative branch provides opportunities to differentiate learning.

ELL and Special Needs

Give your ELL and special needs students a bill to view. Have students draw a picture of what that bill would look like in action.

Gifted Learners

Challenge gifted learners to go online to the Washington State Legislative Web site to view bills that have been introduced. Divide the students into committees. Have each committee choose a bill to discuss and report on to the other groups.

See **www.ExperienceStateHistory.com** for a link to this site.

The Representatives Vote

For the bill to become a law, a majority (more than half) of the representatives must vote for it. However, even if the bill passes and gets a majority of votes, it is not a law yet.

The bill has to be sent to the other group in the legislature. It has to be talked about and passed by a majority once again. Even if it passes this time, it is still not a law. There is one last step.

The Governor Signs the Bill into a Law

Washington's governor has to sign the bill into law. This act makes it a new law for the people of the state.

What if the governor does not agree that the bill should become a law? She has the power to **veto** it. This means she says "no" to the bill. If this happens, the bill might be changed in some ways. Then it might start over in the senate and in the house.

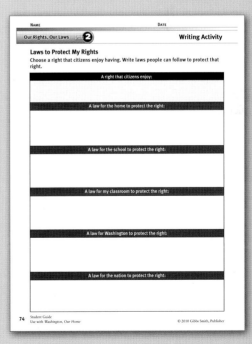

LESSON 2 What Did You Learn?

1. What are some of the rights described in our state constitution?
2. How do laws protect our rights?
3. Explain how a bill becomes a law.

What Do You Think ❓

You can see that it is not easy to pass laws. How does this process protect our rights?

Our Government

REFLECT

Reflect on students' understanding of the role our state's constitution and laws play in supporting freedoms and rights. They should also understand that governments create and carry out laws. You can evaluate students' understanding through discussion or evaluation of activities completed in this lesson. The following activity will serve as another way of assessing students' understanding of the key objectives of this lesson.

✏️ Writing Activity

Laws to Protect My Rights

As a class, discuss how laws protect our rights. Encourage students to think of examples from the lesson. Have students think about a right they enjoy having. Ask students to imagine what it might be like to work for the government and write laws. Tell them to think of laws they would like to have to protect the rights they enjoy. Have students complete the organizer for the Laws to Protect My Rights activity available in the *Student Guide*.

LESSON 2 What Did You Learn?

1. *Possible answers include the right to life, liberty, and property, the right to free speech and ideas, and the right to religious freedom.*
2. *Laws are written to make sure that no one person becomes too powerful and takes rights away from people. Laws are also written to tell people what they can and cannot do so that peoples' rights are protected.*
3. *A bill is written by a representative. The bill goes to the House of Representatives and to the senate to be voted on. More than half of both groups have to pass the bill. The bill then goes to the governor to either be approved or vetoed.*

Standards

GLE 1.4.1
Understands that civic participation involves being informed about public issues and voting in elections.

PREPARE

Activator

A Helpful Town

Tell students that each citizen has *responsibilities* or actions they take for the good of everyone. Have students study the drawing of a town from the activity A Helpful Town, available in the *Student Guide*. Ask students to think of ways that people, places, and things in the drawing help citizens as they complete the activity.

Word Study

Picture Dictionary Part 3

Have students add the Words to Understand for this lesson to the Picture Dictionary started in Lesson 1 (see page 152). Encourage students to think of other words having to do with citizens' responsibilities.

Caption Answer

Adults can stay informed by watching the news, reading the newspaper, attending town and city meetings, and talking with other citizens.

LESSON 3 Our Responsibilities

Key Ideas

- Citizens have responsibilities.
- Citizens can work together to make a difference.

Words to Understand

citizen
civic
duty
election
politics
responsibility
volunteer

Think of the adults you see every day. **How do they stay informed? Do they vote?**

A Citizen Has Responsibilities

A **citizen** is the legal resident of a state or a country. You have learned that our citizens have many rights. We also have **responsibilities**. These are actions citizens are supposed to do for the good of everyone.

Adults' Responsibilities

Adults have many responsibilities. They have important civic duties. The word **civic** has to do with being a citizen of a town or country. A **duty** is an action a person is expected to do. What should adults do?

- Take care of children.
- Work to earn money for themselves and their families.
- Obey all rules and laws.
- Keep homes and yards clean.
- Get involved in **politics** (government).
- Stay informed about political issues.
- Vote.

170 Washington, Our Home

Words to Understand

citizen (p. 170) *a legal resident of a country*
civic (p. 170) *having to do with being a citizen of a city or a town*
duty (p. 170) *an action a person is expected to do*
election (p. 171) *the process of voting people into government office*
politics (p. 170) *having to do with government*
responsibility (p. 170) *a duty you have to do; something you are supposed to do*
volunteer (p. 173) *a person who chooses to work without pay*

A Words to Understand activity is available in the *Student Guide*.

Voting

Adults have a responsibility to help choose who will lead their town, state, and country. They do this by voting in *elections*.

Voting is a very important civic duty. It is our say in the government. By voting, we help shape the future. If we don't like the way our representatives and other leaders do their jobs, we can elect someone else next time.

Staying Informed

It is important that adults understand the issues in their community. Laws are made about these public issues. One issue might have to do with using water and land. Other issues might have to do with smoking, schools, or seat belts. These things affect everyone.

To keep informed, people should:

On election day, voters enter the voting booth. They use a special machine or computer to mark the ballot.

- Get the news. Newspapers always have stories about public issues. People can read newspapers online, have them delivered to their homes, or buy them on the street. They can watch the news on TV or listen to it on the radio. Morning and night, public issues are in the news.

- Attend a town meeting. Town leaders have meetings to talk about issues of their town. Adults and children are always welcome at these meetings. They can listen and ask questions. They can give suggestions.

Newspapers not only have news reports, they have pages where people give their opinions on issues. They have stories about people and places. **Why do you think this girl will make a good voter someday?**

Our Government

171

Talk About It

A Citizen Has Responsibilities
(*From page 170*)

Why do you think it is important for each citizen to have responsibilities?
If each citizen has responsibilities and does their part, we can stay safe and things will go well in our communities.

Adults' Responsibilities
(*From page 170*)

What are some responsibilities adults have?
See the list on page 170 for possible answers. Encourage students to come up with other answers.

Voting

How do adults help choose who will lead their city, town, and country?
Adults vote in elections to help choose leaders.

Staying Informed

Why is it important for adults to understand the issues in their community?
The issues affect everyone.

How can adults stay informed?
Adults can get the news from the newspapers, articles online, and news on the TV and radio.

 Writing Activity

Character Traits

Being a person of good character is the best way to be a good citizen. Have students choose one of the following character traits to write about: citizenship, caring, fairness, responsibility, respect, or trustworthiness. Students should write how they are trying to develop one of these traits in their life. Encourage students to provide at least two examples of how they are developing the trait.

Reading Strategy

Using Note-Taking

Taking notes is a great way to focus a reader's attention to the details of a text. Teach students that taking notes is not copying the text word-for-word, but rather finding key thoughts or words that are important. Explain to students that some students' notes will be short, concise, or full of abbreviations. Remind students that there is no right or wrong to note-taking. Have students read the lesson and practice their note-taking skills. Have students complete the Using Note-Taking activity in the *Student Guide*.

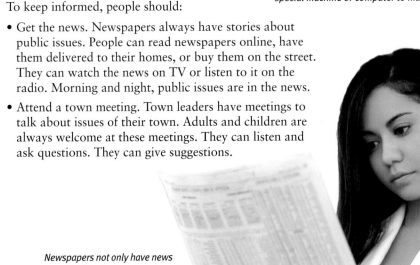

NAME _____ DATE _____

Our Responsibilities Lesson **3** **Reading Strategy**

Using Note-Taking

Read Chapter 7, Lesson 3. Choose a heading in the lesson and read the section underneath it. Take notes about the important thoughts and ideas in the section. Use the notepad to take your notes.

TITLE OF SECTION: _____

Notes About People:
_____
_____

Notes About Places:
_____
_____

Notes About Things:
_____
_____

Notes About Ideas:
_____
_____

© 2010 Gibbs Smith, Publisher

Student Guide **77**
Use with *Washington, Our Home*

Talk About It

Children's Responsibilities

How can you be a good citizen wherever you are?

You can do your part to make home, school, community, state, and county great places to live.

What are responsibilities children have?

See the list on page 172 for possible answers. Encourage students to come up with other answers.

Do Something Great—Volunteer!
(From page 173)

Why is it important to volunteer?

There are a lot of things that need to be done that people don't get paid to do. We can be good citizens by volunteering.

What are some ways that you have volunteered in the past?

Encourage students to share experiences they have had volunteering and how it made them feel.

It's Up to All of Us *(From page 173)*

How does being a good citizen help us to enjoy where we live, work, and grow?

If we all do our part, our cities and state will be safer, cleaner, and better all around.

Caption Answer

The children are doing their part to help. The girl is helping her mom with chores and the boy is walking his dog.

Literature Link

Being a Good Citizen

Read a simple picture book like Virginia L. Kroll's book *Good Citizen Sarah* to the class. Have students write their own character books to share with younger students. Students should write about the character trait they described in the Character Traits activity

Children's Responsibilities

What responsibilities do you have at home? Do you make your bed and help wash the dishes? Do you feed your dog or cat every morning? You have responsibilities in school, too. What are they?

It is your responsibility to be a good citizen wherever you are. This means you will do your part to make your home, school, community, state, and county great places to live.

What can you do?

- Obey all of your family and school rules.
- Tell the truth.
- Be polite and helpful.
- Respect other people's property.
- Study in school to learn all you can.
- Talk with adults about what is going on in your town.
- Write a letter to the editor of your city's newspaper. (Letters from students like you often get printed!)
- Never litter, and always recycle.

You are part of Washington's story. People hundreds of years from now could be affected by the choices you make today. By being a good citizen, you can make your community a better place. You can contribute to the story of Washington. **How are these children showing that they are good citizens?**

172

Washington, Our Home

Reading Activity

Reading Buddies

One volunteer idea that benefits all students is to set up a reading buddy program with one of the lower-grade classrooms. Reading buddies read to and listen to younger students read. This could be an ongoing project or a one-time activity. After students have met with their reading buddies, talk about how it felt to volunteer.

Social Studies Activity

Lend a Hand

As a class, talk about some of the ways students can volunteer in the school or community. Make a list of some of the ideas students come up with. Choose one of the ideas and have the class do it. This may be as simple as picking up trash on the playground to involvement in a community-wide program.

The next time you rake leaves, think about your neighbors. Do they need help raking? **What else could you do to help make your community a better place?**

Do Something Great—Volunteer!

Good citizens not only do the things they have to do; they do more. They look for ways to help out. People who help without getting paid are called *volunteers*. Children and adults can be volunteers.

Think of a way you could help out by volunteering. Could you offer to read a story or play a game with younger children? Could you pick up trash around your home and your yard? Could you clean the bathroom or set the table without being asked?

As you get older, you might mow a lawn or shovel snow for an elderly person. You could help out at a food bank or gather warm coats and donate them.

Look around and see who is volunteering. Volunteers make our lives better.

It's Up to All of Us

We all want a happy life in a free country. Keeping our state and our country strong is important to all of us. Only by being good citizens can we enjoy a great place to live, work, and grow. Do your part. Remind others to do the same.

WASHINGTON

PORTRAIT

YOUR NAME HERE!

YOUR PICTURE HERE

Who are you today? What kind of person will you become? You can write your own story with the choices you make each day. How will you become part of Washington's story?

LESSON 3 What Did You Learn?

1. What are some responsibilities adults have?
2. What are some responsibilities children have?
3. Why is it important for all of us to be good citizens?

Our Government

LESSON 3 What Did You Learn?

1. *Possible answers include to take care of children, work to earn money for themselves and their families, obey all rules and laws, keep homes and yards clean, get involved in politics, stay informed about political issues, and vote.*

2. *Possible answers include to obey all family and school rules, tell the truth, be polite and helpful, respect other people's property, study in school to learn, talk with adults about what is going on in your town, never litter, and always recycle.*

3. *We all want to be happy where we live and enjoy our rights as citizens. It is important for us to do our part to be good citizens so other citizens will want to do the same.*

Chapter 7 Lesson 3

REFLECT

Reflect on students' understanding of the responsibilities that citizens have and what we can do to make a difference. You can evaluate students' understanding through discussion or evaluation of activities completed in this lesson. The following activity will serve as another way of assessing students' understanding of the key objectives of this lesson.

Writing Activity

Responsibility—What's That?

Students and adults both have responsibilities. What would life be like if people didn't have responsibilities? Have students complete this creative writing exercise to write about what life would be like without responsibilities. A Responsibility—What's That? activity is available in the *Student Guide*.

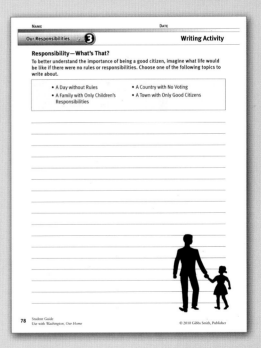

Caption Answer

Encourage students to share their ideas about what they can do to make their community a better place. Make a list on the board.

173

Washington Social Studies Skills

Standards

GLE 5.4.1

Draws clear, well-reasoned conclusions and provides explanations that are supported by artifacts and/or primary sources in a paper or presentation

Washington Social Studies Skills

Identify a Problem and Solve It

Activate

Tell students that good citizens are problem solvers! Ask students to think of a problem they had and solved in a positive way. Share an experience you had solving a problem in a positive way.

Teach

Tell students that it is important to solve problems in a positive way. If a problem is solved right, you are less likely to have to deal with the same problem again in the future. Write the steps to solving a problem on the board:

1. Learn as much as you can about the problem.
2. Brainstorm a list of different ways to solve the problem.
3. Think about your list and choose the best idea.
4. Write your plan to solve the problem.
5. Put your plan into action.

Discuss each step with the class.

Practice

Choose a problem the class faces, such as students not turning homework in on time. As a class, go through each of the steps to solving a problem. Be sure to have students give input in each step of the process.

Apply

Have students identify a problem and solve it, following the directions on the Social Studies Skills Page.

Identify a Problem and Solve It

IDENTIFYING A PROBLEM

Good citizens are problems solvers. If a problem comes their way, they work hard to solve it. Sometimes they look for problems to solve, for the good of the community. Follow the steps on this page to learn how to identify a problem and solve it.

1. Choose one of these topics related to Washington:
   • Hiking trails in the mountains
   • Washington's coast
   • Logging
   • Salmon fishing
2. Brainstorm a list of problems people might face in the topic you chose.
3. Study your list and choose a problem you can help solve.

SOLVING THE PROBLEM

1. Learn as much as you can about the topic. This will help you to come up with the best solution to the problem. Visit your city or school library, talk to people in your community, and do research on the Internet. List your sources on a sheet of paper.
2. Brainstorm a list of different ways to solve the problem.
3. Think about your list and choose the best idea.
4. Write your plan to solve the problem. Create a paper or presentation to explain your plan.
5. Share your plan with your class and then put your plan into action.

Chapter Review 7

Reviewing What You Read

1. What are the things that government does for us?
2. Describe each level of government.
3. List some of the rights you have as a citizen.
4. Draw a conclusion about what life in Washington would be like if there were no laws.
5. Why do citizens have responsibilities?
6. What can you do to be a good citizen?

Becoming a Better Reader

Find the Details

Details are facts that help good readers understand the main idea. Details can be found in headings, pictures, captions, and words of a book. Select a chapter in a story book and a chapter in this book. Make a list of important details you find in each chapter and where you found them. Share your list with a partner, and discuss the different places that you found details in each books.

Spotlighting Geography

National and State Capitals

On a map of the United States, locate our nation's capital, Washington D.C., and our state capital, Olympia.

1. About how many miles do our representatives have to travel to get to Washington, D.C., from Olympia?
2. What methods of transportation might our representatives use?
3. Choose two other states and find their capitals. How far do their representatives have to travel to get to Washington, D.C.?

Our Government   175

Reviewing What You Read

The Reviewing What You Read questions are leveled according to Bloom's Taxonomy and will help students achieve a higher level of thinking. These questions will also prepare students for the chapter assessment. The following are possible answers to the questions. Focus on students' ability to understand and apply the concepts.

1. **KNOWLEDGE** Government makes rules and laws, it protects our rights, and provides services.

2. **COMPREHENSION** National government makes laws for everyone in the country, tribal government makes laws for American Indians on tribal lands, state government makes laws for people who live in each state, and local government makes rules and laws for people who live in towns, cities, and counties.

3. **APPLICATION** Possible answers include the right to life, liberty, property, free speech and ideas, and religious freedom.

4. **ANALYSIS** Students' answers should show an understanding of the role that laws play in maintaining order and keeping people safe.

5. **SYNTHESIS** We have responsibilities for the good of everyone. If we all do our part, the world will be a better place.

6. **EVALUATION** Students' answers should show an understanding of their roles as good citizens and should be a thoughtful reflection on what they learned from the chapter.

Becoming a Better Reader

Find Details

Have students share what they found with a partner. Encourage students to compare and contrast the different ways to find details in the different books. You may want students to complete a Venn diagram to compare their two books. A Venn diagram is available in the Graphic Organizers section of the *Teacher Guide*.

Spotlighting Geography

National and State Capitals

After answering the questions from the activity, have students share their information from number three in a bar graph. This will be a good visual to compare the distances from the different states to Washington, D.C.

Interactive Chapter Review

An Interactive Chapter Review is available online at www.ExperienceStateHistory.com. Have students use this review to prepare for the assessments.

Chapter Assessment

Chapter Assessments are available to preview on pages 148G–148H. Assessments can be found in the *Teacher Guide*. They can also be found online at www.ExperienceStateHistory.com.

8 Working in Washington

CHAPTER PLANNER

CHAPTER OVERVIEW	WASHINGTON SOCIAL STUDIES GLEs
This chapter focuses on the economy and how Washington's geography and resources affect the economy.	GLE 2.2.1 GLE 2.2.2 GLE 2.4.1 GLE 3.3.1 GLE 5.1.1 GLE 5.2.2

CHAPTER RESOURCES	
ELL/Modified Chapter Plan, p. 176I	
Books and Web Sites, p. 176J	

CHAPTER ACTIVITIES	WASHINGTON CURRICULUM INTEGRATION
Tools of the Trade, p. 176E	**Communication** GLE 1.1.1
■ A Resume About Me, p. 176E	**Writing** GLE 2.4.1
What Do You Like?, p. 176E	**Technology** GLE 1.2.1
Small World Industries, p. 176E	**Reading** GLE 3.2.1
■ Math at Work, p. 176F	**Math** GLE 4.5.F
Science at Work, p. 176F	**Technology** GLE 1.2.1
Advertisement, p. 176F	**Visual Arts** GLE 2.2.1
Open for Business, p. 176F	**Writing** GLE 2.2.1

CHAPTER OPENER	WASHINGTON CURRICULUM INTEGRATION
Which Job Would You Choose?, p. 176	**Writing** GLE 2.2.1
Tulips for Sale, p. 176	**Visual Arts** GLE 1.1.2

► Indicates an activity page located in the *Student Guide*
■ Indicates an activity page located in the *Teacher Guide*

The BIG Idea | How are Washington's geography and resources important to the economy?

CHAPTER REVIEW   pp. 198–199

SOCIAL STUDIES SKILLS PAGE	WASHINGTON SOCIAL STUDIES GLEs
How to Read a Graph, p. 198	**Social Studies** GLE 5.1.1, GLE 5.2.2

REVIEWING THE CHAPTER	WASHINGTON SOCIAL STUDIES GLEs
Students show what they have learned by completing application activities and answering chapter review questions. Assessments for this chapter can be previewed on pages 176G-176H. Select the assessment option that best suits your goals for this chapter. Assessments are available in the *Teacher Guide* or online at **www.ExperienceStateHistory.com.**	GLE 2.2.1 GLE 2.2.2 GLE 2.4.1 GLE 3.3.1 GLE 5.1.1 GLE 5.2.2

CHAPTER ACTIVITIES	WASHINGTON CURRICULUM INTEGRATION
Reviewing What You Read, p. 199	**Reading** GLE 2.1.3
Becoming a Better Reader, p. 199	**Reading** GLE 2.4.1
Spotlighting Geography, p. 199	**Social Studies** GLE 3.2.3

CHAPTER ASSESSMENTS	WASHINGTON CURRICULUM INTEGRATION
■ Multiple Choice Assessment, p. 77	**Reading** GLE 1.3.2, GLE 2.1.3
■ Reading Assessment, p. 78	**Reading** GLE 2.1.3
■ Writing Assessment, p. 79	**Writing** GLE 3.3.6, GLE 3.3.7
■ Project Assessment, p. 80	**Communication** GLE 3.1.1

LESSON 1

The Elements of Our Economy pp. 178–183

LESSON OVERVIEW	WASHINGTON SOCIAL STUDIES GLEs
KEY IDEAS • Geography, natural resources, and climate are part of our economy. • We need workers, or labor, to keep our economy healthy.	GLE 2.2.1 GLE 2.4.1

LESSON ACTIVITIES	WASHINGTON CURRICULUM INTEGRATION
▶Goods and Services, p. 178	**Reading** GLE 2.3.2
Picture Dictionary, p. 178	**Reading** GLE 1.3.2
▶Words to Understand, p. 178	**Reading** GLE 1.3.1
Needs and Wants, p. 179	**Writing** GLE 1.1.1
▶Summary Response, p. 179	**Reading** GLE 2.1.7
Resources p. 180	**Science** GLE 3.2.4
Natural Resources Time Capsule, p. 180	**Science** GLE 3.2.4
Grand Coulee Dam, p. 181	**Reading** GLE 3.1.1
Go to the Source: Reading a Graph, p. 182	**Social Studies** GLE 5.1.1, GLE 5.2.2
▶Questions About Jobs, p. 183	**Communication** GLE 1.1.2

LESSON 2
Washington's Industries   pp. 184–193

LESSON OVERVIEW	WASHINGTON SOCIAL STUDIES GLEs
KEY IDEAS • There are many industries in Washington. • Many things come together to make up each industry. • Technology and transportation affect our economy.	GLE 2.2.1

LESSON ACTIVITIES	WASHINGTON CURRICULUM INTEGRATION
▶Places of Work, p. 184	**Reading** GLE 2.1.5
Base Words, p. 184	**Reading** GLE 1.2.2
▶Words to Understand, p. 184	**Reading** GLE 1.3.1
▶Making Generalizations, p. 185	**Reading** GLE 2.4.5
Washington Businesses, p. 186	**Writing** GLE 2.1.1
Planning a Business—Part I, p. 186	**Writing** GLE 1.1.1
Washington Apples, p. 187	**Technology** GLE 2.2.2
An Apple a Day, p. 187	**Writing** GLE 1.1.1
From Idea to Store Shelf, p. 188	**Writing** GLE 2.2.1
How Labor Got Its Day, p. 193	**Technology** GLE 2.2.2
Planning a Business—Part II, p. 188	**Communication** GLE 2.2.1
What's for Breakfast?, p. 189	**Visual Arts** GLE 2.2.1
Planning a Business—Part III, p. 189	**Visual Arts** GLE 2.2.1
Fish Stories, p. 190	**Communication** GLE 1.1.1
Industries in Washington, p. 190	**Communication** GLE 3.1.1, **Technology** GLE 1.3.2
Household Technologies, p. 191	**Technology** GLE 1.3.2
Bill Gates, p. 191	**Writing** GLE 2.2.1
By Car or Plane?, p. 192	**Math** GLE 4.5.F
▶A Business Plan, p. 193	**Writing** GLE 3.1.2

LESSON 3
Global Trade   pp. 194–197

LESSON OVERVIEW	WASHINGTON SOCIAL STUDIES GLEs
KEY IDEAS • Our economy relies on trade with the Pacific Rim. • Our geography helps to make us trading partners with the world.	GLE 2.2.2 GLE 3.3.1

LESSON ACTIVITIES	WASHINGTON CURRICULUM INTEGRATION
▶Where Are Your Things From?, p. 194	**Writing** GLE 2.2.1
Word Tricks, p.194	**Reading** GLE 1.1.4
▶Words to Understand, p. 194	**Reading** GLE 1.3.1
▶Making Inferences, p. 195	**Reading** GLE 2.1.5
Let's Trade, p. 196	**Communication** GLE 2.2.2
▶My Favorite Things, p. 197	**Technology** GLE 1.3.2

Chapter Activities

The focus of this chapter is on Washington's geography and resources and how they are important to the economy. Students learn about different industries in Washington and how Washington's resources help our state be successful. Use the Chapter Activities to help students understand how different components work together to help the economy.

 Set the Stage

Set up a class library with books about economics, industries, and trade. The main goal of this chapter is to help students begin to understand the relationship between the economy and jobs. Provide students with information about a variety of possible business and job opportunities to help them think about what they would like to do when they grow up.

 Introductory Activity

Tools of the Trade

Invite parents and other adults to come to your classroom and share what they do and the tools they use in their jobs. You may want to invite a couple of parents each day over a period of several days or you may want to set up a Tools Day and invite guests to set up booths that students can visit.

 Writing Activity

A Resume About Me

Have students write their own resume.

Prewriting

Have students brainstorm a list of jobs they have at home and at school. Have them make a list of all the different activities they enjoy doing.

Drafting

Have students write their resume. They can use A Resume About Me form available in the *Teacher Guide* to help them organize their experiences. Students should type their resume on the computer.

Revising

Encourage students to read their resume with an adult. The adult should help students choose good action words to describe their experiences.

Editing

Have students use spell check on the computer to correct misspelled words.

Publishing

Have students print out their resumes and post them on a bulletin board.

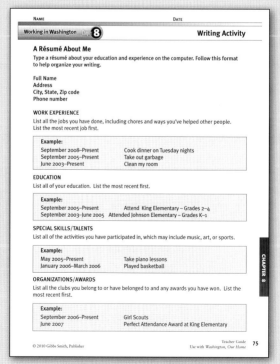

 Reading Activity

What Do You Like?

There is a saying that says, "Do what you love and the money will follow." The idea encourages people to figure out what they like to do and do it as a career. Help students think about jobs in the areas that they are interested in. Have students go online to the Bureau of Labor Statistics Web site. At this Web site, students answer the question "What do you like?" The students' answers to this question will lead them to information about jobs that relate to things they like. This site is also filled with lots of interesting information about specific occupations and industries, types of training and education, and salary potential. For a link to this Web site go to **www.ExperienceStateHistory.com**.

 Social Studies Activity

Small World Industries

To demonstrate the small consumer world in which we live, have students study the movement of goods in your own class. Place a large map of the world on the bulletin board. Have students look at the labels from the clothing they are wearing. Mark the countries where the clothing in your class was made. String yarn from the country of origin to Washington to show the movement of goods around the world. You may want to extend this activity by asking students to look around at home for products from other countries.

Math Activity

Math at Work

Math is used in almost every job. Have students think of five jobs and write about how math is used in each of the jobs. Have students write math problems that an employee in that job might have to solve. Then have students use their math skills to figure out the math problems in the cookie factory. A Math at Work activity page is available in the *Teacher Guide*.

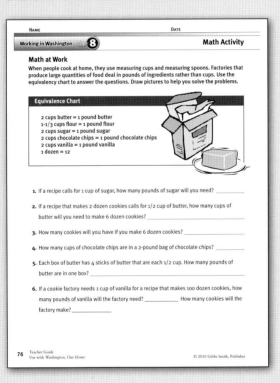

Art Activity

Advertisement

Have students create an advertisement for their business (see the Project Assessment in the *Teacher Guide*). Students should plan a visually pleasing advertisement that will entice consumers to "Purchase" their product or service. Students may want to think of a slogan to promote their product or service.

Culminating Activity

Open for Business

This Culminating Activity is tied directly to the Project Assessment for this chapter. For the Project Assessment, students will create a business. See the Project Assessment in the *Teacher Guide*. For this Culminating Activity, allow students to set up their businesses.

Science Activity

Science at Work

Have students interested in science go to the PBS Cool Careers in Science Web site and read biographies about people who have science related jobs. Have students choose one of the biographies to tell the class about. For a link to this Web site go **www. ExperienceStateHistory.com.**

Assessment Options

The Chapter Assessment options provide opportunities to evaluate students' understanding of the social studies concepts. Choose the assessment options that best meet the needs of your teaching goals. Assessments are available in the *Teacher Guide* or can be individualized at www.ExperienceStateHistory.com.

OPTION 1: MULTIPLE CHOICE ASSESSMENT

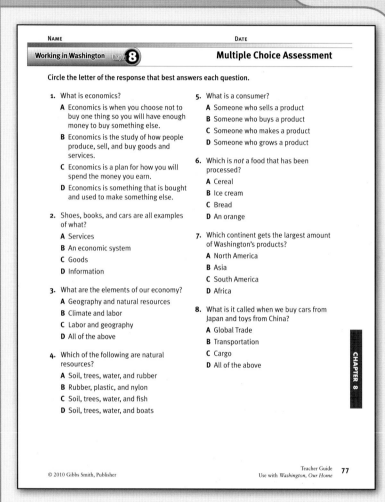

The Multiple Choice Assessment provides a quick way to assess students' understanding of the key concepts of the chapter. Have students read each question and select the best answer.

OPTION 2: READING ASSESSMENT

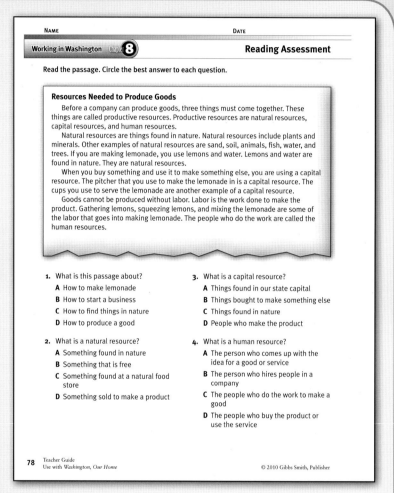

The Reading Assessment provides additional practice for the WASL Reading Test. Have students read the passage and answer the questions that follow.

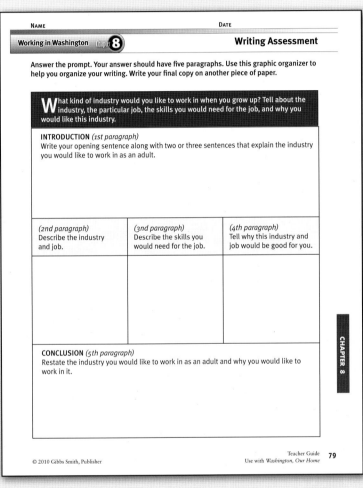

NAME   DATE

Working in Washington **8**   **Project Assessment (Teacher Page)**

OPEN FOR BUSINESS

NOTE TO TEACHER: For this Project Assessment, students will create businesses. You will host an Open for Business Day where students can set up their businesses and patronize the businesses of their classmates.

Here are some suggestions for hosting an Open for Business Day.

1. Schedule a day and time when students can show off their businesses. You will probably want to reserve the gym or cafeteria for two or three hours to allow enough space and time.

2. Decide on the monetary system you will use for the Open for Business Day. You may want to use play money or a bank system where students deposit their earnings into a bank account and write checks on the Open for Business Day.

3. Two weeks before the Open for Business Day, provide students with the Project Assessment checklist on the next page and the Business Plan form found in the *Student Guide*, Lesson 2 activity pages. Talk about things that fourth graders would be interested in and businesses that would provide those things. This chart gives some ideas.

Needs and Wants of Fourth Graders	Businesses
Candy	Sell candy.
Fun	Toss the basketball in the hoop game. Put on a magic show.
School supplies	Sell unique school supplies.
Look good	Do Nails. Do hair.

4. The week before the Open for Business Day, create a task list noting the "money" that will be paid for each task. Encourage students to earn money throughout the week.

5. On the Open for Business Day, have students set up their businesses.

6. Set up a PA system. As students are running their businesses and patronizing other businesses, offer advertising time on the PA system (for a price).

7. At the end of the day, have students clean up their businesses.

8. Talk about the experience of running a business. Discuss the following:

  • How much money did students earn from their businesses?

  • How much money did students spend on goods and services other students offered?

  • Which businesses were the most successful? Why?

  • How would students change their business plan to be more successful next time?

The Writing Assessment provides additional practice for the WASL Writing Test. Have students use the organizer to write a five-paragraph essay in response to the writing prompt about the chapter.

The Project Assessment provides an alternative to the traditional assessment. This interactive Project Assessment allows students to apply what they learned from the chapter to create a business.

ELL/Modified Chapter Plan

Working in Washington

Students will learn that there are many jobs in Washington and that some jobs require special education and skills.

The following pages can be found in the ELL/Modified Chapter Guide on pages 47–51.

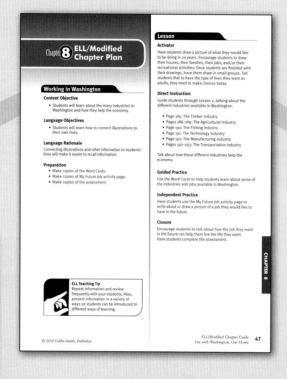

The ELL/Modified Chapter Plan provides a step-by-step lesson in an easy-to-use format. Lessons teach content and language objectives.

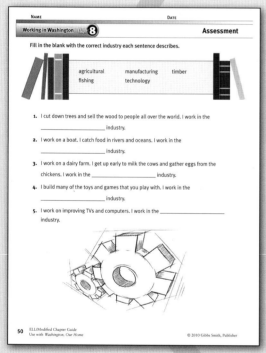

The Modified Assessment for this chapter assesses students' understanding of the key objectives of the chapter.

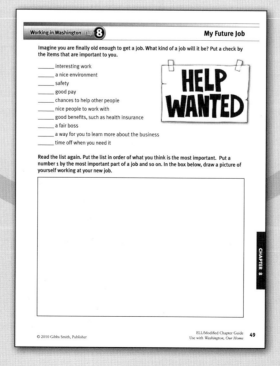

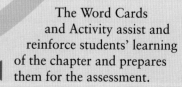

The Word Cards and Activity assist and reinforce students' learning of the chapter and prepares them for the assessment.

Books and Web Sites

Books

Editors at JIST. *People at Work: A Student's A-Z Guide to 350 Jobs.* St. Paul: JIST Publishing, 2005.

McGillian, Jamie Kyle. *The Kids' Money Book: Earning, Saving, Spending, Investing, and Donating.* New York: Sterling, 2004.

Stone, Tanya Lee. *America's Top-10 Construction Wonders.* Woodbridge: Blackbirch Press, 1998.

Tucker, Tom. *Brainstorm!: The Stories of Twenty American Kid Inventors.* New York: Farrar, Straus, and Giroux, 1998.

Viorst, Judith. *Alexander, Who Used to Be Rich Last Sunday.* Bel Air: Aladdin, 1987.

Web Sites

The following Web sites provide resources or lesson plans for teachers and activities for students to help extend the lessons in this chapter. Go to **www.ExperienceStateHistory.com** for links to these Web sites.

Apples4theTeacher

The Apples4theTeacher Web site has an interactive game where students are asked to count money. This site helps students review the value of each coin in our monetary system from pennies to $100 bills.

Bureau of Labor Statistics

At the Bureau of Labor Statistics Web site students answer the question "What do you like?" The students' answers to this question leads them to information about jobs that relate to things they like. This site is also filled with lots of interesting information about specific occupations and industries, types of training and education, and salary potential.

Department of the Treasury for Kids

The Department of the Treasury for Kids Web site has a variety of interactive activities. Students can tour the Bureau of Engraving and Printing, analyze advertisements, "catch" a counterfeiter, and design their own dollar bill.

EconEdLink

The EconEdLink Web site provides teachers with an excellent lesson plan called "How Labor Got Its Day." In this lesson, students will learn the reasons workers formed unions and why we celebrate Labor Day.

KidsBank

The KidsBank Web site has an excellent slide presentation that explains what interest is and how it works.

PBS Cool Careers in Science

The PBS Cool Careers in Science Web site is a place where students can read biographies about people who have science related jobs.

PBS Kids

At the PBS Kids Web site students can go to the "Don't Buy It" site. At this site, students can learn how to be smart shoppers and recognize some of the techniques advertisers use to entice people to buy a product. Teachers can also find a great slide show that explains what interest is and how it works.

ThinkQuest

The ThinkQuest Web site has two excellent resources for teaching economics: Kids Consumer Corner and Investing for Kids. At the Kids Consumer Corner site, students can learn about smart saving and investing. At the Investing for Kids site, students can learn more about the stock market through games and learning centers.

Washington Apples

The Washington Apples Web site is a place where students can explore the Kids page to read fun facts about apples, see recipes, and play fun games.

The BIG Idea

Which Job Would You Choose?

Explain to students that without economics we wouldn't have products to buy or money to spend. Jobs play an important role in the economy. It is important for people to have jobs in order to pay for the things they need. Have students come up with a list of different jobs available in the world. Have students choose a job they would enjoy and journal about it. Why would someone choose that job? What qualities might someone possess that would improve the way they did this particular job?

 Put Yourself in the Picture

Tulips For Sale

Ask students to imagine they are standing in the picture. What would it smell like? What might the temperature be? What little critters or insects would you see while working in this tulip field? Ask students to predict why the people in the picture have jackets, hoods, and gloves on.

Caption Answer

The workers are picking the tulips.

People use our rich soil to farm, feed their animals, and plant crops.

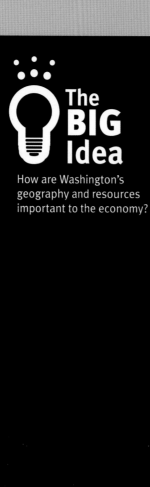

The BIG Idea

How are Washington's geography and resources important to the economy?

People in Skagit County grow colorful tulips to sell. There are many jobs to do. Growers plant the bulbs, make sure they get enough water, and keep them free of weeds and pests. Then workers pick, or harvest, the flowers. Other workers move the tulips from the farm to stores and markets. **Which step are the workers doing in this picture? Can you think of other ways people use our rich soil to make a living?**

176

Working in Washington

CHAPTER

People in Washington have always used the land to meet their needs. Even today, our geography and natural resources help us make a living. They affect the kinds of jobs we have in our great state.

People choose to live and work in Washington because it has much to offer. In turn, Washington's workers produce things they can sell all over the world.

177

Standards

GLE 2.2.1
Understands the basic elements of Washington State's economic system, including agriculture, businesses, industry, natural resources, and labor.

GLE 2.4.1
Understands how geography, natural resources, climate, and available labor contribute to the sustainability of the economy of regions in Washington State

PREPARE

Activator

Goods and Services

Goods are usually things that people make in factories, workshops, or even at home. Services are things that people do for others. Have students use the Goods and Services activity page available in the *Student Guide* to get familiar with the difference between a good and a service.

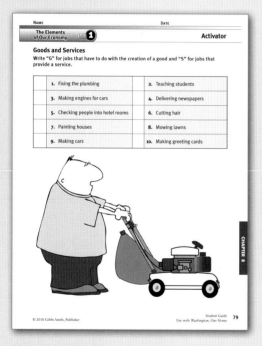

Word Study

Picture Dictionary

Have students make a picture dictionary of words having to do with money and the economy. Students choose a word, write its definition, draw a picture of the word, and write the word in a sentence. Order the pages alphabetically and bind them together in a book.

LESSON 1 The Elements of Our Economy

Key Ideas

- Geography, natural resources, and climate are part of our economy.
- We need workers, or labor, to keep our economy healthy.

Words to Understand

conserve
economics
goods
hydroelectricity
labor
reservoir
services
sustain

What Is Economics?

conomics is the study of how people produce, sell, and buy goods and services. When the economy is strong, there are enough jobs for workers. People have enough money to buy things they need. When the economy is weak, a lot of adults can't find jobs to make the money they need.

Adults do all kinds of work. Some workers make goods to sell. *Goods* can be anything people make that other people want. Workers might build airplanes or computers. They might make medicine or computer games. They might grow wheat or apples. All these goods are bought and sold.

Other people work as doctors or nurses, helping sick people. Some teach school, helping children learn. Some workers might repair broken pipes or broken cars. They might sell food in a store or cook food in a restaurant. The hundreds of jobs workers do for other people are called *services*.

An economic system is a way of producing and selling goods and services.

You can find goods and services almost anywhere you look. **Do doctors provide a good or a service?**

178

Words to Understand

conserve (p. 179) *to protect or save something for the future*

economics (p. 178) *the study of how people produce, sell, and buy goods and services*

goods (p. 178) *things that are made and then bought and sold*

hydroelectricity (p. 180) *electricity produced by water power*

labor (p. 180) *workers; working*

reservoir (p. 180) *an large lake used as a source of water*

services (p. 178) *in economics, work people do for other people for money*

sustain (p. 179) *to support or strengthen*

A Words to Understand activity for this lesson is available in the *Student Guide*.

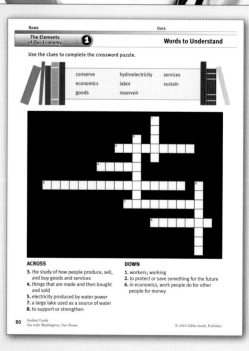

Elements of Our Economy

Many things work together to *sustain*, or support, our economy. Some of these are geography, natural resources, climate, and labor.

Geography

Our location next to the Pacific Ocean helps our economy. Many people who produce goods want to ship them to other places so people there can buy them. Ships go in and out of our harbors every day. Washington is also close to Canada. Canada buys many of the products we make.

Natural Resources

Natural resources are things found in nature that people can use. We use many of them to make a living. For example, water and soil make it possible to raise wheat, fruit, vegetables, and meat. We use trees from the forests to produce logs, boards, and paper.

Rushing rivers give us power to make electricity. We also use rivers for transportation. Fish are a natural resource, too. Fishing provides jobs and goods to sell. Aluminum is a natural resource that is used to make spacecraft.

Will Our Resources Run Out?

We depend on our resources to make a living. What would happen if they ran out? Some of our resources are **renewable**. That means they will probably never run out. If you cut down a tree, you can plant another one. Two of our most important renewable resources are wind and water.

Other resources are **non-renewable**. That means that when those resources are used up, they will be gone forever or they will take millions of years to come back. We may not always have oil or minerals if we do not use them wisely.

Do you take care of your clothes and toys? Why? You probably take care of them so you can continue to use them. We **conserve**, or protect and save, things for future use. Conserving our resources is everyone's job.

WHAT MAKES UP OUR ECONOMY?

GEOGRAPHY

NATURAL RESOURCES

CLIMATE

LABOR

Working in Washington

179

Talk About It

What Is Economics? (*From page 178*)

What are goods?
Goods are things that people make that other people want.

What are services?
Services are things people do to help other people.

Elements of Our Economy

What makes up the economy?
Geography, natural resources, climate, and labor make up the economy.

Geography

How does our location next to the Pacific Ocean help our economy?
Many people who produce goods want to ship them across the ocean to other places where people can buy them.

Natural Resources

What natural resources do people use to make a living in Washington?
People use water, soil, trees, rivers, fish, aluminum, and many more natural resources to make a living in Washington.

Will Our Resources Run Out?

What are two of the most important renewable resources?
Wind and water are two of the most important renewable resources.

What are two non-renewable resources?
Oil and minerals are non-renewable resources.

Caption Answer

(*From page 178*) Doctors provide a service to people.

 Writing Activity

Needs and Wants

Have students take three minutes to write a list of everything they want. After three minutes, allow students to share in pairs the things on their lists. Then have students talk about the things they need. Help students understand that people spend money on things they need and things they want.

179

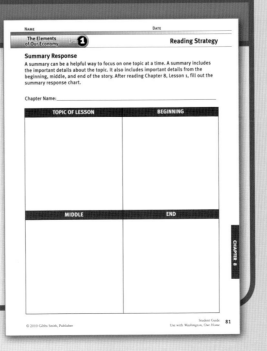

Reading Strategy

Summary Response

Sometimes it's hard for students to write a summary without including every detail about what they read. A summary should include the most important details about the topic and important details from the beginning, middle, and end of the reading. Have students use these guidelines when writing their summary about Lesson 1. Students can practice writing a summary and focusing on the most important details by completing the Summary Response activity page in the *Student Guide*.

DAMS and the ECONOMY

Talk About It

Dams and the Economy

How do we control the amount of water that passes through a dam?
There are parts of a dam that can open and close.

How have dams helped our economy?
Dams have calmed the raging rivers so barges full of goods can be pulled along the rivers to the ocean.

Making Electricity

How does rushing water create electricity?
The rushing water powers generators inside the dams. These generators produce electricity.

Bringing Water to Dry Lands

How does the Grand Coulee Dam help irrigate the Columbia Plateau?
Ditches and pipes carry water from the Grand Coulee Dam to the Columbia Plateau so farmers can grow crops.

 Science Activity

Resources

Discuss with students the fact that Washington has many resources. Below is a list of some of Washington's resources. Have students decide whether each resource is renewable or non-renewable.

Renewable: water, trees, sunshine, air, crops

Non-Renewable: natural gas, soil, oil, minerals

Dams are huge concrete structures built across rivers. They hold back water and keep rivers from flooding. The water that backs up behind the dam forms a lake called a *reservoir*.

By opening and closing parts of a dam, people can control the amount of water that passes through it. Dams calmed the raging rivers so barges could be pulled along the rivers to the ocean. People loaded the barges with logs, wood pulp, and wheat. They shipped these products to other places in the world to sell. After the dams were built, towns like Clarkston became port cities.

Over a dozen dams have been built on the Columbia and Snake Rivers. The dams have changed the rivers. For example, people have had to find ways to help keep fish populations healthy and strong. Dams have also changed the economy.

Making Electricity

Rushing water is so powerful that it can be used to make electricity. Inside the dams are large generators. The rushing water powers the generators, which produce electricity. Electricity produced by moving water is called *hydroelectricity*.

Many businesses have come to Washington because we have a large supply of hydroelectric power. We even sell it to other states, such as California. Producing the electricity provides many jobs. The towns of Richland, Pasco, and Kennewick grew fast once the dams started providing electricity for new industries.

Bringing Water to Dry Lands

The reservoirs behind the dams provide water for farms. For example, the water held back by the Grand Coulee Dam is used to irrigate the dry land of the Columbia Plateau. Ditches and pipes carry the water to the land so farmers can grow sugar beets, potatoes, apples, cherries, grapes, and other crops.

Diablo Dam is one of several dams across the Skagit River. It was built in Bellingham in the 1930s. The work of building the dam gave many people jobs. Today, the dams make electric power for much of Seattle. **How does the water look above the dam? How does it look below the dam?**

180

Washington, Our Home

 Science Activity

Natural Resources Time Capsule

Have students make time capsules to tell fourth grade students in the future what natural resources were available at this time. Have students put pictures, photographs, and artifacts in the time capsule. Students should also write a letter to the future fourth graders describing the natural resources. Time capsules can be made from boxes or cans with lids. The outside should be decorated so that people in the future will know what it is and when they are supposed to open it.

How Irrigation Changed the Economy

Eastern Washington has long been home to different groups of American Indians. In the dry climate, there was not enough rain to grow crops. The Indians met their needs by fishing, gathering camas bulbs and berries, and hunting deer and other wild animals.

In time, more and more people came to settle. They wanted to irrigate the dry land. They built Grand Coulee Dam across the Columbia River. They dug ditches and canals to bring the water held by the dam to crops and fields. Soon the dry land was a lush farming area.

Life changed for Indian people and everyone else. Workers came to the fields and fruit orchards. Agriculture became a large industry in central and eastern Washington:

- Yakima is the second-largest county in Washington. The Yakama Indian Reservation is there. Agriculture is the main industry. Crops love the 300 days of sunshine each year, the fertile volcanic soil, and irrigation water.

- Thanks to irrigation, Whitman County produces more wheat than any other county in the state.

- Chelan County was once home to Wenatchi Indians. They lived on salmon, camas roots, berries, and meat from wild animals. Because of irrigation, the town is now surrounded with apple and other fruit orchards.

- Adams County is rural. Water from the Columbia River irrigates the fertile volcanic soil. Crops include wheat fields, apple orchards, and fields of potatoes.

- Benton County is located where the Columbia, Snake, and Yakima Rivers come together. The Umatilla, Wallowa, Wanapum, Nez Perce, and Yakama tribes once hunted deer and antelope here. Today, farmers grow large crops of wheat, alfalfa, grapes, strawberries, and potatoes.

Working in Washington

The Grand Coulee Dam project put many men to work in the 1930s. It took almost 10 years and over 12,000 workers to finish the job.

The Grand Coulee Dam is said to be the largest concrete structure in North America. It is one of the largest producers of hydroelectricity in the world. It stretches across the Columbia River. **Look at the picture. Why do you think there are so many concrete walls and supports?**

181

Talk About It

How Irrigation Changed the Economy

How did American Indians meet their needs when there wasn't enough rain to grow crops?
The American Indians fished, gathered berries, and hunted wild animals.

How did people finally get water to dry land?
People build the Grand Coulee Dam and dug ditches and canals to bring the water from the dam to the crops and fields.

How did the water change life for many people?
People were able to find work in the fields and orchards.

Which of the five counties listed on page 181 have you heard of? What do you know about the counties?
Allow students to share what they know about the different counties mentioned on page 181.

Do you think people should continue to change the environment to meet their needs?
Allow students to share what they think in a class discussion. Encourage students to support their opinion with details from the chapter.

Caption Answer

The dam holds a huge amount of water and needs many supports to keep the dam from collapsing.

Background Info

Grand Coulee Dam

The Grand Coulee Dam is located on the Columbia River in Central Washington. It is one of the largest concrete structures in the United States. Grand Coulee produces huge amounts of electricity for Washington and many other states. The dam has created the reservoir, Franklin Delano Roosevelt Lake. Lake Roosevelt was name after the United States President who supervised the completion of the Grand Coulee Dam.

Literature Link

Grand Coulee Dam

Show students select pages from Tanya Lee Stone's book *America's Top-10 Construction Wonders.* This book gives a summary of each of the 10 construction wonders and how each was built. Among these top-10 is the Grand Coulee Dam. Discuss with students the importance of the dam and how lucky they are to have it in Washington. Allow students to share any connections they might have with the dam.

Go to the Source

Standards

GLE 5.1.1
Understands the concepts used in documents and sources.

GLE 5.2.2
Understands the main ideas from an artifact, primary source, or secondary source describing an issue or event.

Reading a Graph

NOTE TO TEACHER: *Before completing this Go to the Source activity, complete the Skills Page at the end of the chapter.*

This graph shows different industries in Washington in the year 2008. The bar graph shows the different industries and how many people work in those industries. It is a great way to visually show students the different industries in Washington.

Talk About It

Climate (*From page 183*)

What is the difference between the climate in Western Washington versus Eastern Washington?
Western Washington is mild and wet while Eastern Washington is very dry.

Why is a wet climate important to the economy?
A wet climate is important to the economy because farms provide work and goods to sell. If there is no water then crops cannot grow and people are out of work.

Available Labor (*From page 183*)

Who produces the goods and services in Washington?
The laborers, or workers, in Washington produce the goods and services.

✖ Go to the Source
Reading a Graph

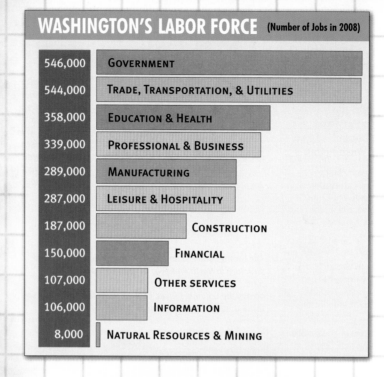

WASHINGTON'S LABOR FORCE (Number of Jobs in 2008)

546,000	GOVERNMENT
544,000	TRADE, TRANSPORTATION, & UTILITIES
358,000	EDUCATION & HEALTH
339,000	PROFESSIONAL & BUSINESS
289,000	MANUFACTURING
287,000	LEISURE & HOSPITALITY
187,000	CONSTRUCTION
150,000	FINANCIAL
107,000	OTHER SERVICES
106,000	INFORMATION
8,000	NATURAL RESOURCES & MINING

Labor is one of the ingredients in our economy. What kinds of jobs do most of our workers do? Study the graph to find out.

LOOK	THINK	DECIDE
What is shown on this graph?	Why do you think the government has the most jobs?	Which of the industries do you think you would find in a rural place?

Washington, Our Home

LOOK	THINK	DECIDE
Possible answers include different industries in Washington and the number of people that work in different industries in Washington.	*Possible answers include the government has the largest need for employees and they have the most job opportunities available.*	*Possible answers include natural resources and mining.*

Climate

Mild weather attracts workers. People looking for jobs come to Washington because of our great climate.

Western Washington has a mild, wet climate. Forests and farms provide work and goods to sell. What would happen if no rain fell for a long time? We depend on climate to sustain our economy.

Eastern Washington has a dry climate. Water must be brought to crops from rivers and irrigation canals. Without irrigation water, the economy of eastern Washington would be different.

Available Labor

We need people to run the dams, farm the fields, ship timber, and work in all kinds of industries. When we talk about the economy, the word *labor* means workers. It takes many laborers to produce all the goods and services of a strong economy.

Many of our workers were born and raised in Washington. Others have come to Washington from other states and countries. They settle where the jobs are. Some workers are needed in urban areas. People who work in businesses or do high-tech research find opportunities in the cities. Other workers find opportunities in the rural areas. If you were a farmer or grower, you would look for work in the rural regions.

Think of the adults you know. **Do they work in urban areas or rural areas? What might happen if there were too many workers available in an area? What if there were not enough workers in an area?**

Climate can affect the economy. It can influence what goods and services we can produce.

LESSON 1 What Did You Learn?

1. Who provides us with services every day?
2. What are some of the elements that make up our economy?
3. Why is it important to be mindful of the resources we are using?

Working in Washington

183

LESSON 1 What Did You Learn?

1. *Possible answers include doctors, grocers, waiters, farmers, and teachers.*
2. *Geography, natural resources, climate, and labor make up our economy.*
3. *Many resources are non-renewable. This means that when they run out they will be gone for a long time and maybe forever.*

Reflect on students' understanding of the things we need to keep our economy healthy. You can evaluate students' understanding through discussion or evaluation of activities completed in this lesson. The following activity will serve as another way of assessing students' understanding of the key objectives of this lesson.

Writing Activity

Questions About Jobs

As a class, discuss how laws protect our rights. Have students interview an adult about the work he or she does, the education and training they received before getting their job, and how satisfying their work is for them. Students should compile notes from their interview and provide at least one picture or poster. They will present their report to the class. Students will use the Questions About Jobs activity page in the *Student Guide* during their interview.

Caption Answer

Answers will show students' understanding of the difference between urban and rural areas. If there are too many workers in one area then certain people will be out of a job. If there are not enough workers in an area then jobs that need to be completed will not get done.

183

GLE 2.2.1
Understands the basic elements of Washington State's economic system, including agriculture, businesses, industry, natural resources, and labor.

PREPARE

Activator

Places of Work

To get students thinking about jobs and industries in Washington, ask them what types of jobs adults they know in Washington have. Have students use the Places of Work activity page to fill out the different jobs they can think of. After students have completed the activity, ask them to share the jobs they came up with. Record the responses on the board. After each student has shared, group the jobs by industry and students can record the information on their Places of Work activity page.

Word Study

Base Words

Challenge students to add suffixes to the Words to Understand to create new words.
consume: *consumes, consumed, consuming*
produce or product: *produces, produced, producing, producer*
distribute: *distributor, distributed*
process: *processor, processed, processing*

LESSON 2 Washington's Industries

Words to Understand

consumer
distributor
livestock
processed
producer
product
technology

Boeing airplanes made in Washington are sold to many places in the world.

Many Industries

You have probably heard of Microsoft, Starbucks, Costco, and Nordstrom. These four very different companies have one thing in common—they are all based in Washington. Each of these companies is part of a larger industry, or type of business. For example, Starbucks and Costco are part of the food industry.

There are many different industries in Washington. Some industries have to do with building homes. Others have to do with making airplanes or cars. Computers make up another industry. Some have to do with farming and food. We have a strong health care industry. In what industry do the adults you know work?

Producers and Consumers

An industry needs to start with two things—producers and consumers. **Producers** make the goods to sell. **Consumers** buy and use the goods. If you eat food, wear clothes, and own anything at all, you are a consumer.

Let's learn about some of the other things that make up our main industries.

184   Washington, Our Home

Words to Understand

consumer (p. 184) *any person who buys goods and services*
distributor (p. 188) *a person or company that transports goods to market*
livestock (p. 186) *animals raised for food, such as cows, chickens, turkey, sheep, and hogs*
processed (p. 189) *made in a factory; having gone through changes in order to produce or manufacture something*
producer (p. 184) *person or company that makes, grows, or supplies goods for sale*
product (p. 185) *something that is made to sell*
technology (p. 191) *the use of scientific knowledge*

A Words to Understand activity for this lesson is available in the *Student Guide*.

The Timber Industry

Cutting down huge trees in the forests was one of the first industries in Washington. Our state is now second in the nation for timber production.

Most logging companies are located in the Puget Sound Lowlands region. People also cut trees in the Rocky Mountain region. The forests are made up of Douglas firs, ponderosa pines, and hemlocks.

People used to cut down trees mainly to use for building. Now they also use timber to make wood **products** such as plywood, wood chips, and wood pulp. They use wood pulp to make paper and cardboard. Selling wood products as well as uncut logs gives a boost to our economy.

There are many components, or parts, to the timber industry. Look at the graphic to learn what they are.

Workers cut huge logs and haul them to the mills. **What type of transportation are these workers using to move the heavy logs?**

WHAT MAKES UP THE TIMBER INDUSTRY?

TREES

WORKERS

PRODUCTION MILLS

CONSUMERS

Working in Washington
185

TEACH

Talk About It

Many Industries *(From page 184)*

What well-known industries are based in Washington?
Microsoft, Starbucks, Costco, and Nordstrom are based in Washington.

Producers and Consumers

What things do you consume on a daily basis?
Possible answers include food, paper, pencils, water, and clothes.

The Timber Industry

What kinds of trees do the logging companies in Washington cut down?
The logging companies cut down Douglas firs, ponderosa pines, and hemlocks.

What do we use the wood from trees for?
People use the wood for building and making wood products.

What wood products do you use at school?
Possible answers include pencils, paper, desks, and books.

Caption Answer

The workers are using semi-trucks to move the heavy logs.

📖 Reading Strategy

Making Generalizations

Many people have different opinions on things in life. For example, some people think that cutting down trees is harmful to the environment while other people think it is okay because you can always plant another tree. Have students make generalizations about some of the topics in the lesson using the Making Generalizations activity in the *Student Guide*.

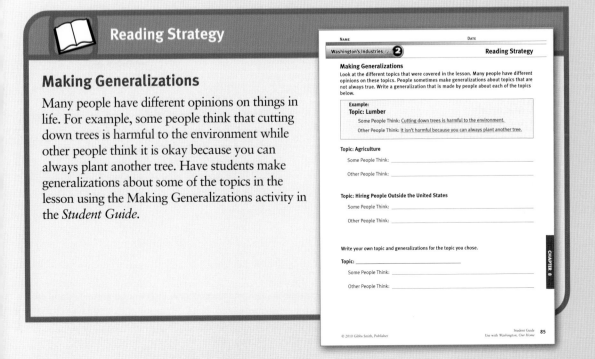

Talk About It

The Agricultural Industry

How much of our state is used for agriculture?
More than one-third of our state is used for agriculture.

What is the difference between livestock and a pet?
Livestock are animals raised to sell as food. Pets are animals raised to live with people.

Have you ever been to a dairy farm? If so, what was it like?
Allow students to share any experiences they have had. Encourage students to share what it smelled like, looked like, and sounded like there.

What materials would a dairy farmer need to produce milk, eggs, and meat?
A dairy farmer would need animals such as cows, pigs, and chickens. They would also need land for the animals to live on and machines or workers to help produce the products.

Caption Answer

Ranchers need water, land, and grass or hay to raise cattle.

Writing Activity

Washington Businesses

Have students call or write businesses in the area to ask for information about the product the business produces, the raw materials they use, and where the raw materials come from. They can also ask for information about the number of employees, the types of jobs the workers do, and who their customers are.

Washington leads the nation in the number of apples grown. We are second in the nation for potatoes, third for winter wheat, and fourth for barley.

The Agricultural Industry

Agriculture is the business of raising crops and animals to sell for food. More than one-third of our state's land is used for agriculture.

In the wet Puget Sound Lowlands, greenhouses and nurseries are built on tiny plots of land. In the dry Columbia Plateau, wheat farms stretch across thousands of acres. In the Columbia River Basin, farmers use irrigation water to grow peach, apricot, cherry, nut, and apple trees. Farmers also grow potatoes, corn, hops, and grapes.

If you've ever visited a farm, you probably heard animal sounds. Animal sounds mean meat, eggs, and milk. These animals are not pets. **Livestock** is another word for animals raised to sell as food. Cattle, pigs, poultry, and dairy products (like milk and cheese) are important to our economy. Dairies and poultry farms are common on the Puget Sound Lowlands. Sheep are raised in the Columbia Plateau region. Cattle ranches are most common in Cascade and Rocky Mountain regions. Animals graze in the mountain valleys.

Let's learn about what makes up the agricultural industry.

In winter, this ranch in Okanogan County is dusted with snow.
What natural resources do ranchers need to raise cattle?

186

Washington, Our Home

Writing Activity

Planning a Business—Part I

Raw Materials
To help students understand how industries are run, tell students they are going to work in groups to make bookmarks to sell. Ask the students what they need to make bookmarks. Explain to students that the materials needed to produce something are called the raw materials. Ask the students where they will get the raw materials they need to make the bookmarks. Explain to students that materials can be used again

(for example, scissors). Other things, such as paper or yarn are supplies that they will use up. Have each group make a list of materials they will need and then divide the materials needed into two groups: consumable and non-consumable. Once the groups have completed their list of materials, have them write the steps necessary to make the bookmarks.

Cooperative Groups

Natural Resources

What natural resources do you think are part of agriculture? Did you think of soil and water? These are very important for farming.

Soil: Plants need rich, fertile soil. Washington farmers are lucky. Our soil is great for growing many kinds of plants. In the Palouse farming region, the soil is made from lava rock. The lava came from volcanoes long ago. Over millions of years, the lava became soil. Because it came from deep inside the earth, it is rich in minerals. Wheat is a major crop there.

Water: Wet climates are great for forests and crops. Farming in dry climates is harder because farmers need to bring water to the crops. They can't depend on the rain to keep their plants alive.

Climate plays a big role in what farmers can produce. If you were a farmer in chilly Alaska, would you grow the same crops as farmers in sunny California? Would the same animals do well in both places?

An orchard owner picks a Red Delicious apple. **Have you ever picked an apple right off the tree? How do apples get from the orchard to your grocery store?**

Working in Washington

187

WHAT MAKES UP THE AGRICULTURAL INDUSTRY?

NATURAL RESOURCES

FARMERS AND LABORERS

DISTRIBUTORS

CONSUMERS

Talk About It

Natural Resources

Describe the soil in Washington.
The soil is fertile and rich in minerals. It is great for growing plants. It is made from lava rock.

What type of climate is best for growing crops?
A wet climate is the best climate for growing crops.

What type of climate do you live in?
Allow students to describe the climate.

Caption Answer

Encourage students to do research on the Internet or by using other sources to find out how apples get from the orchard to the grocery store.

 Technology Tie-In

Washington Apples

Explain to students that Washington leads the nation in the number of apples grown. That is pretty special. Have students visit the Washington Apples Web site. They can explore the Kids page to read fun facts about apples, see recipes, and play games. Challenge students to choose a recipe on the Web site and make it at home with supervision.

 Writing Activity

An Apple a Day

Ask students if they have ever heard the phrase, "An apple a day keeps the doctor away." Have students journal what they think this phrase means. Also, have students write about the last time they had to go see a doctor. What kind of doctor was it and why did they have to go?

Talk About It

Farmers and Laborers

What is a migrant worker?
A migrant worker is someone who moves from place to place as the crops ripen.

Do you think farming would be a hard job or not? Explain why or why not.
Allow students to share their opinions.

Distributors

What would happen if there weren't people to distribute the crops?
The crops could die and the farmers might have a hard time selling the crops.

Caption Answer

Laborers, or workers, are needed to drive the combine and the truck.

Social Studies Activity

From Idea to the Store Shelf

Bring in products from home such as food, shampoo, paper towels, and soap. Divide the class into groups and give each group a product. Have students write about how this product was made and packaged. Have students write a list of the raw materials and the steps of the labor process to bring the product from idea to the store shelf.

Social Studies Activity

How Labor Got Its Day

Go to the EconEdLink Web site for an excellent lesson plan called "How Labor Got Its Day." In this lesson, students will learn the reasons workers formed unions and why we celebrate Labor Day. A link to this Web site is available at **www. ExperienceStateHistory.com.**

A combine harvests wheat in the Palouse region. **Machines do a lot of the work, but who is needed to drive the combine and the truck?**

Farmers and Laborers

You can't have a farm without farmers and laborers. Farmers own their own crops or take care of the owner's fields. Laborers are workers. They might work all year at the farm or come just for the harvest. Workers who move from place to place as the crops ripen are called migrant workers.

Even with computers and high-tech machines, it takes a lot of workers to produce crops. Farmers must till the soil and plant the seeds. They must watch the crops for insects, disease, and weeds. At harvest time, laborers pick the parts of the plant that people will eat. Some crops, such as wheat, can be harvested by machine. Other crops, such as apples and cherries, must be picked by hand.

Distributors

After the harvest, the food doesn't stay at the farm. It has to be packaged and sold to consumers around the world. A *distributor* is a person or company that knows the best way to get the crops to markets near and far. Distributors are important to farmers. Without distributors, the farmer might have a hard time selling the crops.

Labor Means Business

If there are a lot of laborers in an area, a farm can harvest more of its crop. That means it can sell more.

If there are not enough laborers, some of the crops will go to waste. There is not as much opportunity for the farmers to make money.

188

Washington, Our Home

Social Studies Activity

Planning a Business – Part II

Labor
Provide the groups with the supplies they need to make the bookmarks. Talk about where the supplies came from and how much they cost. Have each group assign different students to be in charge of only one of the steps of making bookmarks (for example, cutting the bookmarks out, coloring the bookmarks, punching a hole in bookmarks). Talk about the advantages of doing this.

Consumers of Farm Products

In the agricultural industry, children like you are consumers. You buy and eat the goods that farms produce. People who eat at restaurants are consumers, too.

Some people and animals on farms consume their own food products. For example, farmers may grow grasses to feed their own cows. They might grow corn to feed their own pigs and chickens.

Food Processing

A lot of farm products are used to make other products. These new food products are called *processed* foods. Processed foods are usually made in factories.

For example, a company that makes cereal buys the wheat, oats, and corn from farmers. Then the workers cut, cook, and mash the grain to make cereal. They might add flavors to the cereal. The cereal is then packaged and distributed to stores around the country. Here are some other examples of how food is processed:

- Four mills operate in Spokane, Seattle, Tacoma, and Vancouver. Workers in the mills grind wheat into flour.
- People have jobs cleaning, sorting, canning, and freezing fruits and vegetables.
- Workers and machines make apples into apple juice and grapes into juice and wine.
- Milk is made into 1 percent, 2 percent, or skim milk. Some milk is turned into chocolate milk, yogurt, cheese, cottage cheese, butter, and ice cream.

How much food did you consume this week? Where did your food come from? How did it get to you?

These apples are waiting to be processed. **What foods do you like to eat that are made from apples?**

These workers are cleaning salmon. **What other jobs might there be in this factory?**

Working in Washington

189

Talk About It

The Fishing Industry

What kinds of fish do fishermen catch in Washington?
They catch salmon, albacore, herring, halibut, rockfish, cod, flounder, crabs, and ocean perch.

What is a fish farm?
A fish farm is a place where fish eggs are hatched and where the fish are raised.

Caption Answer

The boat is pulling a net behind it.

Science Activity

Fish Stories

Invite a guest to come to your classroom, possibly a parent, who enjoys fishing. Have them bring pictures, fishing gear, and other things that would be interesting for students to see and touch. You might even ask the guest to wear something that they would wear fishing. Ask the guest to share any fun experiences they have had while fishing and answer students' questions.

*If you live north of Seattle, you might see fishing boats like this one. **What is this boat pulling behind it?***

The Fishing Industry

Washington's coastline and many rivers make fishing a major industry. Fishing crews work on the lower Columbia River, the waters of Puget Sound, and off the coast as far as Alaska. They catch salmon, albacore, herring, halibut, rockfish, cod, flounder, crabs, and ocean perch to sell.

Fish farming is part of this industry. At a fish farm, fish eggs are hatched in special long troughs or tanks. Fish farms along the coastline raise salmon, oysters, and other seafood.

A halibut fisherman prepares a fish. People fish for halibut in the Strait of Juan de Fuca and off the coast of the Olympic Peninsula.

190

Washington, Our Home

Differentiated Paths

Industries in Washington

Divide your class into six groups representing the six industries highlighted in this lesson. Have each group prepare a 10-minute oral report telling about their assigned industry. Students should research information about the kinds of jobs available in the industry as well as other important information about the industry.

ELL and Special Needs

Encourage ELL and special needs students to participate in the groups. Group work provides an opportunity for students to see how other students think and tackle a learning challenge.

Gifted Learners

Challenge gifted learners to be compassionate leaders in their groups. Encourage them to allow the strengths of others to add to the project.

The Technology Industry

Technology is the use of scientific knowledge to accomplish a task. It is using newer, smarter ways to get a job done. In Washington, the computer software industry is an example of amazing technology. All over the world, people use our software to work in the best and easiest ways.

Most of our computer-related businesses are located in and around Seattle. Microsoft Corporation, in Redmond, is the world's leading software manufacturer for personal computers. The company has buildings in about 60 countries and provides jobs for people around the world.

Many other Washington industries also use technology. Workers design machines that get work done faster. They use technology to make better TV sets and sound equipment. If you are sick, you want the best technology to help you get well. Doctors in many places in the world use our medical technology.

Aircraft manufacturers in Washington use the very latest technology. Planes today are safer and faster than ever before.

This is the Microsoft campus in Redmond. People all over the world use Microsoft products every day. **In what ways do you use technology every day?**

Working in Washington

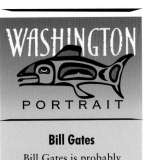

WASHINGTON PORTRAIT

Bill Gates

Bill Gates is probably Washington's most famous citizen. He started programming computers when he was 13 years old. In college, Bill and some friends created software for home computers and started a company called Microsoft. Windows became an important part of their programs. The company has made Bill Gates the world's wealthiest man.

Bill and Melinda Gates and their children live in the Puget Sound area. They have given much of their money to help others. The Gates Foundation gives millions of dollars to support health and learning in poor countries. It also gives college scholarships and develops housing for homeless families.

191

WASHINGTON PORTRAIT

Bill Gates

Who is Bill Gates?
Bill Gates is the creator of Microsoft.

How old was he when he started programming computers?
He was 13 years old.

In what ways has he shared his money?
He founded the Gates Foundation, which has given millions of dollars to support health and learning in poor countries. It also gives college scholarships and develops housing for homeless families.

Help students understand they don't have to be wealthy to make the world a better place. Have students write about a time they volunteered their time or donated money to a good cause. Have them write about what they did and how it made them feel.

Talk About It

The Technology Industry

What is the Microsoft Corporation?
Microsoft is the world's leading software manufacturer for personal computers.

What technologies have been improved in the last 10 years?
Possible answers include computers, TVs, cell phones, video games, DVDs, and cars.

What is your favorite piece of technology and why?
Have students share with a partner their favorite piece of technology.

Caption Answer

Possible answers include phones, computers, TVs, video games, and music players.

Social Studies Activity

Household Technologies

Have students get with a partner. Have each pair select a common, non-electric household item that they believe is important. Have students research information about their item and write down the answers to the following questions:

- What does this item do?
- What do you think the first one looked like?
- How did it change?
- How could it still be improved?
- What might this item look like in the future? (Draw a sketch.)

After students have selected their items and answered their questions, have them give a presentation on their findings. Have a class discussion about how this activity applies to computers and other new technology.

Talk About It

The Manufacturing Industry

What things do manufacturing industries build?
Manufacturing industries build aircraft, boats, trucks, farm equipment, toys, games, and sports equipment.

What is your favorite manufactured thing to play with?
Allow students to share different toys and games that they enjoy playing with.

The Transportation Industry

What is transportation?
Transportation is moving natural resources, goods, or people from place to place.

By Land, Sea, and Air *(From page 193)*

Why are waterways important to our state?
Waterways provide a place for ships and barges to travel. There are also large ports along the coast with harbors, where ships can load and unload goods.

Why are roads and highways important?
Roads and highways connect towns, cities, and neighborhoods together. They allow large trucks to transport goods.

Have you ever been on an airplane or to the Sea-Tac airport to pick someone up?
Encourage students to recall experiences connected to airplanes or airports.

Caption Answers

Answers will show students' understanding of where their city or town is located in relation to the highways on the map.

(From page 193) The roads look like tangled up spaghetti noodles.

What Do You Think

Have students express their opinion on jobs being given to people outside the United States. Why might this be a good thing for our country? Why might it be a bad thing?

Job Losses

Between 1998 and 2004, Washington lost 50,000 jobs in the aerospace industry. The Boeing Company moved to Chicago. It began hiring workers in other countries to build parts. Its planes are still finished in Washington, but fewer workers are needed here now.

What Do You Think

Many companies have started to hire workers in other countries. These workers cost the companies less money than American workers do. Do you think it is better for a company to save money or give the jobs to Americans?

The Manufacturing Industry

Our state's most important manufacturing industry is aircraft, but local companies also build boats, trucks, and farm equipment. Workers make and sell parts to all of these vehicles.

Toys, games, and sports equipment are manufactured in Washington. So are goods made of plastic. Computers are made and sold to the world. Aluminum plants, such as Kaiser Aluminum in Spokane, create aluminum used to make airplane parts and soda cans.

The Transportation Industry

Many industries are near Seattle and Tacoma because these places are close to rail lines, seaports, and a large supply of workers. Transportation is moving natural resources, goods, or people from place to place. It is a whole industry in itself.

By Land, Sea, and Air

Transportation of natural resources and goods is very important for our economy. Without good transportation, most industries would be out of business.

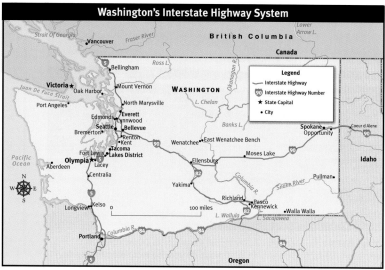
Washington's Interstate Highway System

*Interstates carry goods and people from state to state. **Which interstate highways are closest to your town or city?***

Washington, Our Home

🖩 Math Activity

By Car or Plane?

Explain to students that people pay a lot of money to fly on an airplane because they can get to a place faster than in a car. Have students use a map to guess how long it would take to get from Seattle, Washington to Washington, D.C. by car. Then have students guess how long that trip would take by plane. *It takes 41 hours, almost two days, by car and only nine hours by plane.* Have students choose their own two destinations and find out this same information. Students can share their findings with the class.

Linking the Present to the Past

(From page 193) Have students think about any vacations they have gone on where their family drove. Did it take a long time to get there? How long did it take? Have students imagine what that trip would have been like if they didn't have freeways to travel on.

- **Waterways:** Puget Sound is our most important waterway. Along the coast are large ports with harbors, where ships can load and unload goods. Seattle and Tacoma are our busiest ports. Ships and barges also travel on the Columbia and Snake Rivers.
- **Railroads:** Railroads were important in our history, and they are important to our economy today. Trains carry products to ports and cities around the country.
- **Roads and highways:** Two major highways cross Washington State. I-15 runs north and south near Puget Sound. I-90 crosses the state from Seattle to Spokane. The "I" stands for interstate. These long roads cross many states. Smaller roads and highways connect our towns, cities, and neighborhoods. Large trucks use the roads to transport goods from where they are made to the stores where people can buy them.
- **Airports:** Airports are very important places. They transport people, mail, and goods faster than any other form of transportation. Sea-Tac is the largest airport in the state. There are smaller airports in Spokane and other cities.

Ride on a highway and you will see trucks carrying goods to and from other places. **The places where freeways cross over and connect with each other are often called "spaghetti bowls." Can you see why?**

Linking the Present to the Past

Roads used to be narrow, and driving was slow. Traveling across town took a long time because drivers had to stop at every corner for a traffic light. Today, freeways make it easier to travel across big cities. This means people can sell their goods and services to places much farther away.

LESSON 2 What Did You Learn?

1. How do producers and consumers help the economy?
2. What elements make up the agricultural industry?
3. Which industry is the most important to you, and why?

Working in Washington

193

REFLECT

Reflect on students' understanding of the industries in Washington and how they affect the economy. You can evaluate students' understanding through discussion or evaluation of activities completed in this lesson. The following activity will serve as another way of assessing students' understanding of the key objectives of this lesson.

Writing Activity

A Business Plan

The Project Assessment for this chapter is to develop a business. Have students prepare for the Project Assessment by writing up a business plan for making bookmarks. The business plan should include:

- The idea
- The raw materials needed
- The cost of the raw materials
- The price the product or service will be sold for
- The profit
- The expected steps of labor to create the product or service
- The cost of labor
- The advertising and incentives

A Business Plan checklist is available in the *Student Guide*.

LESSON 2 What Did You Learn?

1. *Producers and consumers are the people who make, buy, and sell the goods. If there were no producers or consumers our economy would fail.*
2. *Natural resources, farmers and laborers, distributors, and consumers make up the agricultural industry.*
3. *Answers will show students' understanding of the different industries discussed throughout the lesson.*

Standards

GLE 2.2.2
Understands that the economy in Washington State relies on trade with Pacific Rim countries.

GLE 3.3.1
Understands that learning about the geography of Washington State helps us understand the global issue of trade.

PREPARE

Activator

Where Are Your Things From?

To get students excited about the lesson, have them complete the Where Are Your Things From? activity page available in the *Student Guide*. This activity will help students begin to understand that many of the things they use everyday come from places other than the United States.

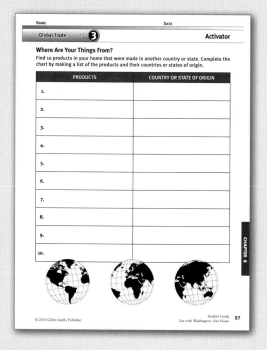

Word Study

Word Tricks

Sometimes words and definitions can be hard to remember. To make it easier for the students, have them come up with "tricks" for remembering each Word to Understand. You may want to do this as a class and practice the tricks throughout the week or have each student make up their own tricks.

194

LESSON 3 Global Trade

Key Ideas

- Our economy relies on trade with the Pacific Rim.
- Our geography helps to make us trading partners with the world.

Words to Understand

cargo
export
gateway
global
import

We Rely on Trade

Trade has always been an important part of Washington's economy. Long ago, people took furs, lumber, wheat, and fruit to other places. They brought goods from those other places back home in return. Today, one in every four state jobs depends on trade with other countries. Computers and the Internet have linked the entire globe and made it easier for us to trade.

You know that a globe is a ball-shaped map of the world. And trade means buying and selling. *Global* trade means buying and selling around the world. That is just what some people in Washington do. They make great products to sell to people who live in other countries.

194

For example:
export—exit
import—into or enter
global—world or globe
gateway—open a gate to get it

Words to Understand

cargo (p. 195) *goods carried on a ship, train, truck, or plane*
export (p. 196) *to ship goods or services out to other countries*
gateway (p. 195) *an opening; a way to enter a place*
global (p. 194) *relating to the whole world*
import (p. 196) *to bring goods or services into a country from another country*

A Words to Understand activity for this lesson is available in the *Student Guide*.

A Natural Trading Partner

What makes Washington such a great trading partner with the world? One answer is our location on the Pacific Rim. Our state is a **gateway**, or opening, for products to go to and from other places in the world. Every day, cargo ships come and go through the Strait of Juan de Fuca and Puget Sound. **Cargo** is the goods carried on a ship, train, truck, or plane. The ships loaded with products pass in and out of the state through the deep, protected ports of Tacoma and Seattle.

You have learned that we enjoy a mild climate and fertile land. We also have many people who work in different industries. They produce all kinds of products and services that people in other places buy.

Washington also has freeways and railroads. Products that come here on ships can be transported across the United States and Canada. All of these things make Washington a great trading partner with the world.

Trade with the Pacific Rim

Back and forth, around and around, huge trading ships carry all kinds of products to buy and sell. The ships travel thousands of miles around the Pacific Ocean. They stop at many countries and unload goods to sell. Then they load other goods to carry to other countries along the rim.

Workers in each country can buy things they want. They can also sell goods they produce. Think about where we live. How might Washington's economy be different if it was not located next to the ocean?

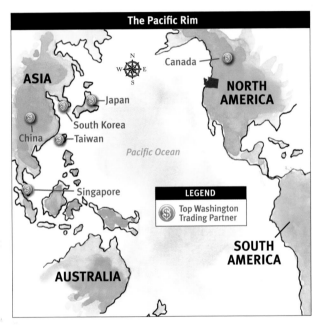

Washington's location on the Pacific Rim has been a big advantage in trade with other countries. **What do the countries in red show?**

The Pacific Rim

ASIA
Canada
Japan
South Korea
China — Taiwan
Pacific Ocean
NORTH AMERICA
Singapore
SOUTH AMERICA
AUSTRALIA

LEGEND
💲 Top Washington Trading Partner

Working in Washington

195

TEACH

Talk About It

We Rely of Trade *(From page 194)*

What technologies have linked the entire globe together?
Computers and the Internet have linked the entire globe together.

What items were traded between people years ago?
Fur, lumber, wheat, and fruit were traded between people years ago.

What is a globe?
A globe is a rounded map of the world.

A Natural Trading Partner

Have you ever visited the Pacific Rim? If so, which city did you visit?
Answers will show students' understanding of the location of the Pacific Rim.

In what ways is cargo carried from Washington to other countries?
Cargo is carried by ship, train, truck, or plane.

Trade with the Pacific Rim

How does trade along the rim help everyone?
Workers in each country can buy things they need and can also sell goods they have produced.

Caption Answer

The countries in red show Washington's top trading partners.

Reading Strategy

Making Inferences

Explain to students that an inference is thinking that goes beyond the facts stated in the text. Inference is a lot like drawing conclusions. Good readers read and think beyond the text. Have students use the Making Inferences activity in the *Student Guide* and the text from the lesson to make these inferences about global trade.

NAME _____ DATE _____

Global Trade   Unit **3**   **Reading Strategy**

Making Inferences
An inference is thinking that goes beyond the facts stated in the text. Good readers read and think beyond the text. The sentences in the chart are from your textbook. Read what each sentences **SAYS** and explain what each one **MEANS** in your own words.

MEANS
SAYS
Computers and the Internet have linked the entire globe.
(pg. 194)
We buy clothing, toys, and electronic products from China.
(pg. 197)
Washington is a natural trading partner.
(pg. 195)

GLOBAL TRADE

CHAPTER 8

© 2010 Gibbs Smith, Publisher   Student Guide **89**
Use with *Washington, Our Home*

Talk About It

Shipping In and Out

What is the difference between importing and exporting goods?
Importing means to bring goods in and exporting means to ship them out.

Why is exporting important to Washington?
Exporting goods allows us to make money on products and services we sell.

Why is importing important to Washington?
Importing goods allows us to buy products we need and want.

Who Buys Washington's Products?
(From page 197)

Which country gets the largest amount of our products?
China gets the largest amount of our products.

What are the top five Asian countries, besides China, that buy our products?
Japan, India, South Korea, Taiwan, and Singapore are the top five Asian countries, besides China, that buy our products.

Washington's Imports

After doing the Where Are Your Things From? activity page, what things did you find around the house that were from China?
Answers will show students' understanding and completion of the activity page.

Caption Answer

Possible answers include aircraft and spacecraft, cereal, oil seeds from grain, fruit, plants, computers and industrial machinery, mineral fuel and oil, electronics, medical equipment, wood, iron and steel, and chemicals.

A ship stacked high with cargo gets ready to leave the port of Seattle. **According to the chart below, what might be in these boxes?**

Shipping In and Out

Two words explain goods shipped in and out of a state or a country.

- To *import* means to bring goods IN from other countries.
- To *export* means to ship goods or services OUT to other countries.

Study the graph. Did you know all of these things were made in Washington?

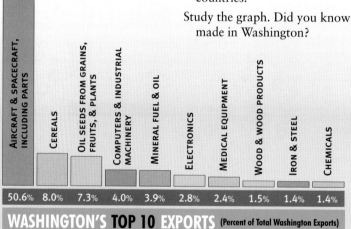

WASHINGTON'S TOP 10 EXPORTS (Percent of Total Washington Exports)

Aircraft & spacecraft, including parts	Cereals	Oil seeds from grains, fruits, & plants	Computers & industrial machinery	Mineral fuel & oil	Electronics	Medical equipment	Wood & wood products	Iron & steel	Chemicals
50.6%	8.0%	7.3%	4.0%	3.9%	2.8%	2.4%	1.5%	1.4%	1.4%

(Source: World Institute for Strategic Economic Research and U.S. Census Bureau Foreign Trade Division)

Washington, Our Home

 Social Studies Activity

Cooperative Groups

Let's Trade

Explain to students that one of the main reasons we trade is to get new resources and goods from other regions of the world and to sell our products as well. Separate students into six groups. Three groups will represent Washington's three largest trading partners, China, Canada, and Japan. The other three groups will represent Washington traders. Ask students to think about items that are unique to their assigned region. Make the computers available for students who need to research products made from their region. After the groups have determined some unique products have them find or create items that represent the products. The China, Canada, and Japan groups should trade with the Washington groups in order to get items they need or want. Explain to students that to make money in the trading process they need to gain additional products from other groups while still retaining as much as they can of their own products.

Who Buys Washington's Products?

Do you know which country gets the largest amount of our products? If you guessed a country in Asia, you are right. China is the state's number-one export market. Five other top Asian markets are Japan, India, South Korea, Taiwan, and Singapore. Together, these Asian countries bought almost half of Washington's exports in 2008.

After Asia, Canada was our second-largest trade market. Europe was next. Countries in Europe that bought our goods were Ireland, France, the United Kingdom (England), Germany, and the Netherlands. Many other countries also bought our products.

Washington's Imports

We buy clothing, toys, and electronic products from Pacific Rim countries such as Japan and China. Workers in those countries make thousands of items and ship them to us. We also import cars from Japan.

Many of the things you use everyday come from other places in the United States. Some come from other countries. Explore your garage, kitchen, and bedroom to see what imports you consume. Where do your food, clothes, and games come from?

(Source: World Institute for Strategic Economic Research and U.S. Census Bureau Foreign Trade Division)

WASHINGTON'S TOP 10 TRADING PARTNERS FOR EXPORTS

2.7% NETHERLANDS
3.1% IRELAND
3.3% TAIWAN
3.6% INDIA
3.9% SINGAPORE
5.1% SOUTH KOREA
5.2% UNITED ARAB EMIRATES
14.8% CHINA
13.8% CANADA
13.5% JAPAN

Percent of Total Washington Exports

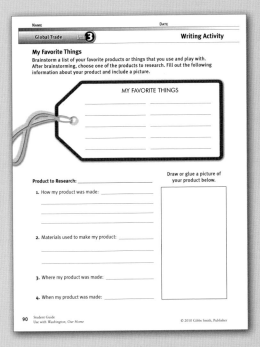

At this factory in China, workers assemble parts for electronic products. The products will begin a long journey across the ocean. **What do you own that was made in China?**

LESSON 3

1. What is global trade?
2. How do products get from one place to another?
3. List some of Washington's trading partners.

Working in Washington

LESSON 3 What Did You Learn?

1. *Global trade is when you buy and sell things around the world.*
2. *Products are shipped in and out of a state or country by ship, train, truck, or plane.*
3. *We do trading with China, Japan, India, South Korea, Taiwan, Singapore, Canada, Europe, Ireland, France, England, Germany, and the Netherlands.*

Reflect on students' understanding of global trade and why importing and exporting goods is important to our economy. You can evaluate students' understanding through discussion or evaluation of activities completed in this lesson. The following activity will serve as another way of assessing students' understanding of the key objectives of this lesson.

 Writing Activity

My Favorite Things

Have students brainstorm a list of their favorite products or things they use and play with. After brainstorming, have students choose one of the products to research. Students should research how the product was made, what year it was made, and where it was made. Students will also need to include a picture of their product.

NAME ___ DATE ___
Global Trade [3] Writing Activity

My Favorite Things
Brainstorm a list of your favorite products or things that you use and play with. After brainstorming, choose one of the products to research. Fill out the following information about your product and include a picture.

MY FAVORITE THINGS

Product to Research: ___

Draw or glue a picture of your product below.

1. How my product was made: ___
2. Materials used to make my product: ___
3. Where my product was made: ___
4. When my product was made: ___

90 Student Guide
Use with *Washington, Our Home* © 2010 Gibbs Smith, Publisher

Caption Answer

Allow students to share their findings with a partner.

Standards

GLE 5.1.1
Understands the concepts used in documents and sources.

GLE 5.2.2
Understands the main ideas from an artifact, primary source, or secondary source describing an issue or event.

Washington Social Studies Skills

How To Read a Graph

Activate

As a class, brainstorm different types of graphs. Make a list on the board of all the graphs students came up with. Ask students to share where they have seen these graphs and what they look like.

Teach

Explain to students that graphs help us to "see" a large amount of information organized into a small space. Many graphs can be very confusing if you don't know how to read them.

As a class, go through the six rules listed on the Social Studies Skills Page. Have students complete the questions about the circle graph.

Practice

As a class, gather one set of data such as your student's favorite colors, favorite day of the week, or favorite subjects. Make a list of this data on the board.

Have students work in small groups to create their own graph using the data listed on the board. You may choose to have them all create circle graphs or a variety of graphs. Remind students to include a title, scale, and other useful information for reading their graph. After students have created their graphs, have them write three questions about their graph.

Students will then trade graphs with another group and answer each other's questions.

Washington Social Studies Skills

How to Read a Graph

Graphs let us "see" information. There are many types of graphs. These graphs can be confusing if you don't know how to read them. The following rules will help you be able to read graphs correctly.

RULES FOR READING GRAPHS

1. Read the title of the graph.
2. Look at how the graph is set up.
3. Look at what things are being represented by the graph.
4. What is the scale of the graph, or how much of something is being shown?
5. Study the legend to the side of the graph if one is available.
6. Interpret the graph by asking yourself, "What conclusions can I draw from reading the graph?"

CIRCLE GRAPH

The graph shown above is a circle graph, also known as a pie chart. You can think of a circle graph as a pie divided into pieces. This particular graph shows Washington's top 10 trading partners for exports. Using the rules listed above, read the graph carefully, and then answer the following questions.

WASHINGTON'S TOP 10 TRADING PARTNERS FOR EXPORTS

Percent of Total Washington Exports

- NETHERLANDS 2.7%
- IRELAND 3.1%
- TAIWAN 3.3%
- INDIA 3.6%
- SINGAPORE 3.9%
- SOUTH KOREA 5.1%
- UNITED ARAB EMIRATES 5.2%
- CHINA 14.8%
- CANADA 13.8%
- JAPAN 13.5%

1. Which country is Washington's largest trading partner?
2. Which country is Washington's 10th largest trading partner?
3. What conclusions can you draw from reading this graph?

Washington, Our Home

Apply

Have students write what they liked about the other group's graph, what was confusing, and how the graph could have been more clear?

Allow the groups to use this information to make their own graph easier to read.

Chapter Review 8

Reviewing What You Read

1. Explain why goods and services are important to our economy.
2. Provide an example of how we can be mindful of the resources we are using.
3. How can learning about the economy help you in the future?
4. How does importing compare to exporting?
5. What would life be like if we didn't have countries to trade products with?
6. In what industry would you like to have a job, and why?

Becoming a Better Reader

Draw Conclusions

You have become a better reader by learning reading strategies. In this chapter, you learned to draw conclusions about what you read. After reading *Washington, Our Home*, write about the most important thing you learned about Washington. Be sure to include facts to tell about what you learned.

Spotlighting Geography

How Geography Affects Business

List two businesses in Washington that are part of each type of industry listed below. To find businesses, you could use this chapter, the Internet, or the yellow pages of the phone book.

Agriculture   Fishing   Timber
Manufacturing   Transportation

Find the following information for one of the businesses you found.
• The business's location
• Nearness to natural resources
• Transportation options

Working in Washington   199

Reviewing What You Read

The Reviewing What You Read questions are leveled according to Bloom's Taxonomy and will help students achieve a higher level of thinking. These questions will also prepare students for the chapter assessment. The following are possible answers to the questions. Focus on students' ability to understand and apply the concepts.

1. **KNOWLEDGE** Our economy revolves around goods and services being provided and used so that people can earn the money they need to survive and have money to spend.

2. **COMPREHENSION** Possible answers include we can turn off lights when we aren't using them, turn off water, use hand dryers instead of paper towels, recycle paper, plastic, and aluminum, and reuse things that are reusable.

3. **APPLICATION** If you understand how the economy works then you will be able to be a responsible spender and make good choices with your money.

4. **ANALYSIS** Importing is when products are brought into a country from another country. Exporting is when goods and services are shipped out to other countries.

5. **SYNTHESIS** Possible answers include we would not be able to make money selling our products and we would have to make all the products we usually buy from other countries.

6. **EVALUATION** Answers will show students' understanding of the industries mentioned in the lesson.

Interactive Chapter Review

An interactive chapter review is available online at **www.ExperienceStateHistory. com.** Have students use this review to prepare for the assessments.

Chapter Assessment

Chapter Assessments are available to preview on pages 176G–176H. Assessments can be found in the *Teacher Guide*. They can also be found online at **www.ExperienceStateHistory.com.**

Becoming a Better Reader

Draw Conclusions

Students have learned many things about Washington throughout the year. Encourage students to look through their projects, papers, and the textbook when trying to decide what was the most important thing they learned about.

Spotlighting Geography

How Geography Affects Businesses

Every business is part of an industry. Encourage students to think about businesses that could be categorized into each of the different industries.

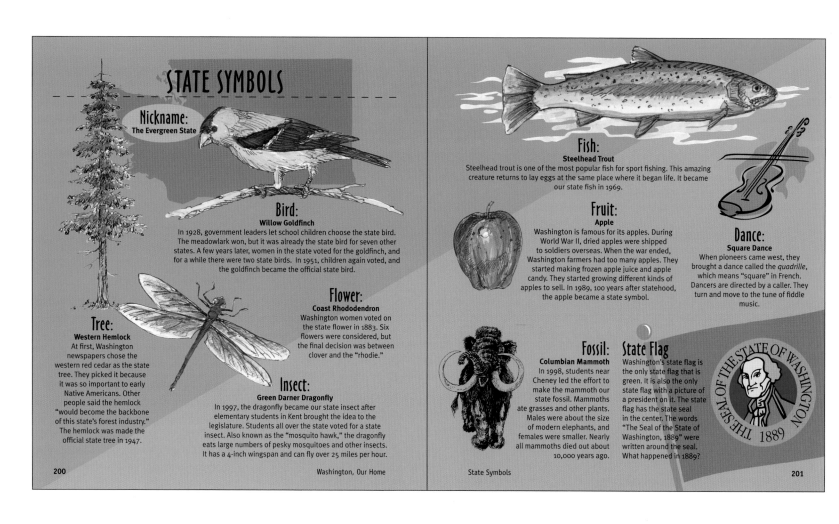

STATE SYMBOLS

Nickname:
The Evergreen State

Bird:
Willow Goldfinch
In 1928, government leaders let school children choose the state bird. The meadowlark won, but it was already the state bird for seven other states. A few years later, women in the state voted for the goldfinch, and for a while there were two state birds. In 1951, children again voted, and the goldfinch became the official state bird.

Tree:
Western Hemlock
At first, Washington newspapers chose the western red cedar as the state tree. They picked it because it was so important to early Native Americans. Other people said the hemlock "would become the backbone of this state's forest industry." The hemlock was made the official state tree in 1947.

Flower:
Coast Rhododendron
Washington women voted on the state flower in 1883. Six flowers were considered, but the final decision was between clover and the "rhodie."

Insect:
Green Darner Dragonfly
In 1997, the dragonfly became our state insect after elementary students in Kent brought the idea to the legislature. Students all over the state voted for a state insect. Also known as the "mosquito hawk," the dragonfly eats large numbers of pesky mosquitoes and other insects. It has a 4-inch wingspan and can fly over 25 miles per hour.

Fish:
Steelhead Trout
Steelhead trout is one of the most popular fish for sport fishing. This amazing creature returns to lay eggs at the same place where it began life. It became our state fish in 1969.

Fruit:
Apple
Washington is famous for its apples. During World War II, dried apples were shipped to soldiers overseas. When the war ended, Washington farmers had too many apples. They started making frozen apple juice and apple candy. They started growing different kinds of apples to sell. In 1989, 100 years after statehood, the apple became a state symbol.

Dance:
Square Dance
When pioneers came west, they brought a dance called the *quadrille*, which means "square" in French. Dancers are directed by a caller. They turn and move to the tune of fiddle music.

Fossil:
Columbian Mammoth
In 1998, students near Cheney led the effort to make the mammoth our state fossil. Mammoths ate grasses and other plants. Males were about the size of modern elephants, and females were smaller. Nearly all mammoths died out about 10,000 years ago.

State Flag
Washington's state flag is the only state flag that is green. It is also the only state flag with a picture of a president on it. The state flag has the state seal in the center. The words "The Seal of the State of Washington, 1889" were written around the seal. What happened in 1889?

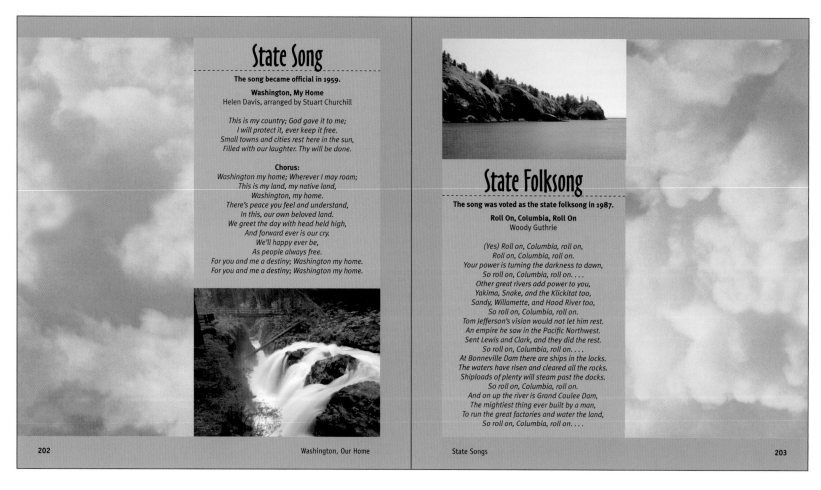

State Song

The song became official in 1959.

Washington, My Home
Helen Davis, arranged by Stuart Churchill

This is my country; God gave it to me;
I will protect it, ever keep it free.
Small towns and cities rest here in the sun,
Filled with our laughter. Thy will be done.

Chorus:
Washington my home; Wherever I may roam;
This is my land, my native land,
Washington, my home.
There's peace you feel and understand,
In this, our own beloved land.
We greet the day with head held high,
And forward ever is our cry.
We'll happy ever be,
As people always free.
For you and me a destiny; Washington my home.
For you and me a destiny; Washington my home.

State Folksong

The song was voted as the state folksong in 1987.

Roll On, Columbia, Roll On
Woody Guthrie

(Yes) Roll on, Columbia, roll on,
Roll on, Columbia, roll on.
Your power is turning the darkness to dawn,
So roll on, Columbia, roll on. . . .
Other great rivers add power to you,
Yakima, Snake, and the Klickitat too,
Sandy, Willamette, and Hood River too,
So roll on, Columbia, roll on.
Tom Jefferson's vision would not let him rest.
An empire he saw in the Pacific Northwest.
Sent Lewis and Clark, and they did the rest.
So roll on, Columbia, roll on. . . .
At Bonneville Dam there are ships in the locks.
The waters have risen and cleared all the rocks.
Shiploads of plenty will steam past the docks.
So roll on, Columbia, roll on.
And on up the river is Grand Coulee Dam,
The mightiest thing ever built by a man,
To run the great factories and water the land,
So roll on, Columbia, roll on. . . .

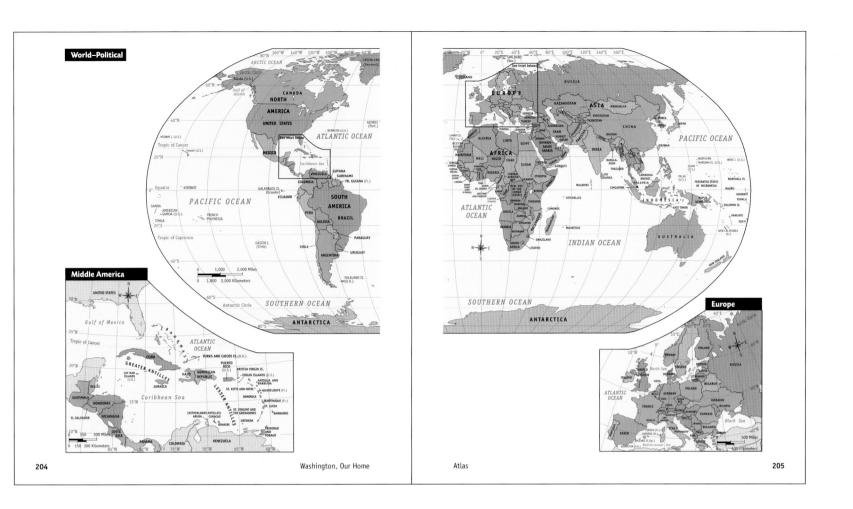

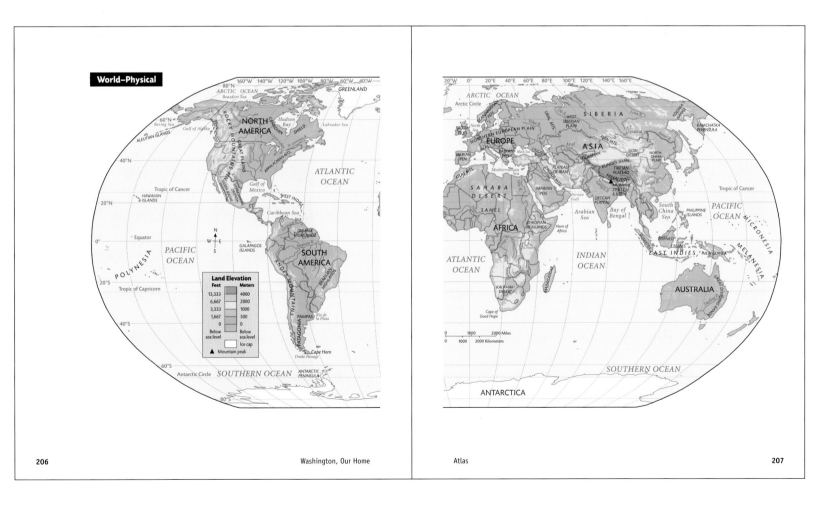

United States–Political

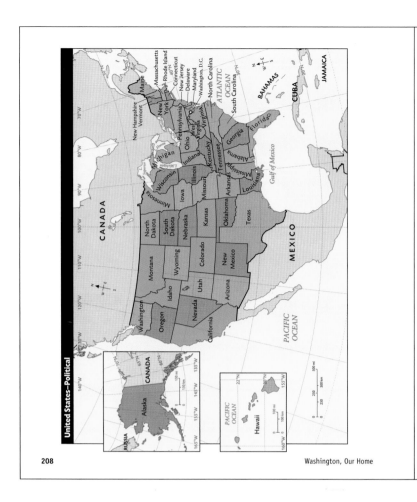

United States–Physical

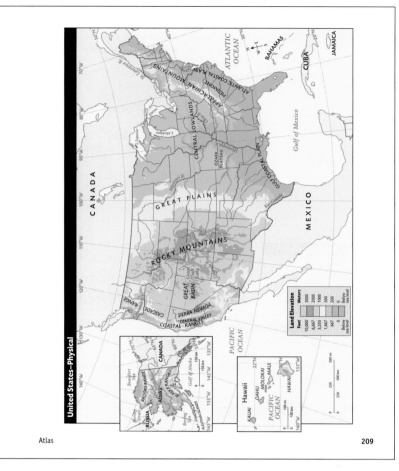

Washington–Political

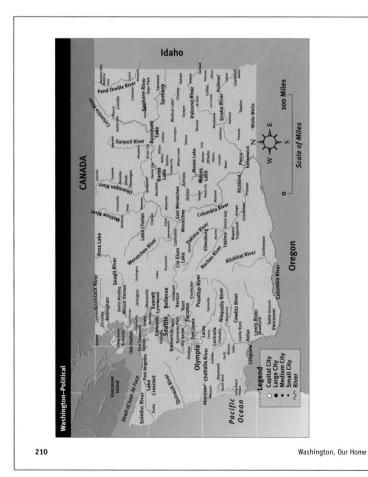

Washington–Physical

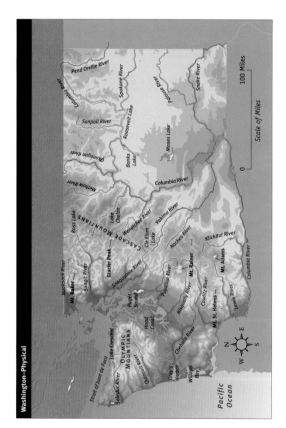

GIBBS SMITH EDUCATION
TO ENRICH AND INSPIRE HUMANKIND

Glossary

The definitions listed here are for the **Words to Understand** as they are used in this textbook.

A

agreement: when both sides agree on what to do

agriculture: the business of raising crops and animals to sell

ancient: relating to a time long, long ago

archaeologist: a scientist who studies clues to learn how people lived in the past

artifact: an object made or used by people of the past

atlatl: a tool used to throw a spear farther and faster

autobiography: a book written by a person about his or her own life

B

barter: to trade without using money

belief: something thought to be true

benefit: what you get in return for paying the cost

bill: a written proposal for a law

biography: the story of a person's life as written by another person

brigade: a large group of trappers or soldiers organized for a special activity

C

cargo: goods carried on a ship, train, truck, or plane

century: a time period of 100 years

ceremony: a ritual; actions done the same way each time for a special purpose

chronological: arranged in the order of time

citizen: a legal resident of a country

civic: having to do with being a citizen of a city or town

civilize: to bring to a higher stage of education and culture

claim: to take as a rightful owner

climate: the weather pattern year after year

community: a group of people living near each other in a place

compass: a symbol that shows direction on a map (north, south, east, west)

compromise: an agreement that is reached by each side giving up something it wants

conflict: a problem between two people or groups

conserve: to protect or save something for the future

constitution: a written plan for government

consumer: any person who buys goods and services

continent: one of the Earth's seven large land areas that are almost completely surrounded by water

convert: to change another person's religious beliefs

cost: what you give up to get what you want

council: a meeting where a group of people makes decisions

country: a land region under the control of one government

county: a government region within a state

cultural characteristic: a feature that has to do with the way people live

D

decade: a time period of 10 years

defend: to drive away danger or attack

descendant: children, grandchildren, great-grandchildren, and so on

discrimination: to treat other people badly just because they are different

disease: sickness

distributor: a person or company that transports goods to market

document: an official government paper

duty: an action a person is expected to do

E

economics: the study of how people produce, sell, and buy goods and services

elder: an older person

election: the process of voting people into a government office

elevation: how high the land is above the level of the ocean

encounter: to meet face to face

enforce: to make sure people obey (a law or rule)

era: a period of years when related events happened

ethnic: referring to a minority race

expedition: a journey taken for a specific purpose

explore: to travel to a new place to learn about it

export: to ship goods or services out to other countries

extinct: no longer living anywhere on the Earth

F

felt: a thick cloth made by pressing and heating fur and wool together

fertile: good for growing crops

frontier: a region on the edge of settled land

fur trade: a business where animal fur is traded for other things or for money

G

gateway: an opening; a way to enter a place

geography: the study of the Earth and the people, animals, and plants living on it

global: relating to the whole world

gold rush: a rush to a new gold field in hopes of getting rich

goods: things that are made and then bought and sold

governor: the top government leader of a territory or state

H

hardship: suffering

harpoon: a long spear used to hunt whales

historian: a person who studies many sources to learn about events of the past

history: the story of the past

homestead: to claim, farm, and improve land

hydroelectricity: electricity produced by water power

I

ideal: an idea about the way things should be; something that is believed to be perfect or best

immigrant: a person who moves into a country

immigrate: to move into a new country or place to live

import: to bring goods or services into a country from another country

industry: a certain kind of business, such as manufacturing, shipping, tourism, etc.

interpreter: one who translates one language into another as someone is talking

irrigation: bringing water to crops from a river or lake

L

labor: workers; working

landform: a natural feature of the land

legend: (1) on a map, a key to the meaning of symbols; (2) story that tells about the past or how things came to be

liberty: freedom; the state of being free

livestock: animals raised for food, such as cows, chickens, turkey, sheep, and hogs

longhouse: long Indian homes where several families lived together

lumber: logs sawed into boards

M

massacre: the violent murder of a large group of people

missionary: a person who tries to teach his or her religion to others

N

native: being born or raised in a certain place or region

natural boundary: a boundary line formed by natural landforms, such as rivers or mountain ranges

natural resource: something found in nature that people use, such as trees, water, or minerals

negotiate: to talk back and forth to reach an agreement

O

opportunity: a good chance for progress or advancement

oral history: a story told aloud and passed down from person to person

orphanage: a home for children who have no parents

overland: across land

ownership: the fact of being an owner

P

pelt: the skin of an animal with the fur still attached

perspective: point of view

---

petroglyph: a rock carving

physical characteristic: a feature that has to do with the natural land and landforms

pioneer: a person who is among the first settlers to move to a new place

point of view: the way a person sees an event

political boundary: a boundary line decided by people

politics: having to do with government

population: all the people who live in a particular area

portrait: a picture of a person in words, art, or a photograph

potlatch: a ceremony of feasting and gift-giving

primary source: an object or writing made by a person who was there at the time

processed: made in a factory; having gone through changes to produce or manufacture something

producer: a person or company that makes, grows, or supplies goods for sale

product: something that is made to sell

profitable: able to make money

R

rapids: a part of the river where the current is fast and large boulders stick out of the water

region: a land division based on common characteristics

religion: relating to beliefs, practices, and worship of God or the supernatural

representative: a person elected to vote for other people

reservation: land set aside for Native Americans

reservoir: a large lake used as a source of water

responsibility: a duty you have to do; something you are supposed to do

rights: the privileges citizens are entitled to

rule of law: the idea that no one is above the law; the law is the highest power

rural: having to do with the countryside rather than a town or city

S

sawmill: a building where logs are sawed into boards

scale: compares distance on a map to actual distance on land

secondary source: information made later, after an event has happened

services: in economics, people who work for other people for money

shaman: a spiritual leader who tried to heal the sick

slave: a person owned by another

slavery: people who are bought and sold and forced to work

sovereignty: self-rule; supreme power or authority

spike: a very long, thick nail

spiritual: having to do with the spirit life and not the physical

state: a part of a country that makes some of its own laws; a political region of a country

stockade: a strong, tall fence made from logs

surrender: to give up

survey: to measure the land

sustain: to support or strengthen

symbol: a mark or design that stands for something else

T

tax: money people must pay to the government

technology: the use of scientific knowledge

terrain: a piece of land; ground

territory: a land region owned and ruled by a country; a region that is not a state

timber: wood (from trees) that is used for building

totem pole: a carved wooden pole made by Native Americans to display family history

trade route: a route of travel over water or land that is used by traders

tradition: a way of doing something the same way your ancestors did it

tragedy: a horrible event

treaty: a written agreement between two groups

trek: an organized journey of a group of people

tribal council: a group that makes laws for an Indian tribe on Indian lands

tule: tall plants or reeds that grow wild in swampy places

tourism: the industry of making money by meeting the needs of visitors

U-W

urban: having to do with a city

veto: to say no to a bill; to prevent a bill from becoming a law

volunteer: a person who chooses to work without pay

wagon train: a large group of wagons that followed each other

weir: a fence built across a stream to catch fish

wilderness: a place in its natural state, where few people live

Index

Credits

Notes

Notes

Notes

Notes